Parent TO Parent: Raising Kids Washington

Photos

We extend a warm note of gratitude to photographer Jerilyn Ray-Shelley, former Board member of the Parents Council of Washington, who provided all of the photos included in this book. That same gratitude is extended to the parents and students of the Washington Waldorf School in Bethesda, Maryland, where the photos were taken over the past several years.

Parent TO Parent:
Raising Kids Washington

DONNA HART, Ed.D., Executive Editor

ISBN 0-9661107-1-4

Library of Congress: 2003100208

Printed in the United States of America
Data Reproductions Corporation

Book design and production
DL Graphics Studio | Bethesda, MD

Cover photos: Jerilyn Ray-Shelley
Cover design: Lynn Springer, DL Graphics Studio

Publisher:
Parents Council of Washington, Inc.
7305 River Road
Bethesda, Maryland 20817

301/767-2385
www.parentscouncil.org

Contents

Contents

Acknowledgements

We are pleased to present the latest edition of the Parents Council of Washington's parenting guidebook *Parent to Parent: Raising Kids in Washington.* The first version of this book, published as *Changing Trends* in 1972, was significantly revised and expanded for the 1997 edition, which was entitled *Parent to Parent: Raising Kids in Washington*. Since then, the guide has been through three sold-out printings.

The choice of executive editor for a project of this scope is critical, and we were blessed in our selection of Donna Hart, Ed.D., for she spearheaded the effort with skill and grace, and was deft in outlining the basic philosophy and determining the topics to be included. Hart's leadership ensured that the project would be educational and enjoyable for all involved. Her enthusiasm, creativity, and sensitivity were critical to the project, and her experience as an educator, researcher, and editor organized and focused the work of producing a remarkably timely, informative, and easy-to-use resource for Washington parents.

Hart, in turn, relied heavily on the wisdom and feedback of literally hundreds of parents and education and mental health professionals to ensure that we crafted the broadest and most inclusive parenting guide possible. In particular, Hart depended upon the insights and advice of Bob Condit, M.Ed. and Sylvia Stultz, Ph.D.

Many educational and mental health professionals and parents contributed to the rich and timely contents of *Parent to Parent* and for their invaluable help, we extend our sincerest thanks to Rick Beizer, Julia Berry, Bojena Buda, Marcy Cathey, Carol Dopp, Pat Douglas, Gerri Fehst, Mimi Fleury, Karen Guberman, Leslie Harps, Elizabeth Hayes, Leonard King, Maria Lopez, Manisha Maniyar, Nina Marks, Susan Messina and the staff of William Wendt Center for Loss and Healing, Bonnie Naradzay, Susan Price, Deborah Roffman, Rita Schonberg, Ph.D., and young people Suzanna Cohen, Taylor Godfrey, and Julia Beizer.

Many others contributed to our effort to ensure the creation of a quality product, including members of the Parent Council Board, who provided invaluable feedback as chapters were written. Very special thanks go to Board member Pat Douglass, who read each chapter for content and style. Thanks, too, to Anna Goiser, who coordinated and polished the many wise voices and formats, ensuring that the book's concepts and strategies came through clearly. Lynn Springer of DL Graphics Studio in Bethesda, Maryland once again went far beyond what was asked of her and provided the very discerning and creative book design.

Parent to Parent: Raising Kids in Washington represents a labor of love by all involved, but none more so than Dr. Hart. She has our deep and abiding gratitude for the innumerable hours of toil bringing the book to fruition.

Board of Directors
Parents Council of Washington, Inc.

Preface

This book is a dialogue between parents working together to share knowledge and experience in order to meet the challenging demands of rearing healthy, independent, competent teens and preteens in the Washington, D.C., metropolitan area. In creating *Parent to Parent*, we worked on the principal that all parents can benefit from the wisdom, humor, and warmth of other parents, as well as from their experience and knowledge when seeking a better perspective on the work we're doing with our own children. As a result, *Parent to Parent* is a deep reservoir of information, support, reassurance, and plain good sense designed to help parents determine what is normal for a given stage of development and to examine the enormous physical, neurological, biological, and cultural developmental changes our teens undergo.

Feedback from parents about the previous edition of the book dictated that we again structure *Parent to Parent* so that it may be read in one sitting, delved into for information about a specific topic, or perused from time to time at leisure. We feel, however, that to reap the greatest benefit from the book parents could use individual chapters as starting points for ongoing discussions of the issues with their adolescents. Invite your teens to read a particular chapter and then solicit their opinions and points of view so that you can make decisions together. We will have been successful if *Parent to Parent* encourages further communication between parents and their children, as well as between and among entire families.

The core belief behind this project is that parents really count and that we are the most important influence in our children's lives. It is often easy to lose sight of the positive force we represent to our children during the turbulent adolescent years. Teens rely heavily upon their peers for support and companionship—it works for them, and it can work for us when we likewise share information and support.

Donna Hart, Ed.D.
Executive Editor

Introduction

Just about every expert we consulted in preparation of this book voiced the same advice: "Teenagers need their parents to be available."

Regardless of what our teens may say, they care deeply about how we parents feel and what we have to say. When they give you "Get lost!" that's probably when they need you most. Ironically, experts tell us the more your teen pushes you away, the more he or she needs you. This is a paradox of adolescence. Our culture encourages a premature separation between parent and child. Teenagers may buy into this separation—parents should not. We should continue to be actively involved in their lives by knowing their friends, knowing where they are, and knowing what they're doing when they're not at home. We need to spend as much time with our children, including our teenagers, as we can—every day.

Parenting a teenager

Adolescence can be a challenging time for parents. Some parents expect the worst, and a few experience it. We should not assume, however, that the preteen and teen years will be an especially trying time for our families. Some parents of teens are confused about how much to parent. Some assume that their teen needs less parenting when, in reality, they may need more!

Parents may feel discouraged, angry, frustrated, or sad during difficult times with their adolescents. Being a good parent does not mean having perfect children, being perfect, or having all the answers. Parenting is an active, evolving process. Children develop and mature, and we parents also continue to grow into our role. While we can expect to experience some difficult months, and sometimes years, with our teens, adolescence can be an exhilarating time—after all, we are watching young adults being formed before our eyes.

We need to remember that parenting is not a popularity contest. Our children may not agree with our views or be happy when we enforce the consequences of their actions, but we are giving them something of great value—active, caring parents who love their children enough to do what's right for them, not what is easy or popular.

Being connected

Being connected to one's parents during childhood correlates with happiness and success in adulthood, observes Edward Hallowell, M.D., in *The Childhood Roots of Adult Happiness: Five Steps to Help Kids*

Create and Sustain Lifelong Joy. Many experts agree that teens who have a connected relationship with their parents are less likely to engage in sex, drugs, and other risky behavior. While teens want to be separate from their parents, they also want to stay connected. Ideally, families provide intimacy, security, and consistency. They should be the ever present safety net in a child's life, always available for support, guidance, and backup. Connectedness and intimacy cannot be scheduled. Parents must provide not just quality time, but real time that includes the routine and repetitive behaviors of an ongoing relationship. By offering ongoing attention parents will know their children better than anyone else in the world.

Parents as consultants

Too often parents think of their role as one of setting limits and restricting, even micromanaging. As our children move into adolescence, our role changes from one of mostly managing or controlling to one of advising and influencing. Parents can position themselves as a resourceful authority available to help clarify issues and steer choices to an acceptable conclusion through discussion.

Finding the balance between supervision and allowing freedom to experience independence may be the true test of effectively parenting adolescents. Counselors emphasize that adolescents rely on peers and media for advice or assistance only when parental assistance is unavailable or inadequate.

The goal of parenting is to teach our children good judgment rather than to police them. Our tools are limit setting, values conveyance, and responsibility fostering. Achieving the goal requires discussion and joint problem solving between parents and children. A skillful consultant knows when to step back, let go, and cede responsibility. We can't make our teenagers do the safe thing, the right thing, or even the sensible thing, but we can give them ample opportunities to learn to be responsible. Responsibility is not something we relinquish, but is the gift we can give to our children.

Parents as communicators

We need to talk with our children often, beginning when they are very young, and practice listening, really listening—nonjudgmentally. It is the most effective way to build the kind of trusting relationships with our adolescents that will encourage them to continue to talk and to listen.

Many teenagers don't talk to their parents on demand, but like to have their parents around in the background, at home, in the car before they come forward with their thoughts, reactions, and feelings. Spending comfortable time together provides opportunities for topics to surface casually and for moments of close, spontaneous, and unplanned connection. We have to be ready to take advantage of the conversational openings our teens provide, even when we may feel stressed-out and overburdened.

Parents do need to express their own opinions. Teens want to know where their parents are coming from on issues. They look to us for values, guidance, reassurance, and information. Psychologist Erik Erikson advises that bringing up our children to be good means you "have to keep doing that, bring them up, and that means bringing things up with them: asking; telling; sounding them out; sounding off yourself."

Bringing out the best

Our words and interactions, acceptance, and unwavering love can bring out the best in our teenagers. Our love can inoculate our children against depression and angst. Parental love influences how children will perceive life as an adult. We need to make sure our teens know they are truly important in our world—more important than clients, customers, or promotion. Make sure your words are consistent with your actions in sending the message that when push comes to shove, you will be there for your kids.

We can love our children but hate their behavior. Because the teen years are a time of individuation, accept that your teen may choose styles of dress, haircuts, music, art, language, and friends that you won't care for. Loving our children includes accepting their limitations while genuinely appreciating who they actually are. Remember Mr. Rogers' reassuring promise: "There's never been anybody exactly like you before, and there will never be anybody exactly like you in the future. You're the only one."

Parent to Parent

We think you will find that each chapter in *Parent to Parent* is like inviting a personal consultant, who has the combined knowledge and expertise of literally hundreds of professional and parental contributors, into your living room. *Parent to Parent* was created on the premise that parents are seeking solutions to everyday issues involving their children. Answers are seldom found in a list of easy steps, but are the result of really knowing our children—recognizing their unique learning styles, personalities, temperaments, and level of maturation.

Final thoughts

If you want the very best for your children—be there for them, with your undivided attention, when your teen seeks it. Listen to them when they want to talk. Talk *with* your children—not to them. "This is the secret of a good relationship between parent and child," says columnist Marguerite Kelly.

1 moving toward adulthood

| 1 |

The Adolescent Brain: Not Yet an Adult

The brain you have when you enter your teen years is not the one you have when you grow out of them. Thank goodness.

SHARON BEGLEY, *Newsweek* senior editor and science writer

We enter adolescence with a child's brain. Over the course of the next ten to fifteen years, that brain matures and achieves an adult's complex abilities. Current research reveals that the brain follows a course of dynamic development until one is about twenty-five years old, thus the adolescent brain is an immature organ and is incapable of adult reasoning, memory, and judgment.

While the adolescent brain is actively involved in construction, it's just that—a work in progress. The equipment is in place, the construction is underway, the structure is being defined, and endless possibilities are on the horizon—but it isn't cooked yet. As a result, teenagers' cognitive processing and other executive functions are unpracticed and unskilled.

For a long time, it was believed that because the brain achieved ninety-five percent of adult size by age six, it was largely developed by that age. However, recently developed brain imaging techniques have expanded our knowledge about the extent to which the brain continues to develop beyond childhood and into young adulthood, and the manner in which this development affects learning. Research provides evidence of the differences between the ability of children, adolescents, and adults to make decisions and take responsibility. Much of this groundbreaking research is being done at the National Institutes of Mental Health (NIMH) under the direction of neuroscientist and practicing child and adolescent psychiatrist Jay Giedd, M.D.

Although children are donning the trappings of adulthood at increasingly younger ages, brain research reveals that the regions of the brain responsible for insight, judgment, and planning are significantly immature throughout adolescence. In light of this immaturity, what are the implications for our teens' social, moral, cognitive, and academic, development? What level of responsibility should we expect of teens? How can parents best support optimal growth?

Early adolescence

Prior to the onset of puberty, the brain completes a period of accelerated production of gray matter or thinking material. Giedd describes this process as a building up or thickening of gray matter that continues throughout late childhood. During this build-up phase, brain cells produce extra branches, twigs, and roots, creating a complex structure for making connections. Prepuberty and early adolescence are thus times of incredible plasticity and enormous potential, as well as being tumultuous in terms of anatomical change, moral and ethical framework building, decision-making skill development, and the identification and exploration of interests.

Gender affects the path, pace, and timing of brain development. Girls' brains develop a little earlier and more quickly than those of boys, as evidenced by MRI scans made of both sexes at two-year intervals by Giedd and others. The build-up of the executive portion of the brain, the *frontal lobes*, peaks at age eleven in girls and a year later in boys, coinciding roughly with the onset of puberty and the possible influence of surging sex hormones. However, the *amygdala*, which guides gut or instinctive reactions and contains many testosterone receptors, develops more rapidly in adolescent boys, while the estrogen receptor-rich *hippocampus*, home to memory storage and retrieval, as well as language, develops more quickly in girls.

Regardless of gender, the job of the middle-schooler's brain is "to start divorcing itself from total dependence on concrete experience, learning to reason about things that can't be seen, touched, or physically manipulated (e.g., a metaphor, a scientific hypothesis, the concepts of ratio, proportion, and probability), and dealing with abstract symbol systems (e.g., rules of grammar, algebraic formulas)," according to Jane Healy, Ph.D., author of *Endangered Minds: Why Children Don't Think and What We Can Do About It*.

The young adolescent also experiences a "spurt in brain areas connected to painful, but necessary, growth in self-awareness, reflection, abstract thought, moral reasoning, and planning," explains Healy. She says this produces a teen who "seems impelled to challenge things he has always accepted, argue with his parents, and take issue even with his own previous self."

During the preteen and even the teen years, the frontal lobes' judgment capacity is very immature, resulting in an uneven connection between feelings, concrete thought, and sound decision making. The prepubescent neural growth spurt is the beginning of an ability to inhibit impulses, link thought and action, manage motivation, facilitate planning, and to develop a more global perspective, observes JoAnn Deak, Ph.D., psychologist and co-author of *Girls Will Be Girls: Raising Confident and Courageous Daughters.*

Some social and emotional issues, however, are simply not appropriate concerns for preteens and teens, as their brains are not yet developmentally equipped to integrate the information and judge the full ramifications of many situations. Giedd is emphatic when he says, "It's not that teens are stupid or incapable of things, but it's sort of unfair to expect them to have adult levels of organizational skills or decision making before their brains are finished being built."

All of this growth and activity in the brain sets the stage for enormous mental potential, and the manner in which teens spend their time appears to have a crucial impact on the development of that potential. The brain develops according to how it is used. Giedd acknowledges that although the "use it or lose it" theory is speculative, scientists generally embrace the notion that when neural connections or synapses are exercised, they are retained, if not, they are lost. The implication is that preteens and teens benefit greatly during this period from an enriched environment with opportunities to explore, question, create, and experiment. By contrast, if a youngster spends this developmental period engaged in MTV, videos, and other couch potato activities, those passive pursuits will become the foundation upon which future development and learning are seated.

Late adolescence

The later adolescent years are a time of thinning or pruning as underutilized connections are eliminated. Beginning in the middle school years, when gray matter production slacks off, kids begin progressively specializing and achieving mastery of a more limited range of skills. Teens begin focusing on that which distinquishes them as special or unique, recognizing their skills, interests, and gifts.

During late adolescence, the frontal lobes undergo major construction building in organization, planning, and judgment, as well as the initiating and shifting of attention. While teens' higher thinking doesn't function at the adult level, the areas of their brains mediating sensory, auditory, spatial, and language function appear to be mature. Teens' impulsivity, emotionality, and hormones, however, offset the frontal lobes' fledgling control, warns Martha Denckla, M.D., professor of neurology, pediatrics, and psychiatry at the Johns Hopkins School of Medicine and research scientist at the Kennedy Krieger Institute. She recommends making fewer cognitive demands on teens while providing them with more structure.

Adolescence is a "time of enormous capacity for development and change, enormous opportunity, and enormous risk," says Giedd, as it coincides with teens' adult urges for sex, drugs, and other risky endeavors. He warns that teens' frontal lobes are probably not well enough developed for them to reliably exercise control over such urges. In fact, the adolescent brain is quite vulnerable to shortsighted, risky decisions, and Giedd counsels teens that the drugs and alcohol they use this weekend may influence their brain development for the rest of their lives.

The cerebellum, long thought to govern muscle coordination, is now known to also be involved in the coordination of cognitive processes and it undergoes the most change during adolescence, not completing the process until about age twenty-five. Just as one can be physically clumsy, one can also be mentally clumsy. "The ability to smooth out all the different intellectual processes, to navigate the complicated social life of the teen, and to get through these things gracefully instead of lurching...seems to be a function of the cerebellum," reports Giedd.

Bonding and modeling

The big question in the minds of parents and educators is: what factors influence or stimulate brain development? Giedd is of the opinion that the more advanced the science becomes, the more "it leads us back to some very basic tenets of spending loving, quality time with our children. The adolescent brain is largely wired for social interaction and for bonding with caretakers."

He asserts that brain imaging substantiates the extremely powerful role of modeling in adolescent learning, and for that reason, one of the worst phrases a parent can utter is, "Do what I say, not what I do." Teens are particularly adept at detecting hypocrisy when their parents' advice on smoking, drinking, partying, and relationships is inconsistent with their behavior.

Factors affecting brain functioning

Giedd observes that everything influences brain development, learning, and intelligence including genes, education, nutrition, stress, exercise, videos, peers, and parenting.

The brain is "just flesh and blood," writes Dharma Khalso, M.D., in his book, *Brain Longevity: The Breakthrough Medical Program that Improves Your Mind and Memory*. It follows, then, that what is good for the heart is good for the brain, and conversely, what is detrimental to the heart is also detrimental to the brain. Khalso recommends parents encourage their children to get adequate rest, eat a healthy and balanced diet, drink ample water, and avoid alcohol, cigarettes, and drugs. Another factor affecting brain functioning is physical activity, as movement stimulates the frontal parts of the brain. William Stixrud, Ph.D., a Washington, D.C area neuropsychologist and learning specialist, points out that patterned programmed movement, such as martial arts, yoga, dance, swimming, or drumming, may be particularly beneficial to optimum brain development.

Stress disorganizes the brain and can significantly interfere with the memory center functioning of the hippocampus, reports Stixrud. Sleep is extremely important for learning and memory consolidation throughout the human life span, he says, and is closely associated with mental and physical health.

Alcohol, smoking, and other drugs each have a negative impact on the adolescent brain. In *Magic Trees of the Mind: How to Nurture Your Child's Intelligence, Creativity, and Healthy Emotions from Birth through Adolescence*, co-author Marian Diamond, Ph.D., reports, "We can only speculate that regular nicotine and carbon monoxide exposure during the brain's final formative years could leave permanent reductions in mental capacity." She goes on to say that "researchers aren't sure whether getting drunk can permanently affect the brain or thinking of a young nonalcoholic, but in testing teens who abuse alcohol, they have detected some significant problems with focusing and maintaining attention." Marijuana, Ecstasy, cocaine, and other drugs "may slow brain development or change it in unknown ways, perhaps altering it permanently," notes Diamond.

Too many parents turn to intensive enrichment programs and activities in an effort to enhance their children's test taking profiles. Curriculum content and demands should be consistent with a child's ability to adequately process and integrate information. Accelerated academics are not necessarily the best choice for most kids, nor is an increased volume of homework better, advises Giedd. In fact, he says, "Things seem to be quite out of balance in terms of what is being asked of kids," especially for gifted students, who are too frequently required to do lengthier, rather than more diverse, assignments. It is crucial to adolescent brain development that teens achieve a balance between learning and relaxation.

Accelerated changes in our day-to-day lives, as well as sensory overload brought about by new technologies, may be permanently altering human brain development. Richard Restak, M.D., a Washington, D.C., neuropsychiatrist, therapist, and author of many books about the human brain, including *The New Brain: How the Modern Age is Rewiring Your Mind,* believes that laptops, cell phones, television violence, and the Internet have irrevocably sped up brain evolution. He believes the accelerated pace of contemporary life renders us more distractible and less able to focus and may contribute to the increasing number of attention deficit disorder (ADD) cases. He suggests that ADD, hyperactivity, and impulsivity may become the norm.

Other intelligences

Parents should be aware that their adolescents' brains are not just the seats of the two intelligences measured on college admissions or IQ tests: the logical-mathematical intelligence of lawyers, researchers, and scientists, and linguistic intelligence of writers, readers, speakers, and listeners. Howard Gardner, Ph.D., Harvard University educator, psychologist, and author of *Intelligence Reframed: Multiple Intelligences for the 21st Century,* introduced the notion that there are a variety of human intelligences.

These other intelligences include the *kinesthetic intelligence* needed by performers, athletes, and builders; the *musical intelligence* inherent in musicians, dancers, actors, and composers; the *spatial intelligence* crucial to surgeons, engineers, sculptors, and painters; the *intrapersonal intelligence* fostering empathy and understanding of oneself and others; the *interpersonal intelligence* so important to leaders, teachers, and service workers; and a recent addition by Gardner, the *naturalistic intelligence* or the ability to identify plants and animals in the natural world.

Martha Cutts, M.A.T., director of the upper school at the National Cathedral School in Washington, D.C., asserts, "If we do more than pay lip service to Howard Gardner's work, we will value the bodily-kinesthetic intelligence of dancers and varsity athletes, as well as the musical intelligence of the choristers, and the interpersonal intelligence of the student government leaders. We will value these gifts just as much as we applaud strong grades in algebra or history. In today's world, the ability to interact well with others or to collaborate with different kinds of people are highly valued and marketable skills."

Teens' remarkable strengths may be any one or more of these intelligences. Parents should support their children's efforts and provide opportunities to gain recognition and appreciation for these abilities. Giedd encourages parents to help their chidren discover their particular array of intelligences by exposing them to a broad variety of extracurricular activities. Thus, children will find their place to shine, find pleasure in learning, and perhaps cultivate friendships with similarly gifted children.

What parents can do

Parents must acknowledge that their teenager, even if physically adult in appearance, is still operating an immature brain, and that means his ability to think, judge, plan, make decisions, integrate and apply information, as well as his ability to inhibit impulses is underdeveloped and not of adult quality. Understanding this, the obvious implication is that teens need their parents to be adults and to provide them guidance, limits, and love.

If everything influences a teen's brain maturation, how does a parent begin to support and strengthen that development? Giedd admonishes parents to avoid "teaching by preaching" and recognize that their own behavior has a great impact on their children's attitudes and values. He observes that the teenager whose parents are seldom home learn that work takes precedence over family.

Michael Gurian, Ph.D., psychologist, social philosopher, and author of many books on child development, including *The Soul of the Child: Nurturing the Divine Identity of Our Children*, elaborates on this notion, saying, "Bonding grows brain cells." He encourages parents to actively encourage bonding and attachment in the family, including "bringing extended family back into the raising of children." He believes that children were meant to have more than one or two parents and that surrogates in the form of grandparents, uncles, aunts, and godparents can satisfy this.

In addition, parents can consider the following strategies.

Acknowledge and support your children's interests and skills. Tell them how proud you are of their special or unique abilities. Encourage them to expand the scope and depth of their gifts. You don't necessarily have to like the chosen interest. Unless illegal or dangerous, accept it and respect your teen's choices.

Encourage your teens to indulge in physical activity, especially those incorporating patterned movements, in part because of the connection between motor and mental control. It is important for children to challenge themselves through the means of a wide variety of activities, including aerobic, strengthening, and stretching exercises.

Encourage your adolescent to learn about the mind-body connection and how each actively impacts the other.

Provide teens with a healthy diet and nutrition, eliminating much of the sugar, fats, and carbohydrates that bloat the menu when teens are left to their own gustatory devices. Gurian says that junk food in large quantities is toxic to brain development and may be responsible for many of our contemporary brain disorders.

Help teens limit stress by identifying strategies that allow them to relax, find comfort, and avoid or bust stress. Stixrud says, "Deep rest heals the nervous system of stress." He also observes that the brain is more vulnerable to stress when dehydrated.

"*Increase the time your children spend in the natural world* by at least double," recommends Gurian. He calls nature the brain's best friend, as it both calms stress and builds brain cells. He also encourages parents to increase the time their children spend in spiritual process, in experiencing joy and a sense of belonging, and in contemplating the mysteries of life. This may include active participation in organized religion, but parents can also encourage and support broad spiritual and philosophical exploration.

Be sure children understand the potential harm to their intelligence and mental performance posed by the use of alcohol, tobacco, and other drugs, especially during these formative years.

Don't be judgmental. If the human brain continues to mature and develop its capacity to think, learn, and judge well into a person's twenties, by what standard can a twelve- or even a seventeen-year-old be judged?

Be interested in your children's emotional development. Daniel Goleman, Ph.D., psychologist and author of *Emotional Intelligence,* asserts that I.Q. contributes only about twenty percent to financial and personal success; the rest is highly dependent on socioemotional abilities. Kids who are happy with themselves and comfortable in their skins are able to learn from their world.

Final thoughts

If we envision the adolescent brain as a work in progress, then we parents have a responsibility to support our teenagers' optimal brain growth during this stage of life. The key ingredient in building better brains may well be the quantity and quality of relationships and connections with others. While teens want to be separate from their parents, they also want to stay connected and have good relationships with them.

As long as new ideas, sensations, and experiences continue to stimulate the brain, the growth and loss of connections is at least a zero-sum game, advises Diamond. While adolescence is prime time for brain construction, lifelong enrichment promotes continued remodeling of our brains throughout our lives. Brain research is in its infancy—stay tuned for more details!

| 2 |

Adolescent Identity: Who Am I?

It's important to accept how other people identify themselves. Never patronize or deny other people's identities. Don't tell someone that they "aren't really Christian" because you rarely see them at church, or that their being gay is "just a phase." Teenagers aren't looking for you to confirm or deny who they are—they are letting you know who they are, who they think they are, want others to believe they are, or who they are experimenting with being.

LESBIAN TEEN

Many of the qualities associated with stereotypical adolescent behavior—unpredictability, rebelliousness, recklessness, impulsivity, irresponsibility—have been scientifically documented to be the result of momentous changes in the developing adolescent brain and the concomitant drive to define self rather than merely raging hormones. The job of forming a stable sense of self is a massive undertaking and is exhausting, aggravating, and challenging for both teens and their parents. Teens use the protected period of adolescence to adjust to their evolving emotions, cognitive abilities, body configurations, and patterns of social interaction. It is a period when our culture allows them to try out different ways of being a member of society without experiencing adult consequences.

Some of the questions teens try to answer during adolescence are: Who am I? What kind of person am I? What kind of relationships do I want? What gives me pleasure? What am I good at? What traits of mine make me proud? What do I want out of life? Which historic role models do I want to emulate? What do I believe in? Am I good enough to be successful (at sports, college, relationships, etc.)? Where is my niche? Where do I belong?

The task of identity formation involves sorting through, selecting, trying on, reshaping, discarding, and fashioning a unique sense of self that includes self-selected beliefs, goals, and values. These efforts sometimes necessitate a certain amount of conflict, observes Rita Schonberg, Ph.D., a Maryland psychologist specializing in children and adolescents.

Parents are understandably troubled by the confrontational, unpredictable, and even irresponsible nature of some adolescent behavior. They wonder how they can offer guidance and boundaries without inhibiting their teenagers' journeys of self-discovery, while at the same time help them establish positive self-concept. How can they help their children learn from mistakes when they're so worried themselves that such mistakes may irrevocably block future options? Parents can begin by appreciating the turmoil in which their teens dwell so much of the time.

Balancing tensions

Famed psychologist Erik Erikson, who developed the concept of Identity Formation, described adolescence as a bridge between childhood and the commitment to adult roles and relationships. Erikson argued that identity formation is a lifelong process with eight themed stages, the first being infancy and the final, old age. At each stage there is a tension between two opposing tendencies, and our task is to establish a balance between the two. During adolescence, the tension is between identity formation and identity confusion. In order to establish a healthy balance, teens must explore new ways of thinking, behaving, and appearing, and consider new ideas, new groups of friends, and new styles of music. Only after exploring a variety of options can teens know who they are and construct integrated senses of self.

It is during this period that teenagers weave together their many threads of self—as sons or daughters, brothers, sisters, students, athletes, friends, and rivals. Adolescence is the critical period of human life in which self-definition coalesces in preparation for adulthood. Teens who do not effectively balance the tension between identity formation and identity confusion will have difficulty meeting the psychological and social challenges to come.

The stage following adolescence is young adulthood, during which the tension is between intimacy, the sharing of life with another, and isolation, or being solitary. Teens failing to construct a sense of who or what they are enter young adulthood confused, lacking in self-confidence, and constantly looking to others for direction, guidance, and decision making. They may feel inept and inferior. They may have difficulty making friends and choices, especially with regard to vocation, sexual orientation, and their roles in life. Establishing intimacy with another may feel very difficult and unrewarding.

Recent research on adolescent brain development indicates that adolescents require a moratorium before taking on certain adult responsibilities. Jay Giedd, M.D., neuroscientist at the National Institutes of Mental Health and practicing child and adolescent psychiatrist, postulates that the quality of a teen's experiences literally sculpts the brain and contributes to the manner in which a young person perceives himself and the world, as well as his potential.

Separation and connection

Children's independent identities are always rooted in the family, but healthy development necessitates they reach beyond the family into the world, especially into the world of their peers. In fact, during middle school, children's collective identity is much more important than their individual identities, observes Elinor Scully, M.Ed., upper school associate director at St. Stephen's and St. Agnes School in Alexandria, Virginia. Most teens strive for incredible conformity with their peers during this period, even while they rebel against their parents, observes Michael Brody, M.D., psychiatrist, parenting consultant, and former Maret School parent.

Teens turn to friends who, for better or worse, are extremely important to their definition of self. "As teenagers change, they frequently change friends or even entire peer groups. They may have different friends for different situations or activities. Making and keeping friends is an ongoing adolescent identity issue," counsels Schonberg. Even though our teenagers are deeply invested in their peer groups, in wanting to be accepted, as well as in appearing to be like everyone else in the group, however, parents are still the most important influence on their children.

A teenager's job is to discover who he or she is, in part by determining which of the values learned from parents, friends, teachers, and the media to retain. "Some tension between parents and children is not just normal but desirable," counsels Patricia Dalton, Ph.D., a Washington, D.C., clinical psychologist. "Teenagers need to determine both how they are like their parents and how they are different—so they can form a coherent, unique sense of self to take into adulthood."

Schonberg says that sometimes a whole new identity seems to form around the pressures of a tragic event like the suicide of a friend, or a routine landmark such as starting high school or turning sixteen. The manner in which teens make sense of it all is much influenced by teachers, friends, the media, and society in general; however, their parents can take the lead by acknowledging and praising their teens for demonstrating laudable qualities and encouraging creativity, curiosity, and kindness.

Visible identity

Defining one's self is, by its nature, a self-absorbing and self-conscious process, especially during middle school when kids perceive themselves as being on stage before an invisible but rapt audience 24/7. While much identity development is an internal or private process, some of the turmoil centers around the external or visible aspects of the physical self—gender, ethnicity, size, and attractiveness.

Gender. Our sexuality, the sense of how we see ourselves and how the world sees us as males or females, is the most fundamental component of our total personality or identity, says Deborah Roffman, M.S., nationally recognized human sexuality educator and author of *Sex & Sensibility: The Thinking Parent's Guide to Talking Sense about Sex*. She goes on to explain that "affixed to us even before we were named or clothed....our sexuality may well have determined more about our [identity and] future course than any other single aspect of our lives."

Body shape, size, and attractiveness. It is not uncommon for teens of both genders to feel they have little control over their bodies. They may have been biologically programmed to be tall or short, have large or small bone structures, or full or thin lips. They may look in the mirror and see only an enormous nose, jug handle ears, or bee sting breasts. It is difficult for a fifteen-year-old to feel good about a body that in no way resembles that of the hottest teen idol. "When teens reach the point where they are able to accept the reality of the features they were dealt by nature, they are then freed psychologically from trying to become the current version of 'perfect'," says Kay Abrams, Ph.D., parenting consultant and Maryland psychologist. "It allows for so many more options."

Sexuality. Along with growing sexual awareness, some teens begin to realize the romantic attractions they feel are for members of their own sex, or for both sexes, or that they aren't comfortable with the gender dictated by their bodies. They are growing up gay, lesbian, bisexual, or transgendered. Even if no one else has a clue that a teen is gay, says Bob Condit, M.Ed., independent consultant and former counselor at Landon School in Bethesda, Maryland, the teen knows it in his heart and often believes he needs to shelter this part of his identity from the world for a while.

"The important thing to figure out is that there is no rush to find out if you are gay or straight," recommends a lesbian student from Georgetown Day School in Washington, D.C. This thoughtful student counsels,

"Take your time and don't put any pressure on yourself. Just know that whoever you turn out to be is okay. It's important for GLBT [gay, lesbian, bisexual, or transgendered] youth to give themselves a break as they try to figure out who they are! Sometimes GLBT youth spend endless amounts of time questioning and analyzing their identity and struggling to find labels for themselves. It's important to relax and realize that it may take you time to find an identity or label you feel comfortable in."

Ethnicity and race. The identity formation process can be more complicated for teens belonging to ethnic and minority groups. "Current conceptions of race and ethnicity can be stereotypical, narrow, and constricting," says Elizabeth Denevi, co-director of multicultural seminars at St. Stephen's and St. Agnes School and an associate with Eastern Educational Resource Collaborative. These constricted conceptions make it more difficult for teens to integrate a positive sense of group membership into their overall individual identity. For many teens, ethnicity or racial identity is merely a fact rather than a defining or motivating force. For others, however, their perception of their race or ethnicity becomes a reality that marginalizes or excludes them. There is no prototypical African-American, Latino, or Asian family. Each varies dramatically in values, economic status, and degree of acculturation to the mainstream. When teens successfully incorporate ethnicity into their identity, it provides a sense of belonging, connectedness, and historical continuity. Being a part of two cultures allows bicultural children to understand their parents' cultures and draw strength from them while making their place in mainstream society.

Explore, experience, and express

Teens use their bodies as canvases on which they unconsciously illustrate their internal journey of exploration and experimentation. They publicize a state of self through clothing, body language, hair color and style, hobbies, and music. By the same token, some teens' external appearance serves as calculated protective coloration, providing an external conformity that shelters their private explorations. Either way, teens use their bodies to make statements, straightforward or protective, and if parents are not thrilled about their children's current styles, they can take comfort in the fact that teens tend to cycle through them and on to the next one rather quickly.

Body decoration. Teens paint their faces or nails, pierce their ears, eyebrows, or noses, and dye their hair, making statements about who they are through the decoration of their bodies. Virginia Beane Rutter, author of *Embracing Persephone: How to be the Mother You Want for the Daughter You Cherish*, calls self-decorating healthy, playful experimentation. Joan Jacobs Brumberg, Ph.D., Cornell University historian and author of *Fasting Girls: The History of Anorexia Nervosa* and *The Body Project: An Intimate History of American Girls*, notes that girls are particularly vulnerable to embracing their bodies as projects and using them as a message board.

Room or school locker decoration is another avenue teens use to project their individuality onto their personal space and expand the canvas of expression. The walls of teens' bedrooms reflect their wishes, dreams, and interests through posters and art. Bulletin boards display important mementos of victories and pleasures. The arrangement of furniture and accessories, the level and nature of lighting, the paint or wallpaper all feather teens' nests with their distinctive touch. At school, teens often use their lockers as mediums of expression, giving much attention to the arrangement of photos and posters to form a collage expressive of themselves for others to see.

The Internet and cyberspace constitute an entire new universe in which teens explore, express themselves, and experiment with their senses of self. Unavailable to previous generations and therefore perhaps not fully understood as the powerful medium it represents to teens, cyberspace provides the ultimate privacy for experimentation. John Suler, Ph.D., professor of psychology at Rider University and author of the online book *Psychology of Cyberspace*, observes that one way in which teens establish their own identities involves the need to keep secrets about themselves from their parents. The Internet is the perfect way to do that. Cyberspace's unique combination of intimacy and anonymity enables teens to discuss things about themselves with others that they would hesitate to reveal in real life and utilize imaginative identities to express hidden wishes, needs, and fears.

He points out that cyberspace allows teens, as well as adults, to invent and reinvent themselves easily and in ways limited only by their imaginations. Teens' online personas can appear as anything from a slightly amended version of their actual selves to imaginative experiments in alternate genders, ages, histories, personalities, and physical appearance. Choice of user names, personal details shared or withheld, information posted on personal web pages, and personas assumed in an online community are all aspects of the manner in which people manage their identities in cyberspace.

What can parents do?

At the same time that teens are deeply, though perhaps somewhat unconsciously, involved in figuring out who they are, the media is aggressively and relentlessly hammering home to them who they should be. Advertising bombards teens with images of how they should dress, the makeup they should wear, the perfumes they should use, the food they should eat, the cars they should drive, and the way their bodies should look. Both film and television programming portray teens as mature and independent and, both explicitly and subtlety, not in need of adult governance or guidance. Experts agree, however, that parents are essential to teens' identity formation because they provide the limits, discuss values, reinforce good decision making, and profoundly love their children.

Parents can celebrate the family and its identities—religious, ethnic, regional, or even institutional, as in the traditions or involvement with a particular college or university. It is no coincidence that rites of passage or initiation into religious or cultural traditions, such the Jewish bar or bat mitzvah and quinceañera celebrations in the Latino community, are held when children are old enough to understand the concept of such identities. To be respectful of the traditions of others, our children need to feel secure in their own cultures.

The dangers of unbridled experimentation are obvious. Teens can endanger their health, their relationships, and their futures. However, the consequences of too little exploration are of concern as well, says Schonberg. Kids who engage in very limited experimentation, who never question or explore paths different than those of their parents, or who don't try on new identities to determine which fits best may well exhibit minimal flexibility in response to opportunities in adulthood. As a result, they may prematurely foreclose on their potential identity, cautions Helen Kivnick, Ph.D., a psychologist who collaborated with Erik Erikson and his wife on their final book, *Vital Involvement in Old Age,* and currently professor of social work at the University of Minnesota. Such young people may turn out just fine, but may nonetheless have missed out on opportunities which could contribute to the formation of a more richly textured identity.

Recognize and encourage those things at which your teens excel. Think beyond academics and sports and help expose them to a wide array of interests so that they have more from which to choose when their curiosity ignites. Support them in pursuing their own interests and ideas. "Look for your children's innate strengths and encourage their three or four natural talents," recommends Marguerite Kelly in a recent syndicated "Family Almanac" column in the *Washington Post.* Think multiple and emotional intelligences. As Kivnick says, "Pay attention to your child's hobbies—they may be where her future lies."

Parents can enhance their children's identity formation by respecting their teens' individuality, taking into account their points of view, utilizing reason and negotiation, and providing—or in some cases tolerating—ample opportunities for them to express their uniqueness. When parents respect, within reason, their teens' right to choose and change, teens learn that love is not contingent on being exactly like their parents. You don't need to push so hard, expect so much, or be so eager for teens to be the adults you want them to be. Your job is to provide acceptance, support and boundaries, limits, empathy, and love.

When your teenager comes to you seeking parental understanding, your child is also looking for validation of his or her goodness and value to you and others, for reassurance that the future is full of possibilities and hope, and that one person can make a difference.

Be sure to tell your children that you eagerly anticipate the marvelous men and women they are in the process of becoming—they need to hear it, and to hear it from you.

Final thoughts

Although we change and enhance our identity in subsequent stages of our lives, it is primarily during adolescence that we have the opportunity for the active exploration that forms the foundation for a meaningful adult life. While many teenagers retain most of their parents' core values, their sense of being individuals, separate from their parents and complete with their own opinions, perspectives, and interests, begins to gel during adolescence. Their challenging of our rules and values, as well as their renegotiating of their positions, are important and necessary to the process.

We have brought our children into a world that changes more rapidly than ever before in human history. We want them to have the inner strength to be flexible, resourceful, honorable, creative, diligent, and devoted amid chaos and change. We want them to recognize and value these attributes in themselves. This is a tall order for all parents and can result in a struggle to balance empathy and support with establishing boundaries and consequences while our children evolve into their own unique selves.

| 3 |

Body Image

Adolescence is filled with angst, and it all has to do with looks. If a teen is "too" anything—too heavy or too thin, too tall or too short, too hairy, pale, or awkward—this can tear at the threads of self-esteem. It all relates to body image, and while not too many years ago the concern was primarily a "girl thing," both boys and girls now almost equally share the angst.

MICHAEL BRODY, M.D., Psychiatrist and parenting consultant

It is not uncommon for teens of both genders to feel they have little control over their bodies. They may have been biologically programmed to be tall or short, have large or small bone structures, or full or thin lips. They may look in the mirror and see an enormous nose, jug handle ears, or bee sting breasts. On the other hand, Kay Abrams, Ph.D., a Maryland psychologist and parenting consultant, says that when teens reach the point where they are able to accept the features nature dealt them, they are then freed psychologically from trying to become the current version of perfect.

Beginning in late childhood, teens of both genders try to cope with a media-driven culture that seduces them into thinking that the body and sexual expression should be their most important projects. Joan Jacobs Brumberg, Ph.D., Cornell historian and author of *Fasting Girls: The History of Anorexia Nervosa* and *The Body Project: An Intimate History of American Girls*, observes that an increasing number of people have come to believe that their bodies are perfectible. She adds that this focus on physical perfection raises teens', especially girls', vulnerability to exploitation.

Self-worth

"Body image involves our perception, imagination, emotions, and physical sensations of, and about, our bodies," says Judy Lightstone, M.F.T., psychotherapist, body image author, and online resource. She says, "It is not static, but ever changing, and is sensitive to shifts in our mood, environment, and physical experiences. It is psychological in nature rather than based on fact, and is much more influenced by self-esteem than by actual physical attractiveness as judged by others. It is not inborn, but learned. And while initial learning about body image occurs in the family and among peers, these lessons are reinforced by what is learned and expected culturally."

Liking one's body and having an appreciation for one's physical needs makes for healthy self-confidence in teenagers. During adolescence, teens try to take ownership of their bodies and need to be able to separate self-worth from appearance. However, both boys and girls may experiment with various self-improvement regimens, including changing hairstyles, working out at the gym, losing weight, trying out different fashion styles, wearing contact lenses, and having, or at least requesting, cosmetic surgery.

The best assurance for positive body esteem is positive self-esteem built on skills, accomplishments, successes, and successful interpersonal relationships. If self-esteem is too dependent upon appearance, teens are at far greater risk of feeling the need to control or change their physical selves. Building strengths in academics, hobbies, and social skills are more important to feeling good about oneself than any competency built around clothes and appearance.

Body loathing

Self-image is extremely powerful psychologically, and when teens are unhappy with what they see in the mirror, that image, and the projected social and athletic consequences of it, is often greatly exaggerated in their minds. It can be extremely frustrating for the parent who pulls her sixteen-year-old daughter in front of a mirror to demonstrate how thin she's become, or to show her how pretty she really is, to have her daughter, looking at the same image her mother's seeing, wail, "Look at all that fat!" or, "I'm sooo ugly!"

According to a study published in the *Journal of Child Development*, dissatisfaction with one's body continues to increase in girls and decrease in boys throughout the course of adolescence. In a survey published a decade ago in the *Journal of Youth and Adolescence*, seventy percent of girls and thirty-three percent of boys reported they would like to be thinner. More than eighty percent of girls responding to the survey said that being thinner would make them happier, more successful, and more popular. Many experts believe the percentages have increased.

Abrams notes that every eating disorder she has encountered in her practice has been the result of clients' body dissatisfaction and a drive for thinness. "All eating disorders begin with negative body image," she observes. While body size issues are often closely linked with eating disorders, many clearly are not. Teens of both sexes who are distraught over body features they find unattractive, are not growing or maturing at the same rate as friends. They may be depressed over the impact of these perceived flaws on their social or athletic lives or wrestling with psychological problems quite different from those causing eating disorders.

Teens' sports participation may also be adversely affected by extreme self-consciousness. Some teens feel as though they are always on stage or under intense scrutiny by others and suffer debilitating humiliation when they appear inept, spend too much time sitting on the bench, or are under too much pressure to win.

When teens feel helpless to change something that has gone wrong in their lives, they often find fault with their bodies and criticize themselves for being too fat, too short, or too anything. Many teens develop an obsessive abhorrence of a single physical characteristic, such as the size of a nose or unruly curls. In the extreme, such self-loathing can result in self-destructive behavior such as cutting, sexual promiscuity, or eating disorders.

When a teen's perception of his body image appears to be truly out of kilter for any length of time, it is appropriate to seek the support and counsel of a social worker or psychologist experienced in dealing with these issues.

Body image and puberty

Body image issues usually flair up at the onset of puberty. Ten- and eleven-year-olds who are either ahead or behind their peers in growing body hair or breasts are likely to feel awkward and self-conscious. Our culture's thinner-than-thou ideal sets up most girls for failure, and many experience anxiety about getting fat rather than taking pleasure in their new female curves.

Rita Schonberg, Ph.D., a Maryland psychologist specializing in adolescents, believes the main threat to self-image is puberty and the changes in appearance that come with it. Teens ask, "What can I do with myself?" "Who am I?" "Who likes me?" " What do I look like to others?" "When will my body stop changing, and what will it be like when it does?" During adolescence, both boys and girls are influenced by the appraisal of peers of both genders.

Some parents mistake a girl's normal pubescent weight gain, necessary not only for feminine curves but also for normal menstrual cycles, for the onset of obesity. When a parent makes a comment like, "Aren't you getting a little heavy?" it can devastate a young girl.

Sexual development during adolescence can be confusing and embarrassing. Wet dreams and menstrual accidents can rattle teens' confidence in their self-control. Parents can assist their children by talking with them early on about the body and the individual pacing of adolescent changes. Encourage questions and answer them honestly and accurately. Parents might also ask an objective third party, such as a child's pediatrician, school counselor, or health teacher, for assistance in obtaining accurate information and achieving a greater comfort level with the material. Such a resource person may also be available to sit in on discussions between parents and their children, as well.

When a boy is aware that the body hair growth rate is different for each kid, or that boys sometimes develop temporary fat pockets resembling small breasts, he may feel more comfortable with his own physical changes and less betrayed by his physiognomy. Bob Condit, M.Ed., independent consultant and former guidance counselor at the Landon School in Bethesda, Maryland, believes boys can be as concerned about body image as girls are. He says, "From the middle of eighth grade through early tenth grade, one of the biggest developmental issues of boys concerns height—'Am I growing?'—and it's not unusual for shorter boys, anxiously awaiting a growth spurt, to measure themselves every night looking for any sign of growth."

By late ninth grade and early tenth grade, many boys are lifting weights regularly in an attempt to build muscle and tight, six-pack abs that they hope will result in greater strength, athletic ability, and popularity. It is not unusual to find a set of weights or gym membership on boys' wish lists.

Media influence

Advertisers don't just sell products, they sell an image, and for our children that image is a terribly unhealthy one, observes Lisa Gray, M.Ed., director of counseling at the Madeira School in McLean, Virginia. The media's message to teenagers is that they not only must dress like sophisticated adults, but to be desirable, popular, and attractive, they must drink alcohol, smoke cigarettes, wear the trendiest clothing, be painfully thin or unrealistically buff, and be sexually enticing at increasingly earlier ages.

Gray adds that while we read much about the negative impact of advertising and television on girls' perceptions of what it means to be attractive and popular, TV and print advertising project an equally unrealistic image of what boys must look like in order to achieve the same status. Calvin Klein and Abercrombie & Fitch ads, Soloflex commercials, and magazines like *Men's Health* and *GQ* do for young men's perceptions of their self-image exactly what advertising from Guess, *Cosmopolitan*, *YM*, and MTV have done to young women. Magazine advertising and articles, billboards, video games, music lyrics, and websites bombard our children with unrealistic, unattainable, and often unhealthy ideals to mimic.

Surgical improvement

Adolescents enter a dangerous realm when they strive to attain the unrealistic physical ideals portrayed by fashion models and movie idols. Some teens consider cosmetic surgery to be the quick, and perhaps only, method of achieving their dream selves.

Numerous ethical questions have been raised regarding teenagers electing cosmetic surgery. While it may help a teen feel better about him or herself, it can set up a child for a fall, says Karen Zager, Ph.D., a developmental psychologist who serves as a consultant on adolescent development to the Public Broadcasting System. The results of cosmetic surgery may not meet a teen's expectations, or the new look may not suit his or her mature appearance. Moreover, the deficient self-esteem that propels a teen toward plastic surgery may stem from other more serious and fundamental difficulties.

Clothes make the teen

Teens use clothes to help represent and define themselves. Adolescents try out personas as though they were clothes and use clothes to flesh out the personas. Younger kids are often eager to look just like their friends, but in adolescence teens begin to question whether or not they want to look just like everybody else, or if they can create a more individual look and still be accepted by their group. Some girls feel the only way to attract boys' attention is to dress up, observes Denise Anderson, parent of a student at Georgetown Visitation School in Washington, D.C. Many girls, however, are more concerned with where their appearance ranks in the pecking order of female peers.

Fashion consciousness is not limited to girls. Boys work to perfect their fashion statements by sporting oversize pants that hang on their hips below the elastic of their undershorts, cut-off t-shirts, tight skullcaps, and sleeveless tops, and by draping themselves with an array of hi-tech gadgets.

Like girls, teenage boys demonstrate a heightened brand awareness, a tendency to buy on impulse, and a predilection for clothes that are both simpler and more blatantly sexy than in the past, reports Ruth Ferla, a *New York Times* staff writer who follows fashion trends. Boys roam the malls in packs, spending their allowances and earnings on the latest fashions, designer sunglasses, logo t-shirts, and expensive sneakers. More guys appear to be shopping and dressing themselves than in previous generations. Boys' personal fashion is greatly influenced by the need to project a masculine image to their peers, in part to discourage homophobic comments and taunts.

Shoes provide teens an opportunity to flaunt a status symbol or make a statement about their individuality, especially for teens attending schools requiring the wearing of uniforms. The cooler a teen is, the more important shoe style, color, design, and of course, brand name becomes. Exotic new shoes allow a teen to become a trendsetter, if only for a short time.

"An interest in fashion, even revealing fashion that makes boys stare and mothers groan, does not preclude an interest in intellectual activities," wrote Northern Virginia rising senior Julia Snyder in a letter to the editor of the *Washington Post*. She apparently speaks for many girls who feel that paying attention to their clothes "does not make them ignorant of other aspects of their lives and certainly is not correlated to the scholarship a girl exhibits."

When parents voice their concerns about their teens' attire, the frequent response from their kids is that they are being "way overprotective." Most parents try to help their teens develop a sense of modesty and decency. Modesty suppresses crudity, signals that what is hidden is worth waiting for, and reflects our instinct to protect what some consider sexual vulnerability.

Body decoration

Another way in which teens express their personalities is body decoration, and their bodies often double as canvases of self-expression in middle and high school. Teens paint or pierce their skins and dye their hair. Self-decorating is healthy, playful experimentation, writes Virginia Beane Rutter in *Embracing Persephone: How to be the Mother You Want for the Child You Cherish*, but it can also veer off into destructive self-injury. Brumberg cautions that girls in particular are vulnerable to embracing their bodies as projects, using them like message boards.

Multiple ear piercing has been commonplace for some time, and the controversy has moved on to tattoos and body piercing, especially the piercing of the tongue, nose, nipple, and belly button. Teens give many reasons for obtaining piercings and tattoos, including the fact that their friends are doing it, for the thrill of it, they think it's attractive, for a boyfriend or girlfriend, to commemorate an event, to be different, to attract attention, and, of course, to annoy their parents. Condit observes that the reason usually has little to do with a teen's parents, contrary to what many believe. In fact, a teen's parents are probably the furthest thing from his mind during the procedure except possibly as a fleeting thought of, "My mom's gonna kill me!"

Despite parents' concerns about multiple piercings and temporary tattoos, as well as bizarre hair color, shaved heads, and garish make-up and nail polish, these are usually just attempts to assert some degree of individuality and aren't often maintained for very long before the next fashion statement evolves. These are generally harmless expressions and rarely cause any damage besides parents' mortification when seen with their children in public.

Permanent tattoos and surgical procedures, however, are quite a different story and should be carefully considered beforehand, including evaluating the risks and possible negative consequences before carrying out any procedure. Parents can suggest to teens contemplating such procedures that they try to imagine how a future mate might react or how their own children might feel about their parent's appearance.

The power of beauty

Our culture recognizes many kinds of power, and physical beauty is the big gun relentlessly aimed at us by marketing and the media. However, as parents, we have the power to diversify our sense of beauty and teach our children to recognize inner beauty as the truest and most lasting variety, as well as the transient nature of sheer physical beauty.

Fortunately, our children's world is generously blessed with people who model inner beauty rather than external show. They are surrounded by adults and older peers whom they love, respect, and recognize as possessing strength, knowledge, and inner beauty, regardless of their physical appearance.

"We give too much power to beauty," Abrams declares. The primary goal of far too many girls is superlative beauty, and guys have a similar goal of being handsome and muscular. While we may avow we value diversity, Hollywood and Madison Avenue certainly don't seem to reflect this. The popular media shows teens, as well as adults, only a very narrow range of desirability.

Brumberg, who writes and lectures in an effort to counteract certain dominant images of beauty, believes that we now recognize a wider range of beauty than the WASP ideal venerated by past generations. She finds that many white Americans now appreciate the beauty of dark skin or ethnic hair, but feels that the spectrum of the feminine ideal is relatively narrow and many girls are excruciatingly aware that they are unblonde, untall, and unlean. The *Washington Post* columnist Donna Britt frequently writes about the media's limited images of African-American women and laments that the absence of images of full-figured and dark-skinned beauties makes it even more difficult for some African-American girls to recognize their own beauty.

What parents can do

The notion that thin is the only way to be and that dieting is a normal way of life permeates the minds of increasingly younger children. Parents have a central role in combating these notions by rearing children with normal eating habits and good body image.

"Healthy body weight is the size a person naturally returns to after a long period of both noncompulsive eating and consistent exercise commensurate with the person's physical health and condition," writes Rita Freedman, Ph.D., in *Body Love: Learning To Like Our Looks and Ourselves: A Practical Guide for Women*. Experts suggest the following ways in which parents can help encourage teens to feel comfortable with their particular healthy body weight.

Talk with your sons and daughters about the difficulty of growing into a teenage body in the current culture. Avoid attempting to accomplish this in one big formal talk. Instead, look for teachable moments, such as when sharing news stories or articles about celebrities' life styles and choices. Discuss with your teens the wide range of factors determining physical size, stressing that while genetics are beyond our individual control, we can rely on nutrition and exercise to optimize our assets.

Parents should probably elect to accept most teen experimentation with clothes, makeup, jewelry, temporary tattoos, and hair dye as temporary choices. Get involved in your teen's body only if invited by them to do so. Schonberg warns that intense parental interest or criticism in this area is usually detrimental.

Remind your teenager of what his or her body is capable of rather than focusing on its appearance. Help your teen focus on what it feels like to be active and energized. Point out that a valid measure of sports success comes from inside the body. Include in the family photo album shots of your teenager in action—dirty, sweaty, and triumphant. Sports participation allows your teen to recognize the body as capable of great feats of dexterity, skill, and grace rather than merely a decorative envelope for the personality.

Establish and enforce a ban on the teasing of anyone, both at home and away, about appearance and eating habits. Don't stop at reassuring your teen, "Of course you're not fat, honey," but take the time to explain that others' ideas about how much one should weigh or eat are subjective opinions and not necessarily fact.

Parents should be careful not to make derogatory comments about their own bodies in front of their children. Many experts agree that some body image conflicts begin at home where there is a parent who speaks disparagingly about his or her own body, or who makes a major issue of dieting. Parents' health habits, body image, and attitudes can greatly affect their teenager positively and negatively. So, examine your feelings about your own body—if you don't feel good about it, you may be serving as a negative role model for your teen.

Be aware of your children's television viewing, magazine reading, and other media exposure, and counter negative body image messages by engaging them in conversation about what they see and hear. Help your children recognize that the media rarely portrays a diversity of physical sizes and shapes, and when they do, it is rarely in a positive manner. Foster in your children a healthy critical disrespect of crass commercialism and the tyranny of beauty.

Don't be a food cop; encourage healthy eating but be relaxed about food at home. Minimize weight talk and dieting behaviors. Emphasize the nutrition needed for energy and good health. Keep in mind that there are no bad foods; bad is an immoderate, extreme, or unbalanced misuse of food. Denying children certain foods will only stimulate an appetite for them. Children need the correct amount and right kinds of fat in their diets for normal healthy growth. Discourage a fat-free diet.

Schonberg says that much of teens' self-image and perception of their own value is derived from real people—loving, attentive parents, teachers, and peers, rather than the media. Encourage your teen to develop healthy passions and interests, as these provide a sustaining breadth of vision that extends far beyond oneself and one's appearance.

Final thoughts

Body image is psychological and not necessarily based on reality. Body dissatisfaction is prevalent among teenagers and is strongly influenced by both media messages and perceived peer opinion. However, parents remain the most important influence on their children.

The teen years are a time of individuation, when your teen may choose styles of dress, haircuts, music, art, and language that you don't care for. Remember, advises John Gottman, Ph.D., author of *The Heart of Parenting: Raising an Emotionally Intelligent Child*, you don't need to approve of your child's choices, you only need to accept them. So many teens' efforts to enhance their images are transient, and parents can remind themselves, and their children, that they love them regardless of their appearance, or to paraphrase the late Mr. Rogers, "There's no one else in the whole world quite like you!"

| 4 |

Communication Between Teens and Parents

God gave man two ears but only one mouth, that he might hear twice as much as he speaks.
EPICTETUS the STOIC

If your voice is the only one you hear, you aren't learning anything you didn't already know.
HAM BERRY, Grandfather of three Washington area teens

Many parents feel out of touch with their teens' lives. Conversations between parents and teenagers typically revolve around the logistics of homework, chores, and the management of busy schedules. We seem to have less leisure to converse with our teens about the day's joys, worries, setbacks, and achievements. While this might not be the case in your home, it's a fact that no matter how in touch we are with our teenagers or how well we feel we know them, we are usually far less informed than we think. And whether we like it or not, they are going to be out there doing things, or, at the very least, will be around others who are doing things, that don't meet with our approval. It makes sense, therefore, to establish the best communication patterns possible with our teens so that we have a chance to be aware of at least some of what is really happening in their lives.

"Where are you going?"

"Out. To Tom's."

"What do you plan to do?"

"Nothing, we're just going to hang out."

"When will you be home?"

"Later. Quit bugging me, I'll be home when I get home."

Exchanges like the one above are frustrating and leave parents feeling excluded and angry. Children begin to shift the focus of their conversational energy away from parents and toward their friends in the latter half of elementary school. Many teens are quite aggressive in pushing their parents away. In *You and Your Adolescent: A Parent's Guide for Ages 10–20*, Laurence Steinberg, Ph.D., and Ann Levine write, "Parents hope to get from children what children crave from parents: unconditional love and approval. And most parents get it, more or less, until their children become teenagers."

When a parent is involved in an exchange like the one above, it is hard not to take it personally. It is useful to remember that adolescence is much like the Terrible Twos of toddlerhood. Remember how often we heard, "No!" and, "*I* do it." Like the toddlers they once were, teens push us away in order to become more autonomous and self-reliant. It is something that must happen for our children to function independently as adults. Ironically, it is during this stage that our teens need our love, without rancor, more than ever, just when they may be least able to reciprocate.

It is tempting to put off working on communication when your conversational partner makes it clear he thinks you're clueless and not worth speaking to, observes Julia Berry, M.A., parent of three teens and director of the nursery program at St. Patrick's School in Washington, D.C. She notes, "The manner in which you manage this new communication dynamic will play an important role in your relationship with your teenager, the atmosphere in your home, and ultimately, how effectively you can guide your child through the tricky and sometimes dangerous teen years." Where to begin? Berry recommends parents begin with improved listening.

Listening

One of the greatest obstacles to good communication with teenagers is our need, and some would call it obsession, to instruct and inform them rather than to listen to them. The instructive or interrogative mode is easily adopted because, as parents, we have much more life experience and wisdom than our teens, and we are so busy that it seems more efficient. It also makes us feel like our kids will be safer. Unfortunately, governance by fiat generally shuts down communication with teens entirely.

Throughout adolescence, our teens begin to think more like adults, and like adults, they crave respect for their ideas and opinions. Their developing ability to think abstractly and hold many variables in mind means that many teens are ready, even anxious, to debate the merits of whom they see, where they go, and what is safe for them to do. Steinberg and Levine point out that the young adolescent may have the mental equipment to "think great thoughts," but he doesn't yet have much experience applying advanced logic to the mundane, practical realities of everyday life. Parents can provide their teens with opportunities to practice thinking things through by taking the time to listen and discuss matters with them.

"Parents have to be smart," advises Washington, D.C., clinical psychologist Patricia Dalton, Ph.D. As children get older, she suggests parents should gradually lessen their protective stance and do less dictating and more consulting.

What does consulting with our teens mean in practical terms? Dalton is not suggesting that parents abdicate their authority over their teens. Rather, she is saying we should capitalize on our teens' willingness to debate and position ourselves as authorities who can help, through discussion, to clarify issues and steer choices to an acceptable conclusion. When our teenagers come to us to talk, we must seize the moment and actively listen. How do we do this?

Be alert for potential conversational moments. Observe your teen's body language; rely on your instincts to know when your child has something important, or even not so important, to tell you. You might then start the conversation with a simple observation like, "Looks like you had a hard day," or, "You look so happy!"

When that moment comes, make yourself available both physically and mentally, i.e., actively. Put down the paper. Stop chopping the onions. Turn off the news. Use your body posture and eye contact to show you're listening and thus granting your teen the respect and importance he or she craves.

Use your instincts. If your child is hesitant, or the topic is sensitive, you might continue with a nondemanding task like folding laundry and ask your teen to help while you talk. Such activity allows for lessened eye contact and provides both of you an outlet for nervous energy.

Be patient. If your teen is hesitant, give him or her some additional time to respond. Acknowledge the difficulty by saying something like, "This must be hard to talk about."

Be encouraging. Say, "What's on your mind?" or, "I'd like to hear about it." Use what Adele Faber and Elaine Mazlish, in their book, *How to Talk So Kids Will Listen & Listen So Kids Will Talk*, call simple door openers—noncommittal interjections like "uh-huh" or "really?"—to encourage your teen to continue.

Be nonjudgmental. Remember, you are trying to hear and understand what your teen is saying so that you can help him solve a problem or make a new game plan. Don't interrupt! If you don't stay quiet long enough to glean the spoken and unspoken information you need, you won't be of much help.

Use active listening. Acknowledge the subtext of the conversation while reflecting upon the salient spoken information. Restate what your child says in your own words to ensure you've understood correctly. For instance, you could say, "It sounds as if you were really upset. It must have been hard to stand up to the whole class when you disagreed."

Parents whose conversational style is not conducive to active listening admit that acquiring the skill takes both practice and patience. However, these same parents report that with regular use, active listening really can promote better understanding between parent and child. In addition, active listening puts the burden of problem solving on the teen. When emotions are high and a parent offers a supportive response like, "Sounds pretty frustrating," the teen must look inside to determine his or her feelings. Even if the parent has guessed wrong, the teen feels less defensive and is less apt to shut out further discussion. A parent can then ask a neutrally worded clarifying question like, "Why is the reading going so slowly?" (rather than the more pointed, "Why aren't you further along?") and lob the ball back to the teen to analyze the situation and identify the true issue.

Acknowledging strong feelings, identifying their source, and taking action are the essence of problem solving. Parents who use active listening effectively and repeatedly instill in their kids an internal problem-solving framework that will hold them in good stead, even when they have to puzzle things out on their own.

Talking to connect and control

Teens, even the best-behaved ones, act foolishly. If parents listen carefully, they are likely to hear things from their teens that frighten or anger them. It is tempting to dream about keeping teenagers locked in a bedroom until adulthood; however, they need experience getting into and out of trouble before they're ready to fully explore life on their own. Parents must try to keep their children safe but also help them develop a sense of reasonable risk. Deborah Tannen, Ph.D., professor of linguistics at Georgetown University and author of many books about communication, advises parents to try to find "the balance between connection and control."

A good strategy for countering your teen's pressure for permission to do something or go somewhere questionable is to give yourself permission to delay your response, especially if your first inclination is to respond with, "Are you out of your mind?" Instead, tell your child, "You know, I'm not sure how I feel about that idea. Can you give me ten minutes (or two hours or until tomorrow) to think this over?" Then, get back to your teen at the end of the agreed upon period and present your thinking in a reasoned fashion. Try to keep your vocal tone calm and reflective. Be honest about your worries and fears. Don't forget to listen. Some teens will continue to lobby or nag at a parent during this period of reflection, but others may actually withdraw the request when given time to reconsider the merits of their case. Avoid overresponding and overexplaining. Many kids want just the bottom line, yes or no, and they tune out parents who talk too much.

Know your child's style. Less really can be more. If teens learn they can trust you to keep your cool and not go on and on, you have a much greater chance of hearing from them when there is big trouble. If your child needs to be rescued in the middle of the night from a party or the police station, you want him to feel he can call you. With practice, you will be able to say in your most soothing voice, "I'll be right there and I'm glad you called. We can talk about it tomorrow," while you bite your tongue on the drive home.

Another important element of ensuring and maintaining open communication is to use information wisely. Bob Condit, M.Ed., independent consultant and former counselor at the Landon School in Bethesda, Maryland, provides this example to parents in his communication workshops: your ninth-grader returns home after a party and, when asked, tells you that a few guys there were drinking beer, but he didn't. Two weeks later, when he asks your permission to attend another party with the same group, you respond, "No, I'm afraid I can't let you go. I remember you told me last time that there was alcohol there. I really can't allow you to be in a situation where you might be tempted to drink." Condit points out that in this exchange, the parent has inadvertently, but effectively, taught the child to lie, or at least to withhold information, so as not to be prohibited from doing "what everyone else does." That parent has created a situation where the child must be untruthful or silent in order to have a normal teenage social life.

Maintaining the dialogue

If your habitual response to your teen in conversation has been more harangue and less than Zen-like, you may have some recovery work to do in order to reestablish a trusting communication between the two of you. A good first step may be to acknowledge that you haven't been the calmest listener in the world and that you would like to change your style of response. This kind of candid self-disclosure has the paradoxical effect of earning your teen's respect. It may also provide you with some leverage when you need to stop your teen's nagging or buy time to calm yourself before responding, as in, "This has really upset me, but I want to listen and think carefully. You'll have to give me a minute to collect myself before we finish this conversation." One note of caution: once you have established a better rapport with your teen, refrain from asking about emotionally laden issues like sex, alcohol, and drugs, or scrapes with the law unless you are absolutely certain you can remain calm upon hearing the answer.

There will be times when, although your teen has not asked your advice, you are nonetheless compelled to give it. Again, choose a suitable time and place to tackle a sensitive topic and begin by saying, "You haven't asked for my advice, but I do have some thoughts on this topic. May I share them with you?" If your teen says no, schedule a better time, perhaps after dinner or when homework is done. Allowing your child to control the scheduling of a difficult conversation increases the likelihood that it will come to pass, and that he will listen to what you have to say.

When you can no longer contain your feelings about an issue, take the advice of an experienced local mom, who says, "Freak out with your friends, not with your kids." Talk with other parents about their take on the teen scene. Rant and rave to a friend who can sympathize. It's important to remember that all families weather crises and challenges similar to your own, no matter how perfect they appear to the outside observer. Parents who share information and experiences with one another connect, and through the many connections they form a network, which ultimately helps them look out for each other's children.

Barriers to good communication

Parents may find it difficult to generate interest in the kinds of issues about which their teens feel passionate. They may be impatient with, and frustrated by, adolescent indecision and egocentrism. Teens' stinging criticism of parents can feel unfair and hurtful. There are several things we can do, however, to make communicating smoother when we feel distanced, irritated, or annoyed by our teens.

Don't take your teen's mean remarks personally. Their criticism is part of the separation process. Don't let such interactions shut you down or succeed in making you give up. Teens are works in progress—sometimes the thirteen-year-old who shuts out her parents is ready a year or two later to open up and enjoy sharing with them.

Try not to get angry when your teen talks like a teen. Indecision and egocentrism are normal adolescent characteristics—not character flaws. Learning how to use complex reasoning and apply ideals to everyday life takes time and repetition. Your grandmother probably soothed your own parents during your adolescence by saying, "It's just a phase." And that's what it is—temporary. Short-term. You and your teen will grow through it.

Don't be afraid to tell your teen your feelings have been hurt. By saying, "That really hurt me," or, "Let's try to stick to the issue and not get personal," you can redirect focus back to the problem when in the heat of an argument.

Learn more about your teen's interests. Parents expect their children to value the things they value. Relationships are built on reciprocity, so turnabout is fair play. Make time to watch a favorite television program with your teen and let him fill you in on what's happening in the series; ask to sit in on his latest computer game and invite his opinion about its merits; or listen to a CD she's fond of with her and encourage her to talk about the group and their work. While you don't have to embrace the values their interests represent, demonstrating a genuine interest will help strengthen the bond between you.

Establish ground rules for respecting private information. Make sure both you and your children have the right to determine whether information is for private or public consumption, and respect those determinations. Indiscriminate disclosure of your teen's personal problems to others is guaranteed to infuriate and embarrass your child and seriously damage his ability to trust you. Likewise, there are undoubtedly many things about you that you would prefer your teen not share with friends, friends' parents, or teachers. Respect for confidentiality makes for more honest communication.

Do not correct or make fun of your teen in front of other people. Wait until you can speak to him or her privately. Public criticism or mockery is painful for anyone, but can be devastating to a teenager.

Create availability

Good conversational skills are learned over the course of many years and with much practice. Many teens need more practice with the exchange of ideas and opinions that constitutes meaningful adult conversation. Berry provides the following suggestions for generating and fostering interesting and rewarding conversation between you and your teen.

Be a model for sharing thoughts. Rather than asking your child about his or her day, begin with, "My day contained some real surprises. May I tell you about them?" Share important details about a highlight, or a lowlight, including how you felt and what you did to solve a problem. Listen to your teen's responses and comments, and when the conversation ends, don't forget to tell him you enjoyed the conversation and thank him for talking with you

Eat dinner together as often as you can. Even if you're having something simple for supper, create a pleasant ambiance. Studies indicate that kids who experience companionable family dining and who talk with their parents regularly score significantly higher on their SATs. Be sure to make the dinner table a snipe-free zone with no tolerance for criticism of others as a conversational gambit.

Take advantage of time in the car with your teen. Your teen is a captive audience when you're together in the car. Perceptive parents sometimes plan to bring up difficult topics on a long drive. Many teens find the car a safe place to discuss embarrassing issues like sex because it's private and they can't be overheard. The side-by-side seating reduces the impact on each other of anxious body language and lessens eye contact. Consider banning cell phone calls, both incoming and outgoing, while in the car with your teen so that riding time is associated with conversation. If you really want to know the lowdown on your teen's scene, volunteer to chauffeur for as many teen social events as possible—and keep your ears open. You will overhear every detail of an event, especially if you can remain quiet during the ride.

Create availability. Put down the newspaper if your child sits down with you on the couch. Offer to watch TV together. Provide a neck rub or a back scratch over homework. Ask for help with chores that can be done together, like putting away the dishes, walking the dog, or cooking. Ask for help with your computer or with editing a piece you're writing for work. Keep jigsaw puzzles, board games, decks of cards, or photo albums near to hand in the rec room to serve as shared activities that can be aids to conversation. When your teen goes out in the evening, Berry suggests you take a nap after dinner so you can be up baking cookies at 11:00 p.m. You'd be amazed at how conducive warm cookies, milk, and a dimly lit, cozy kitchen are to satisfying conversation.

Final thoughts

You and your teen can talk together in real and important ways if you are an effective, attentive listener—if you remain calm and open-minded, use active listening, find a balance between control and risk, use information wisely, and create opportunities to talk together. Know your children. Trust your instincts. Let them know you. Enjoy your fabulous, fascinating children—they are in your care for such a short time.

2 teens on the move

| 5 |

Friendships

A son told his mother that he felt he was a loser. His mother recognized that he often appeared ill at ease with his peers. The problem seemed to grow more acute as he got older.

A mother asked her eleventh-grader why she was crying. When pressed, the girl confessed that she was jealous of the relationship between two of her frieneds and felt left out. To get back at her friends, she had spread rumors about them, and they had confronted her about it at school.

Friendships—too many, too few, or somehow just not right—can create almost as many problems for parents as they do for adolescents. "One hundred percent of kids have trouble with friendships at some point in their lives," observes Sylvia Stultz, Ph.D., a Washington, D.C., psychologist specializing in friendships and social relationships.

In fact, middle school "is about social life," writes Mary Pipher, Ph.D., author of *The Shelter of Each Other: Rebuilding Our Families*, "and the main thing kids need is help learning to deal with each other, with the opposite sex, learning to manage their social anxiety, negotiate conflict. and so on. And this means they need to have adults involved with them—in ways that help them learn social interaction."

The importance of having friends

Friendships play a crucial role in an adolescent's development. The value of a friendship reaches far beyond the relationship itself. Friends teach each other social graces, communication skills, and conflict resolution. They give kids someone to confide in and to learn from. "Friends replace parents as the ones on whom kids depend," Stultz notes. Importantly, friendships enable kids to form a sense of self that is separate from their parents. "Among peers, the adolescent comes into his own as an individual, on the way to becoming a member of the adult world," writes Kenneth Rubin, Ph.D., in his book *The Friendship Factor: Helping Our Children Navigate Their Social World and Why It Matters for Their Success and Happiness*.

The nature of friendship changes as children mature. For example, in their drive to separate from their parents, young adolescents—those aged eleven to perhaps thirteen—"have clingy, passionate friendships," Stultz notes. Young adolescents have a new awareness of popularity and experiment with best friends, finding someone who helps them analyze life, with whom they can share a worldview, she says.

"Typically, the nature of peer groups evolves from middle school to the end of high school," Rubin observes. "Same-sex cliques, which demand a high degree of conformity from their members, predominate and shape the social organization of a school or class through the early teens. By later adolescence, the boundaries of those groups are more permeable. As membership in groups waxes and wanes, the behaviors that define them become less fixed, and older adolescents, in general, display kinder, gentler feelings toward all their peers. 'In' and 'out' matter less."

Close friendships tend to develop between teens who are more similar in nature, interest, social class, and ethnic background, according to an article on relationship development by the Children's Hospital of Pittsburgh, Pennsylvania. "While childhood friendships tend to be based on common activities, adolescent friendships expand to include similarities in attitudes, values, loyalty, and intimacy, as well as common activities. Teen friendships also tend to be more similar in level of involvement in academic and educational interest."

Rubin observes, "For the typical teenager—the boy who has a friend or two he's comfortable confiding in, the girl who turns to her friends with comparative ease—a peer is someone to talk to without experiencing anxiety, embarrassment, or guilt." Invested in shedding family dependencies and loosening the ties to their parents, teens are often reluctant to share highly personal events and feelings with their parents.

To establish and maintain adolescent friendships requires fairly sophisticated social skills, according to Rubin. "To be well liked," he explains, "adolescents, much more so than younger children, must be able to strike up conversations, offer interesting comments, follow up on casual social suggestions, call friends and arrange to get together with them, and adjust to changes in plans with equanimity."

Popularity versus friendship

"The good news is that Mary now has a lot of friends," the mother of a tenth-grader observed to another parent. "The bad news is that she has a lot of friends!" Rosalind Wiseman, consultant to local public and private schools, is also the founder and president of the Empower Program, a Washington, D.C., based, nationally recognized project created to empower youth to end the culture of violence. She writes in her book *Queen Bees & Wannabees: Helping Your Daughter Survive Cliques, Gossip, Boyfriends & Other Realities of Adolescence*, "For some girls, popularity is magical. Popularity conveys an illusory sense of power. Some girls think that if they achieve it, all their problems will disappear. Some become obsessed and measure the popularity barometer daily, then issue constant weather reports. Others dismiss it, thinking the whole thing is ridiculous. Some are angry and deny they care, although they really do. Some feel so out of it they give up."

Every school has an in crowd. "Typically, they're the most visible kids in the group—everyone is aware of them, and the confidence they appear to possess is much envied," writes Rubin. One study of popular versus rejected adolescents found that teens who were well-liked were described as cheerful, friendly, humorous, attractive, and athletically able (especially the boys), and that they initiated games and activities. Teens who were rejected were characterized as restless, over-talkative, too quiet or shy, unattractive (especially those who were overweight), and "different."

As Rubin points out, "Popularity is not a characteristic that belongs to the individual. It's bestowed on a child by his or her peers." Perhaps one out of five or six kids is popular and well liked, he says. As many of us know from painful personal experience, the popular kids aren't always the nicest ones. Rubin describes two types of popularity, the first being *popularity by dominance*. Teens exhibiting this form of popularity may be athletic, attractive, affluent, or wield some type of power, which may even be negative in nature. He describes the second variety as *popularity by decency*. Teens popular in this sense are likable, kind, and fun to be with.

Help your child recognize that popularity is often fleeting when attained through dominance. Most teenagers lack the maturity and experience to realize that success and popularity in high school have very little to do with how much success they will enjoy in the adult world. Rubin suggests you can help your child think through the differences between friendship and popularity and explore popularity issues by asking questions such as, "What are these kids like?" "Do you feel okay about the way they act?" "Are you comfortable being around them?"

Boys and girls as friends

Don't be afraid of cross-gender relationships. Not all boy-girl relationships are of a sexual nature. Michael Kimmel, Ph.D., professor of sociology at SUNY, Stony Brook and author of *Manhood in America: A Cultural History* and other books on men and masculinity, observes that cross-gender friendships can be very rewarding for teens, but can be troubling for parents who assume that the girl-boy relationship is more than a friendship. The first step is to understand the true nature of the relationship, then to define clear guidelines for behavior. In addition, Kimmel cautions parents to avoid sending the message that the only acceptable way for teens to relate is as a couple and to avoid hosting parties encouraging romantic pairing-off.

Recognize the gender differences in friendships. In general, "the female bond is extremely close," notes Denise Anderson, a Georgetown Visitation School parent. "My daughter's friends are practically the most important element in her life." In *Queen Bees & Wannabees*, Wiseman describes a group of girlfriends as hanging out, sharing secrets, acting silly, sitting on each other, doing each other's hair, and usually thinking that they will be supported no matter what, but, she adds, "something in the way girls group together also sows the seeds for the cruel competition for popularity and social status."

On the other hand, society's mixed messages about friendships between boys means that "many boys may feel conflicted about friendships," notes William Pollack, Ph.D., clinical professor of psychology at Harvard Medical School and author of many books, including *Real Boys: Rescuing Our Sons from the Myths of Boyhood* and *Real Boys' Voices*. In a world that requires boys to be manly, he says that "too often boys find it difficult to be honest about their feelings of friendship with other guys, to openly show their compassion and empathy toward male friends, and to connect with other boys in meaningful ways." According to the Children's Hospital of Pittsburgh, while girls' relationships with friends may be very close and intimate, "boys are more prone to form an alliance with a group of friends who validate each other's worth through actions and deeds rather than interpersonal disclosure."

Friendliness isn't always easy to learn

Some kids are likable and make friends easily; others just don't seem to know how to do so. The ease with which friendships are formed depends upon the individual child's personality. The New York Longitudinal Study, the seminal work on temperament begun in the 1950s by Stella Chess and Alexander Thomas, identified distinct temperamental traits, including activity level, distractibility, intensity, persistence, and adaptability. These innate personality traits are a child's way of responding to the world around him, his characteristic disposition. As with adults, some children can be classified as easy, while others are difficult or slow to warm.

Temperament isn't the only factor that makes a difference in the ease with which a child makes friends. Some learning and developmental issues make friendships complicated. Language disorders, which may make it hard for a person to take in information or to speak quickly or smoothly, put a child at a disadvantage. Likewise, problems with muscle tone or coordination can contribute to clumsiness not only in sports but also in the subtleties of nonverbal communication. Some children and even older teens have difficulties in reading facial expressions and gestures. Children with attention problems may have difficulty managing impulses, staying focused, and being persistent in their relationships, as well as their schoolwork.

Stultz observes that parents of children who have problems with friendships can provide the extra help they need to learn how to establish and maintain more successful relationships. Indeed, a parent may be the only one a child can approach on this issue—or the only one to recognize that there may be a need for some help with skill development. Children who report feeling left out may give the impression of being aloof or unfriendly, so that other teens hesitate to make the first move toward friendship. These children may need your help to work out the reason friends are so hard for them to come by and to find ways to improve their ability to make friends.

For example, you can help your child consider himself from other people's perspectives. Some possible questions for self-analysis are:

- Do you try to start a conversation or arrange a social activity?
- Do you always wait for someone else to make the first move?
- Are you more critical than supportive of others?
- Can you be counted on as a friend?
- Do you feel inferior or always put yourself down?
- Would others perceive you as warm and open—or detached, cold, or withdrawn?
- Do you offer help, even volunteer to help, without being asked?
- Do you try to see things from the other person's point of view during an argument?
- Are you a good listener or do you tend to monopolize a conversation?
- Are you kind—if someone seems sad do you try to cheer them up?
- Do you ever talk to kids who seem shy or alone?

• Do you expect exclusivity—are you jealous if a friend socializes with someone else?

Honest answers to these questions can reveal the reasons your child is having difficulty making friends. Helping your teen consider these issues, identifying where changes might be made, and developing ideas for making changes can improve his chances of making friends.

If, however, your child doesn't have someone he identifies as a friend, doesn't know how to organize an activity, complains or aches about being lonely, or engages in inappropriate behavior to get friends—whether passing out candy, bragging, cheating, or smoking—Stultz feels there may be reason to be concerned.

Not being able to make friends is like not knowing math—developing both skills is a critical part of growing up. Children who don't have friends are at higher risk of problems as they get older. When a child has a social problem, it tends to get worse over time, and the gap between the child and his or her peers widens. If your child doesn't have any friends, counsels Stultz, you'll at least want to investigate why.

Adolescent specialists encourage seeking professional intervention early. If the problem is with peer socializing, it may be best addressed in a group setting with professional guidance. A number of local psychologists and language therapists specialize in helping the child who doesn't fit by using role-playing and other strategies. These services, which can also be obtained on an individual basis, are often best in small groups of kids the same age. In these sessions, children learn about communication skills, such as how to really listen, how to interject comments into an ongoing conversation, how to avoid inappropriate interruptions and comments, how to maintain eye contact, how to avoid standing too close, and how to use phrases that redirect the conversation or change the subject. Parents can reinforce those skills in family conversations, encouraging and celebrating even small successes.

A note about shyness

Some shyness or social discomfort is biologically based—it is likely that a shy child has at least one introverted parent. Children learn how to make and keep friends, at least in part, by watching their parents. Children in a home where friends seldom call and guests are not sought out may not develop the social skills needed to make friends.

Shyness can also stem from low self-esteem due to factors such as a learning disability or poor school performance, which may cause a child to avoid social situations. Some socially inept children may suffer from dyssemia, a recently identified learning disability that interferes with one's ability to properly decode and understand nonverbal cues and communication. Others may not be able to follow the subtleties of a conversation due to language processing problems. Whatever the cause, the impact of feeling left out or excluded can exacerbate undesirable behavior, which in turn may drive potential friends away and thus compound the situation.

There is a small percentage of teens whose sense of isolation is so severe it might indicate the presence of an actual disorder, such as social phobia or an anxiety, that interferes with the way they approach peers. It is essential that the parents of such young people find specialists to provide the help their children need to be socially confident and competent.

"Shy or isolated children have difficulty because they're less exposed to other kids' judgments of themselves," notes Rita Schonberg, Ph.D., a Maryland psychologist specializing in adolescents. "Kids who don't spend time with peers, whether at single-sex sleepovers, parties, or just hanging out somewhere, miss out on hearing other kids' insights and experiences. As a result," Schonberg observes, "they might be vulnerable to staying stuck with perfectionist or idealized notions of themselves."

Parents who were shy as children, who felt lonely or excluded, may pressure their own children to become gregarious and popular. A more effective approach is to gently encourage your shy child, focusing on her strengths, celebrating successes, and not getting impatient or referring to her shyness in a way that makes the child feel bad. Parents can encourage their child to get involved in a regular group activity that engages her interests and natural talents. This will allow her to spend time in semi-comfortable surroundings with peers who share her interests.

Sometimes, preteens go through a shy period as they become more self-conscious and fearful of making mistakes in front of their peers. This is different from lifelong shyness and usually eases with the passage of time and empathetic conversations with parents.

Finding friends on the Web

Some teens, particularly those who are socially awkward, are more comfortable relating to others via computer rather than in person. At a time when they really need to be interacting with live people in real time, they're tucked away on the computer rather than learning and practicing the social skills they need.

"More than anything else, adolescents are drawn to cyberspace because they make friends there," says John Suler, Ph.D., professor of psychology at Rider University and author of the online book *Psychol-*

ogy of Cyberspace. Just being online can automatically make teens feel like they are part of an in crowd—in a place where they belong where everyone knows their names. Suler observes that "Internet relationships can feel safer to teenagers than face-to-face relationships. Some teens feel that they can be more open in how they express themselves and may worry less about rejection because they can't see or be seen by the other person."

Of course, there can be problems with joining groups in cyberspace. Many cyber friendships can be shallow or transient and as disappointing as live relationships. It can be painful to be dumped by the click of a mouse—without even being told good-bye. And, there will be a few teens who find online friendships so much more satisfying than personal relationships that there is the possibility of their becoming addicted to them. Parents may need to establish some limits on their teen's computer use and encourage offline activities in order to promote a balanced life.

Friendships you don't like

You can't dictate whom your children will like; trying to discourage a friendship may actually heighten the attraction. Early adolescence begins the period when children select friends who they feel help define their emerging identities. If you discourage friendships they have chosen, they may perceive your action as criticism of them and may rebel against you.

If your child has a friend you don't like, ask yourself what it is that bothers you about this particular kid. You may need to explore your own perceptions of the friend for unfounded prejudice or bias. If you find that your reasons are essentially superficial, such as discomfort with the kid's hairstyle, language, or clothing, a good tack is to try to ignore your feelings and trust your child's judgment. If the other kid is outlandish in some way, recognize that your child may be using the friend to continue separating from you. Absent dangerous behavior, you can console yourself that, while peer influence may reveal itself in superficial ways, parental influence remains powerful in the most crucial areas.

Talking with your child about an undesirable friend's behavior or qualities that alarm you can underscore your family's views, beliefs, and standards without openly criticizing those of the other child or his or her family. The delicacy required in this situation demonstrates, yet again, that saying no is not always easy, especially if your child really enjoys the friend and wants to stay connected. If your teen is secure in his identity, he won't be so dependent on the approval of friends.

A frequent adolescent issue is peer pressure. If your child is vulnerable because he wants so badly to belong, if he is persuaded to join a rough crowd or do something thoughtless, dangerous, or illegal, then you do need to be concerned. Children who haven't received firm, positive direction from their parents and haven't established strong family bonds are most susceptible to negative friendships.

While it is important to monitor our children's friendships, even, and perhaps especially, during the teen years, we must remain respectful as well as aware. Adolescents benefit from knowing kids from different backgrounds and with different points of view. If you model having a diverse group of friends, your children can comfortably follow suit. Overall acceptance of your children's friends indicates your overall acceptance of them and their growing social independence.

Advice and sensitivity

As a parent, you are in the best position to help your adolescent gain social skills and learn how to be a friend through the following means.

Act as a role model for your children by inviting guests to your home, engaging in hobbies or activities with other adults, participating in community or school events, and investing time and effort in maintaining relationships with friends.

Stay current with your adolescent's social situations and friends. Knowing the key players will enable you to ask the right questions, which will, in turn, make it easier to know when your children are experiencing difficulties.

Encourage your children to pursue their interests and skills. Feeling competent builds your adolescents' feelings of self-worth, which will enhance their social skills. You can help by supporting their involvement in non school-related activities, such as Scouts, sports, summer camp, or religious organizations, which provide opportunities for making friends outside of the school circle.

Find a way to support your teenager without intruding. "Provide a place for friends to gather; buy a pool table; do things that increase the chances of your child being in a safe and comfortable place," advises Stultz.

With discretion, discuss your child's shyness or social problems with his teachers and counselor. Sometimes, a simple accommodation, such as seating a child next to a prospective friend or assigning a special partner for a group project, can make an enormous difference. Many schools are aware of the devastating consequences that can result from exclusion and have created conflict resolution and diversity training programs for the classroom.

Accept your children for who they are. Although you may be very sociable, have many friends, and enjoy a whirl of social activities, your child may be perfectly content with one or two friends and a slower social pace. "If she seems reasonably happy and content with life, apparently enjoys school (or at least shows no aversion to going there), has a couple of reliable friends, and expresses no deep distress over her relative status in the peer group, it's probably not a big issue," observes Rubin.

Meet your child where he is. Teens with social problems often have uneven development, with some skills at advanced levels and social skills at lower levels. For example, a ninth-grader may have sixth grade social skills. "You may need to help them plan their social life as you would a younger child," Stultz observes. "Buy tickets to a game. Help them make the phone calls. Seek relationships with families with similar needs. Find replacement social groups for naturally occurring ones. Find ways to coach them." However, adopt a supportive, rather than leading, role in a way that enables your adolescent to feel independent.

Understand the socializing value of the phone and Instant Messages. When kids spend hours talking on the phone or e-mailing each other, recognize that they are working hard on developing their friendship and communication skills.

Consider allowing your child to have a pet. Owning a pet can convey responsibility and fosters expressions of intimacy and empathy that your adolescent may be able to transfer to peers and others.

Support an adolescent who loses a close friend. Teens may define themselves in terms of their friends. Losing a friend due to a fight, a move to a different school, or the natural evolution of a relationship can be devastating. Recognize and respect the magnitude of the loss and support your child as much as he or she will allow.

Recognize that the core of an adolescent's life remains the family, says Stultz. "Good times with the family can energize the kid regarding friendships."

Final thoughts

A feeling of belonging to a community, of being part of a strong, supportive network of family and friends, is among the most important buffer your child can have against peer pressure and depression. Kids who are socially vulnerable need a lot of support. If they don't get it from their parents, they probably won't get it. We must remind our children of their strengths, that they are worthy of love and friendship, and of our confidence that they will acquire the skills to overcome any difficulties they have—and, if they need help acquiring those skills, we need to make sure that they get it.

| 6 |

Hanging Out

They sprawl and eat. They congregate, walk around, watch movies, regroup, and talk. They laugh, commiserate, check out and comment on others, and spend money. There are no adults. The kids bond and connect.

Malls and Starbucks are kid magnets the way the neighborhood vacant lot used to be. Other favorite hangouts may include a music store, outside a multiplex theatre, or the neighborhood parking lot. These are the places to see, and be seen by, peers. In some circles, the phrase "hanging out" is synonymous with dating in the sense that it is used to describe young people spending loosely organized, undefined time together, not infrequently in a group of peers, without making their interest in one another explicit—if it even is. They can shop, eat, play video games, or watch movies. They can catch up with the latest, and, protected from the elements, walk around and look good. Today's young people cruise mall corridors the same way some of their parents once cruised the main drags of small towns.

Separating and connecting

Preteens and teens need relaxed leisure time with peers. In his book *The Second Family: How Adolescent Power is Challenging the American Family*, Ron Taffel, Ph.D., describes the phenomenon of individual teens building relationships with a group of friends who function as their second family. He suggests that teens are seeking acceptance and comfort. While teens may use their peer group to explore sex, drugs, alcohol, and vandalism, for the vast majority, hang out time is about seeking association and belonging. There is emotional, and even physical, comfort in being surrounded by their friends. They are happy to be with people who know what they are talking about when they mention the new hair color of an obscure band member. It is soothing to be with people like yourself, and at this age, more fun if not at home, observes Maryland psychologist and adolescent specialist Rita Schonberg, Ph.D.

It is also about solving problems and negotiating the nonstructured world, says Schonberg. In this world, without adults who know them and out of earshot of parents, teenagers learn to solve practical problems like what to do when adults are rude to them, how polite they're obligated to be to peers they don't like, or how to handle being served something other than the Grande/Skim/Decaf/No Whipped Cream they ordered.

Hanging out with peers is paramount to adolescents as they pull away from family and start exercising their ability to be social without adult supervision or intervention. It is about tasting independence and separateness. Taffel writes that teens are not so much rebelling against adult life as deriving the comfort they need from peers and the group culture. He recommends parents earmark space for this "comfort time" in their teens' schedules, which is distinctly different from quality time with the family, and balance that time with responsive family behavior.

Trouble

Generally, the places teens want to hang out are fairly tame, usually quite visible, and are often policed by security guards or local police. Some parents are concerned that the combination of peer pressure and unstructured time constitutes a temptation and an opportunity for trouble. Sometimes this is, indeed, the case, which is why parents must discuss with their teens the potential pitfalls and challenges of hanging out in public places.

The trouble kids can get into at malls and other hangouts has led some local mall managers to implement strict rules for youth under the age of eighteen. Some malls limit group size and closely monitor behavior. In addition, police substations have been established at several area malls and increased uniformed security is present. Mall managers say that large groups of teenagers discourage other shoppers and disrupt business. On the other hand, teenagers have more money than ever to spend and seem to prefer spending it in groups.

While kids alone in a mall may be vulnerable, kids in groups can get into kinds of trouble that would never occur with parental supervision. The increase in police and security guards in malls and around other public places may lead parents and teens to believe that these are safe places for their children to meet. This is probably the case as long as kids stay in a group and in populated areas. Area police report that shoplifting by teens is much more prevalent than crimes committed against them.

Will your child find trouble at the mall or will trouble find your child? The answer, as with so many aspects of childhood social development, lies in parental preparation. A child with a time limit and a purpose to be at the mall is more likely to have a safe and satisfying visit and less likely to encounter problems. Planning, preparation, and communication with your child and other parents are the keys to successful and positive hanging out.

Parents should discuss their safety concerns with their teens and script an arsenal of appropriate responses for use in unexpected situations. Topics should detail expectations for behavior, including courtesy toward others, respect for surroundings, and specific safety issues, as well as transportation, time limits, the means to call home, and a meeting place. All kids will need to be reminded that stores have a purpose: they are in the business of selling things. Although they are filled to the brim with interesting and entertaining things, one cannot behave in them as though they are playrooms existing only for one's amusement. Talk about behaviors adults find objectionable, such as littering, loudness, and blocking access. These behaviors are always rude and unacceptable.

Kids of all ages need to understand the concept of guilt by association and that they may be blamed if a teen with them or their group misbehaves. Parents should brainstorm with their children about how to get help if a problem arises, such as being approached by a stranger or inadvertently breaking merchandise. Make sure your children know the ramifications of shoplifting. Don't forget working out what to do if one of your child's friends shoplifts, or if your teen is approached by a security guard.

Emphasize that, under no circumstances, should your child ever leave the mall with anyone except a previously agreed upon person. Kids hanging at a mall, coffee shop, or other selected location should stay in well-populated areas, avoiding secluded halls or stairwells.

Beyond a discussion of good manners and common sense, make sure you and your teen know the rules of the mall or theatre. There may be specific rules about acceptable clothing, including the banning of wearing baseball caps backwards. Smoking is usually prohibited inside a mall, and alcohol and drug use is never allowed.

Special considerations for ten- to twelve-year-olds

Mall visits should have a purpose that may be as simple as purchasing a hair accessory or birthday card. Preteens' mall time should be limited to maybe as little time as an hour, and they should have an agreed upon meeting place for parental pick-up. At least one parent should be at the meeting place and all the children in the group should have that adult's cell phone number. The kids should know the adult's plans, and parents should know the kids' numbers if they have cell phones.

Let your child know that you are there for him no matter what kind of problem should occur. Help your child and his friends develop a shopping plan, and what to do should they become separated from one another. Preteens should have at least one friend along. Many parents recommend that preteens never go to the restrooms or sit in movie theatres alone.

Final thoughts

Developmentally, our middle and high school children need time to congregate with peers. They need to discover that no one has a perfect family and to explore their shared angst over being twixt-tween, neither child nor adult. They need time that does not involve adults, to play, gossip, flirt, to learn different ways to hang out.

The parent's job is to support separation and attachment to this new world of rich adolescent relationships, not just to limit and protect their children. Parents can be with their children in spirit by planning with them, expressing interest in their adventures, and providing practical support like transportation.

| 7 |

Driving

Driving is another example of the separation work that is done during adolescence. The parents give up driving their child everywhere, and instead wait at home in total terror worrying about their teen's driving abilities and the inept, immature friends she's traveling around with—not to mention all the crazies on the roads.

MICHAEL BRODY, M.D., Psychiatrist and parenting consultant

"Every time my son gets ready to slide behind the steering wheel and pull out on the streets of Washington, I think that I should put an announcement out on the radio to clear the streets until it's safe," remarked one Washington, D.C., father ruefully when his teen was first learning how to drive.

"Teen drivers have the highest crash risk of any age group," says *Beginning Teenage Drivers*, a joint publication of the Insurance Institute of Highway Safety and the National Highway Traffic Safety Administration (NHTSA). "The problem is worst among sixteen-year-olds, who have the most limited driving experience and an immaturity that often results in risk-taking behind the wheel." Eight out of ten fatal crashes with a sixteen-year-old driver involve driver error.

For teens driving in the Washington, D.C., area, the risks of inexperience are seriously compounded by notorious congestion, complex traffic regulations and driving conditions, faster cars, road rage, cell phones, elderly drivers and tourists unfamiliar with the area, drugs and alcohol, and other teenage drivers. The following sobering statistics should put these risks into perspective.

- Young drivers are involved in fatal traffic crashes at more than twice the rate of the rest of the population, according to the National Safety Council (NSC). Although young drivers represent only 6.8 percent of the nation's licensed drivers, they are involved in 15 percent of fatal crashes.
- Motor vehicle crashes are the leading cause of death for fifteen- to twenty-year-olds, and more than one-third of all deaths of people aged fifteen through twenty resulted from motor vehicle collisions, according to NHTSA.
- Among sixteen- to seventeen-year-old drivers, the risk of a fatal crash increases with the number of passengers in the car, according to research by the Johns Hopkins Bloomberg School of Public Health, the Insurance Institute for Highway Safety, and the Johns Hopkins University School of Medicine.
- Teens who have attention-deficit hyperactivity disorder (AD/HD) have abnormally high rates of traffic violations, collisions, and incidents of driving without a license.

Good drivers don't just happen

Experts suggest that a major reason so many young people are involved in collisions is that they are poorly trained and haven't developed good driving skills. Parents shouldn't expect drivers' education classes to give their kids all the tools they need to be safe on the road. "Ultimately, it's the responsibility of parents, not that of a complete stranger, to ensure that their child has the most driving experience possible," notes Cathy Gorrell, Virginia parent of two teenaged drivers.

It is extremely important that parents be realistic about the amount of time required for a new driver to become skilled. Some experts suggest teens be required to drive 500 or more miles, in a variety of weather and road conditions, with a parent in the car before being allowed to drive on their own. Despite the difficulty of scheduling time for it, parents and their teens need to make time available to train and develop young people's driving skills.

Parents cannot expect teen drivers to be experts even if they've logged hundreds of miles behind the wheel. The American Automobile Association (AAA) suggests the amount of time necessary for one to become a good driver is five years, and they offer some helpful tips for teaching teens to drive.

Use a graduated approach to driving. When children receive only six hours of behind-the-wheel training, there's no way they can gain the experience needed to be a safe driver, notes Norman Grimm, director of driver and safety services for AAA Mid-Atlantic. If graduated licensing doesn't exist in a given jurisdiction, parents can enforce their own form of it by restricting their teens' driving while they gain the training and experience needed to survive on Washington area roads. For example, teens must be accompanied by an adult until they have driven x number of miles and cannot drive with passengers for a certain amount of time, taking into consideration the types of roads, weather, time of day, and traffic congestion.

Take it one step at a time. Edmund Burke School parent Tom Hart, who taught his two children how to drive, advises parents to take an incremental approach, providing kids with plenty of practice and information in small steps so that they can develop confidence and skills. Hart began with each of his children in a large, empty parking lot for an initial session focusing on braking. "I felt strongly that the most important thing was for them to develop the confidence that they could stop the car quickly," he explains. He had each teen learn to find the brake before they put the car into gear. "I then had them exercise finding the brake quickly, moving the car forward a little then hitting the brake quickly, and doing it again and again until finding the brake and stopping the car quickly was instinctive."

Hart then had his drivers-in-training get accustomed to turning by doing figure eights in the parking lot. Next, he had them practice driving straight across the full length of the parking lot, then backing up. When this was mastered, Hart had his teens practice driving around the parking lot, staying within lanes, using the turn signals, and turning, all in preparation for driving on a residential street. When he was confident of the teens' skill with the basics, he had them drive around residential neighborhoods, first during the day and then later at night. Finally, in off-hours, he introduced them to I-270 and the Beltway.

Gorrell says she and her husband were very careful about where and when their teens practiced driving, getting up at 7:00 on Saturday mornings to drive on the Beltway. Driving during off-peak hours helps minimize teens' risk and stress in learning how to drive on highways. "You can say, 'No Beltway; no highways,' but they're a fact of life," Gorrell says.

Ron Shaffer, columnist for the *Washington Post,* better known to area residents as Dr. Gridlock, recommends that family or friends supplement drivers' education classes and provide basic training to include: driving on the Beltway; merging onto an interstate from a dead stop; passing a slow-moving vehicle on a two-lane road; knowing how to respond to tailgating; turning into the correct lane; bringing an errant vehicle back onto the road from the shoulder; and driving in heavy rain, snow, and ice, and at night.

Parents should make sure their teens experience driving in a wide variety of environments and under many different conditions. Take teens to a parking lot when it snows and teach them to counteract skids. Have them drive on country and city roads, highways, and through shopping center parking lots, both at night and during rush hour. Most important, parents should remain involved, even after their teens have graduated to driving on their own.

The basics when driving

The Maryland Motor Vehicle Administration offers the following important tips for parents teaching their children to drive.

- Teach the young driver defensive driving—how to anticipate problems and be prepared to react.
- Stress that laws, signals, and signs exist to help drivers better predict the actions of others.
- Work with young drivers on time and space requirements and judging gaps when they are entering and exiting traffic. Emphasize that within lanes, they must make adjustments for speed and positioning.
- Teach teens to gather and select visual information efficiently. When they are driving, direct their attention to road conditions, signs and signals, potential conflicts and problems, and other road users.
- Teach them to scan for cyclists, pedestrians, animals, and behavioral clues from other drivers by being aware of, to the best of their ability, the hidden areas behind shrubs, buildings, trees, and parked cars.
- Have teens practice the above tips when driving at night—two out of three traffic deaths occur after dark.
- Have teens practice driving in bad weather on a vacant parking lot—twenty-one percent of all reported crashes involve skidding.

Other things parents can do

Model the desired behavior. As in most other areas of childrearing, parents are most effective if they model the behavior they wish their teen to exhibit. Children's behavior and attitudes are shaped when they're very young. Learning to be a good, safe driver doesn't begin when a child is fifteen or sixteen years old. It happens over time as children observe their parents' driving habits. We should seriously ask ourselves if we want our children to drive the way we do! If you, the parent, say to a child, "It's okay for me to do this; I've been driving for so long," as you speed through a yellow light, ignore your side view mirrors, don't bother using turn signals, or pause at stop signs without coming to a full stop, your teen may copy that behavior.

Be current on traffic regulations. Parents should learn, or refamiliarize themselves with, the traffic regulations in their jurisdiction before beginning to train their teens to drive. Chances are rules and regulations have changed significantly since parents first learned to drive. For example, the recommended position for the placement of one's hands on the steering wheel is no longer the traditional ten and two o'clock position. Grimm says that placing the hands at eight and four o'clock are now understood to be the best grip on the steering wheel. He goes on to explain, "That's to lower the hands and get them out of the way of an inflating airbag, so that wrists and thumbs are not broken, and so the air bag doesn't knock the wrists, arms and hands into the head."

Practice driving commentary. As teens near age sixteen, parents can help prepare them for their time behind the wheel by raising their awareness of all that goes into driving. Parents driving with their teens can make use of a running driving commentary, relating what they're seeing and thinking as they drive, and explaining the decisions they make in response. Articulating all of the decisions and actions that most adult drivers do almost automatically, and describing the thought processes behind them, helps young people better grasp the concept of proactive, defensive driving.

Educate your children about the effects of alcohol. Talk with your children about the way alcohol affects driving abilities. Tell them the likelihood of a car crash increases *before* one is legally intoxicated! Even one drink impairs a young person's abilities, perceptions, and judgment. Tell them if they are stopped by the police for any reason and are found to have alcohol in their systems they will lose their licenses. NHTSA reports, "In 2000, twenty-one percent of the young drivers fifteen to twenty who were killed in crashes were intoxicated." The organization further states that on weekends, almost half of all youth traffic fatalities are alcohol related. Even a small amount of alcohol impairs a young driver's newly learned skills.

Establish a no-fault pick-up policy with your children, whether your child is the driver or a passenger. Let your teens know you want them to call home for a ride or that you'll pay for a cab, no questions asked, any time they feel they should not drive home or should not be a passenger in a car driven by a peer.

Avoid power struggles. Battles for control can complicate the driver education process, which often takes place just as your teen is in the throes of separating from you. "My parents had to let go of teaching me how to drive themselves," observes one teen. "We fought too much. I found a very patient neighbor with young kids who was happy to take me driving in exchange for babysitting. This saved me and my parents a lot of stress!"

Not every sixteen-year-old is ready to drive. Some parents want to make the sixteenth birthday a rite of passage that includes the granting of a driver's license. Make the decision about your own child's readiness based on his maturity, kinesthetic and visual coordination, skills, attitude, and confidence. Take a cue from your teen. He may feel peer pressure to drive, but may be apprehensive because he really doesn't feel ready to take on the responsibility. Reassure your teen that individual readiness varies greatly and that his time frame is something the two of you can best judge together.

One Washington teen, a reluctant driver, didn't feel comfortable behind the wheel until she was well into college. "The life and death responsibility was really sobering," she says. Today, she enjoys driving and reports that her anxiety has become "a healthy respect for the power of a car."

"Driving is a privilege, not a right," observes Gorrell. Kids should know they have to earn, and keep, the privilege. Be prepared to take the keys away if the situation warrants it.

Define your family's driving rules

Establish rules for driving and be clear and firm about your expectations regarding:

- drinking, drug use, and driving,
- use of seat belts,
- number of passengers allowed in the car, if any (some parents say no passengers until the teen has driven for a certain number of miles; others require that any passengers have their parents' permission to ride in the car),
- restrictions on car use, such as nighttime driving, driving on the highway, in the city, or during hazardous weather conditions,
- the driver's responsibility for reporting collisions and traffic violations,
- for what the car may be used and how far it may be driven,
- the teen's responsibilities with respect to automobile maintenance, such as buying gas, checking the oil and tire pressure, washing the windows, and
- the consequences for not adhering to the established rules.

Parents should clearly define the driving rules their kids must follow. Many experts recommend spelling out family driving rules, especially regarding the combination of drinking and drug use with driving, in a safe-driving contract signed by parents and their teens. One such contract is the Students against Destructive Decisions'

(SADD) "Contract for Life: A Foundation for Trust and Caring," which is signed by the teen and parent or caring adult.

Another contract is the American Automobile Association's "Vehicle Use and Operation Agreement," available through AAA's Teaching Your Teens to Drive program, which spells out a range of teens' responsibilities. These include expenses such as fuel, insurance, registration, maintenance, fines and penalties, collision damage, etc.; the maximum number of miles a teen is allowed to drive per week and if that number is linked to the teen's grades; behavior that will result in loss of driving privileges, such as traffic offenses and at-fault crashes; and absolutely nonnegotiable rules, such as mandatory seat belt use, no drugs or alcohol, and whether or not to lend the car.

Some families tie teen driving privileges to other family rules. The Gorrell family, for example, requires their young drivers to follow both the rules at home and specific driving rules, as well as maintain excellent grades. An added incentive for parents requiring good grades as a requisite for driving privileges is that some insurance companies have reduced rates for young drivers maintaining good grades. In addition, Gorrell says, "For the first six months, our kids were not allowed to have anyone else in the car except the parents." She goes on to explain that while her girls carry cell phones in the car, they understand the phones are for emergency use only and not for conversation. Radio stations can be changed only when the car is at a full stop at a traffic light or stop sign.

More to consider

Parents should take a close look at the cars their children will be driving. How well will the vehicle protect your teen driver in case of a collision? Is it safe? Well-maintained? Is it equipped with important safety technology, such as air bags and antilock brakes?

Help your teens understand the dangers of speeding. According to NHTSA, "speeding was recorded as a factor in thirty-three percent of fatal crashes occurring in 1999 involving fifteen- through eighteen-year-old drivers." Make sure that your teen does not become a statistic.

Remind your teens that red light cameras at major intersections in many local jurisdictions will capture them on film running red lights and speeding. The fines for these offenses can be in excess of $100.

Seat belts in cars and helmets for motorcyclists are required by law, and parents should make the use of them by their teen drivers mandatory. According to NHTSA statistics, sixty-four percent of teens aged fifteen through eighteen killed in motor vehicle collisions in 1999 were not wearing seat belts. Make buckling up a must—no exceptions—for drivers and passengers.

After your teens have obtained their unrestricted licenses, ride with them occasionally to observe driving habits and skill levels, both good and bad. From time to time, ask your young driver for a ride to the store or to drop you off somewhere. Use these occasions as opportunities to further coach them on good driving methods and decision making.

Teach your teens how to ensure their personal safety, especially when they drive alone at night. Give them a cell phone for use in emergencies. Remind them to always lock the car doors once they are inside. Advise them to pay attention to their surroundings and to keep their keys in their hands when approaching their car at a parking garage or a shopping mall. Talk about what to do in potentially unsafe situations, such as being stopped. If, for example, your teen is pulled over by a person in an unmarked car claiming to be a policeman, he or she should keep the windows closed and the doors locked, ask the person to show I.D., drive to a gas station or police station, or call 911 or #77, if that service is available. If someone gestures at your teen's car, as though to indicate that there's something wrong with it that cannot be seen from inside the vehicle, advise the young person to drive on to a gas station rather than getting out on a lonely road to check.

When teens are prescribed medication, parents should determine if the drug causes them to feel drowsy or light-headed and, therefore, may interfere with their ability to drive safely.

Teens with ADHD will need more parental observation of their driving habits and skills than their peers. Young people with ADHD are easily distracted behind the wheel, reports Russel Barkley, Ph.D., a longtime expert on ADHD now at the Medical University of South Carolina in Charleston. Barkley reports that while the teens know the rules of the road, they just don't know how to apply them. They run lights, cut off other drivers, drive on the shoulders, and become easily frustrated and emotional. Parents and their teens might agree that they must be on medication for the disorder while driving.

Monitor your teen's fatigue levels. A Maryland parent points out that "one of the most important responsibilities of a parent is defining how much sleep their child needs in order to be able to drive." Since falling asleep at the wheel is a danger for drivers of all ages, parents should monitor their young drivers' fatigue levels. The Federal Highway Administration warns that because young people are disproportionately represented in this category of fatalities, parents of teens and adults should be urged to let their children's visibly sleepy friends sleep over just as one would urge a visibly drunk person to avoid the road until their condition improved.

Parents would do well to invest some time in familiarizing their young drivers with the major streets and highways they're likely to travel. Use local maps to give them an overview of the area roads and their relation to familiar landmarks and introduce them to the street layout in your jurisdiction. Help them keep abreast of road construction in the area and help map out alternate routes for avoiding construction or traffic tie-ups. For trips to unfamiliar locations, help your teen plot a course on an area map and write out clear directions before he or she takes to the road.

Explain the consequences of distraction to your teen. A study conducted by the University of North Carolina Highway Safety Research Center (UNCHSRC) and funded by the AAA Foundation for Traffic Safety found that an estimated 280,000 distracted drivers are involved in serious crashes each year. The study reports that fifteen percent of drivers participating in the study weren't paying attention while driving. Young drivers under twenty were especially likely to be distracted by tuning the radio or changing CDs, according to UNCHSRC. Set rules for use of the radio, CD player, and cell or car phones.

Teach your kids how to share the road with trucks. Truck drivers cannot swerve or stop their vehicles as quickly or safely as the driver of an automobile. According to the American Trucking Association (ATA), trucks have four large blind spots where cars literally disappear from the trucker's view in any of his mirrors. A good rule of thumb for teen drivers is that if they cannot see a truck driver's face reflected in his side mirror, then the trucker cannot see them in their cars. In addition, make sure your teen knows not to cut abruptly in front of a truck. According to the ATA, a fully loaded semi may require as much distance as the length of a football field, one hundred yards, in order to come to a complete stop.

Make your teenager aware of his legal rights and responsibilities, such as what to do and say in case of a collision regardless of who is at fault, or if he or she is stopped by the police.

Consider the advantages of not buying a car for your teen. Having limited access to a car lengthens the driver's learning period, allowing for a more gradual gaining of experience. However, parents who are considering purchasing cars for their teens should think big and boring—as in solid, midsize, and stocked with safety features. Large-car drivers suffer half the risk of fatality as drivers of small cars. In addition, the Transportation Safety Group of the NSC does not recommend that teens drive any size sport utility vehicle (SUV), because inexperienced drivers are less capable of compensating for the potential stability problems of SUVs and are less likely to wear the seat belts which would provide some protection in the event of a crash or rollover.

Passengers at risk

Teens are not just at risk of their own driving inexperience and judgment. As passengers, they are at risk when their friends are behind the wheel. According to NHTSA, young people aged fifteen to twenty account for almost one-fourth of all passenger fatalities. With the following tips parents can work at improving their children's safety when being driven by peers.

- Know your children's drivers. Make sure that they have the same levels of driving experience and expertise that you expect of your own child.
- Insist that your child not get into a car driven by someone who has been drinking or drugging, or exhibits reckless behavior.
- Role-play with your teen about different ways to gracefully turn down offers of a ride from a friend.
- Establish a code phrase your teen can use to call you for a ride when he's concerned about a peer's ability to drive safely.
- Urge your teen to always wear a seat belt, both when a passenger and driver. According to NHTSA, "Failure to buckle up contributes to more fatalities than any other single traffic-related behavior."

Final thoughts

Six out of ten parents say driving safety is their top concern when it comes to their teens, far outranking fears of drug and alcohol abuse, pregnancy, and suicide, according to a new survey commissioned by the Chrysler Group. Overwhelmingly, parents report that they know their teens engage in unsafe driving behavior. Chrysler has teamed with Mothers Against Drunk Driving (MADD) and the NSC in a research-based initiative called Road Ready Teens for the development and publicizing of guidelines to aid parents in shepherding their kids through a graduated driving program. The program also includes a web-based video driving game for teens.

Parents' concern about their teens' drinking and driving is, unfortunately, a very realistic fear supported by tragic statistics. Wendy Hamilton, president of MADD, says that on a typical weekend an average of one teen dies every hour in a vehicle crash and forty-four percent of those crashes involve alcohol. Most parents also say they worry when their teenage driver ferries multiple teen passengers late at night. The Road Ready Teens program recommends parents limit their teens' unsupervised driving after 9:00 or 10:00 p.m., limit them to a single passenger, implement a zero tolerance policy for alcohol and drug use, and insist their teens and passenger always wear seat belts. By enforcing these guidelines, parents can help lessen the risk of accidents for their inexperienced teen drivers—and their own worry.

| 8 |

Dating

If you are looking for a short list of "Eight Simple Rules for Dating My Teenage Daughter," you could take some advice from the television show of that title. Included among the TV dad's rules are: "Use your hands on my daughter and you'll lose them later," "Safe sex is a myth. Anything you try will be hazardous to your health," "Dates must be in crowded public places," or, "You want romance? Read a book."

Beth Bailey, author of *Sex in the Heartland*, writes that the relationship scene for young people is "all so complicated, not just because no one can agree on a name for what single people do, but because people don't all subscribe to the same rules. That makes—well, whatever it is—really hard." In addition to a lack of rules, we lack a culture of courtship and romance—of learning to love, commit, trust, of experiencing the satisfaction of cherishing another and being cherished. These components have traditionally been the social processes that guided teenagers and young adults toward marriage, something the majority of college students report they want, someday. And yes, we parents are also confused. When we aren't sure what vocabulary to use and what the words mean to different people, it is even more difficult to guide our children through the process of building relationships.

Preteens: too young to date?

Today many parents seem to think the earlier their children develop, the better, be it toilet training, walking, talking, or dating.

Dating early, particularly between older boys and younger girls, can make an already difficult pubescence even more precarious. Psychologist Karen Zager, Ph.D., a developmental psychologist serving as a consultant on adolescent development to the Public Broadcasting System, advises, "Putting the brakes on preteen dating is something virtually every expert endorses. For kids ages ten through thirteen, dating is developmentally inappropriate. It's like trying to drive an eighteen-wheel truck before you even know how to drive a car. There's too much information and too many complicated feelings for kids that age to integrate." An adult's definition of dating, however, may be quite different from that of his child, as, for example, a coed group going to movies or bowling together may go a long way toward promoting positive interactions between the sexes without unnecessary grown-up stereotypes.

Young adolescents need friendships with members of the opposite sex, and when their parents view all boy-girl relationships as romantic, they're inadvertently pushing their children into traditional dating relationships before they are perhaps ready. Children as young as eleven or twelve may announce they're "going with" someone, but they're actually just reveling in the security of knowing someone likes them and thinks they're special. By contrast, the strong preteen same-sex friendships, minus the social or sexual pressures, are the relationships in which they learn important skills, like sharing emotions and give and take, which will come into play later when they begin dating. According to David Elkind, Ph.D., author of many books including *The Hurried Child: Growing Up Too Fast Too Soon*, "If children this age spend too much time in opposite sex relationships, they don't get to hone these skills."

Preteens are exposed to much more mature material on TV and in the movies than were their counterparts of even a generation ago. Today, the media message, as well as that of their peers, is that even preteens need a steady boyfriend or girlfriend in order to be accepted. In television teen and preteen romances, everything seems to be under control. If the girl gets pregnant, she keeps the baby and life goes on. If the boy's girlfriend dumps him, there is another, just as lovely, girl waiting to ask him, or be asked, out.

Parents may also be a source of even more subtle pressure on their children to date. Some parents organize dances for elementary-age children, describing their preteen dating rituals as "cute," while their children view these events with nervousness. Single sex independent schools sometimes push the dating issue by sponsoring frequent dances for their middle school students and inviting students from other schools to attend. Parents report social events of this nature stress those girls who aren't developmentally ready for coed social occasions but who attend out of fear of ostracism by more socially mature classmates. In dating, earlier is not better.

Define dating with your preteen

If a preteen wants to date, the parents' response should be dependent upon their comfort with dating as the child and his or her peers define it. Does dating mean kids seeing each other on weekends or after school? Where do they go on dates—to the movies, video arcades, or skating rinks? Do they go alone, in groups, or with other couples? While some preteen outings may resemble traditional dates, preteen dating is usually far more innocent and informal. Sometimes kids who call each other boyfriend or girlfriend actually don't spend all that much time together, even on the phone. However, to be the first girl in middle school to start dating does usually earn one a certain status among one's peers, and may later evolve into a bad reputation.

If a preteen wants to be alone with his girlfriend, his parent can say, "You're not ready for this. Someday you will be, but not yet, for the same reason you're too young to drive a car. There are some things you can't do until you're older." It's common for younger children to want to mimic the seemingly more exciting actions of older teens and to feel grown up. However, if parents allow younger children more freedom than they can handle, they are setting them up to fail. Each child matures at a different rate, and parents need to be observant of their children's development and tailor a dating policy appropriate to each child. Observant parents may be able to tell when to loosen or tighten the policy as they note maturing behaviors in their child.

When approached by their children about dating, parents can offer compromises or alternatives. If they are comfortable with their preteen daughter talking on the phone with her boyfriend but don't want them going to a movie together, they can suggest an alternative better suited to their age, such as going to a sporting event or amusement park. If the child is one of a coed group going to a movie, limiting the outing to one location, with an adult present at both the beginning and the end, may be most comfortable for all concerned.

Dating as teens

Dating is a brand new adventure for parents and teens alike. Dating carries multiple meanings for today's teens—going out, getting together, and going steady are terms parents may hear their kids use to define the phenomenon. A provocative report entitled *Hooking Up, Hanging Out, and Hoping for Mr. Right: College Women on Dating and Mating Today*, conducted by the Institute for American Values, a think tank exploring family issues, and funded by the Independent Women's Forum, an advocate for the interests of women, found several common meanings for the term. Dating can be synonymous with hanging out, in which two people "spend loosely organized time together without making their interest in one another explicit, unless they hook up, at which point dating and hooking up become the same thing," reports Elizabeth Marquardt, M.Div., co-investigator of the study. She found that forty percent of college women had hooked up at least once, a minority but a large minority, and states that "it's not possible to say whether middle or high school students do it more or less."

Dating can also refer to a couple in a fast-moving, highly committed relationship that includes sexual activity, studying together, and more, but rarely going out on dates. Then of course there is hooking up, or a physical encounter, which can be anything from kissing to sexual intercourse without commitment, that is engaged in by a minority of young people. College women say it is rare for guys to ask them on dates or to acknowledge when they have become a couple. Many parents report that their teenager does not date at all or only in casual groups of peers. Other parents say they know lots of high school and college students who have steady boyfriends or girlfriends and go through the same dating and breaking-up routines as they did in their teens.

Parents of children who don't feel ready to date should be available to offer reassurance and assistance as they get ready to take the next step. "I know you're growing up, and I want you to be independent and enjoy yourself, but it's my job to help you make decisions that won't be harmful to you or to anybody else," is a way for parents to outline their dating protocols for their children. Then parents can explain why it's important to know who is going where, and with whom, who is driving, and when they'll be home. If parents aren't comfortable with the arrangements, further discussion is in order. To the children of parents who have made a practice of keeping their children informed of their plans when they aren't home, keeping their parents equally informed when they are on a date won't seem inappropriate. This creates an atmosphere of mutual concern while allowing for growing independence.

While some experts are of the opinion that teens are generally not ready for paired dating until the ages of fifteen to sixteen for girls and sixteen to seventeen for boys, coed group outings and activities in middle school and high school have become a common venue for exploring changing interpersonal interactions. While paired dating certainly occurs among high school students, it appears to be of a more intermittent and less intense variety than that remembered by most parents from their own youth. It's not uncommon for friends to become romantically and sometimes sexually involved for a while and then go back to being just friends, though not without some difficulties.

Adolescent dating is often short-lived, and breaking up can be awkward or even embarrassing for some teens. One fifteen-year-old boy attending a northwest Washington, D.C., school said he wanted to meet and date girls from other schools so he could avoid discomfort or humiliation when a relationship ended. His comment is a reminder of how exposed and vulnerable some teens feel when dating.

Susan Reimer, *Baltimore Sun* columnist and parent of two teenagers, observes that parents are usually more comfortable with their child attending an event like homecoming because it is scripted, structured, and public, believing these conditions reduce the possibility that their child will be involved in something sexual. She cautions parents that "by endorsing these romantic pairings, we are sending a message to our teens that this is the only acceptable way for them to relate—as a couple, as boyfriend and girlfriend."

Many parents are more comfortable if their teen chooses to date someone whose family practices the same religion as they do and is from the same ethnic or racial background. Parents may want to clarify their own expectations for their teens and discuss the possible reactions of family members or others who may or may not support the relationship for whatever reasons. However, parents should recognize that the odds of a teenage date becoming a long-term, serious relationship are slim. By requiring that their teens date only a certain type of person, they may be fueling rebellion and should remember to choose their battles thoughtfully.

Parents need to recognize that a small percentage of teenagers have no interest in dating someone of the opposite sex. Gay, lesbian, and bisexual youth know that the majority of their peers express romantic attractions to the opposite sex and that this attraction sometimes leads to dating. Some teens, says Carol Dopp, M.Ed., family life counselor at the Potomac School in McLean, Virginia, will question their sexual orientation while in middle or high school. Others will feel same-sex attraction and want to share this awareness, or "come out," with others, including parents. Dopp advises parents of gay, lesbian, and undecided youth to set dating rules similar to those set for a heterosexual child. She cautions that parental pushing of gay, lesbian, and undecided youth into heterosexual dating can damage their self-worth.

The dating games

The greatest change in the age-old dating game is the girl's role. Contemporary girls learn about relationships from TV talk shows, MTV, the Internet, and teen magazines in which teenaged girls are often portrayed as sexual aggressors. It is not uncommon for girls not only to initiate phone calls to boys they like, but also to ask for a date, make the romantic moves, and even prompt sexual activity. When younger girls wear tight, skimpy, or suggestive clothing and spout sexual innuendo, boys may assume that they are interested in a sexual relationship. If girls don't follow through, boys may spread the word that they are teases, or may aggressively push for sex.

William Pollack, Ph.D., clinical professor of psychology at Harvard Medical School and author of many books, including *Real Boys: Rescuing Our Sons from the Myths of Boyhood* and *Real Boys' Voices*, reports that some boys want casual relationships with girls without their parents warning them against sex or their friends insisting on it. Pollack describes how boys like to talk to girls and find out what makes them tick, but will engage in sex before they're ready if it seems the only way to solidify a relationship.

Teenagers of both genders can get some useful dating advice from a website called *Grrl.com*, an entertaining and informative website for girls created by Bonnie Burton, editor, writer, and web celeb. In a frank, no-nonsense manner, Burton ladles out advice for contemporary teens, such as, for the boy and girl who have been best friends and are debating a romantic or sexual relationship, she advises, "Make *damn* sure that you *both* know what you want from each other before you dive in head first. What may be vague to you could be sincerely cut-and-dry to him. It's important that both of your views of the relationship are crystal clear to each other. This will save you plenty of tears in the future, and may actually help you realize that this isn't such a good idea after all."

Casual dating or "scouting"

Casual dating, "scouting," or short-term serial dating of different people without intense sexual activity provides teens with opportunities not just to develop social skills, but also to enhance their sense of identity, value, and confidence. It's a way of chalking up non-threatening learning experiences about flirting, risking rejection, and considering the personality and interests of another in order to select an activity or destination the invitee is likely to accept and enjoy. It allows one to practice holding the door for dates, seating them, or respectful slow dancing. Casual dating provides for addressing such dilemmas as whether or not to hold hands, put one's arm around another, allow one's self to be embraced, and whether or not to kiss. Such dating allows kids to explore and learn the difference between love and lust. While teenagers are still learning the decision-making skills that will enable them to handle these situations more easily, neglecting to address them at all until one is in one's twenties makes the lessons more difficult.

Falling for the person one is dating, and then being rejected, is painful. Washington, D.C., clinical psychologist Patricia Dalton, Ph.D. reminds us that there are emotional costs of repeated breakups that are difficult to calculate. She is convinced that breakups are much harder when the couples have been sexually intimate. Breaking up is also more difficult for those teens for whom dating provided an enhanced identity, teens with an unstable or weak sense of their own value, or those who took emotional, and perhaps sexual, risks and feel discarded and humiliated. This is especially true if one's partner has been unfaithful.

Compounding the pain of breaking up is the fact that many teens are children of divorced parents. Dalton reports she often hears her teen clients say, "My parents divorced when I was...," and too often these teens have real difficulty trusting the people they date. They seem without direction, unable to take hold of life, and are afraid of the future, having seen so much go wrong with their own families in the past.

Advantages of romantic dating

Paired or romantic dating, or exclusively seeing one person for a longer period, allows teens to learn enticement, seduction, and courting. They feel the anxiety of pleasing someone to whom they're attracted, and learn how to work through it and balance it with their own needs and wants. In the comfort and security of a relationship, teens come to enjoy pleasing their partners—holding hands, exploring the pleasures of touch, being concerned about each other, trusting, respecting one another, compromising on social plans, as well as all the lovely romantic sharings—taking leisurely strolls, giving flowers, having candlelit dinners, bestowing small tokens and surprise gifts, and marking anniversaries.

Teenagers who date as a couple for several months are quite likely to become sexually involved. The decision to do so leads the couple into a new area of decisions and responsibilities about such issues as exclusivity, parental knowledge, closeness, safe sex, and birth control. Teenagers in an exclusive relationship are often included in family activities and events by their partner's families, particularly if the parents are pleased with their child's choice. It is just as likely, however, that parents may be concerned their teen isn't playing the field, chalking up the learning experiences, or is getting too serious, too soon.

Teen couples in a reciprocal loving, comfortable relationship may be able to relax somewhat about the social scene, having no need to struggle with whether to ask someone out or with whom to get together on the weekend and suffer no angst about not being asked or included in the social whirl. A teen in an exclusive relationship needn't question any longer his or her desirability and achieves a certain level of security, of being loved and valued. The consistency and structure of the relationship can enhance a teen's academic productivity and his or her sense of self. Long-term dating provides opportunities to learn discernment, empathy, and patience, all necessary elements of an enduring marriage later on in life.

Parents' role

There are many ways in which parents can help children safely learn and enjoy the dating game, including setting reasonable curfews with allowance for extensions on special occasions, waiting up until they return home from a date, or being awakened by their teens upon returning home.

Experts agree it is best to allow kids to attend only chaperoned parties and to obtain the host parents' names, address, and phone number before the event in order to call ahead to verify details and ask questions about supervision and the family's alcohol and drug policy. Parents should also speak regularly with the parents of their teen's friends in order to keep current on their children's world and to let their teens know they care and are informed.

The initial premise for a phone call to check into the circumstances of a party a teen wishes to attend can be to thank the hosts and offer support for the event. It's amazing how many parties are suddenly canceled when unsuspecting parents find out from another parent that they're hosting a party—while they are scheduled to be out of town. Some mothers of teenage daughters say they try to check casually with the parents of the boys their daughters are dating to be sure of plans for big events, such as dances or proms. At a minimum, these mothers say they at least want to introduce themselves and open the lines of communication to the other parents.

It is important that parents also talk with their teen about what makes a good, mature relationship. In his book *How to Keep Your Teenager Out of Trouble and What to Do if You Can't*, Washington, D.C., clinical psychologist Neil Bernstein, Ph.D. outlines some essential points for parents to make, including that good relationships require hard work, trust, and commitment; establishing closeness takes time; mutual respect is necessary; and excessive criticism, coercion, and bickering erode a good relationship. When teenagers are in a positive relationship, they feel better about themselves and about their world rather than pressured or controlled.

Some experts recommend that going steady should be discouraged. Going steady limits a teen's options and greatly increases the likelihood of sexual intimacy. High school and college years are ideal for meeting, learning about, and dating many people. In this way, kids can gather information about the kind of person they're most comfortable with.

Sexual activity while dating

Marguerite Kelly, author of the syndicated "Family Almanac" column and several parenting books, says teens need clear guidelines about sex from their parents rather than restrictions because, while "restrictions make sex inconvenient...they don't, of course, turn a sexually active young couple into a celibate one. Sex is much too addictive for that." According to a recent study, most teenaged sex occurs at home and parents should feel comfortable making rules such as not being alone with a date at any house—yours, the date's, or a friend's—and no going into the bedroom with a date, even if an adult is downstairs.

Parents need to talk with their teens about sexual activity. It is not unusual for a teen couple, after dating exclusively for a few months, to contemplate and consummate a more intimate physical relationship. Teens need to hear their parents' positions on such issues as birth control and oral sex. Bernstein recommends they be asked the hard questions, like how will they avoid pregnancy and sexually transmitted diseases (STDs), or how they think they're likely to feel afterward should they either decide to have sex or abstain. Do they think they'll respect, or regret, their decisions?

Kelly asserts, "A few dates and a lot of togetherness at seventeen often turns into a heavy relationship, with all the joy and sorrow that can entail. There is perhaps no love as sweet or intense as a teenage romance, or as scary for grownups. While adults know that young love is full of pitfalls and pain—and sometimes pregnancy—it's a miracle to smitten teenagers....who think they'll live happily ever after, if they're thinking at all. At times like this, the adults have to do the thinking for them."

Parents seeking some tricks of the trade might employ the antics of Annie Johnstone, a Silver Spring physical therapist, the eighth of eleven children, and parent of two young children. She relates that when she was a dating teenager, her father made a practice of cleaning his hunting guns on the dining table just as her date arrived to pick her up or her mother would be sleeping in Annie's bed when she returned home from a date. She reports that "no one ever tried anything."

Parents can ensure they have input and exert a positive, reasonable influence in this most private area of teenage life by following these guidelines.

- Establish an atmosphere where anything can be discussed in a non judgmental manner.
- Be available and encourage conversation. While teenagers might try to push us away, they very much need and want the wisdom of our experience and guidance.
- Work with your school or community to provide activities where teens can have socializing experiences without romance.
- Accept that your teenager may not be interested in dating even though his or her peers have begun to date. Don't push dating on your child. He will do so when he feels comfortable.
- Include teenagers in developing rules about curfews, driving, and paired or group dating so they will understand the need for limits.
- Help your teenagers explore issues about relationships, including what to expect, how to decide what they want out of a relationship, what is negotiable and what is not, and how to talk about things without being threatened or self-centered.
- Review your own approach to interpersonal relationships. Parental relationships are the most influential models for teenagers.
- Share stories about your own early dating experiences. When appropriate, talk about a prom or special occasion, or talk about an embarrassing time—like when you spilled soda in your date's lap. Then discuss how you handled the situation and the outcome. By sharing your faults, you give your children permission to learn from their mistakes.
- Check up on them. If kids know you may appear at a dating event, they are less likely to engage in unacceptable behavior.

What children should know before dating

Parents can prepare their children for the dating experience by helping them set up the following guidelines in advance.

Communicate well with your date. Be clear about significant likes and dislikes, your principles and values, and try to listen to one another in a non judgmental manner.

Recognize which areas are negotiable and which are not. Three things are non negotiable: physical safety; the extent, if any, of physical intimacy; and issues involving drugs and alcohol.

Make decisions in advance. Where are you going? Who are you going with? What are you going to do? Who's going to pay? Who's going to drive? Who else will be there?

Girls, make sure you tell your parents where you're going. Bernstein recommends girls tell parents, and maybe friends, exactly where they're going and when they expect to be home. He also recommends that girls "avoid situations where it is just the two of you such as a parked car in a deserted area. Always carry a cell phone or enough change to make several calls. If you are dating someone who loses his temper often, or gets violent when he is angry, or acts possessive and controlling toward you, or even if you just get a really bad gut feeling, bail out as fast as possible."

Boys, treat girls kindly and with respect. Take seriously what they have to say and place more value on substance than appearance. Bernstein advises, "It is never, under any circumstances, appropriate to take advantage of a woman for the purpose of having sex. Using deceit, alcohol, or even coercion to have sex is cruel, dangerous, and illegal."

Final thoughts

Dating remains one of the primary methods by which teens explore romantic feelings and develop the interpersonal skills necessary to ensure later success in long-term relationships. Peter Spevak, Ph.D., director of the Center for Applied Motivation in Rockville, Maryland, notes, "Besides fun, clear communication is one of the most important elements in dating. This includes communication between parents and adolescents about dating and...between dating partners." Children learn much about dating relationships from observing their parents' behavior. They learn about romance, affection, intimacy, and love through our example—traits too seldom presented in the movies or on television.

| 9 |

S-e-x

Sex is not about a single act, nor about the juxtaposition of any particular body parts, but a uniquely intimate way of touching and enjoying your own and another person's body. All of these ways of touching are important and real, and none of them should occur outside of a context that is caring, mutual, private, respectful, responsible, and age appropriate.

DEBORAH ROFFMAN, M.S., Human sexuality educator and author

As tough a job as parenting is, dealing with our children's sexuality can seem especially tricky. Many of us post-sixties parents assumed we would have much less difficulty handling the matter than did our parents, but find that when addressing the subject as it applies to our own children we, too, often feel unsure and uncomfortable.

Talking about s-e-x

Parents face a formidable challenge when helping their children sort through the hash of family values, personal beliefs, media messages, and peer pressure about sex. Children desperately need accurate, honest, and compassionate information and guidance that speaks to them personally—to their hearts as well as their minds. "Hard, cold facts," such as the physical changes a prepubescent child goes through in preparation for adulthood, are very different from the "warm, fuzzy, touchy-feely facts" about such things as the emotional roller coaster of sexual desire. Teens need to understand the characteristics of a healthy sexual experience, as well as those of an abusive one. They need to know about the joys of love and intimacy, as well as methods for handling the rejection and disappointment of failed relationships.

Our goal as parents is to prepare our children for the future changes in their sexual interests, experience, expectations, and perceptions, and to help them develop a positive attitude toward their sexuality. The core message for parents to communicate to their sons and daughters is that sexual pleasure is an activity that is shared equally between partners, and something to which both partners involved are entitled.

Parents talk and listen

Before talking to our children about sex, we first need to examine any emotional baggage we may be carrying in terms of our own sexuality. We must be careful not to decide what our children need to know and when they need to know it solely on the basis of our own personal experiences, counsels Bob Condit, M.Ed., independent consultant and former counselor at the Landon School in Bethesda, Maryland. Instead, we need to think about, and maybe even rethink, our own sexual experiences, views, opinions, expectations, disappointments, and joys before determining what to pass along to our children.

Talking with our kids about sexuality is not something we can necessarily schedule and is best accomplished through many conversations over a long period of time, beginning when our children are very young. Quite often, it's our children who inadvertently broach the subject for the first time, beginning with that initial heartstopper, "Mommy, where do babies come from?" As they grow older, parents can continue to use their children's questions to initiate teaching moments. Parents can also draw upon the all too frequent sexual exploits of a sitcom character or the way a passerby is draped around his date to initiate a conversation about sex. Our teens might make casual comments. We might follow with open-ended responses. Conversation begins.

Waiting for the "right moment" to bring up the topic of sexuality with our teens may well put their health and lives at risk. We parents must recognize that sexual desire is a normal and healthy part of growing up and realistically expect our children to have sexual relations at some point. While we hope the experience will be satisfying and enjoyable for our children, we would like for their involvement in sexual activity, particularly intercourse, to occur later—maybe a lot later. Now, however, is the best time for us to begin the dialogue about sexual responsibility with our children, so they will be well briefed if "later" comes earlier than we would have hoped.

Teens whose parents have been talking with them about sexual responsibility are better prepared to make a mutual decision to be sexually active with their prospective partners. "When teens are contemplating engaging in sexual behavior, they must talk with each other—discuss the whether, why, when, etc.," advises Michael Kimmel, Ph.D., professor of sociology at SUNY, Stony Brook, and author of *Manhood in America: A Cultural History*. "If they can't talk and plan together," he says, "they're not ready for sex."

Current studies indicate that, on average, teens engage in sexual activity approximately four years earlier than was the norm for their parents' generation. Researchers at the University of Minnesota Adolescent Health Center report that half of all mothers of sexually active teenagers mistakenly believe their teens are still virgins. Parents should realize that they will not be party to their children's decision to engage in sexual activity. It is imperative, therefore, that our teens have all the accurate and appropriate information they need ahead of time to help them make the best possible decisions and protect themselves and their partners from harm.

Condit counsels that parental admonitions and criticism are less likely to effect changes in our teens' behavior than they are to cause teens to avoid discussions about sexual issues at home, so that they can better hide their feelings or activities from parental scrutiny.

Being honest with our children doesn't necessarily mean being totally open with them, particularly with regard to sharing explicit details of our own sexual experiences. The goal is to be a parent, counselor, and supporter—not a peer. However, it is quite appropriate to relate some of our experiences with disappointment, confusion, or loneliness, for example, to demonstrate our experience with, and understanding of, what they are feeling. Likewise, sharing with our teens the fears and possible ramifications of a traumatic experience such as date rape can be accomplished without divulging explicit, personal details.

Family values and expectations

What our kids need most, counsels Deborah Roffman, M.S., nationally recognized human sexuality educator and author of *Sex & Sensibilities: The Thinking Parent's Guide to Talking Sense about Sex*, is more discussion of moral values with their parents. Teens do want adults' views on values, more than they want yet more lectures about the dangers of early sexual activity and the best forms of contraception.

We need to reexamine our values with regard to sexual behavior and, most importantly, identify the core values we would like our children to embrace so that we will be able to articulate them clearly. What kinds of sexual experiences, if any, do we think are appropriate for our children before marriage? At what ages and stages of development and under what circumstances are they appropriate? What are our views on homosexuality, birth control, abortion, monogamy, cohabiting without benefit of marriage? How should we respond if our children tell us they don't share our views? The point is not to have all of the answers or even to anticipate all of the questions, but rather to prepare ourselves to explore with our children the complexities of this dynamic, powerful, and most human of subjects.

In order to speak openly and freely with our children about sexuality, we need to be aware of the manner in which we talk and listen to them. Reflection, introspection, acceptance, honesty, and compassion will be the most helpful qualities parents can exhibit when speaking with their children. Professional counseling may help parents overcome anxiety that interferes with their ability to communicate effectively with their kids. If discussions with a child will be in tandem with another parent or significant adult, then both adults should work together to determine each other's point of view and, if they differ, present the differences as rational opinions rather than as disagreements.

As parents, we have the responsibility of sharing with our children not only our values, but also the rationales behind them. If the concept of multiple sexual partners is unacceptable to us, for example, we need to explain this value in a context our children can understand. Likewise, if our children call us on an aspect of our behavior that doesn't appear to be in line with our stated values, we need to explain the reasoning behind our actions. For example, a girl may observe that her divorced mother has more than one concurrent sexual partner and question the reason she can't do likewise. Her mom can either fob her off with, "It's okay for adults to behave like this, but not young people," or, better yet, she can carefully talk with her daughter about the complex issues and dynamics involved.

Similarly, when sharing our values with our teens, we also need to honestly make clear to them our expectations. If we expect our teens to remain virgins until graduating from high school or later, then we should say so. Our statements of expectation may prompt our teens to share their own expectations and the reasons behind their thinking, and a constructive dialogue can then ensue.

If we suspect or discover that our teens are engaging in risky sexual activity, such as unprotected sex, engaging in sexual activity while under the influence of alcohol or other drugs, or if they are abusive or victims of abuse—direct action is called for. We should preface our remarks by reiterating our genuine concern and fear about the behaviors in question. If we focus the discussion on the issue of safety rather than that of sex, our teens are much less likely to become defensive or otherwise uncooperative. Hopefully, we can then enlist their input and tackle the safety concerns together. We can introduce or stress alternative methods to minimize their risk. This may also be the time to have our daughters consult with a gynecologist and our sons with their primary care physician.

Teens talk about sex

We want our children to enjoy their youth, to be reasonably popular, and to feel they fit in. To do so, however, they may face formidable peer pressure to engage in sexual activity, very possibly to the extent of having intercourse. Much of the pressure felt by girls is applied by other girls, and many boys report feeling under pressure from other boys to be sexually active. For some boys, the fear that others might think they are gay can be the motivation for sexual activity.

Teens who are willing to speak openly about their experiences say that they regularly engage in sexual behaviors at home while their parents are asleep or away, and they frequently engage in impromptu encounters at small parties rife with alcohol and other drugs. They say their sexual activity is a natural response to a sexually inundated culture and crushing peer pressure. However, a recent survey conducted by SexSmarts, an ongoing public information partnership between the Henry J. Kaiser Family Foundation and *Seventeen* magazine, found that "nine in ten teenagers agree that most young people have sex before they are really ready, and nearly two-thirds say once you've had sex with a partner it is hard to say no in the future." While teen sexual activity crosses all racial, religious, and socioeconomic boundaries, a significant percentage of teens have limited, or even no, sexual experience during high school.

Casual sex without commitment

Casual sexual activity without commitment, also known as "hooking up," is reportedly more prevalent than traditional dating relationships, says Elinor Scully, M.Ed., upper school associate director at St. Stephen's and St. Agnes School in Alexandria, Virginia, speaking of the boys she teaches. Hooking up can include kissing, as well as more intimate behaviors, such as oral sex and even intercourse. These casual encounters occur at dances, parties, and informal gatherings. Hooking up requires no commitment of time or emotion, and constitutes what Washington, D.C., clinical psychologist Patricia Dalton, Ph.D., characterizes as "sex as sport." Scully's students agreed that most hook-ups were not kept private, but were discussed openly in the school. Boys reported feeling pressure to hook up and related that most of such encounters occurred while the partners were under the influence of alcohol. The link between alcohol and this type of casual sexual behavior "implies a loss of control over the sexual decision-making process for both parties," observes Scully.

Among the teens willing to speak candidly are some who report they view sex as a recreational sport, with all the attendant thrills and entertainment value that entails. It's fun. It grants them an added cachet of maturity and daring among their peers. It provides them with an element of control and an opportunity to defy parental authority.

"Hooking up isn't healthy if it's teens' only type of intimate relationship, for years at a time," cautions Marsha Levy-Warren, Ph.D., Manhattan psychologist and author of *The Adolescent Journey: Development, Identity Formation, and Psychotherapy*. She also notes that while many guys report feeling more mature and socially confident in the wake of multiple sexual encounters, girls may feel the same way initially, but some begin to believe something is wrong with them if they have not experienced a more prolonged dating relationship by college graduation. There is an emotional downside to hooking up, including feelings of rejection and exploitation. Dalton warns that casual sex robs some young people not merely of their innocence, but also of hope and optimism that are difficult to restore.

Real dangers

Levy-Warren warns that many teens put themselves at risk when they hook up, because the spontaneous nature of such an encounter requires they make snap judgements about their partners' sexual health status and about contraception. According to the SexSmarts survey, the longer teens are in a relationship, the more likely they are to discuss their sexual histories and sexually transmitted disease (STD) testing, and to use some form of birth control. On another note, habitual participation in casual sex makes it much more difficult to prove rape.

Parents must take responsibility for ensuring their teenagers have accurate information about the possible health risks of sexual activity. Girls are more knowledgeable and tend to worry more about sexual health risks than boys, reports the SexSmart survey, although both boys and girls harbor some dangerous misperceptions. Many teens surveyed, for example, were unaware that STDs can be spread by partners presenting no symptoms or by engaging in oral sex; that birth control pills provide no protection from STDs; or that condoms are effective in preventing HIV/AIDS and other STDs.

Adolescent specialists warn that teens engaging in sexual intercourse are potential victims of psychological distress, abuse, disease, and even death. According to the Centers for Disease Control and

Prevention, between 2.5 and 3 million teenagers are infected with STDs annually. By the age of twenty-one, one in four young people has contracted chlamydia, syphilis, gonorrhea, herpes, genital warts, or HIV/AIDS.

Sexual orientation

Condit observes that among the toughest sexual issues with which some teens wrestle are questions about sexual orientation. Teens as young as thirteen identify themselves as gay, lesbian, or bisexual and many others are deeply conflicted and agonize over whether they are gay or straight.

Sexual orientation is, at least in part, determined by genetics, and it is now well accepted that the propensity of one's sexual orientation is already in place by age three or four. Growing up, we gradually recognize our romantic attraction to others. For most of us, the attraction is heterosexual—we are drawn to members of the opposite sex. For perhaps eight to ten percent of the population, the attraction is either for members of their own sex or to both sexes.

Acting upon these romantic and sexual attractions is a matter of choice. The gender of those to whom one is consistently attracted determines one's sexual orientation. One's sexual behavior comprises the sexual activities in which one chooses to engage with another.

No one, including parents, can say or do anything that will effectively change a teen's fundamental sexual orientation. What parents can influence is how their children feel about themselves when questioning their sexual orientation.

The manner in which parents react to gay characters portrayed in television programming, news stories about gay, lesbian, or transgender issues or demonstrations, or same-sex passersby observed holding hands or kissing in public speaks volumes to children about their parents' feelings and is a clear indication of whether they might ever be able to comfortably speak with their parents about same-sex attractions or relationships. Many teens question whether their parents would love them were they homosexual. Likewise, parents' body language, as well as their words, can have a tremendous influence on the manner in which their children view and treat others, both teens and adults, who are gay, lesbian, bisexual, or transgendered.

Gay teens, as well as those wondering if they might be gay, are in need of the same practical advice as straight teens—appreciate the benefits of abstinence and postponement of sexual behavior, explore sexual behaviors gradually and safely, and be aware of hazardous sexual practices. All teenagers deserve parents who will help them grow into healthy, loving adults.

When and what

Patrick F. Bassett, past president of the Independent School Association of the Central States, observes that a teen's decision to abstain or postpone intercourse is both wise and deserving of support, because the physical, emotional, and psychological dangers of early sexual intercourse increase the younger children are when they first engage in it, due to the likelihood of multiple partners and increased exposure to risks. Young people whose parents communicate openly with them about sexuality are more likely to opt for abstinence or postponement, significantly delaying sexual intercourse as compared to their peers. Recent findings of an ongoing national survey of twelve- to seventeen-year-olds concludes that if teens perceive that their mothers strongly disapprove of their being sexually active at a given age, they are more likely to delay their involvement.

Kimmel notes that teens who receive abstinence training may perceive the absence of penile-vaginal penetration as virtual virginity, and deem many other sexual behaviors of a very intense nature—oral sex, for example—as not counting as sexual activity. In recent years, there has been concern about teens, particularly middle schoolers and even preteens, engaging in oral sex. Adults are often mystified by young people's notion that oral sex isn't really sex. Parents, however, often unwittingly contribute to this attitude, both by emphasizing the dangers of sexual intercourse at every turn and by using the word "sex" as a synonym for "sexual intercourse." If parents either aren't clear as to whether or not oral sex is actually sex, or if they are, fail to properly define their terms when speaking with their children, how can young people be expected to think any differently?

Final thoughts

Talking with children about sexuality requires a willingness to address sensitive and potentially embarrassing subjects like masturbation, sexual orientation, and physical intimacy. Recognizing the difficulty adults can have with the subject matter should help us understand our children's reluctance to broach the subject with us. Our responsibility as parents is to take the lead in discussing sexual responsibility with our children and helping them to understand and appreciate the potential consequences of their choices. When we initiate the dialogue, our children will have the benefit of another point of view—ours!

| 10 |

Home Parties and School Dances

A planned coed sleepover following a homecoming dance changed course when kids brought in drugs and alcohol after the chaperoning parents went to bed. These parents had given their guarantee that the attendees would be safe and everything would be aboveboard in their house. One of the kids who didn't like the situation left and informed his parents, who were then left with the dilemma of remaining mum or confronting the hosting parents and exposing their son to the wrath of his peers.

RAYMOND COLEMAN, M.D., Pediatrics and adolescent medicine specialist

Parties and dances are opportunities for teenagers to have fun, hone social skills, expand their circles, and take the risk of rejection—all essential to adolescent development. The prospect, however, of hosting or having their children attend parties gives some parents pause. The media and the rumor mill have portrayed teen parties as dreary and frightening undertakings with potential for disaster. As children grow older, factoring in the "fun" quotient is quickly overshadowed by concern for finding safe, age-appropriate activities. Schools face the same challenge as parents when planning student dances and other social events. Teenagers, who should, and usually do, have a hand in planning their own parties, are not always able to identify potentially risky situations and are sometimes persuaded by peer pressure to do things they know they shouldn't.

Providing a safe social climate for children tests the efficacy of some basic parental input: the setting of limits, conveying of values, and the fostering of a sense of responsibility, all of which involve discussion and joint problem solving between parents and children. The general rule of thumb for parents is to make it as difficult as possible for children to get into trouble, whatever their ages.

Some parents are caught up in whether their children are social butterflies; they feel embarrassed if their children aren't in the popular group or aren't invited to the homecoming dance or the prom. Often parents equate their children's social success with membership in a particular group, although, unfortunately, that group may be the very one that is drinking, doing drugs, smoking, and attending unsupervised parties.

Parties can be a major pitfall. Each year raucous behavior and police intervention are the result of gatherings that get out of hand or chaperones who fail in their roles. At inadequately supervised or unsupervised parties, there is an increased risk of alcohol poisoning, violent behavior, or teens having planned or spontaneous sex. There is an excellent chance that your teen will attend parties that are not supervised by responsible adults, or that drugs and alcohol may be available even if a chaperone is on site.

Preteen parties

Parents should always be central to planning a party for the preteen crowd. Different rates of maturation call for these events, especially if they include dancing, to have small guest lists and well-defined activities. "There are so many other ways for preteens to socialize," says Jeff Jones, dean of students at Georgetown Preparatory School in Bethesda, Maryland, and goes on to say that if his school included a middle school, it would hold no dance parties for middle school students.

If your children attend such an event, it is important for you to discuss with them the nature of the party, chaperone rules, and the time and length of the party. Host parents should know who is invited and should make it clear that a chaperone will always be on hand, whether sitting behind a group of kids at a movie theater, nearby at a pool party, or in and out of the room on a frequent basis.

Guidelines for hosting parties

Here are some well-established parental guidelines for hosting a party for preteens or teens. The points outlined may also be useful when talking with the parent hosting a party your child wishes to attend. Remember, the goal is to teach our children good judgment rather than to police them.

- It is illegal to serve alcohol, or allow it to be served, to anyone under age twenty-one. Any person injured by an intoxicated or impaired minor driver, even the intoxicated driver himself, may sue whoever knowingly provided the alcohol. The supervising adult may be legally responsible even if he or she didn't know there was alcohol being consumed on the premises. Furthermore, local law enforcement has zero tolerance for any degree of alcohol in a minor's bloodstream.
- Parents should be at home for the entire party and should look in regularly. They can serve snacks in small bowls or baskets which require frequent refilling. They should be alert to signs of alcohol and drug use, keeping their eyes open and breathing deeply when refilling the bowls. If punch is served, parents should taste it occasionally, circulating and letting their presence be known. The host family may wish to invite other parents to help chaperone. Some parents recommend a ratio of one adult for every ten guests.
- Establish rules ahead of time and be ready to enforce them. These might include no drinking, no smoking, lights on, and some rooms of the house designated as off-limits. Parents should discuss with their teens ways to handle unexpected situations.
- Notify the family of any guest who arrives at the party with, or under the influence of, drugs or alcohol. Those guests should not be allowed to attend the party. Parents should be prepared to ask a guest to leave if he tries to bring in drugs or alcohol, or fails to observe other rules. Adults should not allow a teen suspected of drinking to drive himself from their home.
- If teens are discovered drinking, parents should determine if the drinking teens are in need of medical attention, then should consider calling the police. By doing so parents may limit their legal responsibility and protect themselves from possible lawsuits.
- Admit only specifically invited guests. Invitation-only parties allow parents to control the size and guest make-up of the planned gathering and make it easier to turn away uninvited guests at the door. Of equal importance is the fact that small groups are easier for parents to handle.
- Parties should have clearly stated beginning and ending times. Open-ended parties are difficult to control. Guests' parents will appreciate being able to anticipate and arrange for pick-up.
- Enforce the "once in/once out" rule. This discourages teens from leaving the party to drink or use drugs elsewhere and then return. Parents should be aware that teens can be extremely resourceful about smuggling alcohol into a party, including passing it through open windows to a friend inside and bringing it in in water bottles.

- Alert neighbors of a scheduled party. In the interests of good neighborliness, let neighbors know the date of a party in advance, as well as the number of people invited, and if parking or outside noise is a consideration. Informed neighbors can also be helpful spotting suspicious activity going on outside the host home.

Guidelines for attending parties

The following guidelines for children's safe attendance of parties should be discussed and finalized long in advance of the first invitation so that kids can accept and internalize the knowledge that the rules are for their safety.

Transportation. Agree with your child on the means of transportation to and from the event. Emphasize the importance of not driving while under the influence of alcohol or drugs and of not riding with a driver who is under the influence of either.

Provide contact phone numbers. Exchange phone numbers with your child and make sure you know how to contact each other. Establish when to expect each other to arrive home.

Confirm overnight invitations. If your child is invited to stay overnight at a friend's home, you might want to confirm this and the arrangments with the host family beforehand.

Leave if there is no chaperone. Make sure that your children know that if they arrive at an unchaperoned party, they should call home for assistance. Make contingency plans with your child in advance.

The bad cop excuse. Give your child permission to make you the bad guy—"My parents are soooooo neurotic!"—as an excuse for not going somewhere or doing something he knows probably isn't safe. Work with your child on developing the skill to refuse drink or drugs gracefully but firmly. Make sure that your children know that if they find themselves in difficult circumstances, they can call you for noncritical help.

Make sure your child actually attends. Some teens will wave goodbye to the parent who transported them to the party and then never even enter the building, taking off instead for activities about which you have no clue.

Home alone

It is never a good idea to leave a preteen or teen at home alone overnight—especially on a weekend. If you must be away overnight and leave your child at home, have a clear understanding that the home is off-limits for parties. Be aware that both planned and spontaneous "open" parties occur when parents are out of town and have left a teen home alone. A few invited friends can quickly evolve into a disaster with tens, or even hundreds, of gate crashers, alcohol and drug use, and property damage.

Do not make the mistake of believing your teen and your home will be just fine if only a few buddies come over, or that your teen will be able to turn away uninvited guests. Teenagers are not able to control what their friends, and particularly a group of other teens, do. They get embarrassed about having to restrain them or are unable to effectively stop fighting, noise, or kids pairing off into bedrooms.

We need to help our teens learn how to avoid problems by calling a responsible adult to help at the first sign of a party invasion, as their primary protection is an adult consistently on site. If at all possible, do not leave your teenager home alone overnight and thus avoid the risk of an impromptu party in your home.

Parent networking

If your teen is going to a party, informal parent networking beforehand can be extremely helpful. An increasing number of community coalitions and police departments offer advice on party strategies and even publish monthly lists of recent teen parties warranting police attention and the addresses where they were held. Some parents associations ask parents to sign pledges promising that if they host a party, it will be an adult-supervised gathering that is alcohol- and drug-free, and publish a list of pledged parents in the school newsletter. Several area schools have assigned administration the task of monitoring the student grapevine in order to warn unwitting parents that their house is an intended party site.

Sleepover parties

Sleepovers present parents with a different set of considerations than parties. Having small numbers of boys or girls for a sleepover can be great fun for all ages. However, coed sleepovers or all-nighters ending with breakfast for the guests following a school dance, a prom, or graduation, can easily get out of hand. After-prom parties at which the guests are all seniors work best if dozing space is well defined, adequately chaperoned, and with enough carpeted floor and comfortable furniture for sleeping. Many parents buck the current trend entirely and politely decline to either host or allow their teens to attend coed sleepovers.

School dances

School dances are always actively chaperoned. Jones, believing that total chaos would erupt were dance chaperones to go outside and leave the kids to themselves inside, predicts the same result for unchaperoned home parties. Society is loose enough, and he feels we do not need schools and homes to be equally loose. One area school has the faculty chaperones form a receiving line at the event entrance to greet and shake hands with guests. The receiving line allows chaperones an opportunity to observe each guest as he or she arrives, as well as providing teens with a scenario for practicing the etiquette of formal introductions and behavior.

Some parents and teachers are disturbed by what they perceive as dancing that is so close and intimate as to be lewd. Jones says students at Georgetown Prep are reminded, "If you wouldn't do it in front of your parents or a priest—don't do it here."

In response to concerns voiced by parents and heads of school about lewd dancing and inappropriately clad teens at school-sponsored dances, the Parents Council of Washington sponsored a dance symposium at which representatives of twenty-eight independent schools exchanged ideas and developed a set of recommendations to govern dances. The guidelines addressed the number of attendees, admission cut-off time, leaving and reentry, coat and bag check, dress code, chaperones, acceptable dance styles, and DJs and bands.

Ask your school administration or parents association about your school's guidelines for dances and social event. Of course, not all teens are into dancing and either don't attend them at all, or only go to hang out and talk with friends or to listen to the band.

Final thoughts

Parents and schools need to consider proffering a wide range of social activities in order to provide kids of all levels of social interests, needs, and skills ample opportunities to enhance their social abilities. Remember, if we keep the lines of communication open and work with our children, they can be happy, confident partygoers, and we can be comfortable with their social activities.

| 11 |

Clubs, Concerts, and Music

When the friend my fifteen-year-old daughter was expecting to join her at a Bare Naked Ladies concert called two days before the event and said she wasn't going to be able to attend, my daughter invited her father, who also really liked the group, to join her. They had a fabulous time, good bonding, buying CDs and a t-shirt, laughing at all the crazy-obsessed folks around.

DONNA HART, Ed.D., Educator and editor

So much of teens' social lives revolves around music. An adolescent risks being out of the loop if unaware of new hit songs on the radio or so-and-so's new video on MTV. In our digital age, children have access to a wider variety of music than ever before through Internet trading and band websites. The sheer diversity of music available to teens allows them to develop their aesthetic tastes and connect with others who share their enthusiasms.

The culmination of teens' zest for music often is attending live concerts of favorite artists or groups. There they can experience the thrill of a live performance and the community that such an event creates. Before allowing your teenager to bounce out the door with friends to attend a concert, however, there are a few things you should discuss together. Even if you and your teenagers have attended concerts at arenas, coffee houses, or clubs together, your children will still need a reminder of some of these issues.

General advice

Go with friends. Music lovers should attend concerts or clubs with at least one friend—better still, with a small group of friends. It is not recommended that anyone, preteen or teen, attend such an event alone.

Locate the venue. Both you and your teen should be familiar with the exact location of the concert. Often you can find this information through the venue's or performer's website. If your teen is driving, map out a route to and from the venue together and make sure he or she has enough money to pay for safe parking. If you are driving your child to the performance, be aware that a few venues have waiting areas for parents.

Select a meeting spot and time. Encourage your child to make sure everyone in his party agrees on a time and landmark, such as a vending booth or restroom, as a meeting place in case they are separated. Everyone should also know where the car is parked so they can reconvene after the show should they be separated. Each member of the party should be responsible for carrying his own ticket at all times.

Check the regulations. Some concert venues don't allow attendees to bring in cameras, or food from any source other than the venue concession stands. Make sure your child knows what he's allowed to bring. Illegal substances are, of course, not permitted. Kids risk ejection from the venue, as well as arrest by police, if they fail to comply with these rules.

Find out the size and nature of the venue. Concerts usually take place either at larger arenas/pavilions or small-scale clubs. The nature of the venue greatly affects the scene at the show, as well as the precautions you and your child should take.

Carry a cell phone. When kids attend a club or concert as a group, at least one member of the party should carry a functioning cell phone. A cell phone is useful for a teen to call home to let parents know the traffic leaving the venue parking lot is jammed and he or she may be late getting home, as well as for calling the police in the case of a serious situation, like being under threat in the parking lot. Sergeant Jacques Croom of the Tactical Operations Division of the Montgomery County, Maryland Police recommends teens carry small, twelve channel, one-half mile radius walkie-talkies so they can stay in touch with one another in large, noisy, and crowded concert venues.

Wear earplugs. The amplified music in most large arenas is in the 105 to 120 decibel range; ear damage can begin at eighty-five decibels. Small clubs, especially those occupying converted row houses, basements, or industrial locations with exposed brick or concrete walls and low ceilings, are also extremely hazardous to one's ears as there is nothing to absorb the sound. Important symptoms of ear damage in the music scene are muffled hearing, "stopped up" ears, or a ringing sound in the ears following a concert or club date. These warning signs, if repeatedly ignored, can result in partial hearing loss or deafness. Music instrument stores or ear specialists can provide discrete earplugs which filter out the majority of the harmful sounds without muffling or distorting music or conversation. As it is very difficult for one whose hearing is fading to be aware of the loss, it is important for parents to explain the insidious nature of ear damage, what living with a hearing loss is like, and to make sure their teens wear ear plugs when listening to loud music.

Small clubs

Ensure that your teens bring proper identification. While some clubs admit people of all ages inside for concerts, serving alcohol only to those of legal age, others limit admittance to people eighteen or twenty-one years of age and older. Parents can research a given club's admittance policy with regard to age and required identification either through its website, by calling the club, or, less often, by checking the websites of the scheduled performer or group.

Warn your children of the danger of using false identification showing them to be older than they actually are. In the past two years, local law enforcement has cracked down on false identification among young people, and clubs are much stricter in their scrutiny of patrons' identification. Some of the doormen and bouncers checking I.D.s at club entrances are actually moonlighting police officers, and, as such, are both more experienced and rigorous in their examination of identification than the average club employee. Were your teen able to finesse his way into a club with a false I.D., he still runs the risk of being caught in one of the increasingly frequent police raids of area clubs. Presenting a false I.D. is against the law, and underage teens found carrying false identification can be charged. In the process, they may be forced to forfeit their driver's licenses for the period of a year; earn twelve points against their driving records, a penalty that takes years to work off and may result in a significant increase in their parents' insurance premiums; and be required to pay civil fines of at least $500. Parents, concerned their teens may be attending adults-only events and drinking alcohol, might consider Croom's recommendation that they periodically check their teens' wallets for false I.D.s.

Coats and purses. Teens run a greater risk of having their possessions stolen at events held in smaller venues. Advise your children to leave their coats in the car, avoid carrying bulky purses, and not to leave any possessions unwatched in a club, no matter how safe it may seem. Smaller venues often offer coat checking services for a nominal fee, and though long lines for retrieving coats can be a hassle at the end of a show, it's preferable to a stolen jacket.

Alcohol and drugs. With stringent and vigorously enforced laws on the books about the sale of alcohol to minors, area small clubs are extremely vigilant about not doing so. Advise your teens of the possibility of date rape drugs slipped into drinks. Teens should not accept drinks from strangers and, to guard against someone either spiking or exchanging them, should never allow their own drinks to be out of their sight or hands. Though the possibility of being drugged is rare, the consequences can be dire so the simple act of taking care of one's own drink limits the risk.

Crowding. Often concert attendees crowd up to the stage to be close to the action. This crowding is more common at smaller venues where there is no assigned seating and it's easier to get close to the performers. While some kids thrive on the jostling crowd in front of the stage, others find it distasteful. Warn your children that if they do not like being pushed or jostled gently or, depending upon the type of music, roughly, they can avoid it by watching from the sides or back of the hall. Also, warn your teens of the possibility of their being groped or pickpocketed in crowded situations. Suggest they conceal their valuables and discuss possible ways to deal with unwelcome roaming hands.

Larger venues

Getting lost. Your teen runs a greater risk of being separated from friends at a larger venue than in a club. In indoor arenas, assigned seating lessens this risk, but during the summer months, venues are more likely to offer outdoor lawn or pavilion general admissions seating. In the latter case, advise your children to enter with their group and set up a home base with a lawn blanket. Some people even set up flags or banners so that they can find their way back after going to the concession stand or the restroom. Make sure everyone in the party knows how to find this area, as well as where the car is located, so that they can meet up should they be separated.

Weather. If your teen's group has lawn seats or is attending an outdoor concert, be sure they are prepared for all types of weather. Being stuck out in the rain can be lots of fun or very messy, depending on one's gear, and sunblock or shade umbrellas can prevent a summer daytime concert from having uncomfortable consequences.

Parking lot drama. Leaving the parking lot after a large concert can be quite an ordeal, sometimes taking as much as two hours to get out and on the road. If your teens are driving, make sure they are aware of this phenomenon and factor it in at the end of an already long, and probably pleasantly exhausting, evening. Advise your kids that sometimes it is more prudent to stay parked for a while and let the traffic die down before attempting to leave the parking lot.

The opportunity to see live music is very special to most kids. By making your teens aware of these precautions, you can help ensure their time in clubs and at concerts will be safe, as well as enjoyable.

Check for safety

In the light of a number of recent disasters resulting in fatalities in crowded clubs, teens should be aware that a group of ordinary people having a good time can turn into a trampling, panicked mob in mere seconds should a fire or a fight occur. Similarly, kids cannot depend on fire, emergency, and crowd control procedures of a given indoor venue to be effective, indeed, even adequate. Their safety and their very lives can depend upon their knowing survival techniques should they be caught in a stampede of frightened people. Upon first entering a venue, patrons should automatically:

- locate the exits and check to see they aren't locked (check the exit doors even if they have been unlocked on previous visits as management or staff may have changed the policy since the last visit),
- avoid overcrowding, especially being caught in a crowd and pushed up against the stage, and
- in case of a fight or any disturbance with a capacity for escalation, leave immediately, but in an orderly fashion that draws as little attention to one's self as possible.

A word about music

Music is an integral part of many teens' lives. The Internet and MP3 technology allow our children to easily download and burn their own CDs. Sometimes this music includes racist, homophobic, degrading, or sexually violent lyrics which many parents find disturbing, although many teens report they don't really like, or even listen to, an artist's lyrics, they just like the beat or the melody. Parents wonder if an artist or group singing about violence or about abusive behavior, whether physical or verbal, toward women will influence their teens' attitudes or behavior or if hateful lyrics prompt children to indulge in hate crimes. Research findings and opinions on this issue are mixed.

Forbidden fruit being by its very nature alluring, it is wise for parents to carefully choose their battles with their children. Therapists caution that fighting with children over a musical genre or a specific artist is a battle parents just can't win; however, most encourage parents of "tweens" and young teens to monitor and restrict exposure to certain artists or songs that they find offensive. A parent simply announcing that they abhor rap and refusing to have it played in the home is not a move most therapists would support as wise. Criticizing or making fun of your teen's musical taste is not constructive either unless you find it too crude, profane, or violent to countenance. Parents whose children seem well adjusted and happy can ask the kids to use headphones when listening to music they do not appreciate or do not wish to share.

Adelaide Robb, M.D., medical director of the adolescent inpatient unit at the Children's National Medical Center in Washington, D.C., advises that if a teen is depressed or suicidal it isn't good if his musical fare consists entirely of music by artists or groups who expound only on suicide and self-destruction. Most therapists agree, however, that if parents have reared their children to be respectful, nonviolent, rational people, lyrics alone will not lead to acts of violence, promiscuity, or suicide.

Final thoughts

The young people of every generation in modern times have enjoyed music that many of their elders found reprehensible and tried to censor, or at least limit. Parents can elucidate for their teens the reasons for their own musical tastes and encourage their kids to explain what it is they like about theirs, listening carefully to the teens' comments. A teenager's favorite music is an extension of who he or she is. Music allows teens to express themselves, to protest parental or societal values they do not support, vent their anger, or let out excess energy.

12

Beach Week

Beach Week is one of those traditions—like bullying and hazing—that seem to have no redeeming merit. Expect the kids to do every form of alcohol, sex, and drug until they fall out, pass out, or give out.

HIGH SCHOOL ENGLISH TEACHER

The most important thing about Beach Week to me was that it was a time for me and my friends to bond. We spent an entire week together just relaxing, partying, and enjoying ourselves. There are so many little inside jokes and experiences we share now, both good and bad, that it changed all of our friendships for the better. We have become like brothers.

SEVENTEEN-YEAR-OLD SENIOR BOY

Each June thousands of Washington area teenagers flock to beach resorts in Maryland and Delaware for the annual ritual of Beach Week. While Beach Week traditionally attracted a "seniors only" crowd, the event has become popular with high school juniors as well, and even some sophomores and freshmen. The social value of this rite of passage is a matter of opinion and varies widely depending upon the speaker. Teenagers usually love the experience. Parents, on the other hand, are rarely enthusiastic, with most expressing feelings ranging between apprehension and strong disapproval.

It is possible for this ritual celebration of the end of school to be relatively safe, yet fun and exciting, but ensuring safety and peace of mind requires parental involvement early in the planning stages, says

Bob Condit, M.Ed., independent consultant and former counselor at the Landon School in Bethesda, Maryland.

Certainly, there are teens who trek to the beach simply for an idyllic week of fun and camaraderie in the sun, surf, and sand. Many, however, are drawn by peer pressure and the lure of excitement into serious partying, which, during Beach Week can mean unbridled drinking, drugging, smoking, and sex.

Two words that should be foremost in the minds of every parent of a teen attending Beach Week are "responsible chaperones." No teen should be allowed to spend the night at the beach without a supervising adult present. Chaperones help keep the partying under control. Without them, the picture is not pretty from any adult perspective. Many chaperones acknowledge that their responsibility made for a grueling, but very satisfying, week—especially if their availability and attentiveness prevented major problems.

What Beach Week represents

During Beach Week, kids rule—or at least believe they do—if for no other reason than their sheer numbers. The parents' restrictions don't apply because "they're here, and Mom and Dad are there, and that's what this week represents," explains Marc Fisher, *Washington Post* columnist who spent a Beach Week at Myrtle Beach, South Carolina, with a group of Northern Virginia students.

Boys usually outnumber girls at Beach Week. Girls are more likely to have had to swear to abide by a long list of parental restrictions—no drinking, drugs, driving, sex, tattoos, piercing—in order to obtain permission to go, while boys are more likely to have only had to agree to not drinking and driving. Once at the beach, however, both sexes seem to feel that just about anything goes.

Several years ago, while researching patterns of teen drinking, Regina Milteer, M.D., medical director of the general pediatric inpatient unit of the Inova Fairfax Hospital in Fairfax, Virginia, co-authored a study of teen drinking and Beach Week. One of her findings was that binge drinking, getting as drunk as possible as quickly as possible, was one of Beach Week's dominant themes.

The study found that three-quarters of the girls got drunk at the beach, with almost two-thirds reporting that they consumed eight or more glasses of beer or wine during a typical party. While more than half the girls reported abstinence from drugs and sex during their week at the beach, more than fifty percent smoked cigarettes daily and only twelve percent abstained from getting drunk. Approximately half of the twenty-seven girls included in the study reported they had sex, four of them for the first time. The majority of their sexual partners were steady boyfriends.

Not always appropriate

Most teenagers attending Beach Week remain at the beach anywhere from a long weekend to ten days. Even accompanied by dedicated chaperones, attending Beach Week is not appropriate for high school sophomores or freshmen. Promise younger teens a week at the beach with you later in the summer, but keep them away from the influence of older teens during Beach Week revelries.

Many parents feel that their juniors, and even seniors, shouldn't attend Beach Week either. Saying no to a high school junior who insists attending Beach Week is an important rite of passage may be difficult. Juniors eager to attend the event will work hard to convince parents of their maturity, pointing out how conscientious they have been in school, that they deserve a fun break, and that they are rising seniors. Whether you allow your older teen to attend Beach Week should depend, in part, on your child's maturity, sense of responsibility, willingness to accept joint adult and teen planning, and a number of other factors discussed in this chapter.

Some Beach Week statistics

According to the Ocean City, Maryland, Convention Bureau, only a small percentage of the thousands of teens invading the resort for Beach Week are arrested or suffer serious injury. Police records indicate the police receive an average of 6,000 calls per week during the Beach Week season, resulting in an average of 600 arrests a week.

The Ocean City Police Department reports that during the three-week period in June comprising Beach Week (June 4 through June 28), approximately 100,000 to 150,000 teens descend upon the city each week. Police statistics indicate that "no more than one-half to one percent of beach goers are either arrested or suffer serious injury" weekly, which translates to between 500 and 1,500 each week—numbers no parent should find reassuring. While these numbers seem small relative to the large influx of teens, any one of those statistics could be your child. Remember, too, that these statistics represent only teens whose behavior was so egregious as to attract police attention.

Beach Week destinations

Beach Week destinations include most area beaches, especially Ocean City in Maryland and Rehoboth, Bethany, and Dewey Beaches in Delaware. Also popular are Virginia Beach, Fenwick Island, Lewes, the North Carolina Outer Banks, and Myrtle Beach, South Carolina.

Dewey Beach seems to be more popular with the college crowd; thus, to allow high school teens to go there for Beach Week is to cast them into an older crowd. Because area public schools end the school year at least a week later than do independent and parochial schools, the private school Beach Week takes place one week earlier and before the crowds peak at area resorts.

Of all the area beach resorts, the jurisdiction that appears to have done the most to both attract high school students and ensure they have a positive and safe time is Ocean City. The Ocean City website, in addition to listing accommodations, restaurants, and events, has a link to "Senior Week Housing," which lists city-approved accommodations for high school students. These have all been checked for safety and for the management companies' ability to successfully handle groups of young people.

Each spring, the Ocean City police and parks and recreation departments distribute a free booklet called "Play It Safe: Passport to Fun" that lists a schedule of more than thirty alcohol- and drug-free city-sponsored events and contains discount coupons for food, miniature golf, and specials from area merchants. The booklet also includes a list of pertinent Maryland state laws and information about the consequences of underage drinking, drugging, sexual activity, and body piercing. For parents, it includes information about the Parent Network, a 24/7 hotline for parents that operates from mid-May through the end of June. The purpose of the Parent Network is to provide assistance in Ocean City to anxious parents seeking information, or worried about their vacationing teen. While they make no promises, the Parent Network will attempt to locate teens if parents can't contact them, and encourage them to call home.

Parental involvement in Beach Week

Make your active participation in all Beach Week preparations one of the conditions of your permission for your teen to attend. Discuss your concerns and expectations of behavior. Work, not only with your teen, but also with the entire group that will be staying together.

Accommodations. Research and approve accommodations in advance. If your teens are going to Ocean City, begin with the approved housing list on the Visitors Center website. Don't allow your teen to take off for the beach without having first secured firm accommodations. You should know the address, and contact the chaperone before your teen leaves home in order to verify he or she will be welcome, safe, and have a place to sleep. Some parents drive to the beach to check out potential accommodations themselves and to determine if there is a manager on site 24/7, obtain the property address and the manager's phone number, as well as a viable number for reaching their teens.

Don't deceive a property owner or manager reluctant to rent to minors by renting a place in your name, or by misrepresenting who will be occupying the property. If you rent the property, you are legally and financially responsible for any damage or breaking of rules, in which case, you might wish to consider chaperoning the group to protect both yourself and your teen. In some jurisdictions, the person named on the lease must be present as a tenant. In such a case, if a problem arises that requires the attention of the landlord, property manager, or police, everyone staying on the premises is liable for eviction unless the signer of the lease is among them.

Roommates. Know with whom your teen will be staying. Are these all friends of your child? What is the age range? Do you have misgivings about any member of the group? Voice reservations early in the planning when issues can be addressed and changes made. Remember that responsible roommates encourage responsible behavior.

Don't agree to allow your teen to stay in a coed accommodation and lobby hard to ensure the house rules include no coed sleepovers. Encourage members of the group to use the buddy system and promise to go nowhere alone. If only one member of the group wants to go somewhere, then no one goes. Be aware of the possibility, in the case of an all-boy group, of a fight erupting between members of the group and boys from a rival school.

Chaperones. While your teen may not like the idea of live-in chaperones, having a responsible adult on site is one of the most effective methods for ensuring a safe Beach Week. The recommended ratio of chaperones to teens is 1:10. If you sense that the teens in the group are at increased risk for getting into trouble, increase the number of chaperones.

Explain to your teens that while you want them to have a good time, your primary concern as a parent—a concern that is nonnegotiable—is their safety. One experienced parent-chaperone recommends chaperones stock the house with lunch food and prepare at least one full meal per day. She got up each day by 6:30 a.m., shopped for food while the rest of the house slept, and was back and cooking a big breakfast when her nine male charges rolled out of bed. Her breakfasts may well have been the only healthy food consumed all week as the guys were on their own for meals during the rest of the day.

Some parents of Beach Week attendees call upon each of the group members' parents to serve as chaperone for a twenty-four hour shift. When one shift ends, a new chaperone arrives, is briefed, and takes over while the off-duty chaperone heads for home.

An alternative to having adult chaperones staying in the house or apartment with the teens is for them to rent a second place right next door. This certainly is less intrusive than the chaperone staying in the house itself, but chaperones should nonetheless make their presence known and felt as often as possible.

Select for chaperones people who are firm and consistent, as well as capable of standing down a teen who declares, "My parents let me drink at home," or, "They don't care if I have sex with my girlfriend." Older siblings of a group member are rarely good candidates for chaperones, and parents should be extremely cautious if their teens offer this as a supervisory solution.

Be certain the parent who agrees to chaperone will be able to resist flashbacks to his or her own Beach Week adventures. In a situation that occurred several years ago, a chaperoning father proceeded to get drunk with the kids, then moved out to the street, stopped traffic, and was arrested.

Essentials. Give the teens in your child's troupe a checklist of essentials to bring with them to Beach Week, including SPF 8 and higher sunscreen; toys such as frisbees, beach balls, books, playing cards, radio, videos, boombox and CDs, etc.; bedding and bed and bath linens; and toiletries. Be sure the chaperone or someone in the group is responsible for bringing a first aid kit and sunburn remedies. The checklist should also include these essentials: legal identification, sufficient money and/or a bank card, prepaid phone card or a cell phone and charger, phone numbers for reaching parents at any hour of the day or night, a medical release form or power of attorney authorizing emergency medical treatment, and the name and cell phone number of the chaperone.

If you are the chaperone, try very hard for a no alcohol or drugs policy among the group members. Be aware, however, that if your group's house is dry, the kids may troop down the street to party at another house that isn't. Plan safe and healthy recreational activities for the week, like chaperoned visits to area amusement parks or other places of interest.

Parents should insist their teens not drive or be driven by anyone other than the chaperone while at the beach, particularly if teens are drinking. It is strongly recommended the chaperone collect and keep all car keys and rule on all use of cars except in emergency.

Parents should check in with their teens while they're at the beach. Insist your teens call you occasionally, and call them at unscheduled times. Use the calls to gently reinforce the importance of responsible behavior and making good choices. Let your teen know the chaperone has your permission to contact you at any time, day or night.

Have a rational discussion about alcohol and drug use and abuse with your teen well before Beach Week begins, being sure to point out that the lowered inhibitions resulting from alcohol or drug use can lead to dangerously poor judgment and risky behavior. Also talk with your teen in an honest, straightforward, and nonjudgmental manner about sex. This discussion is not only necessary, but to be effective, it must be far more extensive than, "Don't do it." While you certainly may advise your teen to abstain or postpone sexual intercourse and other intimate sexual contact, understand that many seniors and juniors have already engaged in some degree of sexual activity.

A Beach Week contract

Some parents have found a successful Beach Week strategy is to write up a simple legal contract that remains in effect during the entire time the teens are together at the beach. Each teenager in the group, as well as his or her parents, must sign the contract with the chaperone(s) as a condition of inclusion.

Use the contract to spell out the rules and regulations by which the teens are expected to abide while at the beach and list the consequences for noncompliance. Consequences should be simple and straightforward. An example of the consequence for a major infraction is the chaperone has the right to call the teen's parents to come retrieve their child within a stated matter of hours if he or she feels the teen is in violation of the contract. The contract should also stipulate that if the teen being expelled drove to the beach, the parents will bring along someone to drive the kid's car home. Not allowing a dismissed teen to drive home reinforces the consequence, while ensuring that he or she actually gets home rather than moving in with another party farther down the beach; it also eliminates the possibility for anger or clouded judgment to impact negatively on the ability to drive safely.

Other items recommended for inclusion in the contract concern the cost of groceries, with an estimated amount collected up front by the chaperone and additional costs collected at the end of the stay, and rules for the cleaning and maintenance of the house.

Groups who decide to use a contract should call teens and their parents together at one of their homes to hammer out the details; however, the chaperone is the person who must be ultimately satisfied with the final document.

Beach Week alternatives

There are many alternatives to your teen attending Beach Week. Parents may find peace of mind by planning an activity with their teens instead. Any plan parents concoct will be more appealing to their teen if they allow him or her to include one or two friends on the adventure. A family trip planned to coincide with Beach Week, or for later in the season, is a good alternative. The location doesn't neces-sarily have to be exotic, but should be something different and of particular interest to your teen. If you have access to a home at a less frequented beach, you might plan a Beach Week trip there for your teen and two or three friends, with adult supervision, of course. Your teen can indulge in Beach Week fever, and you can avoid the anxiety.

One option is, of course, to simply tell your teen that you're sorry to disappoint him or her, but Beach Week is out of the question. While your response will seem unreasonable and harsh to the teen who views Beach Week as the high water mark of his entire life to date, it's certainly one that hundreds, probably even thousands, of kids hear every year.

If you feel strongly your child shouldn't participate in Beach Week, you might network with other parents to determine who else has said no to their teens. You may not feel the need for support, but it can be helpful to have some names handy when your teen wails, "Everybody else is allowed to go to the beach but me!"

Some area schools, such as the Waldorf School in Bethesda, Maryland, sponsor annual senior trips, and other schools are considering or initiating them. Waldorf graduating seniors have traveled to Italy, France, England, Canada, Mexico, and California in the past eighteen years. The teens raise money for the trip throughout the school year with a lunch program, a yard sale, a senior recital, and the senior play. School-sponsored trips such as these have the added advantage of taking place before graduation and students not following the rules risk being excluded from the graduation ceremony.

Final thoughts

It certainly is possible for teens to have fun and be safe during Beach Week. Careful and thoughtful planning and conscientious chaperoning are probably the most important assurances of a positive experience. While there are never any guarantees, anticipating problems before they occur and working in partnership with teens to make sound decisions enables parents not only to help their teens prepare for a safe Beach Week, but also teach valuable lessons in planning future events. Assisting in the planning, and knowing that your teens will be under the watchful eye of an attentive chaperone, should allow parents some degree of comfort.

3 | under the influence

| 13 |

Media

Forget about religion and politics, the fiercest battles on the home front these days probably concern electronic media—how much, and what kinds of, television to watch, which movies are okay, what CDs to buy, how much and what Internet access is acceptable.

Between television, cable, music, the Internet, video games, videotapes, and films, today's children are plugged in as never before and exposed to influences, ideas, and images that we parents may find objectionable. In addition, as children mature, it isn't simply a matter of turning off the set or not shelling out the bucks. It's a big world out there—kids will hear lyrics and see programs that we probably won't like or approve of.

Media use, listening to music and playing video games, or watching television, music videos, or rented movies, consumes an enormous amount of a teen's free time. These activities can be relaxing and help a teenager get over powerfully felt emotional hurdles. For the most part, though, pastimes such as these are intellectually passive and probably contribute little to neural development relative to the time invested by teens.

Many parents are oblivious to the media images bombarding their children daily. What needs to be of utmost concern to parents, counsels Lisa Gray, M.Ed., director of counseling at the Madeira School in McLean, Virginia, is the impact of the media as it relates to present and future alcohol and tobacco use, body image, and sexual activity among youth. It's not just the programming parents must consider, but also the commercial messages. "Advertising hurts our children in a number of very serious ways," says Gray. "We are a consumer-driven society in which most of our children want more and more things, but advertisers are not just selling us a product, they are also selling us an image, and for our children that image is often a terribly unhealthy one."

The message slammed home repeatedly to our teenagers is that for them to be considered desirable, popular, and attractive, they must drink alcohol, smoke cigarettes, wear the trendiest, most sophisticated clothing on painfully thin or unrealistically buff bodies, and present themselves as sexually enticing at progressively earlier ages.

How can parents even begin to get a grip on an issue that has provoked so much national debate and emotional rhetoric? One organization dealing with the overall scope of media issues is the Institute for Mental Health Initiatives (IMHI), a Washington, D.C., based group whose goal is to present the latest behavioral science research to the creative community of television and movie producers and music industry professionals.

One of the organization's initiatives focused on the manner in which portrayals of language, sex, and violence can either pose risks to, or help, children between the ages of seven and thirteen as they grow into adolescence. Children in that age range, experts agree, are increasingly receptive, and therefore vulnerable, to influences outside their families. Teachers, coaches, and other adults they meet, as well as the characters they watch on the screen, become increasingly important models of how to act, react, and think.

Teens on TV

According to research completed by Katharine Heintz-Knowles, Ph.D., professor of communications at the University of Washington and longtime researcher on the effects of television on children, for the Frameworks Institute in Washington, D.C., young characters are included in about one-half of all prime network programs. The teens on television are more likely to be female and are overwhelmingly white. They are shown dealing with concerns related to their immediate experiences—school, peers, romance, and family. Major social problems are almost never discussed or acted upon, reinforcing the common stereotype of self-absorbed teens. TV teens are loyal to their friends and show compassion when friends face problems.

Most teens portrayed on TV exist in a world devoid of parental or family involvement, their parents being absent, uninvolved, or ineffective. They are often shown as capable of solving their own problems without help from individual adults or social agencies, businesses, or government. This programming can convey the message to both adolescents and adults that young people do not need connections to their families or the larger community.

Television teens are talked about most often in terms that set them apart from adults, observes Heintz-Knowles. Both teen and adult characters describe adolescents as "kids" or "girls." The use of terms connoting immaturity is in stark contrast to the images of teens as self-reliant problem solvers. "This duality does seem consistent, however, with public opinion data showing that adults are not often sure how to define adolescents," reports Heintz-Knowles.

Relationships

Children pay close attention to how others deal with emotions like anger and frustration, as well as sexuality. They are still developing the capacity to manage their own behavior and to consider the risks, goals, and consequences of their actions. Consequently, media portrayals suggesting quick and easy answers to the tough work of building relationships, reining in strong feelings, and acting responsibly are often misleading and sometimes destructive. In contrast, programs with characters dealing with real life issues in a realistic manner can be very inspirational for kids and provide them with role models to emulate.

The characters on shows targeting young people become "pseudo-peers" to many teenagers, reports Marisa Nightingale, director of media programs for the National Campaign to Prevent Teen Pregnancy. She says children come to know these characters inside and out, they email each other about them and talk about them the next day at school. The relationship between children and the characters is complex, for they care about what an individual character does and they ponder his or her motivation. Parents can talk with their children to discover why they are fond of certain characters and what they think about the choices the characters make.

A survey of adolescent contentment conducted by the Henry J. Kaiser Family Foundation found that children who watched TV, or spent excessive amounts of time on the computer, were far less content than their peers who did not. The report concluded that "indicators of discontent, such as not getting along with parents, unhappiness at school, and getting into trouble a lot, are strongly associated with high media use."

Some part of this discontent can be attributed to programming subject matter. Sex, violence, and obscenities abound. It is widely believed, however, that the antisocial nature of television viewing contributes greatly to discontentment as well. Excessive viewing results in kids feeling isolated, depressed, and out of touch with other human beings. Media use "has become an increasingly isolated activity," notes Vicky

J. Rideout, vice president of the Henry J. Kaiser Family Foundation, director of the Program for the Study of Entertainment, and director of the Kaiser study. While TV and the movies have the potential to supply admirable role models for young people, viewing cuts into time that children might better spend socializing with others and improving their communication skills. In short, electronic media are never a substitute for actual human interaction.

Language

Crude language can be an issue as kids reach adolescence and begin aping role models in expressing themselves, whether these models are from television, film, the school halls, or their own homes. Regarding this tendency among teens, IMHI concludes, "If their models sound more like Howard Stern than Ted Koppel, so, too, might they." During this stage, kids are likely to pick up on language that mocks, bullies, or puts others down. When they experience no repudiation of such language, they may also accept the attitudes and beliefs about relationships that these forms of expression imply.

Children in this age group are also learning to substitute language for action, to listen, to joke, and to communicate thoughts and feelings effectively. They use language to define and assert who they are, and their choices and humor may not always please parents. Shows like "Home Improvement" have been popular with children of this age because of the way the characters interact. They share concerns and feelings; they listen, and they temper their teasing with love. As they do, they demonstrate acceptance and the ability to express strong emotions without meanness, which are relationship skills seven- to thirteen-year-olds need to master.

Sex

Studies of young teenagers indicate a connection between watching sexually explicit programs and the early initiation of sexual behavior. IMHI, in the organization's newsletter *Dialogue*, reports, "Those that depict sexual conquest, and even rape, as the measure of manliness, or seduction as a means of manipulation, may lead young viewers to see sex as a route to power rather than as an expression of love. Portrayals in which love and intimacy are absent, and especially where women are shown as the victims of sexual violence or disdain, can influence viewers' images of their own sexuality and that of the opposite sex." Moreover, the strongly heterosexual bent of today's media may leave many homosexual teens feeling alienated and abnormal, though shows such as "Will & Grace" and "Queer as Folk" challenge the stereotypes tacitly promulgated by popular entertainment.

Perhaps what is most troubling is the desensitization of adolescents regarding sexual acts. In a world where sex is used to sell everything from clothing to watches to alcoholic beverages, it has become trivialized. As sexuality and sexual acts are increasingly portrayed in a casual, off-hand manner by the media, adolescents have a tendency to engage in it with little forethought and prudence. The tales of Marsha Levy-Warren, Ph.D., Manhattan psychologist and author of *The Adolescent Journey: Development, Identity Formation, and Psychotherapy*, make this point painfully clear. "I see girls," Levy-Warren says, "seventh- and eighth-graders, who tell me they are virgins and they're going to wait to have intercourse until they meet the man they'll marry, but they've had oral sex fifty to sixty times. It's like a goodnight kiss to them, how they say goodbye after a date."

Another Kaiser Family Foundation study, "Sex on TV 3," finds that two-thirds of all television shows include sexual content, but more recently programming features waiting, protection, or the consequences of sexual behavior. This survey indicates that the sexual content of television programming may actually be conducive to parent-child discussions about sex. One in three fifteen- to seventeen-year-olds reported they'd had a conversation about a sexual issue with at least one of their parents as a result of something they saw on TV. Among teens' twenty most popular programs, eight in ten episodes included some sexual content, including one in five with sexual intercourse; however, one in three of those included a safer sex reference—nearly double the rate found in programming only four years earlier. Nightingale works with the entertainment industry to integrate teen pregnancy prevention messages into shows targeting adolescents, recognizing the influence those programs have on teen behavior.

Violence

Research into the impact of viewing on-screen violence is consistent—children and teens who view a lot of TV and film violence are more likely to become desensitized to real world violence, to view the world as more violent than it is, and to behave aggressively themselves. In fact, such sentiments seem to remain with troubled adolescents into adulthood.

As a study recently commissioned by University of Michigan social psychologist L. Rowell Huesmann, Ph.D. revealed, individuals who watched a significant amount of violent TV as children, including seemingly innocent material like "Loony Toons," were more likely to behave violently in later life toward spouses and other individuals around them. Children are most likely to imitate violent behavior when it is effective, rewarded, has no consequences, and is easy to mimic. "Most on-screen violence is like this. It suggests that the fist or a weapon is mightier than the word, and that nothing much bad happens when you use either. Children need to learn that this is not true," advise professionals writing for IMHI.

That said, violence on TV, in the movies, and in computer games is not the sole reason for aggressive behavior among adolescents. Holman Jenkins, Jr., M.A., notes, in a *Wall Street Journal* editorial entitled "What's Worse, Imaginary Violence or Real Sex?": "We...know there is little evidence for the belief that our youngsters are like yogurt cultures that can be spoiled by exposure to the flickering images of Hollywood. That's not to say some of what appears in the media isn't reprehensible, but when one child in ten million takes a gun to his school chums, something else is going on."

As comforting as it might be to identify a single scapegoat for the violence to which our children are exposed and sometimes mirror, it is unrealistic and won't contribute to the resolution of the underlying problem. As Jeff Kaufman, a member of a Boys and Girls Club in suburban Maryland, noted in a *Washington Post* article about children and the media, violent behavior among teens is more influenced by their peers than by the programs they watch. While it is the opinion of only one teen, Kaufman's observation does give parents an important sense of just what does influence adolescents and underscores the fact that media violence alone cannot be blamed for aggressive behavior.

Challenging censorship

Is the answer more censorship? Jon Katz, media critic and author of many books, including *Virtual Reality*, believes it is not and recommends that censorship and bans should be the last resort in dealing with children rather than the first. He maintains, "Parents who thoughtlessly ban access to online culture or lyrics they don't like or understand, parents who exaggerate and distort the dangers from violent and pornographic imagery are acting out of their own anxiety and failing to prepare their children for the world they'll have to live in." What's more, telling adolescents they are prohibited from seeing certain things imbues the forbidden with allure, making it all the more tempting for teens. "I think if you put more restrictions on it, kids will just want to go to it even more," said fourteen-year-old Kristin Finamore when asked whether she thought tougher guidelines on admission to R-rated films would be effective.

"Parents should exert the influence available to them," advises Washington, D.C., clinical psychologist Patricia Dalton, Ph.D. She cautions parents about permitting their children and young adolescents to be surrounded with violent and sexually provocative material until they are more developmentally mature. Parents can decide whether to subscribe to cable and, if so, whether or not they want to make added channels like HBO available for their children. They can use the V-chip. While kids may see programs away from home that their parents would find objectionable, they will notice the contrast between the lives depicted in the shows or movies and those of the less dramatic families they know personally.

Agreeing there are dangers in the media and that the influence of TV can be pernicious, Tom Raneses, parent and director of arts and technology at The Woods Academy in Bethesda, Maryland, suggests the "job of parents is to insure their children understand their family values and how certain programs do not support those values." He further points out that many schools assist parents in this endeavor with media classes focusing on such issues as the purpose and effect of advertising. He encourages parents to find out what their children's school is doing and get involved.

Tempering media's impact

Gray offers some suggestions, the first of which is to teach your children and teens media literacy. Intelligent consumerism and skeptical viewing can be initially taught as a game parents and kids play while watching television. Asking your children, yes, even your teenagers, questions like, "How many people do you know who live like that?" or, "What do you think the advertiser is trying to get you to believe?" is a good way to help your children spot the manipulation inherent in commercials. Asking teens to determine whether they're intrigued by something advertised because they actually need it, or they believe the commercial actually proved a product was better than that of a competitor, or they were just amused and entertained by the commercial helps them sort out the informational from the emotional part of advertising.

Parents can encourage critical thinking by asking, "Where do you think they got that fact or statistic? Do you think it's true? Can you prove it one way or the other?" and then make a game out of fact checking to find out if, indeed, the information is true, skewed, or erroneous. Parents can also induce critical thinking in their children by making a practice of voicing their own thoughts about what they see and hear on the screen and then eliciting their kids' opinions and thoughts. Even when just passing through the room where your kids are watching TV and commenting on the attire, behavior, or language of the characters on the screen is helpful, if done casually and is used as a prompt for later informal discussion. Since you can't always be around to look over teens' shoulders and see what they see, helping them develop such skills is an absolute necessity in today's media-driven world.

Final thoughts

Gray suggests parents talk to their kids about issues such as sex and drugs. If we parents don't teach our children about these things, they will learn about them from television, movies, and popular music, and what they learn may not be what we would wish for them.

Every single day reinforce the message that you love and value your child just as he or she is. Parents must counter the battering our children take from advertising's primary message, repeated incessantly day in and day out—"You are not good enough the way you are."

Finally, Gray counsels that parents should not forget that they are the single most powerful and persuasive force in their adolescent's life. Your child may not seem to be listening, but he is and cares deeply about how you feel and what you have to say. Never give up such an important advantage.

| 14 |

Eating: An Issue of Control

A high school wrestler starves himself throughout the season so he can compete in a lighter weight category where he can take advantage of his greater overall size.

A busy teen skips breakfast, eats soda and snack foods for lunch, and then lacks energy to get through soccer practice and homework.

Parents are up against some powerful cultural forces when it comes to food. We live in a nation obsessed with looking thin or muscular, and which equates a "good" body with success. On the other hand, obesity in children and adolescents is on the rise, the fashion industry designs clothes for anorexics, and a billion-dollar diet industry urges us to restrict our food intake in ways that lead to compulsive overeating.

The general nutrition of time-strapped families juggling the multiple commitments of members often suffers from the lack of a set family mealtime and the tendency to resort to readily available, but less nutritious, fast food. Parents find it difficult to monitor exactly what their children eat because most of the food eaten is consumed at school, in the company of friends, or at home alone. Many young children, unable to play outside without supervision, or teens with fewer activities options, spend hours in front of the TV consuming the snack foods they see advertised on the screen or turn to food for comfort when stressed.

Rita Schonberg, Ph.D., a Maryland psychologist specializing in adolescents, says parents have to acknowledge that they are helpless when it comes to controlling much of their teens' eating habits and should recognize there is a normal range of eating "mess-ups" which require little intervention from parents. Whether you desperately want your obese teen to lose thirty-five pounds or you desperately want to keep your twig-thin teen from losing the five pounds she thinks make her look fat, you lack the power to make it happen. Serious eating issues are some of the most difficult for a family to work through; however, with professional assistance they need not have tragic outcomes.

No more food fights

Setting rigid rules about food may lead to power struggles with our children, and because our teens consume so much of their daily intake out of our sight, we have very little control over what that food consists of. What we put into our bodies is a highly individual decision. Our job as parents is to educate ourselves about the nutritional needs of our family, then to stock the cupboards and fridge with healthy snacks, and serve nutritious, yet appetizing and appealing, choices at mealtime. Forget about "good" foods and "bad" foods. Growing kids, especially those who are athletic, need the energy that comes from a balanced diet encompassing all the major food categories.

Dinner together is an important way family members can stay connected and allows parents the opportunity to observe their children's eating habits. Keep dinner free of distractions by turning off the TV and letting the answering machine catch any telephone calls. Keep conversation positive. This is not the time to lecture kids about their picky eating, table manners, or a less than stellar report card.

Eating breakfast is important, too, stresses Ann Litt, M.S., R.D., L.D., Washington, D.C., area registered dietitian and author of *The College Student's Guide to Eating Well on Campus*. "Skipping breakfast shortchanges your body, your brain, and your attitude and can make you feel crabby come mid-morning," she warns. Encourage your kids to get up a few minutes earlier on school days for a bowl of cereal and juice, or at least send them off with a portable breakfast—yogurt, a banana, and a bagel—that they can eat on the way. Be sure to set a good example by eating breakfast yourself.

Pay special attention to your child's calcium needs. Most teenagers do not meet recommended calcium intake requirements, in part because they drink more sodas than milk. Inadequate calcium intake increases the risk of bone fractures. The long-term health implications are serious, as well, since failure to build bone mass when young increases the risk of osteoporosis in later adulthood. Encourage your kids to eat dairy products and to drink milk, even if it's the flavored variety.

Despite the sugar, flavored milk is still a better choice than soft drinks. When selecting breakfast cereals, buy those that are calcium fortified.

When your teen adopts a food fad or diet on her own, you should be aware of what she's doing but allow the teen to experiment, understanding that this particular interest may be short-lived. If possible, recommends Schonberg, support your child's attempt to do something new and self-improving. If the child abandons the project, she suggests not fussing unduly about it because your child should feel comfortable about trying new things and being able to quit without fanfare or embarrassment.

Parents should not be too concerned if their adolescents are among the growing number who have adopted vegetarianism. The choice of a vegetarian diet can be a healthy decision as long as it includes a wide variety of foods that meet nutritional needs, including some that may be high in fat and calories. However, in some cases, vegetarianism may disguise an eating disorder, especially when, according to Litt, "being a vegetarian becomes a legitimate reason to exclude whole categories of food." Encourage your adolescent vegetarian to routinely select nonanimal foods from all the categories on the Food Pyramid and to take a multiple vitamin pill daily.

Dangers of dieting

With all the emphasis in the media and pop culture on achieving the perfect body, it's no wonder that children as young as second and third grade begin to be judgmental about their bodies. How kids feel about their body shape and size is crucial to their approach to eating. Mary Lynn Duvall, R.D., a Northern Virginia registered dietician and consultant to area private schools, says, "Unfortunately, we are seeing an explosion of body hating and dieting." Her observation is mirrored by Mary Pipher, Ph.D., author of *Reviving Ophelia: Saving the Selves of Adolescent Girls*, when she says, "When unnatural thinness became attractive, girls did unnatural things to be thin." The same phenomenon occurs in boys around the issue of looking buff.

Ironically, obesity is also skyrocketing and part of the reason is dieting, according to Duvall. She cited a recent study of high school girls who dieted, in which it was found that the girls who dieted ended up weighing more when they graduated than did those who hadn't dieted at all. Crash diets can achieve a short-term, but difficult to sustain, weight loss but rarely achieve the desired outcome because they most often result in inefficient metabolism and a subsequent craving for high-calorie foods. Parents need to model and encourage sensible eating and an active life style. Kay Abrams, Ph.D., parenting consultant and Maryland psychologist specializing in eating disorders, points out that we all, adults and children, should develop a greater acceptance of a range of body types and sizes.

Darlene Atkins, Ph.D., director of the Children's National Medical Center's eating disorders clinic in Washington, D.C., suggests parents prepare their kids for the changes their bodies will go through during puberty and explain that they and their classmates will each develop along their individual developmental timelines. Some will undergo growth spurts earlier than others. She warns us to "watch out especially for girls who mature early, because that sometimes triggers dieting" or restricting food intake in order to retard their developing curves so they don't appear different from their less-developed friends. It is natural to put on an extra layer of baby fat just prior to puberty, explains Abrams, and often this normal weight gain is a prompt for ill-informed young teenagers to perceive themselves as being fat.

There is still much we do not know about the impact of genetics, the environment, and various other factors upon our shapes and sizes. Parents should help their children understand that few people have perfect bodies, nor is an ideal form the key to a happy life. The best way to instill this knowledge is to be a good role model. Don't criticize your own body or discuss fad dieting. Don't express regret about having eaten that special dessert or deliberate whether you will allow yourself to eat a particularly high calorie food. Our need to be more active and to model moderation is as important as supervising and teaching our children not to fill up on processed snack food. The best formula for maintaining a healthy weight and preventing eating disorders is sensible nutrition, an active lifestyle, and a supportive family.

Eating disorders

Eating disorders occur in children of both sexes, although girls are ten times more likely to develop them than boys. Teens with eating disorders spend a lot of time thinking about eating, food, weight, and body image. They may count calories, weigh themselves frequently, or place themselves on severely restricted diets regardless of their weight. They may start out truly overweight or they may feel fat when they hit puberty. Young girls may stop eating because they are uncomfortable after consuming a normal-sized or small meal. Generally, those at risk may categorize food as "good" or "bad," and make judgments about themselves based on how well they control what they eat. Believing that others are also judging their food intake, they may feel anxious eating in front of others and begin eating compulsively or in secret.

Abigail Natensohn, M.A., L.C.S.W., B.C.D., recognized psychotherapist and author of *When Your Child Has an Eating Disorder: A Step-by-Step Workbook for Parents and Other Caregivers*, lists some questions for parents who suspect their child of an eating disorder. Does your child bring her own food to the dinner table or family gatherings? Does she pick at foods, cut food into very tiny pieces, refuse to eat certain foods, or claim to have already eaten or not be hungry at mealtime? Does she disappear into the bathroom during or immediately following meals?

Duvall observes that parents often notice if their child is losing weight, but may fail to recognize that their child simply isn't undergoing the normal weight gain that accompanies growth. Either circumstance can indicate that a child is malnourished or has an eating disorder. More significant is when a child refuses to eat foods containing fat, displays an obsession with calories and the fat content of food, or exhibits a dramatic increase in regimented exercise.

Types of eating disorders

Anorexia nervosa. Anorexia nervosa is identified as a condition in which a person weighs less than eighty-five percent of the accepted normal weight for his height, build, and age. The symptoms of the disorder include:

- an obsession with fat and calories,
- compulsive excessive exercise,
- mood swings, depression, and anxiety,
- lying about food intake,
- the abuse of laxatives and forced vomiting (as evidenced by abrasions on the fingers),
- the absence of regular menstrual periods,
- obsession with fashion magazines,
- withdrawal from family and friends, and
- preoccupation with cooking and recipes without intake.

Bulimia. Bulimia is a condition in which a person eats and then purges the intake almost immediately by means of vomiting or abusing laxatives and/or diuretics. The bulimic may lose weight, but may also maintain normal weight. Symptoms include:

- menstrual irregularities,
- the hoarding of food,
- fasting or excessive exercise to combat weight gain,
- binge/purge episodes often following a period of restricting, and
- mood swings, depression, and anxiety.

Other signs of a possible eating disorder occur when a parent notices evidence of vomitus in the teen's bathroom, that the teen is regularly purchasing over-the-counter laxatives, or when the family dentist remarks on the deterioration of the child's tooth enamel.

Binge eating disorder. The binge eater binges but doesn't purge afterwards and an excessive weight gain is the primary symptom of the disorder.

If you suspect an eating disorder

Speak to your child privately about your concern for his or her health if you suspect an eating disorder. Remain calm and honest in talking with your child about the situation, the behavior, and its consequences. Your expression of concern, rather than condemnation, could make the difference in your child moving from denial toward admitting there is indeed a problem. Obtain professional help for your teen and learn all you can about the specific disorder.

Remember to be patient. Eating disorders take a long time to develop, and recovery does not occur overnight. Try to accept setbacks and relapses calmly and with understanding and avoid arguments about food. Keep a positive attitude, encouraging everyone to work together to improve the situation rather than blaming individuals. Include your child in activities that she enjoys and encourage new interests and an active lifestyle. Take an inventory of the family's emotional well-being and make adjustments for improving emotional health.

It is obvious that all eating disorders are not alike, and they are usually best treated by a multidisciplinary team of specialized health professionals. Such a team could include a physician, psychologist, social worker or other mental health professionals, and dietitians or nutritionists. The aim of successful treatment, counsels Abrams, is to increase adaptive ways of coping, develop better self-identity, and increase social skills to enhance a secure sense of belonging and social confidence. The extent of treatment, recovery, and outcome varies and involves many social, familial, and biological factors. Moreover, your teen needs to want it—not just you.

Preventing eating disorders

Parents should first check to see if their own notions about nutrition are sound, or if they need to learn more about how to develop a healthy, moderate approach to food. What might have once been perceived as a healthy diet, a generation later is recognized as an extremely unhealthy diet. Be willing to educate yourself and to change patterns of food selection and preparation. Do not forget the importance of ritual mealtimes and homemade meals.

Heading off eating disorders in our children begins early on when young children are beginning to notice and remark on the differences in the weight and body structure of people they see. Set a good example by accepting your own appearance and eating a well rounded, balanced diet. Teach your children to recognize and respect their bodies' indications of hunger and satiation. Don't avoid fats like the plague—there are many healthy foods that contain fats. Restriction of fats leads to dissatisfaction and a craving for carbohydrates. Fat restriction can also lead to amenorhea, the absence of menstruation. For overweight children, practice portion control, slowing down when eating, and regular meal times combined with increased activity.

Work hard at teaching acceptance of body diversity, explaining that one's body is just a small part of the entire person. Be careful about the messages you send your child about body size, dieting, and beauty. Avoid criticizing or putting down others because of their size or physical features. Discuss how the media influences our sense of the ideal figure, face, and hair. Compare and contrast magazine and TV portrayals of life with that of newspaper reportage and of people your children know, distinguishing the real from the idealized. Help your child define his own values and determine what is really important about himself. Engage your teens in activities that build mastery and esteem from the inside.

Sports nutrition

Student athletes require greater amounts of nutrients than the average adolescent to compensate for their high energy expenditure. Unfortunately, inherent in some sports and physical arts is pressure to achieve and maintain a certain look in addition to a certain level of performance. Pressure from a coach to lose body weight or fat may be justified in some sports; however, there is a fine line between what could, and should, be reasonably and safely expected of a child without putting him or her at risk for developing the sort of distorted body image that leads to eating problems.

There is also growing concern about high school athletes, mainly boys, who are using sports supplements to increase muscle mass and boost energy. The safety of such supplements for teens has not yet been adequately studied, and both parents and coaches should discourage their use.

Know where your children's coaches stand on dramatic weight loss. Activities with the greatest risk of promoting unrealistic, and therefore unhealthy, weight expectations are gymnastics, track, wrestling, ballet, swimming, and diving. Some student athletes may resort to dramatic techniques in order to achieve some idealized body form, seriously stressing a growing system with laxatives, diet pills, diuretics, or excessive exercise. None of these is healthy or effective, and all are damaging to growing bodies.

If your child's coach encourages your teen to lose weight, discuss with him a safe plan for doing it. The American Academy of Pediatrics recommends undertaking a weight-reduction program only when truly necessary and advises that it should be done during an activity's off season. It is unwise to add the stress of weight reduction to a child's body during a period of extended peak physical performance. Consult a sports nutritionist or a sports medicine specialist for advice.

Challenge the coach if you feel that excessive or unrealistic demands are being made on your child. You know your child best, and you are his greatest advocate. Remaining silent in the face of disturbing efforts to accomplish weight loss serves as a form of endorsement and can jeopardize your child's health and future.

Roots of disordered eating

On the surface, an eating disorder can look like an obsession for thinness or binge eating for comfort. In our culture, where appetite is rarely about real hunger, Joan Jacobs Brumberg, Ph.D., Cornell University historian and author of *Fasting Girls: The History of Anorexia Nervosa* and *The Body Project: An Intimate History of American Girls*, observes that more and more frequently people's appetites act as a voice expressing their unhappiness, anger, or need for control. Experts agree that disordered eating is a very complex phenomenon involving physical, psychological, social, cultural, and/or familial components. Current theories about how one develops an eating disorder vary. Factors that can play a role include anxiety, perfectionism, depression, feelings of inadequacy, troubled personal relationships, difficulty with major life events such as loss or transition, biochemical imbalances, and genetics.

Many overweight children with a genetic propensity for weight problems are put on restrictive diets by their parents. Compulsive overeating and binge episodes are a natural reaction to feeling deprived and guilty about eating. Cravings for carbohydrates are also a normal reaction to restrictive dieting. There are also many overweight children who do not have effective regulatory signals for satiation. Commercialized foods high in salts, sugar, and fats are easy to eat and gratifying. Such foods are less likely to activate fullness signals.

Binge eating and subsequent weight problems may mask a distorted body image resulting from a traumatic incident such as sexual violation, cautions Abrams. Eating disorders can also be complicated by addictive tendencies, obsessive-compulsive disorder, or problems with impulse control. If there is evidence of depression or other neurological issues, a mental health assessment is recommended. A consultation with an endocrinologist may be advisable if your teen is obese and if adolescent hormonal development could be a contributor.

Don't overreact

Parents can't make their teenager lose weight. Schonberg notes there is only so much a parent can do because of the teen's need for autonomy and independence. She recommends that parents acknowledge their lack of power to their teen. She reminds parents to be aware that children gain or lose weight at various stages of adolescence because of biology or between seasons of the year. If this is the case, be sympathetic but don't get involved in any eating plan.

When it comes to losing weight, teens have difficulty deferring gratification. Most teens won't be interested in an eating regimen that promises the loss of two pounds a week over months, especially if they need to lose twenty-five or more pounds for their health. They want improvement fast. Many teens also don't want to be bothered with counting grams and calories, they want simplicity. For girls, especially, this can mean resorting to fasting, crash diets, and bulimia—extreme measures not requiring pacing, regulation, or delay. Boys more frequently prefer the super-workout method, although some boys may eschew swimming or other sports which require removing their shirts because they are concerned about their physical appearance.

Any plan promising fast weight loss is alluring to teens. They don't really care about nutrition, being more interested in appearance and feeling good. When adults try to warn them about the health hazards, the warnings fall on deaf ears. Teens just cannot think that far ahead. Parents should not try to fool themselves or their teenager that losing long-accumulated extra pounds will be anything but difficult.
One mother of an overweight daughter has found that the healthiest thing she can do emotionally, besides quietly throwing out the junk food her teen brings home, is to say things like, "I'm concerned about your health. I believe you would have more energy if you were not so heavy," or, "If, not when, you decide to lose weight, I'll be as supportive as I can and will help you find the best professional help available."

Final thoughts

How teens feel about their body shape and size is critical to their approach to eating. Too many are influenced by commercials for supersized fast foods and weight-loss products. It is important to remember that most adolescents who want to lose weight do not have an eating disorder. Setting rigid rules about what, and how much, to eat only leads to power struggles. What parents can do is provide regular, healthy meals and snacks, and work at making mealtimes pleasant occasions. Our job as parents is to make the items essential to good nutrition and growth available in a physically and emotionally comfortable setting.

| 15 |

Smoking

I have often wondered how a cigarette stays lit as one frolics in a waterfall with ten fantastic-looking male and female best friends. The ad slogans tell us, "You've got what it takes." "Alive with pleasure." "B Kool." "What you're looking for." "There's no slimmer way to smoke."

LISA GRAY, M.Ed., Director of counseling, Madeira School, McLean, Virginia

By telling smokers that smoking is a personal choice, the tobacco industry has helped to keep its customers in denial about the true extent of their addiction. If smoking is a choice, then what's the rush to quit? The tobacco companies have used this spin to help keep millions of customers buying their deadly products.

THE FOUNDATION FOR A SMOKEFREE AMERICA

Nearly all children under the age of ten have intensely negative opinions about smoking. Ask and they are happy to tell you with a grimace, "Smoking is stupid." "Smoking is disgusting." "Smoking can kill you." "I would never smoke." However, something happens to many of these same kids when they reach middle school and they try their first cigarette. The average adult smoker had his first cigarette around the age of thirteen and was a daily smoker by fourteen. What happens between nine and thirteen to change a child's perception about smoking, and what can parents do to ensure that their children can resist the lure of cigarettes and remain tobacco-free?

While our teens seem to appreciate the dangers associated with drugs and driving after drinking, it is difficult for many teenagers to understand how deadly smoking is. They don't feel the occasional cigarette will hurt them and believe lung cancer and emphysema are for old people. Neil Bernstein, Ph.D., Washington, D.C., clinical psychologist and author of *How to Keep Your Teenager Out of Trouble and What to Do if You Can't*, says that smoking, to teens, seems like a social, enjoyable activity and notes that "though few would admit it, many teens think it does look cool to smoke and view smoking as a sign of maturity and sophistication." The U.S. Department of Health and Human Services estimates that one-third of all teens smoke, while the National Cancer Institute sets the figures somewhat lower at 27.9 percent of white, 12 percent of Hispanic, and 4.4 percent of African-American teens, indicating perhaps cultural biases toward smoking as cool behavior.

Risk taking

Five thousand teens begin smoking every day. Many teenagers don't understand smoking really is a matter of life and death. Tobacco is responsible for the deaths of 400,000 Americans every year—more than alcohol, cocaine, crack, heroin, murder, suicide, car accidents, fire, and AIDS combined. In fact, the Environmental Protection Agency rates nicotine as a Class A carcinogen, in the same category as asbestos.

For parents, the most troubling tobacco statistic is that nearly all smokers began their habits as children despite the fact it's been unlawful to sell tobacco products to a minor since 1997. David Kessler, M.D., former commissioner of the Food and Drug Administration, changed the way policy makers thought about tobacco by calling smoking "a pediatric disease." Illness and death may not occur until adulthood but it is children who become addicted.

In the face of medical evidence, the tobacco industry insists smoking is an adult choice, and some parents may discount the seriousness of their children's smoking by thinking they can quit later when they achieve maturity and wisdom. The reality of nicotine addiction, however, is that it is extremely difficult for addicts who do try to quit. Four out of five teen smokers have tried to quit but few succeed, while seventeen million adult smokers try to quit each year with only ten percent succeeding. Seventy percent of teens who smoke say that if they had it to do over again they would never have begun. These are sobering statistics for parents who recognize the wisdom of carefully choosing their battles during their child's adolescence.

As parents and former teenagers ourselves, we all know that adolescence is a period of experimentation, definition, and separation—all normal activities along the developmental road to adulthood.

Our role as parents is to help our children arrive at adulthood as effective self-advocates, able to make good choices on their own behalf. In the course of doing so, parents must cope with their teens' impulsivity, difficulty imagining longterm consequences, and their tendency to be somewhat cavalier about risk. Numerous studies show the average teen either underestimates, or is unaware of, the health risk and addictive potential of nicotine.

Smoking can be a red flag

That the passionate, nine-year-old antismoker may become a fifteen-year-old smoker can be the result of a combination of peer pressure, rebellion, academic failure, anxiety, or depression—all ingredients of the adolescent emotional soup. For girls, smoking can be one of an array of behaviors that include eating disorders. A teen's decision to smoke can be a warning to parents of their child's low self-esteem or inability to resist peer pressure.

Chevy Chase, Maryland, clinical psychologist Sharon Stoliaroff, Ph.D., believes teen smoking is ultimately a willingness to engage in self-destructive behavior. While rebellion and peer influence may be common elements of adolescent development, they don't necessarily result in unhealthy choices. A teenager can rebel without smoking. Connections can be made with nonsmoking peers since seventy percent of teens don't smoke.

Understanding that smoking can be a sign of trouble should help transform a parent's reaction upon realizing that a teen has become a smoker from one of anger and hostility to compassion and helpfulness. Only a few of our teenagers smoke just to get a rise out of us, and the way we respond will depend on our parenting style, attitudes about smoking, and our child's age and personality. Although parents may sometimes feel helpless in their struggle with adolescent behavior, studies have shown that parents have much more influence than they realize and should try to take comfort in the power of their ultimate influence on their kids.

Selling us "kool"

While smoking among teens has begun to decline somewhat in the past five years, sixty percent of smokers begin by age thirteen and ninety percent by age twenty, and the younger kids are when they begin, the more likely, by far, that they will become addicted. Research is showing that it is not unusual for children to have their first cigarette at age nine.

The reason alcohol and tobacco companies target young people is because the addicted consumer is the ideal consumer, and they hire the best and most creative advertising talent to develop campaigns to capture very young children's imaginations, associating a fascinating persona with the act of smoking. An example of this is the recent R. J. Reynold's Joe Camel ad campaign and its astounding impact on children's smoking in the three years of its existence. Prior to the debut of Joe Camel, less than one percent of smokers under eighteen smoked Camels as compared to thirty-three percent choosing Camels subsequent to the campaign. Illegal sales of Camels to minors jumped from $6 million before the campaign to $476 million afterward. While Joe Camel has been pulled as a result of parental pressure, the Marlboro Man is still with us and he's aiming for children. Few adult men yearn to be cowboys but young boys do, and they find in the Marlboro Man someone to emulate, accepting the cigarette in his hand or the corner of his mouth as just another part of the overall package.

Lisa Gray, director of counseling at the Madeira School in McLean, Virginia, observes that tobacco and liquor companies target teens' social anxieties and need for approval. To better understand the insidiousness of their intent, she suggests parents take a good look at a cigarette ad in a magazine. If one looks carefully, one observes that the ad depicts what teens are looking for—romance and rebellion. "The models in the ads are always good-looking and apparently fit, exuding what every preteen and teen fantasizes about being—independent, confident, daring, hip, and sassy." Young people in commercials are usually pictured in exciting settings with their awesome boyfriend/girlfriend sailing, snowboarding, or building snowmen, and are always surrounded by a loyal clan of equally stunning friends.

Advertising is effective because it hawks not the product, but how the consumer will feel or expects to be perceived if he uses the product. Tobacco companies are telling our kids in many subtle ways that smoking is a part of success, worth, popularity, and normalcy. They are telling our kids who they should be—lifelong addicts.

Peer pressure

During middle and high school years, fitting in with friends and being accepted by the peer group is of overriding importance. In a bid for acceptance, children may indulge in risky behavior, including smoking. A teen doesn't usually smoke by himself, observes Robert Roth, M.F.C.C., coordinator of adolescent services at Montgomery General Hospital in Olney, Maryland. Teens indulge in risky behavior in the company of their friends, and it serves as bonding behavior.

Who is most likely to ask your child to try cigarettes? A friend. How does it feel to say no to a friend? Explain to your children that when they decline, the rejection is of the tobacco, or alcohol, or the drugs, not of the friend. It is important to emphasize that our kids can say no and keep their real friends. Their saying no may help their friends follow their lead and say no, too.

It is a myth that most kids in high school smoke, in fact, it is perfectly normal not to. The trick is to avoid having smoking become a young person's ticket to fitting in. Some teens can't imagine a social life without smoking. It is such a rite of passage that many students may be afraid not to smoke. Teenagers who get through high school without smoking have consciously decided not to smoke and have developed strategies for avoiding it early on, frequently with their parents' help.

Help your teen learn refusal skills

Whether parents themselves smoke or not, they have a responsibility to teach their children refusal skills. An adolescent's ability to say no is the simplest way to prevent the use of alcohol, tobacco, or other drugs, advises the Community of Concern, an independent nonprofit organization whose mission is to encourage partnerships between parents, students, and schools to prevent alcohol, tobacco, and other drug use among young people. The better you prepare your adolescents, the better they will be able to gracefully deflect the pressure of peers offering them cigarettes, alcohol, or drugs.

Bethesda teen Lauren Szcudlo suggests parents tell their teens to blame them when they refuse a cigarette from friends or acquaintances. Parents can work with their teens to create scripts so when offered a drink or other drugs, the teen says no, and then adds:

"I don't want any...I'm not into it."

"My dad will smell it on me, and I'll lose my car privileges."

"I've got to stay eligible for the team."

"My parents'll ground me for a month—it's not worth it."

"If I smoke and my parents find out, we'll all be in trouble because you know our parents all talk to each other—if someone's parents find out, they'll call everyone else's parents."

The Community of Concern recommends you tell your children that the first time they say no is the hardest, but that it gets easier with practice. Often, the person offering cigarettes to your teen will interpret a weak no as a possible yes. The more firmly your teen can say no, the less likely he will be asked again.

Parents can make a difference

Adolescents often tell counselors their parents never took a decisive stand on the matter, and that they often wish their parents had said no clearly and firmly. Counselors also say that parents' failing to follow through on a promised consequence is often more damaging than their having stated no consequence at all.

Many parents hesitate to discuss tobacco, alcohol, and other drug use with their children. Some of them want to believe that their children simply won't be tempted. Others delay because they don't know what to say or how to say it, or are afraid that by introducing the subject they might inadvertently trigger an unhealthy curiosity about it in their children. However, many young people in treatment programs confess they used tobacco, alcohol, or other drugs for at least two years before their parents became aware of it.

Prevention is best

The primary reason teens give for not smoking in high school is that they don't want to disappoint their parents. Parents have the greatest influence on their kids' decisions about smoking *before* their kids begin to smoke. For this reason it is important for parents to make their expectations and rules about smoking clear to their teens long before they try their first cigarette. By the time a smoking problem is recognized, a teen's ability to quit is greatly diminished by the powerful hold of addiction.

A teen with one smoking parent is at much greater risk of smoking himself. However, even if a parent smokes, he or she can still express concern over a teen acquiring the habit. Bernstein recommends parents who smoke to share how difficult it is to quit, how discouraging it is to fail to break the habit, and their regrets about ever having begun. When talking to children about smoking, one can always use the example of an acquaintance who has died of a smoking-related illness.

Parents can try to dissuade their children from spending their allowances or spending money, most of which is parentally dispensed, on cigarettes by demonstrating the cumulative cost of smoking in the context of the kids' weekly and long-range financial planning.

Parents can actively support politicians favoring restrictions on young people's access to tobacco products, as well as on tobacco advertising aimed at them. It is neither coincidence nor accident that eighty-five percent of the adolescents who smoke buy the three most prominently advertised brands.

Helping a child quit

Parents who suspect their children are smoking should "engage in a dialogue, not a battle," suggests Stoliaroff. The manner in which parents approach any problem with their adolescents determines, to a greater or lesser degree, how successful they are likely to be. Stoliaroff recommends that, first and foremost, parents listen thoughtfully and respectfully to what their children have to say. Parents' attitudes can help strengthen their teens' confidence in themselves as reasonable people and their trust in their parents as compassionate advocates.

When discussing your child's smoking with him, try to hear and understand what smoking means to him, how it started, why it continues. Respond to underlying self-esteem issues with alternative coping strategies and therapy, if necessary. Express pride and confidence in your child's effort to quit, even in the face of setbacks. Remember to be patient, optimistic, and encouraging. Set appropriate limits. For example, cigarette smoking should not be permitted in your home or car, or in your presence.

Giving up cigarettes may be one of the most difficult challenges a teen undertakes. On average, it takes smokers seven tries before they are able to quit for good, reports *QuitNet*, an online guide to smoking cessation. A good resource for help is the website of the Foundation for a Smokefree America, which offers very helpful tips beginning with the advice, "Do not try to go it alone. Get help, and plenty of it." Parents can be the first lines of support, offering encouragement. They can help their teen develop a plan, and seek advice about products and medications from the family health care provider, if necessary. Parents should understand that part of the difficulty in trying to quit smoking is that quitting is like losing a good friend, cautions *TobaccoFree.org.* Teens shouldn't have to pretend smoking isn't enjoyable—it is, and they will grieve the loss of it. If smoking wasn't pleasurable, or didn't answer some strong psychological need, it would be easier to give up.

Final thoughts

Cupid may be the best ally to keep teens from starting to smoke or being able to quit successfully. According to some experts, young love can be a great motivator. Kids respond to the fact that the combination of bad breath, smelly hair and clothing, yellow teeth, and a hacking cough is a major turn-off to the opposite sex.

| 16 |

Alcohol and Other Drugs

My friend's older children were home from college for the holidays. They planned a get-together at their home, which was to include younger high school kids. My husband and I had just attended an alcohol and other drugs education night at our son's school and had been told about the importance of networking, and when we told our son we were going to give the host parents a call, he became very upset and claimed our calling would mean we didn't trust him. Our son had never given us a reason to be concerned, and we almost backed off. We assured him that we did trust him, but our job as parents was to "trust but verify."

"Oh, absolutely, it's going to be a great time for all of them," the host parent assured me. "We know the kids will be drinking anyway, so we'd prefer they drink here, safely, in our home. We'll be sure to take their car keys."

Our son did not go. The first calls about the accident began coming into our home at 7:00 a.m.

When teenagers are invited to a friend's house, many parents don't have the nerve to call the friend's parents to ask important questions like, "Will adults be at home?" "Will you be serving alcohol?" "Will you call me if my child leaves your house?" Parents' best offense in the battle against alcohol, tobacco, and other drug use among preteens and teens is to know what's going on. Many teens find themselves in situations, sometimes with other parents' knowledge, in which they may have the opportunity to indulge in alcohol and other drugs. Do not fool yourself that your children will somehow be immune to temptation. Likewise, don't kid yourself by thinking that having only one discussion about drinking or drug use with your children is enough--it's a topic that must be revisited a number of times as children grow up and their worlds expand.

Alcohol laws and liability

Many parents are ignorant of the legal ramifications of underage drinking for both adults and teens. Throughout the country, it is illegal for young people under twenty-one years of age to purchase or to possess alcohol. Maryland law allows parents to serve their own teenagers alcohol in their home or at religious ceremonies; however, it is illegal to serve alcohol to any other minor. The penalties in Maryland for serving liquor to a minor who is not one's own child are severe. Virginia's policy is even more restrictive. It is against Virginia law to allow, aid, or abet underage persons to possess or consume alcohol. Adults may face legal charges for providing or allowing minors, including their own children, to use alcohol in their home. Punishment may include one year in jail and/or a $2,500 fine.

The Community of Concern, an independent nonprofit organization whose mission is to encourage partnerships between parents, students, and schools to prevent alcohol, tobacco, and other drug use among young people, advises, "If you say to your children, 'It's okay to break the law as long as you do it here with me,' you are sending them a basic message that individuals can decide whether or not, or when, to obey the law. Instead, we can educate our kids about the medical, legal, and other consequences of underage drinking and drug use so they may make responsible decisions not to drink or 'use.'"

Legal ramifications aside, underage drinking can result in untold psychological suffering should someone—whether the driver or a passenger—be maimed or killed in an accident resulting from the driver's being under the influence. Parents can help their teens imagine the lifelong, horrific guilt that shadows a person responsible for the death or maiming of another while drinking, and point out that the guilt and pain is shared by the entire family. The irresponsible use of alcohol and drugs can be costly, dangerous, and even deadly, thus it is even more imperative that parents discuss their values, expectations, and safety concerns with their teenagers.

Substance ambivalence

Every family should carefully consider the issues of alcohol and drug use among young people in order to determine how best to deal with them—and each will reach a different conclusion. Some families will decide it's okay to allow their children the occasional glass of wine at a family celebration. Others would rather have their teenagers drink at home than somewhere else and then attempt to drive home. There are parents who not only tolerate their teens' drinking, but also provide the liquor for their parties. Many parents believe they need to teach their kids to drink responsibly before they go away to college, while others take a zero-tolerance position, instituting random drug tests at home. A number of teens report they drink their parents' liquor or help themselves to drugs from their parents' stash, with and without their parents' knowledge. On this particular issue, do not be surprised if your personal values and those of your family contrast starkly with those of your children's friends, or even with other parents you have known and respected for years.

Some parents are ambivalent about teen drinking. It is interesting to note that those same parents are not ambivalent about cocaine use or smoking. While most parents believe no thirteen-year-old should drink, they may find it more difficult to believe a sixteen- or eighteen-year-old shouldn't have a glass of wine or beer. There is hardly any ambivalence on the part of parents, however, when it comes to their teens drinking for the sole purpose of getting drunk, and all are concerned about alcohol abuse.

Rita Schonberg, Ph.D., a Maryland psychologist specializing in adolescents, confirms that when thinking about teenage drinking, most parents would agree on at least the following four points.

Binge drinking. All parents are frightened of their children engaging in binge drinking with the potential for alcohol poisoning, brain damage, and death.

Alcohol and drug dependency. Parents don't want their children to become dependent upon substances in order to get through their days. It is a well-documented fact that a certain percentage of drinkers will become addicted and no one wants their child to fall into that percentage, especially if there is a family history of alcoholism.

Dishonesty. To a greater or lesser degree, underage drinking is a sneaky, deceptive way of life, and a flaunting of the law. Parents don't want their children to hone such life skills.

Danger. Parents fear their teens don't fully recognize the degree to which their judgment is impaired by liquor consumption and dread the increased risk for their children of the consequences of bad decisions about driving, assault, falls, unplanned and unsafe sex, violence, and peer influence.

Negative consequences

The Community of Concern warns that "drinking by kids under twenty-one can have serious consequences, among which are addiction, brain damage, and risky behavior. Learning to drink during adolescence is neither a rite of passage nor a part of growing up." The group reports, "The younger a person is when introduced to alcohol, the more likely he or she is to develop lifelong alcohol dependence."

Recent research indicates the adolescent brain responds differently to alcohol than does that of an adult. Some researchers believe adolescents may be able to drink more than adults before becoming sleepy enough to stop; however, their mental ability to judge and make decisions is severely impaired at lower levels of alcohol consumption than adults. A teenager may be awake enough to get behind the wheel after drinking, but incompetent to make the necessary judgments to drive safely.

Alcohol and other drug use are often a factor in acquaintance rape. Deborah Roffman, M.S., nationally recognized human sexuality educator and author of *Sex & Sensibility: The Thinking Parent's Guide to Talking Sense About Sex*, reports that surveys of college students have determined that at least seventy-five percent of males and at least fifty-five percent of females involved in rape had been drinking just prior to the incident. She warns that the direction of causality in situations involved sex and drugs is not clear: is it the drinking or drug use that leads to the sexual behavior? Do teenagers deliberately use alcohol or drugs to ameliorate guilt or anxiety about sex? Does engaging in one type of risky behavior correlate with a likelihood of engaging in others? Whatever the answers, the combination of sex and alcohol or drugs increases adolescent risk of pregnancy, rape, and sexually transmitted infections.

Binge drinking and alcohol poisoning

Alcohol poisoning, or acute intoxication, is a drug overdose that kills more than 4,000 kids every year and can result in irreversible brain damage in survivors. Some teens drink with the express purpose of getting drunk. They drink fast, or binge drink, attempting to ingest as much alcohol as quickly as possible. Binge drinking is defined for boys as the consumption of five or more beers or drinks in one sitting at least once in a two-week period; for girls the amount is four beers or drinks. Binge drinking is increasing among teens. While chronic drinking is considered a disease, binge drinking is too frequently thought of as a rite of passage or an appropriate form of celebration. The Centers for Disease Control and Prevention reports that half of the 100,000 alcohol-related deaths each year can be blamed on bingeing, and that binge drinkers are fourteen times more likely to get behind the wheel than nonbingers.

Sargeant Jacques Croom of the Tactical Operations Division of the Montgomery County, Maryland, Police, explains that while alcohol initially feels like a stimulant to the drinker, it actually is a depressant, and to stay "high," some drinkers down energy drinks like Red Bull as pick-me-ups and then switch back to liquor. Other young drinkers try "beer bongs"--downing four to six beers in a few minutes. These dangerous behaviors quickly raise the alcohol level in teens' blood far above the level of legally drunk. In his book, *How to Keep Your Teenager Out of Trouble and What to Do if You Can't*, Washington, D.C., clinical psychologist Neil Bernstein, Ph.D., writes, "The amount of alcohol it takes to make you pass out is dangerously close to the amount it takes to kill you."

Parents and kids both should know the signs of alcohol overdose, including mental confusion, stupor, difficulty being aroused, slow or irregular breathing, low body temperature, and bluish skin color. Be aware, too, that someone who has passed out from drinking too much too fast can die. If you think a person may be suffering alcohol overdose, call 911 and do not leave the person alone.

Do not give the person food; let him sleep it off, or give him a cold shower. Never encourage vomiting due to the risk of tracheal blockage or aspiration of vomit, either of which can cause death.

Why do teens drink or use other drugs?

Why, despite all the warnings and education about the consequences, are dangerous substances so appealing to teens? Bernstein cites several reasons, including the eternal teen shibboleth, "Everybody's doing it." He says for many teens, to party means drinking and smoking pot. Some teens turn to chemicals for solace, to feel wonderfully happy, blissfully oblivious, or energized and confident. Some long to escape their daily existence and sedate themselves, while still others seek excitement. Robert Roth, M.F.C.C., coordinator of adolescent services at Montgomery General Hospital in Olney, Maryland, reports that he sees too many teens, even basically good, healthy kids, who say of drugs, "There's nothing else to do." The combination of poor judgment, impulsive behavior, and lack of experience leaves many teens vulnerable to the temptations of drugs and drinking.

Teenagers are drawn to that which is forbidden, reports the Mothers Against Drunk Driving (MADD) website, and are especially intrigued by that which may be acceptable for some, but not for themselves. "They rebel against adults' message, 'It's okay for me, but not for you.' They watch adults consume alcohol and want to find out what the all the fuss is about."

Many adolescents long for instant gratification and want to be rid of bad feelings immediately. Unfortunately, most substances that initially elevate a person's mood leave the user even more deflated, sad, or depressed as they wear off. Insecure teens drink or use drugs to boost confidence. They believe they won't be able to dance, sing, or kiss someone at a party unless they're a little drunk. Bernstein says that teens who feel bad about themselves are more susceptible to substance abuse, but the false sense of security provided by alcohol or drugs is short-lived. In addition, a teenager may make poor decisions while under the influence, further undermining his self-confidence.

There are always teens who drink simply because it's available. Croom reports he has seen too many parties where the alcohol set out for adult guests is placed immediately adjacent to the soft drinks intended for younger guests and notes certain teens will take advantage of the proximity. For that reason, he recommends that hosts don't invite teen and adult guests to the same function if planning to serve alcohol.

Peer pressure

During middle and high school years, fitting in with friends and being accepted by the peer group is of overriding importance. In a bid for acceptance, children may indulge in risky behavior, including the use of alcohol or other drugs. A teen doesn't usually drink or smoke by himself, observes Roth. Teens indulge in risky behavior in the company of their friends, and it serves as bonding behavior.

Who is most likely to ask your child to try beer or other drugs? A friend. How does it feel to say no to a friend? Explain to your children that when they decline, the rejection is of the alcohol, tobacco, and other drugs, not of the friend. It is important to emphasize that our kids can say no and keep their friends, sometimes. Their saying no may help their friends to follow their lead and say no, too.

It is a myth that most kids in high school use alcohol or drugs. In fact, it is perfectly normal not to. The trick is to prevent the use of alcohol and drugs from becoming a young person's ticket to fitting in. Encourage your teens to find two or three kids who do not drink and with whom they would like to be friends.

Teenagers who get through high school without drinking have consciously thought about how not to drink and have developed strategies for avoiding it early on, frequently with their parents' help.

Media influence

Among many teenagers, drinking is socially acceptable. This is not surprising considering prevalence of images of drinking portrayed in the media. By the time young people attain legal drinking age, they will have seen approximately 75,000 alcohol commercials and advertisements. Lisa Gray, M.Ed., director of counseling at the Madeira

School in McLean, Virginia, says the liquor ads and commercials portray exactly what adolescents are looking for--romance and rebellion. "The models in the ads are always good-looking and apparently fit, exuding what every preteen and teen fantasizes about being--independent, confident, daring, hip, and sassy." Young people in commercials are usually pictured in exciting settings with their awesome boyfriends or girlfriends sailing, snowboarding, or building snowmen, and are always surrounded by a loyal clan of equally stunning friends. These idealized young drinkers are never shown getting drunk, vomiting on the sofa, or being arrested.

Gray says the Internet poses an entirely new venue for encouraging children's interest in alcohol. She explored several alcohol marketing websites where she was required to enter a birth date, ostensibly to prove she was of legal drinking age, although there was no way for the birth date she input to be verified. Nearly all of the sites included glitzy interactive games and contests, as well as free merchandise targeted for young people, such as screen savers, music audio clips, and baseball caps. Other websites outline methods for defeating police intervention and obtaining fake identification. Croom says kids don't realize the local police are also surfing the Net and are aware of those same tips. In the course of surfing, police occasionally uncover plans for underage drinking parties and sometimes prevent them by dropping by the prospective venue in advance and informing the parents.

Help your teen learn refusal skills

Whatever stance parents ultimately take on teenage drinking, be it to teach their children to drink responsibly or abstain until attaining legal age, they have a responsibility to teach their children refusal skills. Developing an adolescent's ability to say no is the simplest way to prevent the use of alcohol, tobacco, or other drugs, advises the Community of Concern. The better you prepare your adolescents, the better they will be able to gracefully deflect the pressure of peers offering them alcohol, cigarettes, or drugs. Parents can work with their teens to create scripts so when offered a drink or other drugs, the teen says no, and then adds:

- "I don't want any...I'm not into it."
- "My dad will smell it on me, and he'll never let me drive again."
- "I've got to stay eligible for the team."
- "My parents'll ground me for a month--it's not worth it."

The Community of Concern recommends you tell your children that the first time they say no is the hardest, but it gets easier with practice. Often, the person offering alcohol or drugs to your teen will interpret a weak no as a possible yes. Your teen need not argue or discuss. The more firmly your teen can say no, the less likely he will be asked again.

Know the signs and symptoms of abuse

Beth Kane Davidson, M.Ed., director of the outpatient addiction treatment center at the Suburban Hospital Healthcare System in Bethesda, Maryland, says the first sign of a young person's alcohol or drug use is often a change in the level of family involvement. "When your kids start withdrawing from the family, being secretive about their whereabouts and new friends," she says, "parents need to be concerned."

Other telltale signs a child is involved in liquor or drugs include negative changes in academic performance and motivation to perform, sleeping in class, curiosity about alcohol and drugs, loss of interest in personal appearance, fatigue, and depression, as well as a sudden spate of phone calls from new acquaintances. Parents need to be on the lookout for disappearance of alcohol from the home, unfamiliar smells on clothing, the burning of incense, and the use of eye drops. Be aware that prescription drugs, such as Ritalin, and even over-the-counter medicines can be abused. Physical symptoms may include bloodshot eyes, weight loss or gain, a dazed look, and changes in sleeping habits.

Parents can make a difference

Parents *can* make a difference, and there are many reference works and resources available to help them learn how, among which is the Community of Concern's handbook, *A Parent's Guide for the Prevention of Alcohol, Tobacco and Other Drug Use*.

Model the desired behavior. Parents can have a lasting influence on their children's attitudes about drinking and drugs by modeling responsible alcohol consumption, as well as providing for alcohol-free, yet enjoyable, family occasions like birthday parties, christenings, graduations, team parties, and Sunday afternoon football games where children may observe adults enjoying themselves either with moderate drinking or none at all.

Avoid mixed messages. MADD advises that parents need to avoid giving their children mixed messages about drinking. They report that nine- to thirteen-year-olds hear alcohol prevention messages as, "Anyone who consumes alcohol will be hurt or possibly die." As they get older and realize this isn't always the case, they may feel conflicted and confused about the veracity of warnings. Conflicting messages increase the likelihood of children doubting the credibility of important messages in the future. Older teens may interpret "Don't drink and drive" as "It's okay to drink; just don't drive." Still other teenagers perceive their parents' message to be that drinking, in and of itself, is not a punishable offense, but to do so irresponsibly results in punishment.

Many parents hesitate to discuss alcohol, tobacco, and other drugs with their children. Some of them want to believe that their children simply won't be tempted. Others delay because they don't know what to say or how to say it, or are afraid that by introducing the subject they might inadvertently trigger an unhealthy curiosity about it. However, many young people in treatment programs confess they used alcohol, tobacco, or drugs for at least two years before their parents became aware of it.

Establish guidelines. Know where your children are and make sure they know how to reach you. Agree upon a code phrase, such as, "I have a game tomorrow," or "I forgot that I need to start work on that huge project," that your children can use as a cue for you to come pick them up and discretely remove them from an unsafe situation. Be willing to be unpopular—accept that there will be times your children won't like the rules you set, but be assured that kids interpret limits as love. Be at home when they are getting ready to go out and be awake when they arrive home.

Know your children's friends and their parents. Attend school-wide or grade-level meetings and establish relationships with the parents of your children's classmates. Offer, along with other parents, to host fun, alcohol-free get-togethers. Ask for help by giving other parents permission to call you if they see your child participating in activities they know you would not approve of. Call the parents of any boy or girl you perceive to be high or drunk and be willing to provide a ride to protect the teen or to call the police, if necessary.

Confronting an intoxicated child

What if, despite all your teaching and precaution, your child comes home drunk or stoned? Your best response is to put your emotions on hold while you try to determine your child's condition by:

- finding out what your teen has ingested,
- calling a doctor or taking your child to a hospital, if he/she is incoherent or quite ill,
- telling him/her you'll discuss the incident later on, and
- sending your teen to bed and checking on him/her frequently.

It is very important that you do not respond by shouting at, accusing, or physically abusing your child. It accomplishes nothing and only exacerbates the situation while reducing your chance of turning the incident into a positive learning experience.

On the following day, when your teen has recovered, you should:

• have him/her assume responsibility for his actions, including any cleanup,

• try to determine how he/she came to ingest the drugs or alcohol and who else was present at the time,

• follow through on the consequences, but only if they have been clearly established in advance of the incident,

• make it clear you do not condone such behavior and will be watching closely henceforth,

• set new behavior guidelines for your teen, including a curfew, and insist upon compliance, and

• help your teen come up with alternative activities that would lessen the exposure to alcohol and drugs.

Don't begin this discussion with your teen if you are too angry to control your emotions--wait until you can discuss the incident calmly. Also, do not try to hide the incident from other family members.

If you feel overwhelmed, seek help. Many resources are available in the Washington metropolitan area for helping children and their parents deal with alcohol and substance abuse.

When your child is a "user"

It is frequently in middle school that children first experiment with drugs and alcohol. For some, it is simply that--experimentation. For others, however, the consequences are far more serious. The earlier a person predisposed to addiction takes a drink or smokes, or uses other drugs, the more likely he is to use it to provide solace, eliminate stress, or manage his life.

Parents who suspect their teen of alcohol or drug use must be wary of falling into denial, which is a coping mechanism into which many people retreat in order to avoid confronting a painful or difficult problem. Denial may work for parents in the short term, but, over the long haul, it can result in a high cost for their children. If you suspect an alcohol or drug problem, confront it and agree on a course of action with your spouse or other adult family member before talking with your child. Be open and honest about your feelings, but remain in control of your emotions. Do not let anger or fear overwhelm your effectiveness to communicate.

When coming to grips with a child's alcohol or substance abuse problem, remember to:

• make it very clear that while your love for him is unconditional, you will not condone the behavior,

• let him know that you will be a supportive advocate and will help him to turn the situation around, and

• do not be afraid to seek the help of a substance abuse counselor or medical doctor.

The need to consult professionals is imperative when alcohol or drugs become a daily preoccupation for your child. There are several effective models for adolescent substance abuse treatment from which a family can choose. Some individual therapists or programs view the problem as addiction, disease, and dependency. Others perceive teens as "abusers" or ill, the message being "You aren't able to stop right now, and we want to keep you safe." Substance abuse problems don't occur in vacuums; family dynamics are contributing factors, which means that parents may need help as well.

Recovery can be very hard work and requires the commitment of the entire family, especially the teen. Roth cautions that, upon review of the situation, a therapist or treatment program may determine your child isn't ready to make a change, and that until he or she is, there isn't anything they can do to help.

Final thoughts—build your own Community of Concern

As a founding member of the Community of Concern, the Parents Council of Washington, Inc., believes that keeping kids free from alcohol, tobacco, and other drugs is a community effort, and that parents, students, and schools can be powerful partners in this effort.

Our goal as parents is to rear confident, self-sufficient young people capable of making sound decisions. We teach our kids good judgment by communicating with them, establishing rules and consequences, teaching them refusal skills, and modeling responsible behavior. We are the most powerful and persuasive forces in our adolescents' lives. Our children care deeply about how we feel and what we have to say—we should never give up such an important advantage.

4 | focus on parents

| 17 |

Saying No, and Meaning It

EXPECTATION:
"Be home by 11:30 and you'll be able to discuss extending your curfew."

RETALIATION:
"If you're not home at 11:30, I could just make it earlier next weekend."

A teenager is as eager for independence as a toddler, and both may become stubborn, defiant, argumentative, and explosive if their parents don't adjust to this innate need, cautions Marguerite Kelly, author of the syndicated "Family Almanac" column and several parenting books. The right curfew for a fifteen-year-old may enrage a sixteen-year-old. "The more parents ignore the new signs of maturity in their teenager, the more he or she will explode," warns Kelly.

That is not to say that parents should let their teenagers do whatever they want, whenever they want, but they should listen to their teens' ideas and consider very carefully their points of view. In this way, we give our children what they want most—respect for their thoughts and feelings. Parents can prevent many unpleasant scenes if they regularly assess their teens' growing sense of responsibility and ease the restraints as their children are ready for more freedom, rather than waiting until they harbor major grievances.

Limit setting, discipline, and consequences are not punishment; they are tools for teaching acceptable behavior that enable our children to function productively in society. Setting limits is a method of imparting our values to our children, as well as a demonstration of our commitment and caring. Parents must remember that beginning in early adolescence, our children are struggling to define personal values and direction. For some teens, dependence on their parents is summarily dismissed in favor of what they may think of as freedom, which, in reality, is a slavish conformity to the dictates of their peers.

Why set limits?

The primary purpose of setting limits for young people is to demonstrate that life is composed of choices and that every choice has its ramifications and consequences. Robert Roth, M.F.C.C., coordinator of adolescent services at Montgomery General Hospital in Olney, Maryland, encourages parents to promote their children's autonomy by providing them with choices. He says, "Supporting autonomy does not mean condoning irresponsibility, nor does it mean allowing your children to engage in dangerous or harmful acts. Central to promoting autonomy is encouraging our children to understand where their rights end and other's rights begin. Setting limits is a way of communicating about people's rights and about constraints that exist in the social world." To ensure that limit setting does not undermine autonomy, Roth, along with most therapists, encourage families to collaborate with their teens in establishing the limits.

"Kids feel safer when they are given clear limits," observes Sally Smith, Ph.D., nationally recognized educator and founder of the Lab School in Washington, D.C. "Even if they revolt against the rules, children feel better knowing that there are parameters and boundaries," she affirms. Helping our children behave in an acceptable manner is a necessary part of rearing them properly. Changing our children's unwanted behaviors, or preventing potentially undesirable ones, helps them develop the self-control they need to accept responsibility and be considerate of others. Limit setting also helps children develop the resourcefulness necessary for coming up with solutions that are palatable to them yet fall well within parental boundaries.

It is important to understand that adolescents, especially, live in an exciting and, for some, long-anticipated time of "firsts"—the first date, the driver's license, the awareness of emerging sexuality, the first prom, the first evenings out of the house alone—all occasions for solidifying appropriate expectations. Most parents have learned by the time their children are teenagers that preventing unwanted behavior from happening in the first place is much easier than stopping it after it has begun. Making a practice of negotiating limits early on with our children is one key to their successfully mastering self-management.

"Parental guidance translates into love, and children appreciate limits," says Joanne Ricciardiello, former president of the Parents'

Association to Neutralize Drug and Alcohol Abuse (PANDAA). When we set limits, we must be prepared to explain the reason for them to our children. There will be times when it will be necessary to say, "No, because I am the parent," or, as one quick-thinking mother replied in answer to her teenage son, "Because that's my job." With parents guiding the process by setting consistent, reasonable limits, self-control increases throughout the school years. Teenage experimentation and rebellion may occur, but the vast majority will safely pass through this period and become responsible adults.

Jane Annunziata, Ph.D., Northern Virginia psychologist and co-author of *Sex and Babies: First Facts*, points out that setting limits for our children helps them to accept the limits in life, explaining, "Life is filled with disappointments and rejections, and children need to learn how to tolerate and manage situations that don't go their way. Children who don't have enough limits set for them can have more emotional difficulties than those who do. They can't tolerate things not going their way; they have difficulty in peer relationships; and they have difficulty if they are not the center of attention."

Determining consequences

Determining consequences commensurate with a child's offense is another essential component of effective limit setting. Roth explains that when setting limits, parents are defining the givens in the negotiation with their children so it is important to be very clear about the consequences of disobedience. "Consequences are not the same things as punishments," he says. "Punishment is a means of controlling adolescents, but limit setting is not about control; it's about encouraging responsibility. It is the child's choice. If you get caught in a power struggle, then you have moved beyond limit setting into fighting, pressuring, or struggling."

"Children who learn from an early age that they must experience the consequences of their choices and actions will grow into thoughtful adults with the confidence and ability to solve their own problems," advises Linda Jessup, founder of the Parent Encouragement Program (PEP) in Kensington, Maryland. While parents need to have the final say, it is essential that they elucidate consequences early on, as part of the limit-setting process. If given the opportunity, teens will often come up with surprisingly suitable consequences for their offenses.

Parenting consultant and Maryland psychologist Kay Abrams, Ph.D., observes that parents too often threaten consequences they cannot, or will not, enforce. Whenever possible, parents should communicate to their children the behavior they expect, rather than focusing on the behavior they won't accept. It is also more helpful to highlight the rewards for cooperation rather than threaten the loss of privileges.

Consequences for misdeeds have to be logical and should not be so strict as to suspend a child's belief in his parent's intrinsic love and good intentions. One should not ground a child for a month, for example, if he arrives home once fifteen minutes past curfew. Similarly, it makes no sense to deny a teen telephone or computer privileges for an extended period in response to a minor infraction. Children of overly strict parents are just as much at risk for dangerous behaviors as are the children of overly indulgent parents. Parents who emphasize control, rather than teaching the causal relationship between action and consequence, rob their children of the learning experiences necessary for them to become responsible adults skilled at informed decision making.

Get to know the parents of your children's classmates in order to avoid awkward or unpleasant surprises due to differences in parenting styles. It is helpful for parents to know the consequences other families have established for their children—being aware that other parents are experiencing similar challenges with their children helps reinforce the parents' need to consistently enforce limits with their own children.

Control

Annunziata urges parents to distinguish between controlling and setting reasonable limits on their children, since young people perceive dictatorial or harsh limits as arbitrary. Sometimes parents have to choose to dispense with some limits. She also advises parents to choose their battles, assuring them it is alright to take time out to think about the issues with which they are struggling. There is absolutely nothing wrong with a parent saying to a teen, "I have to think this situation through so I can make a good decision. I'll get back to you on this."

Parents work against themselves if they try to force their children to comply, says Roth, pointing out that to succeed, children must choose to stay within the limits. If you control your children enough, he observes, they begin to act as if they want to be controlled. In an effort at self-protection, controlled children may focus outward, looking for clues about what their parents and teachers expect from them, looking for what will keep them out of trouble. While this parental strategy may prevent kids from acting out, it doesn't help them internalize the knowledge of what is right as their behavioral motivation, but rather instills in them the twin external motivations of pleasing others and not getting caught.

Parental control can appear to be the solution to adolescent misbehavior, based as it is on the assumption that the promise of reward or the threat of punishment will force offenders to comply. Control sounds tough and feels reassuring to parents who are fearful that things are not going well with their teen. However, control simply does not work and there is mounting evidence that rigid authority exacerbates, rather than ameliorates, problems.

Children respond to control in two ways: they either comply—the ideal response to the authoritarian approach—or they defy the control and do the opposite of what is expected simply because they are told to do it. Rebellion is the consequence of teens' determination to defy controls.

Where to draw the line

We must always remember that it is our right and responsibility as a parent to say no. There are certain situations where no is not negotiable, usually in situations having to do with our children's health and safety. The following are examples of instances where a parental no should be nonnegotiable.

Destructive relationships. In this case, the parental no must be very carefully delivered, perhaps with the help of a professional counselor, so as not to alienate the child and drive him or her even deeper into a destructive relationship.

Core Values. Parents should never compromise a core value, no matter how much resistance they encounter from their children and no matter what others say or do. Resistance is normal. Never forget how important our value systems and we parents are to children, especially as they experience the confusing changes and intense emotions of adolescence.

Activities compromising academics. Parents must say no to activities that seriously interfere with academic success, such as part-time jobs of more than fifteen to twenty hours a week and overly demanding hobbies, sports, theater, or other extra-curricular activities.

Washington, D.C., clinical psychologist Neil Bernstein, Ph.D., offers parents more specific issues he feels should be nonnegotiable in his book *How to Keep Your Teenager Out of Trouble and What To Do if You Can't*, including drinking, helping around the house, drugs, school attendance, dangerous situations, school dress codes, and treating others with politeness and respect. He also identifies situations that warrant discussion, including: curfews, TV, telephone, and computer privileges, the appearance and cleanliness of one's living space, study habits, and dating rules.

A positive approach

There are some important positives to keep in mind when setting limits. Roth advises that parents make limits as broad as possible, allowing for a certain degree of individual latitude within the boundaries so as to prevent adolescents from feeling restricted. He suggests parents dispense with unnecessary rules so a child can remember the really important ones. This advice, frequently given to parents of preschool children, is equally relevant to parents of teens.

After agreeing on behavioral expectations for their children, parents may find it helpful to write them down, along with the consequences for not meeting them, and give their children a copy or post it in some prominent place. Parents should regularly reinforce their children's good behavior and encourage them. It's much easier for kids to avoid doing wrong when they're consistently recognized for making good decisions and doing right.

Parents need to be willing to admit their mistakes and acknowledge they are sometimes in error, for example when they realize limits they have set are unreasonable, unrealistic, or inappropriate. Adults do teens an invaluable service when they model humility, flexibility, and willingness to negotiate.

Fairness, good listening skills, consistency, and what may seem a superhuman fund of patience are critical tools for successful limit setting. A healthy sense of humor and perspective are also invaluable when establishing limits, when clarifying for teens the family's values, and when making clear the line beyond which certain behaviors will not be acceptable.

Why parents have a difficult time saying no

Parental authority has diminished over the past years. Setting limits and sticking to them is seldom easy. Many parents have difficulty saying no and even more difficulty following through. Agnes Underwood, former headmistress of the National Cathedral School in Washington, D.C., says, "Parents, like schools, have to decide on the most important issues on which to draw the line. With adolescents, there are many issues that provide opportunities to teach decision making and its consequences."

Annunziata notes that limit setting is more difficult for many area parents because their affluence guarantees their ability to lavish their children with material things. The age-old parental excuse of not being able to afford something a child wants is rarely a factor anymore, and parents have to find other reasons for saying no to their children. She suggests parents' increased sensitivity to their children's emotional and psychological needs also increases the difficulty of telling them no. Fearing to hurt their children's feelings, disappoint them, stifle their creativity, or tolerate their anger, along with their own responses, often makes giving in and avoiding conflict seem attractive to parents.

Washington, D.C., clinical psychologist Patricia Dalton, Ph.D., reports, "Some parents become more concerned about their children's happiness and self-esteem than about their sense of morality and basic decency." When parents view no as a dirty word and believe that punishment or consequences should be avoided because they might harm the child's fragile self-esteem, Dalton says there is an "unspoken assumption that a child who feels good will never need to behave badly."

Another reason some parents avoid setting limits is that, after spending long hours in demanding, stressful jobs, they want to spend their limited family time in peace and harmony. Setting limits on their teens' behavior can mean confrontation and feeling miserable. Dalton observes that tired, guilty parents make poor disciplinarians.

Annunziata comments that parents also experience pressure from their peers to allow their children to do things they really don't feel are appropriate, like go to the mall, see certain movies, or participate in certain after-school activities. Susan Reimer, *Baltimore Sun* columnist and parent of two teenagers, agrees that sometimes parents fail to enforce rules because they are clueless or too worn out to fight about it, but she suggests another reason for parental reluctance to follow through on limits—popularity. Parents want to be liked by their kids and their kids' friends. Parents were once teens themselves and well remember how much it hurt when given the ice treatment by the popular girls or belittled by guys in the cool set. "We do not want our teens to be ridiculed because of our rules," reports Reimer, who goes on to explain, "This makes for very conflicted parenting, and it turns on its head one of the more familiar parenting aphorisms—don't be your kids' friend. Be their parent."

There are still other parents who take the tack of not sweating the small stuff. Dalton warns that if parents find it difficult to enforce the more mundane limits, they will be lost when it comes to dealing with the big issues. It takes a confident, purposeful parent to say to a pleading fourteen-year-old daughter, "No, you aren't going to that concert," and to remain resolute if there is fallout. Saying no may well cause some tension, but it won't permanently damage the bond between parent and child.

As parents today, we have to be vigilant against the many dangerous opportunities available to our children. Peer pressure can be intense, media messages are frequently unhealthy, and participation in risky behavior is often perceived as evidence of being cool. We must not be so concerned about our children's popularity and their affection for us that we condone questionable behavior. Parents worrying about losing their children's love would do well to heed the observations of experts who warn that teens whose parents did not set limits often reject their parents and may never learn how to create their own limits.

If your child breaks the rules

When a teen's performance falls short of the standard, parents should not view the situation so much as a basis for criticism, but rather as a problem to be solved. In other words, Roth advises, don't jump to the immediate conclusion that the cause is your child's behavior. Perhaps the standards were inappropriate; perhaps unanticipated obstacles arose. Even if the difficulty was largely caused by the child's behavior, viewing it as a problem to solve, thinking about how this can be improved next time, rather than simply being critical, will usually produce more positive results.

Parents need to support a child who is caught cheating, shoplifting, or speeding without excusing the behavior. Psychologists recommend that such a child receive not only the legally mandated punishment, but also an additional consequence designed and agreed upon by the teen and his or her parents.

Final thoughts

Teens demonstrate their independence and individuality by questioning, arguing, disputing, and, at times, rejecting their parents' opinions and beliefs. Despite their occasionally rebellious postures, however, teenagers still value their family and clear rules more than they are likely to admit.

Parents can, and should, allow their children latitude for self-expression and individuality, within firm limits, and choose their battles wisely. As part of the normal separation process, we should expect our children to adopt dress, language, and behavior different from our own, but within reasonable limits. If unsure about what constitutes reasonable limits, parents can talk with other parents with similar values and consult with their children's school. Consistently inappropriate behavior, such as lying, rule breaking, school problems, moodiness, withdrawal, and excessive time spent away from home may be signs of more serious problems that should be addressed immediately by a professional.

The good news is that it's never too late to begin setting and/or enforcing limits for our children, according to Annunziata. Setting limits may be more difficult as our children get into their teens, but they will afford us many opportunities to do it.

18

Push for Success

Try to see your child as a seed that came in a packet without a label. Your job is to provide the right environment and nutrients and to pull the weeds. You can't decide what kind of flower you'll get or in which season it will bloom.

ANONYMOUS

Whether success is spelled by the number of zeroes in a signing bonus or salary or the number of advanced degrees from prestigious institutions that follow a person's name, parents need to appreciate that parent-driven success, rather than that which is child-propelled, often comes at great expense.

"If only parents could witness the suffering I see in kids all the time in my work, and the depression caused by parents who are pushing their kids on to success," laments Washington, D.C., area neuropsychologist and learning specialist William Stixrud, Ph.D. He notes that parents who consider such things as school acceptance the pinnacle of success often pressure their children because they love them and want them to experience the widest possible life choices. He notes, however, that the academic pressures parents apply from preschool onward greatly increase the likelihood of burnout, physical ailments, depression, eating disorders, sleep deprivation, and alienation.

Behind the push for success are parental fears that their children will miss out, says Washington, D.C., clinical psychologist Patricia Dalton, Ph.D. Yet, it is misguided to believe that if children don't do well from the earliest years through high school, they won't be accepted into a good college and later won't land a good job and ultimately will miss out on the good life. As parents, we need to examine what we mean by a good life and if our definition dovetails with that of our children.

Wendy Mogel, Ph.D., in her book *The Blessing of a Skinned Knee: Using Jewish Teachings to Raise Self-Reliant Children*, says that parents' most important job is to prepare their children for life not just for the forums for success, such as schools. There is no denying the competition is tough; in fact, many parents could not get into their own alma maters were they to apply today. However, our children are smart enough to get into a good enough school and have a good enough life, says Mogel, who advocates more time for play, more time for rest, and more time for reflection by both parents and children.

The push for success occurs in many areas besides sports and academics. Many parents enroll their kids in private lessons, classes, camps, and traveling sports teams, loading them with schedules that fuel the competitive spirit but leave little room for kids to dream or stumble onto discoveries of their own personal passions. These schedules reinforce the achieving, dominating side of the child's personality, but neglect the dreamy, creative, imaginative side of a child, says Dalton. Where is the hang-around-the-house time? What about family meals together? What happens to a child who isn't tied up in all the family activity?

Learning from mistakes

The pressure to win imposed upon children and teens, whether individually or on a team, in sports or in academics, in making new friends or risking new adventures, closes the door on personal development. Playing for the fun of the game or taking a new course for the thrill of discovery may be lost. The grade point average may be saved but the atmosphere changes; the only rush is in winning.

"Children who are not afraid to fail, are not afraid to try," write local authors Sandra Burt and Linda Perlis in *Parents as Mentors:A New Perspective on Parenting that Can Change Your Child's Life*. Carol Weissbrod, Ph.D., clinical psychologist and professor at the American University, says that parents play a vital role in helping children understand what happens when they make mistakes, fail, or disappoint themselves or their parents in some way. For example, when a child fails a math test, rather than having the child interpret the result to mean he's stupid, parents can help the child analyze what happened. Perhaps the teacher was too tough; perhaps the child did not study hard enough; or perhaps math is not the child's greatest strength.

This is not to suggest that a child avoid taking responsibility, but rather to understand there are more useful insights to be gained than wallowing in damaging global self-assessments like, "I'm stupid," or, "Nobody likes me." Weissbrod reminds us that it is empowering to examine the various causes for a child's lapse because then the child can take the appropriate, positive action. Arrangements can be made for a tutor; one can study an extra thirty minutes; or the teacher can be sought out in advance of an exam for guidance or extra help.

Weissbrod suggests encouraging children to be optimistic and to believe they can accomplish what they set out to do, no matter the difficulty or discomfort. It is counterproductive to pressure children to do better in some nonspecific way, whether it be in school, in sports, or in friendships. We need to help them learn what it takes to face the task, learn that they can rely on themselves, and realize the value of approaching difficulties with a plan rather than with avoidance.

The good life—the search for self-awareness

Overscheduled children and adolescents are less likely to develop time-management or decision-making skills, both of which take practice and should be encouraged from the earliest age. Dalton warns that micromanaged children are at greater risk in adulthood of not knowing what career is right for them or what kind of mate they want, because they're not accustomed to thinking for themselves and, therefore, don't rely on their own instincts or judgment.

The best emotional support parents can provide a child, advises Washington, D.C., psychologist Trish Calvert, Ph.D., is to create a family environment that encourages the child to set his own goals, know his own desires, and take responsibility for his own decisions, all of which contribute to increasing the child's self-awareness. Calvert believes many parents do not allow their children to struggle enough, experience disappointment, or ultimately find their own way.

Bob Condit, M.Ed., independent consultant and former counselor at the Landon School in Bethesda, Maryland, says that one of the greatest growth experiences a parent can provide is to step back and allow the child to fail at something. As painful as this is to watch, some of the greatest opportunities for personal and emotional growth follow significant disappointments and failure.

For an intriguing conversation, Calvert suggests asking children what they think it means to be a successful person and how someone should feel once he becomes successful. Ask them how they imagine people find meaning in their lives, how they learn to relax, to know themselves, to say what they mean. Ask them so they start asking themselves the same questions, exploring their own feelings on the subject.

Children bent on compulsive overachieving, whether to please parents and teachers or to satisfy an inner drive, can lose touch with their own desires and never really know what they want for themselves. Calvert says that our children may know how it feels to be driven but suggests we ask them, "How does it feel to be inspired?"

The good life—it's theirs

What's a parent to do to aid a child in choosing his or her own good life? Parents can advise their children to acquire life skills and broaden their perspectives through summer jobs, after-school jobs, internships, community service projects, and networking with former teachers. Parents can facilitate introductions to adults who work in various professions. High school students, even those who know what they want to do as adults, can schedule informational interviews with successful adults working in the fields they are considering and ask them to describe ideal job candidates and the future of the field so as to determine if that is, indeed, the path they wish to follow. They can also arrange to shadow a professional on the job in order to experience a typical day and get a sense of such things as the atmosphere, workload, variety, and pace.

Kaye Cook, M.P.A., a Bethesda, Maryland, career counselor who works with adolescents and adults, says that parents should play a major role in this planning process. Parents should not resist their child's ideas and desires, especially if those ideas do not match the parents' hopes or expectations. Allowing your child to control his destiny is especially difficult when the child's intellectual curiosity, personal style, or competitive spirit is not the same as your own. "Kids sing their own song from the minute they are born," says Cook, "and parents need to be sensitive to their children's strengths and interests and explore with them what is out there, rather than decide for them which way is best for them to go."

What are your child's interests, passions? Parents should be willing to take the time to ask the right questions and be astute observers of their children. Children who make their own choices about what they want to do will be motivated to do what it takes to be successful. Research shows that children who have input in arranging their own schedules feel more supported by their parents and maintain more interest in the scheduled activity. Ideally, a parent will express enthusiasm to match that of the child.

How can parents contribute to the success of the child who is ready for college? They can take a very active role in helping children acquire all the information about choices for college, whether it be a two-year, four-year, technical, or vocational institution. They can make sure their child has access to all the aptitude and assessment tests available. Cook encourages parents to say, "You may choose not to act on any of this information about college or career choices and vocations, but not knowing about it all is not an option. You must at least inform yourself."

Help your children focus on their gifts, interests, and values throughout their school years. Encourage them to explore options that interest them and then collaborate to find a middle school, high school, or college that provides an environment and curriculum to nourish and develop these interests. Parents and children both should research and experience the school cultures carefully to ensure there is a comfortable match between a child's personal qualities and the strengths of the school. "Be careful where you place your child, because that will be the air they will breathe," Dalton says.

Listen to your children. Join them for regular meals and dinner table discussions. Studies show this is the single most important act a parent can perform to ensure a grounded, successful child, according to Garry Ripple, Ph.D., author and former admissions director at Lafayette College and the College of William and Mary. Perhaps most importantly, parents can help children learn to trust their instincts. Support their decisions. Value who they are and how they are. Children need to be encouraged as they learn to make choices in their lives and be allowed to experience the positive and negative ramifications of their actions. As they do, they become better acquainted with their own needs and are more likely to find not only the path that is right for them, but also the confidence to follow it.

Young people need the freedom to experiment, to fail, and to try again—and again. Through our words and our example, we teach our children that trying, and failing, and learning is the way to genuinely satisfying success.

| 19 |

Gender: Rearing Boys and Girls

Boys are still trapped in their own gender straightjacket that…calls upon them to perform a constant acting job. Males must pretend to be confident when they may feel afraid, sturdy when they feel shaky, and independent when they may be desperate for love, attention, and support.

WILLIAM POLLACk, Ph.D., Author

The image being sold to our girls is that to be considered popular, attractive, and desirable they must wear the trendiest clothes on painfully thin bodies, use alcohol, smoke cigarettes, and present themselves as sexually enticing at progressively earlier ages.

LISA GRAY, M.Ed., Director of counseling, Madeira School, McLean, Virginia

Before looking at the ways in which boys and girls are both different and the same, we should define what is meant by gender, suggests Deborah Roffman, M.S., nationally recognized human sexuality educator and author of *Sex & Sensibilities: The Thinking Parent's Guide to Talking Sense about Sex*. She outlines four fundamental dimensions of human gender.

Biological gender is determined by one's external genitalia and is something people are born with; it is something they have.

Gender roles are defined by society, our culture, and family and are primarily learned behaviors. These are the roles we play every day, and they determine how we behave.

Gender identity is the gender with which each of us identifies internally—what we feel ourselves to be. This develops from within and is something we experience.

Sexual orientation concerns the gender to which we are attracted romantically, affectionately, and sexually. We may be attracted to individuals of the opposite gender, the same gender, or both.

Rearing boys and girls

Rearing children of either gender is a major undertaking. Parents and teachers cannot ignore the differences between girls and boys, nor should they be bound by stereotypes that constrain expectations for children. We want our children to be themselves, be happy, make their own decisions, feel fulfilled, and move beyond sexist and racist attitudes and behavior.

The need to overcome society's gender stereotypes is as important for boys who dream of becoming teachers or nurses or dancers as it is for girls who dream of careers in electrical engineering, finance, or commercial construction. Sexism is a two-edged sword, and boys, as well as girls, pay a price for it. In school, boys are more likely to need special education services, and they have a slightly higher dropout rate. While girls lag behind on some critical standardized tests, boys continue to receive lower report card grades than girls.

Peer conflicts are another area in which boys and girls differ. "Girls manage conflict using social and emotional aggression, whereas boys are socialized to act out their aggressive feelings, sometimes physically," notes Amye Fried, M.S.W., counselor at the Edmund Burke School in Washington, D.C. Neither of these means is constructive. Fried recommends teens be taught assertiveness skills, as well as an understanding of the reasons they resort to aggression. She says, "For girls, aggression can be a defense against the fear of losing a friendship, coupled with the fact many have been socialized not to show anger directly. For boys, aggression is the way they often have been socialized to manage conflict—no words, just action."

Considerable research is currently available comparing and contrasting the very real developmental differences between boys and girls. Researchers and authors such as JoAnn Deak, Michael Thompson, Mary Pipher, Michael Gurian, Carol Gilligan, William Pollack, and Michael Kimmel, to name but a few, address these differences clearly in very readable, available books aimed at parents. A list of these can be found in the resource section for this chapter at the back of this book.

Boys are different

Although many girls feel pressured to live up to various images of femininity, their sense of gender is not fundamentally questioned in the same way that masculinity often is, says Elinor Scully, M.Ed., upper school associate director at St. Stephen's and St. Agnes School in Alexandria, Virginia. "Girls are born female," she explains. "While they may have to prove what kind of girl they are, their gender is taken for granted. Boys, on the other hand, must earn their masculinity. It is not simply enough to be born male; masculinity must be demonstrated and proven."

Michael Kimmel, Ph.D., professor of sociology at SUNY, Stony Brook, and author of *Manhood in America: A Cultural History*, suggests that the "strength" of boys' and girls' voices, incorporating their levels of confidence, are quite equal until preadolescence when girls begin to "lose voice." About this time, boys usually gain new and stronger voices, but they are anything but authentic. They have at their roots deep feelings of insecurity that are masked by constant posturing, posing, and bravado. Unfortunately, these masks often prevent boys from being able to express their more sensitive, tender inner voices through much of adolescence and contributes to the apparent emotional shallowness exhibited by many boys. Kimmel calls this limiting construct forced by society on our sons the "gender box."

Unfortunately, societal constraints prevent many boys from learning to express the wide range of feelings and emotions that are allowed girls. They are constantly told to "suck it up," not to cry, and are called sissies if their responses aren't deemed appropriately masculine by adults and peers. "Anger is the one emotion that boys are allowed to show," says Craig Windham, L.C.P.C., a Washington, D.C., area independent counselor. "It's a tragedy that boys are forced into a tight box of what others define as being masculine, because these same boys then grow into men who are emotionally challenged, still repressing many of the same emotions they learned to repress as children."

Males are in a double bind, according to Kimmel. If they remain in the gender box, they cannot live up to the idealized image, but if they step outside the box, they're excluded and may even be physically attacked. Neither position is safe. Boys' resulting anxiety and insecurity lead to hypermasculine play, the constant testing of others, and the repeated challenging of peers.

A significantly larger number of boys than girls have learning disabilities, and fewer boys graduate from high school, college, and graduate school. Boys act out more frequently than girls, are more likely to be antisocial, take risks, and are far more prone to fighting. Because boys are less communicative and subscribe to a code of silence, it is often difficult for adults to obtain accurate information from them even when there is a serious problem. Despite the fact that girls show signs of depression and attempt suicide more frequently than boys do, boys commit suicide at least three times more often

Girls are different

Kimmel believes that society forces girls into a gender box, as well. Girls are expected to be attractive, show and express emotions, exhibit artistic abilities, and are allowed qualities like athleticism, organization, and leadership more frequently than boys are allowed to be anything but tough. The consequences for girls of stepping out of the gender box include subtle psychological intimidation and backstabbing by friends.

Much attention has been focused recently on "mean" girls—girls who bully other girls through the use of exclusion, gossip, name-calling, and rumor mongering, according to Rachel Simmons, author of *Odd Girl Out: The Hidden Culture of Aggression in Girls*. She describes girls' aggression as frequently being covert in nature, consisting of the silent treatment, rigid fashion guidelines, death stares, note-passing, and being friendly to a peer in private but humiliating her in public.

Simmons, who grew up in the Maryland suburbs, blames this form of bullying on the cultural restraints imposed on girls, which prevent them from the healthy expression of competition, jealousy, and anger. As parents, we want our daughters to be assertive and adaptive or aggressive when necessary. However, we do not want them to be mean or bullying to others.

"Girls face an extraordinary challenge in our changing world," writes co-author JoAnn Deak, Ph.D., in *Girls Will be Girls: Raising Confident and Courageous Daughters*. Our daughters face more sophisticated issues and life choices with less adult guidance than ever before. Joan Jacobs Brumberg, Ph.D., Cornell University historian and author of *Fasting Girls: The History of Anorexia Nervosa* and *The Body Project: An Intimate History of American Girls*, explains that our daughters "develop physically earlier than ever before, but that development is occurring within a society that does not protect or nurture them in ways that were once a hallmark of American life. Contemporary girls seem to have more autonomy, but their freedom is laced with peril."

Possible consequences of growing up female in such a perilous environment are reflected in these facts: one in four girls shows signs of depression; three times as many girls attempt suicide as boys; one in four girls will be sexually assaulted in college; and girls in coeducational settings are five times less likely than boys to receive attention from teachers. By age thirteen, fifty-three percent of girls report they are unhappy with their bodies; by age eighteen, this number jumps to seventy-eight percent.

Thoughts on rearing girls

If our goal is to rear daughters with the courage to speak their minds and the power to do what they believe in, we need to praise them for their skills and successes in those areas, rather than for their beauty alone.

Make sure your daughter understands that sexual liberation is not about saying yes to advances, but about making thoughtful choices based on her own terms and values. This is not accomplished in a single Big Talk, but should be reiterated over the course of time, and is best begun when girls are in late elementary school. Increasingly younger girls are being drawn into overt sexual activity and acting out. Girls in the seventh and eighth grade, even some in sixth grade, often feel pressured to perform oral sex on boys their own age, explaining casually that it's expected of them.

In general, parents and teachers should avoid rescuing girls. Encourage them, instead, to take risks. Provide them with opportunities to get dirty, disheveled, and sweaty playing sports or climbing trees and create opportunities for them to challenge themselves in areas from which females traditionally have been excluded.

Use television programming to initiate an ongoing, long-term discussion about body image. Watch TV with your daughter and, when appropriate examples appear on screen, express amazement at the old canards as they are trotted out. Are heavy girls shown as unpopular? Do they go out on dates? Are they used as comic relief? Are voluptuous girls only shown as sex symbols? Are sexy girls portrayed as being smart? Through gentle discussion, help her decipher the messages contained in the various portrayals of girls and become aware of how destructive stereotypical female portrayal can be to her and her peers.

Debunk the myth of Prince Charming. Teach girls that most women will work for most of their lives and each girl needs to be prepared to support herself. Provide opportunities for your daughter to meet dynamic women, including women who do it all, combining paid work, volunteer work, and family life. Make certain your daughter is afforded opportunities to pursue leadership roles in one or more activities as she gets older. Student government, sports, drama, extracurricular activities, scouting, and community service all provide excellent leadership opportunities, but let your daughter choose the activity and pursue the role. A girl who has learned to lead is better prepared to take charge of her own education and career.

Promote your daughter's physical and mental health. Be vigilant to identify and prevent eating disorders, substance abuse, and verbal aggression against other girls, each of which can be signs of depression. Watch for changes in what you have come to expect as normal behavior on the part of your daughter and talk with her, as well as with your doctor or school counselor, should you feel concern.

To adequately prepare our girls for the twenty-first century, Brumberg calls for a new era of girl advocacy, in which "multigenerational dialogue speaks to the reality of earlier maturation, the need for sexual expression, and the nature of contemporary culture."

Thoughts on rearing boys

If our goal is to rear sons who respect and support women, have the courage to speak their minds, and the power to do what they believe in, we need to foster our sons' relational skills, such as their abilities to nurture, empathize, sympathize, and feel compassion.

Foster your son's ability to broaden his emotional vocabulary, including feelings of love. Help him to neither discount fear nor be overwhelmed by it, and learn to express, and be comfortable with, feelings of deep sadness and great joy. Dan Logan, an advocate for gender issues and a parent, recommends, "Talk about your tender feelings, and when he talks about his, listen and restate what you heard. This tells him you are really listening and encourages him to talk more. Don't try to 'fix' his feelings. They, and he, are not broken."

Logan suggests parents help their sons understand that gender awareness will enable them to see everyone as indivivuals rather than stereotypes. Gender awareness is not about giving up power, status, or privilege. Explain to him there is no such thing as an "all boy" child or "real men." All boys and men are real, all are masculine, and he is quite validly male without having to prove himself. In fact, trying to live up to the stereotypical hypermasculine models of popular culture is a full-time, unrewarding job that could damage his developing character.

Boys can and must control their sexual urges. Insist that the notions "boys will be boys" and "boys can't help it" are patently untrue and serve as excuses for bad behavior. The belief that boys cannot control themselves ensures they are never expected to be able to learn to do so. It assumes the worst of boys and men and, for that reason, is horribly insulting. It will take a concerted effort by both parents and schools to make headway on boys' issues.

Single-sex education

Given recent gender-focused educational research, what should parents look for in evaluating their children's current school or in considering another school?

The decision whether or not to choose a single-sex school certainly depends on the needs and personality of your child. Many of the characteristics of successful single-sex classrooms are also available in coed schools, except for a separation of the sexes. Most independent schools encourage a profound sense of responsibility for one's own learning, offering an atmosphere of cooperative learning, an environment where students feel free to ask questions, take risks, admit mistakes, and express confusion, all within a supportive environment that encourages strong rapport between teachers and students. Schools should foster an atmosphere of, and create opportunities for, genuine collaboration among students, including group projects no single child can complete without the group members' help.

Parents' expectations and attitudes

Parents, as always, teach as much by unintentional example as they do on purpose. Review your own attitudes and actions about gender awareness. Do you:

- expect girls to be more dependent and less aggressive than boys?
- expect girls to be verbal and artistic, and boys to be mathematical and scientific?
- disapprove of noisy girls more than noisy boys?
- allow boys to use poor grammar and profanity?
- feel critical of unfashionable girls?
- feel critical of unathletic boys?
- react negatively to boys with long hair or girls with extremely short hair?
- use derogatory descriptives, such as sissy, fag, tomboy, chick, slut, wimp, wuss, whore, etc?
- tend to discipline a daughter verbally and leniently, but a son physically and strictly?
- encourage boys to settle disputes physically?
- follow the double standard in terms of your children's sexuality?

Final thoughts

Sexism harms both genders. Too often, our teenagers look to movies, television, magazines, and peers to understand what it takes to be a man or a woman. Many feel pressured to conform to very narrow definitions of femininity and masculinity. We want our children to have the confidence to define their gender in ways most comfortable to them. This kind of self-definition is a work in progress that can take many years, but should begin at home. We need to remember that parents can have the most influence on their teens—should they choose to exercise it. Our words and behavior can reflect our values of equity and fairness. We can and must teach our children to see the value and worth of every human being, and to honor and respect the uniqueness of each person without regard to gender. Yes, boys will grow up to be nurses and childcare providers, and a girl will be president someday.

| 20 |

Communication: Parent to Parent

"We know our son smokes—a lot," said the mother as she sat among other parents of ninth-graders in a mid-year peer group meeting. After a brief, but pregnant, lull in the conversation, another parent blurted out, "How can you let him do it? I just wouldn't let my daughter smoke. I'd make sure she didn't have money to spend on cigarettes; I'd do something to stop her." There was another pause in the flow of discussion; then the first parent said "Cigarettes aren't the worst thing he's doing—and smoking is not a battle we're choosing to fight right now." As the other parents contemplated the many nightmares which could be encompassed by "worse," many realized the problems they had with their own teenagers were actually rather mild.

Many parents wrestle with worry, embarrassment, and feeling helpless with regard to their ability to parent their children. Some dread having their perceived parental shortcomings exposed, others may be at a loss about how to handle a teen's behavior. It can be comforting to speak with parents who are struggling with similar issues, or to be reassured that, although their teens may have their moments, they're basically good kids.

In years past when more parents were at home during the day, casual conversations with friends provided comfort and advice about the challenges of parenting. Today, however, parents have demanding schedules, friends are dispersed over a wide geographic area, and the amount of time spent in the car battling traffic precludes opportunities for casual conversation with other parents. Many parents have come to realize that their children's school community serves as a surrogate neighborhood that functions much as did the contiguous backyards of earlier generations.

Networking

Communicating with other parents can make a difference. If you are wrestling with a problem, or are in need of advice about anything from learning disabilities to curfews, from risky behavior to Beach Week, one thing is certain: other parents are too, and they may well have found solutions that can be of help to you. Networking is just a modern term for an old-fashioned activity—supportive conversations about different ways to solve problems.

Families' beliefs about parenting and appropriate behavior differ, of course, and those beliefs vary more widely as children grow older. However, if we use opportunities to talk with, and listen to, other parents, we will identify those with values similar to our own, as well as those parents whose children are similar to ours. These are the folks to whom we will turn when we need advice or commiseration.

Deborah Roffman, M.S., nationally recognized human sexuality educator and author of *Sex & Sensibilities: The Thinking Parent's Guide to Talking Sense about Sex*, suggests, "Parents would be wise to set up a supportive network with other parents, whether through grade level meetings at their children's schools or, more informally, by actively getting to know and routinely checking in with the parents of their children's friends."

Make opportunities to talk with other parents

Parents can build a support network by making a concerted effort to meet with other parents and getting to know them and their children. Connecting can be more difficult once children are in middle and high school. Roffman observes that if parents of teens have made family-to-family communication an integral and accepted part of the landscape for years, it will be easier to make those contacts as their children move through high school.

School has replaced the physical neighborhood as the community from which parents can draw support. Take advantage of this pool of resources by volunteering at school and attending parent receptions and back-to-school nights, and use such occasions to informally bring up parenting topics of concern to you. Attend school parent peer group meetings at which pertinent developmental issues are discussed. Sit with other parents at school sporting events and performances and ask their opinions about a problem with which you're dealing.

Don't be reluctant to pick up the phone to discuss a specific concern with another parent. While you may find this difficult initially, there are times when it will be advantageous and even necessary. Remember that individual families have their own individual standards, acknowledge the awkwardness of the call, and strive for a diplomatic tone. Your child will undoubtedly be irritated about such a call, and you should acknowledge his feelings and try not to embarrass him. Do not, however, be deterred.

Make connections through school

Parents of children in a given grade at school may well constitute a group personality or culture. The group's characteristics influence the nature and number of gatherings or meetings, as well as the level of attendance and degree of participation.

During middle school it is easier for parents to plan social activities that include both parents and their young teens. Events such as picnics, potlucks, bowling, and theater outings are well attended and often serve to strengthen genuine friendships between parents. Groups of parents might get together to attend events featuring an expert speaking about particularly pressing developmental issues. One parents association president made up and distributed a flyer explaining the tradition of the potluck dinner in an effort to attract parents from other cultures to these social gatherings. Some schools have sports team potlucks and school play parties that include both kids and their parents. These casual, food-centered affairs provide a relaxed social ambiance conducive to parents getting to know one another.

Parent peer groups

A more formal strategy for networking is the parent peer group, organized and led by schools' parent associations, but supported and encouraged by the school. Many parents of middle and high school students will not make time for something that smacks of a "support group," but will eagerly attend a discussion about an issue of current concern, such as driving or the college application process. However, most parents will admit afterwards that the real benefit of these events is the networking and exchanging of ideas with other parents.

The effectiveness of parent peer group meetings is enhanced when participants agree to abide by basic ground rules. Do not discuss those who are not present, thus avoiding adversarial or conspiratorial behavior. Refer to the subjects in general, rather than in terms of specific personalities. Do not tell others how to behave, but offer ideas that have worked for you. Respect the need for confidentiality. Don't gossip with your child or others about information shared in a peer group.

Peer group programs should consider a few generally accepted procedures. Do not allow meetings to degenerate into gripe sessions about school issues. Provide attendees with name tags. Arrange seating so that people are comfortable and can see everyone else in the group. Begin and end meetings on time. Make sure to welcome new attendees.

Be prepared for surprises. Parents' values and beliefs differ widely. A family might permit their ten-year-old to watch R-rated movies while your child is visiting; another might host a coed sleepover or allow teens to drink alcohol at their home if the kids agree to stay for the night; yet another may permit their middle-schooler to visit the shopping mall or Georgetown unsupervised by an adult and invite your child to go, too.

Understand that it is not really your place to tell more lenient parents how to rear their children. By sharing your own views, you may broaden other parents' viewpoints or give them something to think about. In any event, your knowledge about the sorts of things to which your child is exposed will increase, and you will be better equipped to talk with him or her.

Communication pays off

There are many benefits to open communication between parents. You will be in a better position to deal with a crisis if you already know the parents of your child's peers. Others will feel more comfortable confiding in you if they know you. They will be more likely to approach you when your child misbehaves. Sharing problems can relax anxieties and help when you need a reality check. It is of great value for kids to know that their parents are in close touch with other parents. If you know the parents of your child's friends and talk with them periodically, chances are you will discover that many families operate under guidelines very similar to your own. Such knowledge reduces the effectiveness of your child's argument that he's the only kid who isn't allowed to stay up until midnight.

Final thought

Our children have each other to rely on as they pass through this tumultuous time of their lives, but with such hectic lives, casual kaffee klatches for parents are rare. Susan Reimer, *Baltimore Sun* columnist and parent of two teenagers, laments our relative isolation and suggests that we mistake this isolation for privacy. She believes that if we were to connect with other parents on a more regular and frequent basis, we might find comfort in the commonality of our experiences, at the same time we come to realize we aren't in this childrearing venture alone. So—make new friends, have a good time—and don't forget to laugh.

| 21 |

Learning from Diversity

Diversity is who we are. We don't create diversity, for it exists all around us; it is the presence of difference. Only by embracing and understanding diversity can we preserve the differences that make us unique while recognizing the commonalities that bind us together.

RANDOLPH CARTER, Diversity consultant
Founder, Eastern Educational Resource Collaborative

One of the greatest things about sports is that they provide venues in which large numbers of diverse people with little else in common can join together in a temporary community and be part of a grand collective.

UNKNOWN

To respect others is to be open to understanding them and get beyond the ways in which we differ to recognize how much we have in common. Being respectful of others is awareness that we all have aspirations, experience loss, revel in our children, and share the same fundamental needs—safety, comfort, and affiliation.

Respect includes recognizing that individuals and groups develop different traditions over time to meet the basic needs of human community. When we respect such traditions, we open ourselves to new possibilities and can appreciate our own traditions more. Respect for others precludes our making snap judgements, often erroneous, about a person or group of people different from ourselves. Respecting diversity promotes an environment in which everyone feels safe, welcomed, and included.

What is difference?

Skin color, race, ethnicity and gender are the primary differences we note about others, although other characteristics, such as regional speech, physical size, and perceived disability, are some of the visible differences that can influence the manner in which we perceive and interact with one another. Still more differences include less obvious diversities of learning style, sexual orientation, religious affiliation, family income, political affiliation, and level of social conformity. Personal qualities, such as drive or motivation, intuitiveness, or degree of social extroversion or introversion, are differences we encounter in people every day.

Why is it important?

Why should we strive for an inclusive, eclectic community that is safe and welcoming to a diverse membership? What are the benefits to us as individuals, or to the schools, immediate neighborhoods, and larger communities in which we are rearing our children?

We no longer live in isolated communities. In many ways, the world has become smaller, connected as never before by high-speed communication, technology, commerce, and transport. Races and ethnicities are no longer anchored in individual nations or geographic regions but overlap and intermingle at all levels of society and commerce. Thus, longstanding notions of race and ethnicity are changing, as well. Interpersonal relationships are reshaped in ways that were unthinkable just a generation ago, and personal identity can be influenced more by cultural preferences than by skin color or ethnic heritage. A Mexican-American girl may listen to hip-hop, belong to the Asian Club at school, have a crush on an African-American boy, and not identify with any one group or race. It may well be that our children are spearheading the move to a new, more nuanced, global understanding of identity and diversity.

Our children will be living and working in a much more integrated world than the one in which many of us grew up. Schools are making a concerted effort to prepare our children for this complex world, and we can do our part by clarifying our values for them, modeling respect for others, and helping them recognize intentional and unintentional prejudice in the community, the media, and on the Internet.

While encouraging respect for other's differences is appropriate for children of all ages, adolescence is an especially opportune time to work on it with kids because it is a period during which identity development is not only important, but difficult. Teens' attempts to determine who they are and where they fit in is a complicated process.

Bob Williams, assistant principal of Capital City Public Charter School in Washington, D.C., and diversity consultant and associate with Eastern Educational Resource Collaborative, observes that the desire to be included in a cohesive social group can lead our children to make decisions based upon potential group acceptance and approval, rather than on their own evolving values and beliefs. Sometimes, in an effort to establish an identity and boost self-esteem, a child will express discomfort with, or fear of, those who are different from himself by reverting to name-calling—or worse. Often, a lack of self-confidence or esteem is manifested in displays of disrespectful behavior and even hatred toward an individual or group.

Enlightened educational systems have identified two critical concerns: the need for diversity sensitivity and the fight against harassment of those perceived to be different. Respect for diversity, embraced by more schools throughout the country than ever before, "leads to an environment that is safer, and one that is more welcoming and inclusive for all students," says Randolph Carter, diversity consultant and founder of Eastern Educational Resource Collaborative. Safe and inclusive communities don't just happen. Maria Lopez, M.A., director of community life at the Langley School in McLean, Virginia, points out that such communities require vision, initiative, and nurture to take root and grow strong.

Classroom diversity is beneficial in several ways. Students of different backgrounds, cultures, and learning styles contribute to one another's broader education about the world. School curricula and textbooks depicting students from diverse racial and ethnic origins help teens feel connected to their classmates by their similarities rather than separated from them by their differences—a connection which, over time, extends beyond classroom walls to the wider com;munity beyond. Most importantly, learning side by side with students from different backgrounds broadens our children's perspectives, increases their knowledge, and helps them overcome superficial differences to value and respect people unlike themselves. Frequently, to know someone is to find commonality.

Why doesn't it come easily?

If respect for our differences is so important and valuable, why does it seem so difficult to achieve? Why is it so hard for us to engage in discourse about our differences?

Respect for other cultures and ethnicities is a relatively new concept in terms of the history of mankind. For centuries, a small world population, geographical barriers, and limited communication served to keep diverse peoples separate and distinct from one another. While the world has changed dramatically with respect to population, mobility, and communication, all of which make for increased intimacy and interaction with people different from ourselves, we still must struggle against our outmoded inheritance of ignorance, attitudes, stereotypes, and misguided beliefs.

While we are born innocent of prejudice, we are exposed to the likes, dislikes, and prejudices of those around us throughout childhood. Childhood experiences provide the framework from which we determine whom we embrace as being okay and whom we reject. By preadolescence and adolescence, being "like everyone else" is of paramount importance and we seek out friends who are most like ourselves. At this age, Carter says, accepting differences in others can become increasingly difficult for young people, and understanding differences nearly impossible without considerable effort.

Prejudice, whether overt or covert, is a learned behavior. Children most often learn bigotry and prejudice close to home—from parents, siblings, peers, and school. Research shows that we learn more effectively by observation than from what we are told, which is the reason, "Do as I say, not as I do," is ineffective in shaping behavior. Children managing to grow up with few or no prejudices generally have benefited from the active involvement and encouragement of adults who have cultivated and nurtured the values of diversity, acceptance, and respect for all people.

Despite the popular conceit that Lady Liberty summons the world's poor and downtrodden to our shores for succor and a new beginning, the U.S. struggles daily with the legacy of the civil rights violations of the past. Adults are all too familiar with the many infamous stereotypes resulting from slavery and the westward expansion in the early days; the overt prejudice against African-Americans, Irish, Italians, Chinese, and Jews in the nineteenth and early twentieth centuries; as well as those aimed at women who sought to step outside the *kinder/küche/kirche* box in the first two-thirds of the twentieth century. Today's stereotypes seem more subtle and insidious in nature than previously, and parents need to help their children be alert for, and sort out, remarks that demean or ridicule another.

It is human nature to seek common ground and unifying bonds with others. When we believe that we recognize a commonality with another person, particularly racial or ethnic background, we ofen assume the other person innately understands us, as well, and are quick to relax our guard and speak candidly. In reality, we can find many areas of commonality and unity with almost anyone if we are open to looking beyond our obvious, and often entirely physical, differences.

Preconceived notions about others can unrealistically limit or inflate our expectations of them and interfere with our ability to see them clearly for who they are. Stereotypes, or oversimplified generalizations, reflect preconceived notions and can lead people to dislike others before they even know them. Traits and values we attribute to "us" and "them" don't necessarily reflect reality, and false beliefs and erroneous information can lead to prejudice and even hatred. Many people feel uncomfortable, unsure, or even frightened in the face of difference and often lapse into traditional prejudices in their discomfort.

One way in which teens and adults stereotype is to assume that an individual is representative of an entire race, gender, or culture and dismiss or ignore his or her individual uniqueness and distinction. The assumption that all members of a particular group share one set of abilities, interests, values, and roles affects the behavior of both those making the assumption and those about whom the assumption is made. To ask an African-American student to provide the "Black perspective" on an issue in class, for example, is to insult the teen in particular and African-Americans in general, because it assumes there is a single, unified Black perspective that ignores the depth and breadth of diversity encompassed by the African-American culture.

While we cannot blame all bias on the media, it does serve as a melange of ideas and images from which our children pick up notions about others to whom they have limited exposure. People of color, Latinos, and those of Middle-Eastern and Asian backgrounds are too frequently portrayed as one-dimensional—drug dealers, gang members, terrorists, or objects of fear or ridicule. Our children's self images and understanding of the world is greatly influenced by the media and limiting portrayals of various peoples in programming can have an effect on the manner in which our children view themselves, their culture, and their possibilities.

Bob Condit, M.Ed., independent consultant and former counselor at the Landon School in Bethesda, Maryland, observes that conversations about diversity can become tortuous when participants feel the need to be overly tactful. The effort of reviewing thought before speaking and choosing words carefully in order not to offend can be so arduous as to rob such exchanges of all spontaneity and vitality, resulting in a reluctance to discuss diversity issues altogether. Today's teens appear to be more accepting of individual differences than are their parents and grandparents and therefore appear to have less difficulty talking about differences such as religion, race, and sexual orientation with others.

What creates the possibilities?

Creating a community that is safe and welcoming to all is a challenge. Not only is such a goal possible—it's in process. The speed and smoothness of its progress is enhanced by the participation of each person who joins in the effort.

Children secure in their own race and culture tend to be respectful of the traditions of others. Leah Latimer, author of *Higher Ground: Preparing African-American Children for College,* could be addressing Jewish, Japanese, Saudi, or Indian parents when she advises parents of color that "all children need a strong, positive sense of their heritage." Biracial and multicultural children should be made aware of their combined heritages. Latimer further advises, "If you want your children to take a place in the leadership positions of society and move about the country and the world, don't leave them racially, i.e. culturally, isolated. Support your children to feel comfortable with themselves in situations where they are in the minority."

The possibilities of broadening our insights and achieving a safe and inclusive environment are aided by the fact that, for most of us, our values and beliefs are not set in stone, so it is possible to break out of outmoded patterns and attitudes. Ideally, we continually modify our stereotypical beliefs as we absorb new information and experience, thus reaching a deeper understanding of other individuals and groups. Very often, the attitudes that prompt negative comments and behavior toward others can be impacted in a positive manner by actively getting to know the complex and unique individuals behind the flat cartoons of the stereotypes.

Since the mid-1980s, diversity in school populations has been increasingly seen as a desirable goal and advantageous to the education of all our children. Many area schools are far more diverse than apparent at first glance. Beyond the obvious differences in skin color and eye shape, student bodies represent myriad countries of origin and learning styles.

Carol Dopp, M.Ed., family life counselor at the Potomac School in McLean, Virginia, believes that embracing diversity means that we strive to support every student and family, as well as faculty member, who joins our school community. She says, "It is the role of educators to accept, celebrate, support, and strive to nurture all students."

Educators seek to train our children to be a new variety of world citizen who is culturally versatile and competent, attributes that will be invaluable in the increasingly global interaction of their future. Parents and coaches share in educating youth, so it is immensely important that we, too, accept and support the children whose lives we touch, and demonstrate to them how freeing it is to find acceptance and rapport among others and give the same in return.

The probability of a safer, more inclusive environment for our children increases when parents model openness and respect for others in both their language and behavior, not just when outside the home around other people, but also at home with family and intimates. Parents can discourage the formation and perpetuation of stereotypes if they challenge such views in their children and their peers, pointing out the intrinsic fallacies and destructiveness of such views. Parents can use media portrayals of people different from themselves to examine with their children the messages inherent in the programming about the relationships, violence, humor, and occupations of specific racial or ethnic groups. When watching TV together, parents can remark favorably on positive portrayals and point out the similarities, as well as the differences, between the characters and their own family members.

Participating in cross-cultural experiences can bring about an appreciation and respect for others. Again, personal interaction can lead to the recognition of commonality. The Washington, D.C., area is host to many fascinating and enjoyable ethnic and cultural events throughout the year that attract multiracial, multicultural, and multigenerational participants and audiences. Such events are wonderful relaxed occasions providing opportunities for us to learn about others.

There are many resources available in our community offering guidance and strategies to encourage the building of a safe, inclusive, and supportive community. For more information, consult the resource section for this chapter at the back of this book.

Final thoughts

Parents play a critical role in ensuring that their children's developing sense of identity includes not only strong identification with their own family's traditions, but also a respect for and appreciation of qualities contributed to our society by people of divergent cultures, abilities, and experiences. Every child deserves to live in a world that feels safe for his family, his culture, his person, and his unique individualism. Our communities will be safe and inclusive when we respect others, both individually and in groups, and recognize that we have a shared humanity.

5 emotions

| 22 |

Stress: Living with the Inevitable

Parents and their children are on twin treadmills. Parents work more so their families can have more...and the kids are booked into an array of activities to ensure they will have the success that will earn them the money to pay for the lifestyle their parents have provided.

SUSAN REIMER, *Baltimore Sun* columnist and parent of two teenagers

Many might say that stress, or being stressed, is an unfortunate given for most Washington metropolitan area families. Children and parents are encouraged to live 24/7 lives at full tilt, packing as much as possible into each day. Adult Washingtonians log some of the longest average work weeks in the country, and families in which both parents pursue careers are the norm. Consequently, our teens are expected to artfully juggle their multiple roles—to be above average students, team sports captains, presidents of school clubs, and accomplished members of the band studying privately with musical professionals.

While stress is a normal part of every life, when teens talk about being stressed, they are speaking of trying to cope with internal anxiety about everything from school assignments to after-school activities to carpool scheduling to teasing in the school halls. Children who do not learn to anticipate, prevent, and cope with stress become stressed out. Depression is a common psychobiological response to stress. Experts caution that high levels of stress can be dangerous, or even deadly, as stressed-out children turn to smoking, alcohol, drugs, unhealthy eating patterns, or flee into the cyberworld for release. For some chronically stressed teens, the longing for relief from pressure is so great they consider the final escape of suicide.

Teaching a child how to manage stress can be difficult if parents are modeling stressed-out behavior themselves. Parents having difficulty managing their own stress levels contribute to the Washington area phenomenon of families of overscheduled children with burned-out parents.

Child and teen stressors

Stressors vary with each developmental stage of childhood. Teens, for example, view life through an entirely different lens than either elementary school children or adults. The internal and external pressures children feel are age specific and predictable. Younger children tend to be more sensitive to pressures at home and school, while older children are more sensitive to pressures relating to their social and sexual identities. It is important that parents recognize and understand their children's age-related stressors, whether they be the humiliation of playground teasing for a second-grader, or the devastation of a seventh-grader at not being invited to an eagerly anticipated party. To them, these are very significant occurrences.

Stress appears to stem from three sources: one's environment, one's body, and one's thoughts or perceptions. Some teens are sensitive to environmental factors such as noise, light, or temperature; physical factors of hunger, fatigue, constipation, thirst, or prolonged illness; and psychological factors such as fear, pressure, uncertainty, responsibilities, safety, or expectations. These sensitivities may be temporary, occasional, intermittent, or chronic. Some stress, whether short- or long-term, can be anticipated, some prevented, and some lived through. Teens who are more vulnerable to certain environmental conditions, physical discomforts, or stressful thoughts will need adult guidance to recognize the source of their stress and develop coping mechanisms.

Obvious teen stressors include changing schools, the death of a relative or friend, an injury like a broken leg, or parental separation and divorce. Less obvious is the stress some teens feel when they are taking tests, are over committed, or are singled out for an award. The stressors of which parents are even less likely to be aware are those of peer pressure and harassment or bullying. Uncertainty about the future and others' opinions of them can cause our children high levels of stress. Validating children's feelings is important to building trust and helping them learn to make changes or learn ways to cope with the stress and the challenge of life.

Stressed-out signs

Common reactions to stress include self-criticism, a feeling of being overwhelmed, and feeling there is no way one can make a positive change. Signs that children are dealing with more stress than they can handle are:

- inappropriate boredom, fear, edginess, depression, guilt, sadness, and anger,
- headaches, stomachaches, perspiration, rashes, difficulty sleeping, increased urination,
- seemingly unprompted laughter or tears,
- projection of blame for misfortune onto others, and
- resentment of others for their responsibilities.

More subtle indications that it is time to relax are:

- cold hands and feet when others around are comfortable,
- frequent, out-of-character blushing,
- easy emotional upset over something relatively insignificant like a traffic jam, over which no one has control,
- feeling rushed and impatient, finishing other people's sentences, and speaking quickly,
- tight neck muscles and stiffness when moving head from side to side,
- clenching of jaw muscles, and
- constantly feeling burned-out or tired.

You or your child may be chronically stressed-out if the questions posed by Carolyn Hax, author of the *Washington Post* column, "Tell Me About It," give you pause: "When was the last time you laughed at yourself, questioned your worldview, blew off a whole afternoon? Come to think of it, when was the last time you blinked?"

Helping kids cope

Beginning as early as preschool, children need guidance on how to express what is stressing them, as well as how to handle stress. Martha Cutts, M.A.T., director of the upper school at the National Cathedral School in Washington, D.C., says children and teens need to know they can have some control over the pace and turbulence of their lives. Children benefit from anticipating what stresses them—exams, performances, asking for a date, or driving in heavy traffic; knowing what they can do to prevent or avoid some stressors; and developing coping strategies. Parents can help them learn the value of approaching difficult people or situations with a plan.

Problems in the family can be the hardest to talk about. "What we fail to realize is that parents are sometimes the source of a lot of stress," said one parent. "From our expectations for their future to the fact that we scheduled a dental appointment at a time that conflicts with softball practice, we add a lot of stress to our children's lives." It is the wise parent or sibling, acknowledges one school counselor, who encourages his or her teen to seek a spiritual leader, school counselor, or family doctor to talk with when the talking is not happening at home.

It is useful in helping children cope with stress to learn to accept the temperament and personality of each child. All too familiar are the shy children whose parents push them to be more social, the unathletic children whose parents compel them to play sports, or the academically average children with high-achieving parents. Forcing children to engage in activities for which they are developmentally or temperamentally unsuited can lead to anxiety and depression.

Some teens are temperamentally intense perfectionists and are always assessing what constitutes 100 percent so that they can deliver 110 percent. These children need extra guidance in learning to give themselves a break sometimes, to recognize what is "good enough," and to strike a reasonable balance in their lives. Silver Spring, Marland, psychologist Jack Leeb, Ph.D., counsels that stress often prevents people from being able to prioritize or to recognize that they have choices. Teens can be reminded that they cannot please everyone in their lives all the time and it's human and natural to make mistakes occasionally.

Parents: dealing with your own stress

The old saying, "When Mama ain't happy, ain't nobody happy," couldn't be truer for some families. Parents would do well to examine their own stress levels to determine the impact of them on the family dynamic. If, for example, Dad receives constant dinnertime calls from a frantic co-worker that require him to return to the office, dinner uneaten and feeling guilty, leaving Mom upset and the children disappointed, then the entire family suffers. Parental stress trickles down within a family, and consequently, many teens suffer from secondhand stress.

Protecting children from secondhand stress is a parental responsibility. When parents experience difficulties such as spousal conflict, serious illness, or money issues, children are quick to sense the adult tension and frequently assume they are to blame. It is best to find a way to let children in on the fact that the adults are going through a difficult period and, if needed, to obtain a professional's help before the situation results in long-term emotional damage. Open communications, consistent routine, deliberate displays of affection, and simple good humor all go a long way toward dissipating the effects of secondhand stress on children.

Coping strategies for parents and teens

There are a number of strategies parents can teach children to help them recognize and control stress before it reaches overwhelming, paralyzing levels.

Teach a vocabulary of feelings. Parents can help children develop an appropriate vocabulary for describing their feelings. If they are angry, then how mad are they on a scale of one to ten if one constitutes mildly annoyed and ten indicates furious? Explain the differences in ranges of feelings. What does it mean to be irked, exasperated, agitated, nervous, tense, worried? Once children can properly identify how they are feeling, then suitable steps can be taken to deal with the emotion and to react appropriately. If teens are reluctant to talk with their parents, then parents should encourage them to speak with a friend or counselor. Children who respond inappropriately to stress by throwing tantrums or acting out aggressively, for example, should be encouraged to scream in the shower or be given pillows to punch.

Don't dismiss the feelings. When children feel something is wrong, parents should avoid making a dismissive judgement like, "You just can't let that get to you," or, "That shouldn't cause you a problem." Despite whether parents feel the problem is one of significance or not, they should encourage discussion of it. Understanding and trust grow stronger through communication.

Identify temporary or short-term stresses. Much short-term stress, especially that of an environmental nature, such as sensitivity to light, temperature, or noise, can be tolerated, modified, or even eliminated if it is understood the conditions are temporary or short-term. Parents can help children learn to separate out the short-term stresses from the more long standing ones and support them in their efforts to desensitize themselves to the stress.

Avoid overcommitment. Teens sometimes need parental help in learning it's alright to politely decline committing to things they don't really want to do, and how to go about doing so. You can also help them to be more realistic about volunteering to do things they don't have time for or won't be able to complete.

Practice self-calming techniques. Self-calming techniques include such simple activities as walking around the block, running around the neighborhood, or spending an hour at the gym in order to vent frustration and gain some distance and perspective on stressful situations.

For some people, singing at the top of their lungs works, for others, a period of taking regular deep breaths and expelling the air out of their mouths with great force does the trick. Equally satisfying can be munching on crunchy foods. Planning things to look forward to can be a relaxing activity and embraces the notion that life will be easier and fun.

Work at positive diversions. Many people find that working on things or relationships that are important to them and which give meaning to their lives defuses stress. Volunteering, helping others, and visiting with extended family or friends serve to divert one from one's own particular stresses while improving the quality of one's life and that of others.

Dispense with negative self-assessments. Instead of, "I can't do this," or, "I'm never going to make it," Leeb recommends that we change our self-talk, using instead a mantra such as, "How am I going to solve this problem?" or, "Let go of the meaningless stuff." Psychological stress is reduced with the negativity thus jettisoned, making room for positive, creative thought about how best to get through a particular difficulty.

Lighten up. Make time for fun, especially with the family. Carve out leisure time and add life to it. Make dinner dates, movie night dates, or swimming nights with the family. Recreational activities are good stress-busters for children of any age, as well as parents, and help people feel more hopeful about the future.

Eat well and sleep more. Treat yourself well. Eat regular, healthy meals and nutritious snacks. They can be the pauses that refresh both mind and body. Get enough sleep—frequently, things really do look better in the morning.

Set, and stick to, technology-free periods. Marcy Cathey, M.S., parent and director of technology at the Madeira School in McLean, Virginia, recommends setting limits on interference with family time by cell phones, faxes, e-mail, and Instant Messages (IM). She feels most families have become accustomed to allowing the intrusion of outside communication to take precedence over the company and conversation of family members in the same room. Establishing guidelines about when, where, and how often such communication is received enables families to break out of the "on call" mentality. Parents and children may agree upon uninterrupted blocks of daily family time. Allow the answering machine to pick up calls and take messages during dinnertime, for example, and ban e-mail or IM during specific evening hours. For this plan to be viable, however, parents, as well as children, must adhere to the guidelines.

Use hobbies as stress-busters. Many children, as well as adults, can benefit from time spent engaged in a hobby. Knitting, woodworking, gardening, and cooking, to name just a few, are all creative hobbies that allow the mind to function differently than at work or school and serve to aid people in disengaging from everyday angst. Parents can explore with their children the many interest groups and courses available in the metropolitan area that support a wide variety of fascinating pastimes and avocations.

Learn to be comfortable asking for help. Children often need to be assured that they are not expected to be able to solve every problem by themselves. It is important to be able to determine when one needs assistance, and when a child asks a parent or adult for help, he or she presents the adult with an opportunity to acknowledge the wisdom of the decision and reinforce it.

Call a mental health day. Parents should be alert for those periods when their children are dealing with too much stress and call a time-out or a mental health day to provide the young people a break in the action so that they can regroup. A mental health day can be one in which a young person stays home from school to work uninterrupted on a project, memorize lines for the school play, or simply catch up on some much needed sleep. While each school has specific guidelines about absences and school administrators might cringe at the notion, one mental health day per semester could well be just what is needed to reduce student stress. Parents should allow children to decide, after discussing it with them, if a mental health day is in order, because learning to recognize when to say "when," in terms of stress, is an important element of stress management that a young person needs to know.

What schools can do

When children are stressed due to issues at home and are having difficulty coping, parents should make sure they inform the teachers, advisors, or school counselors as to the situation. Ideally, parents partner with the schools to educate and care for their children, and keeping the schools apprised of children's current situations can be critical. While many families will share the death of a family member with a school counselor, they shy away from letting the counselor know that the family is experiencing serious marital or mental health difficulties. Knowing the real source of children's anxiety enables school staff to understand the motivation for behaviors they observe and is vital to the school's ability to take the appropriate action to ensure children's overall scholastic success.

If a child is stressed from school-related issues, it is important for parents to advise his teacher, advisor, or school counselor. As an example, consider the stress teens feel when confronting long-term school projects, something with which they often have difficulty. The planning and execution of a major project is a major stressor for many students from the late elementary grades to senior year, and no parent wants her child in tears the night before a deadline because he forgot the poster board, the modeling clay, or the maps in his desk. Developing a plan, with a detailed calendar of discrete tasks that can be checked off as completed, helps make the entire project more manageable. Older students often have difficulty determining when enough research is enough. Some schools teach these skills and others don't. It's up to parents to familiarize themselves with their children's projects so as to be able to help them learn the process for accomplishing large jobs successfully. Should projects of this nature not be the parents' strong suits, they shouldn't hesitate to ask the children's teachers for help.

Final thoughts

Yes, there is good stress. Some stress can be happy, exciting, and challenging—in fact, life would be dull without a little stress. Most of us need the pressure of competition, one kind of stress, to motivate us to do well at sports, music, dance, work, or even school. Without the stress of deadlines, many of us wouldn't finish projects or get to work or school on time. These everyday, or occasional, stresses are the ones we hope our teens will accommodate with little effort. Parents must, however, avoid thinking that there is only a limited, finite amount of success to be had in life and that if they, or their children, are not actively striving to get a piece of that success, the good life will somehow pass them by.

Some teens are more vulnerable to stress, negative thinking, and low self-esteem than others. Individual children tolerate the stress they create or encounter in vastly diverse ways. Not surprisingly, young people who have confidence in their appearance and their intellectual ability, a sense of humor, and some social ability, report the least stress.

Obviously, managing stress is more than just learning how to breathe deeply, although such strategies can be very important. Professional help may be necessary in determining the causes of a child's stress reaction, discover alternative solutions to stressful situations, reexamine his thoughts and perceptions, or explore creative coping skills.

| 23 |

Afraid, Anxious, and Just Worried

Fear and anxiety are normal reactions to abnormal times.

We all know there are plenty of reasons to be afraid or anxious from time to time; the question is—what are those times? Linda Goldman, Ph.D., area grief and loss counselor and author, answers, "Death related tragedies involving suicide, homicide, and AIDS, and nondeath related traumas, such as bullying and victimization, divorce and separation, assault and rape, abandonment, violence and abuse, drugs and alcohol, and sexuality and gender identification, have left many youth living their lives with overwhelmed feelings and distracted thoughts."

Neither privilege nor fame keeps one safe from violence, disaster, or trauma. At any moment, we can either be on the receiving end of the sort of everyday, garden-variety violence that can touch anyone or become victims of the kind of extraordinary crime that touches only a few. Some instances of violence are caused by forces of nature—others by people using force. How do we parents help our children to feel secure? How can we inoculate them against anxiety? How can we recognize the signs of distress, anxiety, or fear in their behavior that indicate they need either our help or assistance from a professional? How can we encourage confidence and resilience, the ability to bounce back in the face of trauma or tragedy?

Many parents, as well as teens, wonder how much worrying is normal and what is excessive, says Edward Hallowell, M.D., author of *Worry: Hope and Help for a Common Condition*. Hallowell warns that worry, depression, and stress go hand in hand, so a child's appraisal of trauma and tragedy may be further complicated by a powerful mix of emotions and feelings. Some experts warn that if teen anxiety and fear are left untreated, young people are more at risk than their peers of alcohol and substance abuse, as well as of suicidal thought and attempts.

It is particularly challenging for parents to help their kids feel safe and secure when they themselves are not feeling that way. Nationally, adults and children are reporting more depression, separation anxiety, and other emotional problems than ever before. If a parent is a worrier, it may be difficult for him or her to recognize that a child's anxiety or worry is of such an extent as to require treatment. To do so, parents first need to understand how preteens and teens think, how they view the world, and the normal range of angst for the age group. If parents' own anxiety is excessive, they may endow their children with that worry. Those parents may need to seek a professional evaluation even before seeking help for their children.

How preteens and teens view their world

As children move into their middle school years, they begin to relinquish all-or-nothing thinking and begin bringing a deeper perspective to bear on current events. Stanley Greenspan, M.D., local parent and nationally recognized psychiatrist, clinical professor of psychiatry and pediatrics at George Washington University Medical School, and author of many books, including the most recent, *The Secure Child: Helping Children Feel Safe and Confident in a Changing World*, says that middle schoolers are "typically just learning how to recognize gray areas in an issue, or multiple causes of events. If something is scary, it's hard for them to figure out if it's very scary, medium scary, a little bit scary, or just a tiny, tiny little bit scary. So, every fear can feel like a huge fear." Parents can expand their children's gray-area thinking by helping them reason through frightening events, evaluate risks, and see the many potential positive outcomes.

Childhood and adolescence are earmarked by many "firsts," by the challenge of doing so many things for the first time—the first sleepover, the first French class, the first kiss. Each exciting moment, however, carries with it a potential for worry. Of this potential, Hallowell says, "In some ways, worry is what makes childhood so memorable. We remember how much we worried about such little things. Being popular. A pimple. Grades. Hitting a baseball. Being picked for...anything."

Greenspan points out that while developing new cognitive abilities enables teens to feel secure and confident, these same abilities open them up to a whole different category of insecurities. Many teens are aware that their generation will have the task of coping with the problems of the future and of leading the world--a reality of which they were innocent in earlier childhood. They need reassurance that there is going to be a future.

Teenagers are especially vulnerable to insecurity and uncertainty due to all the changes inherent in adolescence and the uncertainties they face as they get ready for adulthood, says Greenspan. In his latest book, he writes, "Because adolescents can understand the gravity of such problems as terrorist attacks, environmental pollution, and nuclear proliferation, their worries cannot be dismissed as fantasy, or with easy reassurance."

Fear of the future is a concern of many teenagers, who may focus on their prospects for college, a career, relationships, or having a family. Greenspan cautions that these very common fears may be intensified by fear for the world's safety and survival. Teens can face some uncomfortable truths about our world and have global awareness, even of such adult subjects as economics and politics. They look at things differently than they did just a few years previously. They feel vulnerable, and some of that fear is justified. Other teens feel helpless, while still others may imagine themselves as quixotically powerful.

On September 11, 2001, area residents experienced the horrific trauma of the destruction of the World Trade Center in New York City and the plane crash at the Pentagon. Many people were personally touched by the events, and many more were affected indirectly. Immediately following the attacks, many children and teenagers, as well as adults, voiced a desire to move away from the area. Many continue to feel vulnerable and uneasy.

Fear

Fear is rational if it is in reaction to what is happening or has happened, but not in advance of what might happen, points out Gavin de Becker, longtime consultant on violence and author of *The Gift of Fear: Survival Signals that Protect Us from Violence*. Fear is part of our emotional sonar, signaling the presence of danger in our lives, and is triggered by a specific object or situation, and, even if excessive, is grounded in reality. If a teen has been in a tragic car collision, she may blanch and cry out every time she hears the squeal of brakes, or she may delay preparing for obtaining a driver's license.

Our fears reflect our vulnerabilities, our belief that we cannot survive or are unable to do something. Teens experience survival fears, which are often linked to physical dangers, such as driving on icy roads, being confronted by a potential mugger, or encountering a snarling dog. They may also experience performance fears that more often revolve around psychologically risky situations and which might include speaking before a crowd, asking someone on a date, soaring out over a river on a rope swing. Most of the time, this sort of fear is an anticipation of rejection, embarrassment, abandonment, or helplessness--all feelings with which adolescents are very familiar.

Fear is more easily aroused in some people than in others, which helps explain why one person may react in terror to a situation that stimulates only mild trepidation in another. Being afraid may trigger any number of defenses, including anger, denial, avoidance, or displacement. Boys are heard to say, "Of course, I wasn't scared," even as they slump, faces drained of blood and hands trembling.

Trauma

Sudden, and apparently random, frightening events are especially traumatic. The essence of one's reaction to random terror or assault is, "Who's next? Me?" About twenty percent of people who experience extreme trauma will develop a debilitating condition known as post-traumatic stress disorder (PTSD). Girls and women seem to be twice as susceptible to PTSD as boys and men, perhaps because they are more often the victims of sexual assault, abuse, and rape. Professional help, including some form of individual and family counseling, along with medication, may be necessary for a full recovery from extreme trauma.

Reaction to trauma can last a long time, even years. During the recovery process, it is common for a person to experience nightmares, restlessness, numbness, detachment, hyper-alertness, or loss of concentration. One may also suffer physical reactions, as well, such as backaches and stomach pains.

Christel Nichols, president of the House of Ruth in Washington, D.C., advises that trauma survivors need consistently supportive people in their lives. It should not be surprising how strongly a new trauma or loss, especially a dramatic or tragic one, rekindles old trauma or loss. While further tragedy often complicates coping, for most people, the general trend is toward resilience and recovery.

Anxiety and worry

Preteens, as well as teenagers, often worry about peer rejection, not doing well enough at sports, academics, performing, not looking good enough, or being bullied by peers. They may be anxious about a piano recital, a test, a bad report card, or meeting their parents', or their own, expectations. They may feel anxious about trying to ski, being in a school play, walking alone outside at night, or they may be petrified of snakes, spiders, or death. If they have had disastrous experiences with any of these, or have experienced blatant rejection or pain, they may have very good reason to be anxious.

Most children and teens worry about a wide range of things. It is when that worry interferes with their functioning at home, at school, or with their friends that help is warranted. Some kids are serious worriers. There appears to be a genetic predisposition for anxiety disorders; the symptoms run in families. Anxiety can overlap with other conditions like depression. However, for anxiety to be considered a disorder, the anxious behavior must be persistent, although perhaps intermittent, over a period of many months.

Children's imaginations can be fertile ground for the growth of worry and anxiety. Some children may need guidance to understand they needn't assume an imagined outcome is inevitable. Brock Hansen, L.C.S.W., Washington, D.C. area therapist and coach of "learnable emotional skills," observes that chronic worriers learn their habit well by practicing constantly for years. Hallowell concurs, noting that the habitual worrier lives with the most toxic worry. It is not easy for some to slow down and sort out the real dangers from the thousand and one potential threats in their minds.

Local psychologist Marilyn Fuchs, Ph.D., counsels that teens may need help to trace their patterns of anxiety, for example, when a teenager fears failing an exam, he may fear that he will flunk out of school, never be able to go to college or get a job, and will end up as a homeless street person. When a teen is anxious, parents can help test the likelihood of their teen's worst case scenarios by posing questions like, "You're worried the coach is going to yell at you—has he yelled before? What happened?" Questions like these will help the teen gain some perspective on his fears and allay some of them, while reinforcing his parents' support of him.

Greenspan warns us that anxiety can also stir up prejudiced feelings that lead to polarized thinking, as in "us versus them," or "that which is outside our circle is bad; that which is inside is good." Children, and some adults, want to see who the "bad guys" are so they know whom to blame, fear, or hate. This reaction is especially prevalent during the middle school years.

While a fear reaction is not voluntary, worry is. In the absence of an actual risk, worry is fear manufactured for a purpose. Worry can be an excuse for avoiding change or admitting powerlessness. Worry can be a way to connect with others or a protection against future disappointment. While worry may well be worth understanding and managing, worry solves nothing, in fact, it is more likely to distract than facilitate finding solutions. Worry can be a form of self-harassment and to give it less space in our lives, we must understand what it really is.

How much worrying is excessive? In *Worry: Hope and Help for a Common Condition*, Hallowell offers a self-assessment quiz that provides adolescents and adults with a tool to rate the intensity of their worrying as compared to that of others. The Freedom from Fear organization's website also offers a screening questionnaire to assess the level of fear or anxiety one is experiencing.

Panic and phobia

Certain kinds of worry are genetically based and amenable to specific treatments. These include separation anxiety disorder, generalized anxiety disorder (GAD), obsessive-compulsive disorder (OCD), social phobias, and intense shyness. Hallowell emphasizes that these are brain based--genetic vulnerabilities or overly sensitive nervous systems--and can be treated effectively with medication and psychotherapy.

A few teens suffer from phobias, which are obsessive, intense, persistent fears. Phobias are irrational and are about loss of control rather than real dangers, reports the Institute for Mental Health Initiatives (IMHI) in an issue of their quarterly newsletter *Dialogue*. Social phobia is an intensified case of shyness in which a child may be fearful of all social situations or only selected ones. Another small group of teens suffers panic attacks, which are sudden, overwhelming waves of terror. Seemingly unprovoked panic attacks are pathological and may have a biological base. If a teen has repeated panic attacks, provoked or otherwise, it is important that he or she receive professional attention.

Controlling worry

Hallowell explains that worry derives from a feeling of vulnerability coupled with a feeling of powerlessness. The more vulnerable one feels, the less control one feels, the more toxic one's worrying will be. It is normal for teenagers to often feel vulnerable and powerless, so when danger, trauma, or disaster strikes, they are at heightened risk for toxic worry. Rational admonitions, however well meaning, usually don't make teens feel more secure.

Hallowell outlines five ways in which teens can reduce feelings of vulnerability and increase feelings of control.

- Never worry alone. Talk to a trusted teacher, the school counselor, parents, and friends, either on the phone or in person.
- Get the facts. A lack of, or incorrect, information needlessly amplifies anxiety.

- Make a plan. With a plan, one's judgment improves and restores the ability to take constructive action.
- Take care of yourself. Nutrition, sleep, exercise, and human contact are essential during times of worry and danger.
- Let it go. Let it go—at least partially.

Parents can play a central role in helping their teens follow these steps by being available to listen, assisting them in gathering accurate information, collaborating with them on a plan of action, and providing for, or encouraging, their child's basic self-care. Experts suggest parents remember the following five points in helping their children overcome fear and anxiety.

Resilience starts with family. Children develop resilience in many ways, beginning with trusting relationships that make them feel safe and loved. Greenspan's advice to parents for helping children feel safe and confident in an uncertain world includes encouraging children's optimism and hope by spending time together, expressing their feelings, reinforcing their children's emerging sense of efficacy and self-respect, and fostering acts of caring and compassion.

Spend time together as a family. Mental health professionals and child/adolescent development experts are united in advising that parents be there for their children, that they spend time with them. Greenpan urges parents to keep nurturing their teens even when they aren't sure they really want it. Get better connected as a family. Hallowell reports that connectedness activates powerful healing forces we are only just beginning to understand. The one remedy he recommends above all others in combating worry is to increase connectedness in your life. This may mean that some parents will need to recommit to family relationships and family time, indeed, in the wake of the many recent frightening national events, many families have pulled closer together.

Parents and children alike are recognizing the comfort found in those we love. Susan Reimer, parent of two teens and columnist for the *Baltimore Sun*, recommends families "embrace one another without restraint. I have confessed to my teenaged children that these calamities have made me feel insecure." She informed her children that she requires long and frequent hugs from them, to be delivered on demand and without protestation. They yield obediently to her embrace, and both Reimer and her children are reassured. Reimer also suggests we say, "I love you," when we bid a family member goodbye. If there must be last words, let those worlds be "I love you."

Express feelings. Parents can help children express their feelings, but should be careful not to overload them with their own, and also be aware of their children's levels of comprehension and tailor discussions to their age and developmental abilities, recommends Greenspan.

Be honest with kids. There are risks in life, and the threats and uncertainty are unnerving. If children express anxiety, parents can validate the reactions as normal, but explain that they rarely persist. Parents' pretending to be unaffected doesn't help allay children's fears, rather they should acknowledge their fear and model courage by moving forward in spite of it. It's helpful to ask children what they need in order to feel less afraid, as well as to make sure they understand that crying is perfectly alright under the circumstances.

By helping a child understand his fears and anxieties, parents actually help soothe the fearful children who dwell within themselves. Greenspan says that in order for parents to be able to reassure their children, they have to assess their own feelings about what has happened and about the future, no matter if the fear or anxiety results from a public trauma, a sexual assault, or a devastating illness.

Provide reassurance. Hallowell counsels that children need to be able to take a sense of "I love you, and I'll be here, no matter what" for granted. If they can't, then they'll begin to worry, and this kind of worrying is bad for kids because it retards their emotional and intellectual growth. *Daughters*, the online and hard copy newsletter for parents of girls, advises parents to reassure their teens by talking with them about what's going on. Parents can ask, "What do you know about this, and what do you want to know?" The more parents talk with their teens, the more teens will learn about their parents' perspectives and moral frameworks, and they'll gain reassurance and control from the exchange. Parents can acknowledge their children's search for understanding by prompting, "I know this is upsetting. I'm here to listen."

Parents should share their perspectives, reminding their teens that for every act of hurt or hatred in the world, there are many, many acts of decency and compassion, saying, for example, "Many good people work for good. They are powerful, too." If parents live with hope, they can tell their children, "There are always things we can't control. That has always been true, but that doesn't mean we live in fear." Undoubtedly, there is violence and evil in the world, but we can carry on with confidence and live with hope. The National Association of School Psychologists advises parents to talk with teens about the difference between the possibility of danger and the probability of it affecting them personally. Remind children that America has weathered many other crises, including natural disasters, war, and terrorism, and has emerged stronger and more united each time.

Parents can help their teens recognize their own strength by expressing confidence in them and encouraging them to think in terms of using their strengths by suggesting, "Now that you know about this, can you think of ways to take care of yourself and others?" or "You'll learn more about how to keep yourself and others safe from harm." It's good to remind children of instances in which they've successfully handled other challenges, which may provide direction and ideas for dealing with current anxieties.

Parents can take advantage of a wealth of instances of courage inherent in family stories by sharing with their children tales of relatives meeting and overcoming challenges, whether they be war, economic depression, or personal tragedy. These stories serve to remind children they come from a long line of brave and courageous people. Family stories of slavery, the Holocaust, immigration, ocean voyages, and poverty help shape children's sense of who they are and what they can be.

By sharing their own faith that the twenty-first century will be a truly extraordinary time, parents can assure their children of the wonderful future they believe to be in store for them. Some teens turn to alcohol and other drugs or to risky behavior because they think, "I have no future, so why not smoke or do drugs? I just want to have some fun while I can." It is important parents restore and heal their children's shaken faith in the future.

Help others. Greenspan says that if parents really want their children to feel safe, they have to help people elsewhere feel secure. "We have to invest in forward-looking plans that will address the root causes of violence, terrorism, epidemics, and pollution." He says unless we are involved in shaping a better, safer future, we "may ourselves convey an attitude of uncertainty and anxiety" to our children.

Greenspan recommends parents participate in building a secure community and form alliances with school, religious organizations, other parents, or neighbors. When teens and parents have a sense of being directly involved in a positive and constructive approach to alleviating a problem, everyone gains in both energy and confidence. Participate in organizations working toward conflict resolution, environmental protection, eliminating homelessness or family violence. Teens will feel they are no longer passive, helpless bystanders and will be buoyed by spirituality and sustaining ties to the community and by the conviction that life has meaning. Encourage children not to overlook opportunities to be kind—to a store clerk, a stranger asking directions, a neighbor, or a peer—because such acts enhance one's reservoir of empathy, faith, and self-esteem.

Evaluate the risks. Greenspan notes that adolescents who can assess probabilities can look at the likelihood of bad or good things happening and are better able to put their worries in perspective. Generally, they will see that the chances are likely they will be safe and secure, at least for the short-term future.

Because worry and anxiety are always caused by uncertainty, improving predictions can greatly reduce them. If a child predicts that, should he have to take the history exam today, he will not get a passing grade and is certain the prediction is correct because he's missed classes and hasn't read the chapter, he won't have anxiety about failing. However, he may be anxious about events he can't predict with certainty, such as the impact of failing this exam. Hallowell says that children must learn how to gather information to inform their worries and to help calculate their risks.

Hurrying and worrying

While help from mental health professionals may be warranted for teens suffering acute and severe anxiety and worry, along with their parents, the first order of business is to decrease the pace of family life in order to better control worry and anxiety. Some chronic worrying may be aggravated or reinforced by a frantic, hurried lifestyle, suggests Hansen. He says it's necessary to break the cycle of hurrying and worrying and to slow down. "We are inclined to confuse urgency with emergency, and deadlines with deadly threats. Constant hurrying generates a steady trickle of adrenaline, keeping us alert to danger and ready to run, keeping us worrying." It is advisable for families to sit down together and discuss the daily and weekly schedule and get input from each member as to how they might slow the pace.

Parents and teens can also experiment to identify effective self-calming techniques. The variety of strategies is almost limitless, so a certain amount of trial, error, and practice are necessary. Hansen suggests that worriers begin by practicing deep rhythmic breathing. Because anxiety causes one to breathe differently than normal, deep, calm breathing helps one break out of the physiological and emotional state of anxiety. He advises people to slow the pace of walking, driving, eating, showering, etc., consciously counteracting the habit of hurry.

Final thoughts

Hallowell says the most important step in preventing and managing fear, worry, and anxiety, and sustaining our children's sense of security, is to, "Connect. Reach out. Commiserate. Brainstorm. Hug. Eat together. Talk. Play a game of cards. Don't let yourself get cut off from others." He suggests children learn how to tolerate a certain amount of uncertainty, to "worry well," and to do so by practicing, rather than by being protected from all danger and all worry.

| 24 |

Depression: When Is It Over the Edge?

A teen asks: My best friend admitted she's taking medication for depression and I feel funny about it. I feel like I can't act like myself around her anymore, and I think it's affecting our friendship. What should I do?

A teen responds: Depression isn't a disease you can catch. Don't abandon her and you'll find out that things are only going to get better.

Adapted from *In the Mix*, Public Broadcasting System website

Being able to discern the difference between the everyday angst of growing up and the darkness of clinical depression could mean the difference between life and death for a child. For parents, this means staying in touch with their children's behavior and emotions, despite "Leave me alone" and "I don't need you" responses. Depression, unlike physical illness, cannot be clearly diagnosed by a medical test, but can sometimes be seen in subtle physical and emotional changes over a period of time.

Teens and adults both describe depression as a pervasive sadness, a sense of utter hopelessness or worthlessness, of immobilization or paralysis, of being drawn ever faster down the vortex of a black hole. An adolescent may feel he or she will never recover and can imagine nothing positive about the future, reports Robert Roth, M.F.C.C., coordinator of adolescent services at Montgomery General Hospital in Olney, Maryland. The bottom line is that depression is much worse than mere sadness or being in a bad mood.

Degrees of teen depression can run the gamut from relatively mild symptoms over an extended period to something akin to having a freak tsunami break over one's head. A large percentage of teens experience low grade depression that can last for months or years—a condition that is particularly difficult to diagnose and is commonly overlooked, observes Bob Condit, M.Ed., independent consultant and former counselor at the Landon School in Bethesda, Maryland. "This is something like running a low grade fever while trying to maintain your normal routine. It's not serious enough to keep you home from work or school, but it certainly affects your level of performance and quality of life."

Depression occurs in people of both sexes. Real men can get real depression, too—and there are real treatments with medications, psychotherapy, and support groups to help manage the pain and reduce the toll. The "Real Men, Real Depression" public education initiative from National Institutes of Mental Health is designed to "break down the macho barrier of denial that says tough guys don't get sick in the head. They do, and keeping quiet can be fatal." Many more men and teenage boys are depressed than get help, and many of them have suicidal thoughts and attempt, or succeed at, suicide.

How to know if it's depression

"How do I know the difference between feeling sad and being depressed?" is a common question from teenagers. Most of us know, even in the midst of a bad time, that we'll get through it and feel better in a while. A depressed person, however, feels there is no end to the pain and doesn't believe he can do anything to make it better.

Condit cautions parents to be concerned with behavior they observe in their children that deviates from that which they have come to expect as the norm. Changes in eating or sleeping habits, withdrawal from friends and normal activities, a sudden nose dive in grades, and a decline in grooming and personal hygiene are all signs of something serious going on in a teen's life. The more of these behaviors that appear concurrently, and the longer they last, the more potentially serious is the problem.

Adolescent depression takes a different form than that occurring in grade school children, notes Stanley Greenspan, M.D., local parent and nationally recognized psychiatrist, clinical professor of psychiatry and pediatrics at George Washington University Medical School, and author of many books, including the most recent, *The Secure Child: Helping Children Feel Safe and Confident in a Changing World*. While a younger child tends to be depressed about concrete, specific situations in his immediate sphere, such as peer rejection, anger at a parent, or rivalry with a sibling, Greenspan warns that "an adolescent will internalize more of his feelings and will be more likely to feel worthless or like a bad person, even hopeless and helpless about the future...he can have many more self-accusatory and negative feelings."

Taking into consideration the adolescent emotional roller coaster—on top of the world one day and staggering under the weight of it the next—how can parents tell the difference between a normal degree of being bummed out and indications of the onset of clinical depression? Condit advises parents to be particularly aware of dramatic mood changes lasting more than seven to ten days as these may indicate the beginning of depression. Greenspan also observes that teen depression can result in aggressive acting out and the hurting of others, which is, in actuality, self-destructive behavior. Radical behavioral changes, including the sudden increase in the use of alcohol or drugs, inconsolable sadness, inexplicable crying jags, and uncharacteristic anger should trigger parents' concern and require close attention and evaluation.

Signs of depression

Adolescent depression is different in appearance from adult depression, too, explains Roth. Depressed teens often appear more as though they are angry and rebellious than withdrawn and sad as adults do, and they present more acting-out behavior, including suicide attempts. Condit urges parents to understand that teens will attempt suicide for reasons that even a depressed adult would not consider valid. Common among them are the fear of disappointing parents, like questioning if mom or dad could ever really love a C student, and being caught in a disturbing dilemma, such as a romantic attraction to members of the same sex.

Roth notes that while adult depression is often treated compassionately by friends and relatives, teen depression, due to its sometimes aggressive tone, is often met with anger, especially from parents and teachers, but also from peers. He adds that depressed adolescents' parents are often stressed and even depressed themselves, although it is often unclear which party triggered the depression—a teen's depression triggering stress in the parents coping with the situation, or overstressed parents triggering depression in a teen.

Adolescence can be divided into three phases, early, middle, and late, and depression is manifested differently in each. Young teens often experience depression as pessimism and withdrawal. The middle group's pessimism is coupled with concerns about the future and general physical complaints. Older teens are likely to feel guilty about what they perceive as bad or tragic events, to be careless or even reckless about their own safety, have nightmares, and experience suicidal ideation. This is not to say that preadolescents and early and middle adolescents do not also feel suicidal, but that suicidal thoughts are more likely to occur in older teens.

The step from depression to suicide

Not all depressed teens attempt to take their lives; however, most suicides and attempts are preceded by depression, in fact, depression is the primary impetus for suicide. According to the Surgeon General of the United States, a young person commits suicide every two hours—every day. While one study found that there are an average of twenty-three suicide attempts for every death from suicide, parents need to be extremely vigilant and concerned following an unsuccessful attempt on the part of their teen, as an unsuccessful attempt is high on the list of indications warning of another attempt.

Teens with undiagnosed or improperly diagnosed bipolar disorder or manic depressive illness are at greater risk of suicide than teens experiencing other forms of depression. Bipolar teens can be effectively treated once correctly diagnosed and properly medicated, but, the characteristic seesawing mood swings of the disorder as it appears in adolescents may be mistaken for typical teen emotional ups and downs.

Triggers to depression

Condit observes that the preadolescent and adolescent years can be rough ones for almost everyone and frequently encompass periods of major unhappiness. Teens attempting to discover who they are and where they fit into the scheme of things are often overwhelmed by conflicting feelings. Those experiencing the loss of a loved one through separation, divorce, or the breakup of a friendship or a romance are especially vulnerable to depression.

The pressure to achieve and be successful is strongly felt by children, and parents need to be especially aware of the manner in which their children are affected by such pressure. When children experience setbacks, they sometimes feel their problems are insurmountable, that no one understands them or their plight, and that they're incapable of resolving the situation. Such feelings can quickly spiral down into an accelerating depressive crisis, especially for teens whose parents are unavailable for regular, daily, meaningful communication.

Adelaide Robb, M.D., the medical director of the adolescent inpatient unit at the Children's National Medical Center in Washington, D.C., urges parents to understand "that teenagers are short on experience; they haven't been through many failures or losses in life that have been followed by successes. They only see the failure and become overwhelmed. A fatalistic thinking pattern combined with a lack of life experience precipitates illogical conclusions; even teenagers who are intellectually gifted often don't have those problem-solving skills."

Parents' own upheavals and reversals, be they financial, career related, spiritual, or marital, can have profound effects on their children. The normal emotional turmoil of adolescence quite often coincides with the time when parents are experiencing their own emotional turmoil about middle age, career progress and options, or the state of their marriages, and teens' normal emotional churnings may be exacerbated by an environment of parental anxiety. Changes in the family, a move to a new house or school, or the greater academic expectations upon reaching high school all constitute the kinds of pressure that can result in teens' depression, as well as that experienced by kids in very structured families, or in tightly scheduled, dual career families where there is literally no time to deal with problems.

A history of depression within the family can predispose a child for depression, as can an episode of mononucleosis or a number of medications for acute chronic asthma that contain steroids. The death of a friend, family member, beloved pet, or an idolized person can trigger depression. Formal rites of passage requiring longterm study and public demonstration of proficiency such as bar or bat mitzvahs can constitute the kind of stressor that can result in depression.

Teens suffering from seasonal affective disorder (SAD) have more difficulty coping with the challenges of adolescence during winter when the days are short and often gloomy. They may experience a decline in motivation and academic performance, as well as either minor or major depression during those months. Once properly diagnosed, SAD can usually be treated through the daily exposure to special lights prescribed by a therapist.

Cultural differences

Western societies accept depression as a relatively common, treatable illness. By contrast, the very concept of depression is almost nonexistent in most East Asian cultures. As a result, Asian-born parents and teens in this country may not recognize depression when they experience it, quite often attributing their feelings to the strain of adapting to a new country, working in a new language, and the stress of heavy course and work loads. As the depression deepens, many Asian teens attribute their symptoms to shameful character flaws and blame themselves for their weakness.

The Surgeon General's most recent mental health report found that African-American families experience the same percentage of per capita depression as the overall population. Marilyn Martin, M.D., Baltimore area psychiatrist and author of *Saving our Last Nerve: The*

Black Woman's Path to Mental Health, observes that African-Americans may be more likely to suffer somatic symptoms, such as fatigue or stress, rather than describe feelings or emotions, saying, "We might talk about how tired we are, and mention headaches, chronic back pain, or irritability." While aware of treatments and interventions for depression, many African-Americans are concerned about "having treatment happen to them."

African-Americans seeking treatment for themselves or their children are hard pressed to find an African-American mental health professional, as only two percent of psychologists and psychiatrists are Black, and only four percent of all social workers are people of color, explains Martin. Other racial and ethnic groups suffer the same paucity of diversity in the mental health professions, as well. Parents of color have the added task of selecting therapists they feel are "culturally competent," committed to understanding the influences and dynamics of diverse communities, and who are aware of the documented range of responses among various minority groups to average dosages of medications, as well as side effects resulting from physiological differences.

Treatments

Depression is a highly treatable condition, and we in the metropolitan area are blessed with a wide range of quality mental health services. Parents seeking a therapist for their child or their family can begin by asking for referrals from trusted friends, the family doctor, or school guidance counselor. They should be aware that there are a variety of counseling styles, and many practices are limited to a single specialty or a specific therapeutic approach.

Selecting the best therapist for your child involves some research and investigation, but it is well worth the effort. Make appointments for you and your child to interview several prospective candidates and take your child's preferences into consideration. A child as young as ten years old will have definite feelings about whether a counselor seems to be the kind of person with whom he or she would feel comfortable talking. When speaking with a therapist, be as honest as possible about your child's difficulty, as well as about any family history of depression, mental illness, alcoholism, and drug abuse. Don't hesitate to ask questions about a therapist's counseling style, the length of time he or she has practiced in the stated specialty, how often your child will be seen and the general pattern of therapy, and the expected nature of your participation in the treatment. Gathering this information is especially important when making the treatment decision for a younger teen or one who is depressed to a degree where self-harm is a distinct possibility.

It is quite possible after a session or two that you and your child may not be completely comfortable with the therapist. Much of successful therapy is dependent upon the fit between therapist and client, so don't be discouraged if your first choice doesn't turn out to be the one. Try another therapist if you're not satisfied, and keep trying until you both feel good about the match. Stick with it—you have everything to gain and so very much to lose.

There are some excellent and effective medications available for the treatment of depression, and while such medications must, by law, be prescribed by a medical doctor, most therapists maintain an association with a psychiatrist for this purpose. A high percentage of adolescent depression is biochemical in nature, and most of the medications used in treatment are designed to restore the chemical balance and elevate a teen's emotional state to a level conducive to effective therapy.

Some parents are uncomfortable when their child sees a therapist, fearing the family and personal information revealed during sessions may expose them as being a contributing factor to their child's depression. None of us wants to feel we've been responsible for our children's pain, but, should we have been, inadvertently or out of misguided but good intentions, it is better for us to know. We may not be able to change our actions or behavior patterns, but being more aware of them and working with the professional to find ways to help our children will make a difference.

Parents of depressed children should consider family or couples therapy if the family is not functioning well, if their children perceive that to be the case, or if their children genuinely feel they are not loved by the parents, all of which are very common perceptions of depressed teens. There may be issues about themselves as a couple or with the family's dynamics that parents need to address immediately in order to put them in a better position to help their children.

School's role

Condit strongly urges parents to consider informing their child's school of his or her depressed condition and the manner in which it is being treated. He also advises that someone at the school should be apprised of the child's situation and be available to serve as an advocate on his behalf with the school, if necessary. Condit explains that the reason for informing school staff is that teachers have very probably been aware for some time that something is going on when a teen hasn't been functioning, or functioning well.

Explaining the reason for a child's behavior helps teachers understand the unsubmitted homework, plummeting grades and test scores, lack of classroom participation, and emotional or angry outbursts. It helps them understand that it is not a matter of an incorrigible teen simply not caring, but of a young person struggling with a legitimate difficulty, upon whom they can have a positive impact. Informed teachers are more apt to work with a counselor who requests postponement of work or extension of deadlines while the child works through particularly difficult times. Parents may also choose to inform teachers when their child is taking medication in case of possible side effects. Teachers can be extremely helpful to parents and therapists, and thus to depressed teens, by being on hand to monitor and chart behavioral changes and side effects during the course of treatment and afterwards.

Some area parents, however, recommend caution with regard to informing a school of a child's depression and treatment and whom to inform. Teens may be embarrassed to have anyone know of their condition; teachers may inadvertently, or even deliberately, betray the confidence; and school staff may treat the teen differently than before, being markedly solicitious and overprotective or setting unnecessarily low expectations for the student's performance. Parents should be guided by the severity of the depression and the degree to which it impacts on their child's school work in determining whether there is a benefit to sharing the diagnosis with school staff. Obviously, the more serious and visible the symptoms, the more essential it is to inform school personnel.

Final thoughts

Depression is an illness and must be treated as such. It is not simply a bad case of the blues, and a depressed person cannot just snap out of it. The illness affects the entire body, including the brain. Remember that depression is not an emotional weakness; it is a serious health disorder, and it is imperative to seek help from a professional as early as possible.

Teenager Carl Holscher on *teenadviceonline.org* gives this advice to depressed teens, " Do not keep all the pain inside...get help. You cannot do it all alone!"

25

Anger

Angry adolescents are skilled in finding the most offensive ways to express themselves to their parents. If you value neatness, your daughter keeps her room messy. If you're proud of your house, your son kicks holes in the wall when he loses his temper. If foul language makes you uncomfortable, your angry teen perfects his vocabulary of obscenities. And one of the most far-reaching angry protests is deliberately failing school in response to parents' demands for academic excellence.

NEIL BERNSTEIN, Ph.D., Washington, D.C. clinical psychologist and author

Intense feelings such as anger and frustration can be scary for adolescent and parent alike; however, anger can provide valuable information. "It's a signal that some need is not being met, that some boundary is being violated or crossed," explains Washington, D.C., therapist Susan Drobis, M.S.W., and it's certainly part of every teenager's life. Unfortunately, parents often don't know how to help their children manage their anger, and, in fact, may not handle their own anger well.

Understanding anger and its triggers

When we perceive a threat, our bodies instinctively react with the "fight or flight" response. We produce a burst of adrenaline, our hearts pump more blood to muscles and, in effect, our body gets ready to either fend off an attack or run away. The reaction to perceived physical or emotional threat is the same.

Adolescents' lives are full of physical and emotional threats. Control battles with parents, restrictions on their freedom, competition with siblings, the pressure of school and homework, anxiety about a test or getting into college, the need to separate from parents, an argument with a friend, feeling fat or stupid or unloved, dating problems, social injustice, the inequities of everyday life, feeling mature but not being treated that way—it's a wonder adolescents and preadolescents aren't angrier than they are!

Helping our children understand what provokes their anger is the first step to helping them manage it. Each person's trigger is unique to them. "If somebody comments on an area that we're struggling with or feel vulnerable about, we feel threatened," points out Britt Rathbone, L.C.S.W., director of Rathbone and Associates, an outpatient mental health practice for adolescents in Rockville, Maryland. "When we feel threatened, we get angry." We also get angry at what we think is not fair or when we don't feel respected. Anger within the family is sometimes activated by stress and sometimes by the individual or collective fatigue of parent and child.

Most often, writes Neil Bernstein, Ph.D., Washington, D.C., clinical psychologist, teenagers' anger reflects one of the following feelings:

- they believe their parents are selfish and don't have time for them,
- they need more attention and caring but are unable to ask for it directly,
- deep down they want limits set on their behavior, and they are not getting any,
- they want to feel understood by their parents, but they aren't,
- they feel burdened by their parents' inappropriate and excessive worries, or
- they're unhappy with their own lives and take it out on their parents.

Understanding what sparks anger is complicated by the fact that the anger may be covering up another emotion. Fear, anxiety, rejection, hurt, or feelings of helplessness may be the initial emotions and anger is the defense mechanism. Professional help is sometimes needed to identify what's truly triggering a child's anger, especially if that trigger has its origins in the family's dynamics.

Anger in men and boys is often viewed as masculine, while girls and women have traditionally been discouraged from demonstrating their anger, which has led to the notion that females have problems expressing anger. June Tangney, Ph.D., professor of psychology at George Mason University, says, "Women don't have a problem with anger—they just manage it differently." She adds that females tend to talk about their anger more and are not as aggressive as men in expressing it. "They are more proactive and use more problem-solving approaches in discussing a problem with a person they are angry with." Parents can aid in dislodging gender stereotypes by giving their children insights and skills to express and defuse their anger.

Managing anger

No matter what produces the feeling, anger itself is a normal, healthy emotion. "Nobody is perfect; everybody feels angry sometimes," observes Rockville, Maryland, psychotherapist Diane Scheininger, M.Ed., M.S.W. Some parents believe that any expression of anger is unacceptable, but, she warns, if there is no room for, or no permission for, anger to be expressed, an emotionally restrictive environment is created, one in which kids may fear voicing any negative feelings. When this occurs, children can't learn to manage or modify their anger and may feel guilty when they do get angry.

Parents can help their children, and themselves, learn to manage anger and channel it into constructive outlets with these steps:

Differentiate between feelings and behavior. When setting limits, separate emotions and actions. Anger, an emotion, is normal. "Anger is not necessarily inappropriate," points out Scheininger. "It's how anger is expressed that may be inappropriate."

Set boundaries on anger. Your child needs to know that it's okay to feel angry and to express angry feelings, but it's not okay to hit or hurt people or damage property. When setting rules about anger, be clear about what behavior is unacceptable. Your family's values will determine what expressions of anger are acceptable. Some people can tolerate door slamming or swearing, while others can't. "Anything that feels abusive, whether directed at a sibling, a parent, or someone else, is destructive," Drobis cautions, and should not be tolerated.

Let your child blow off steam. When kids are most worked up and upset, you can diffuse a lot of their anger simply by listening empathetically, using validating phrases such as, "I can see that you're angry," or, "It sounds like you're really upset."

Avoid becoming agitated while your child is venting. Drobis warns this can be difficult to do, particularly when you disagree strongly with what your child is saying, but you can be empathetic and understand that this is the way they see a situation without having to agree with what's being said. If you want to share your perspective, she advises you to wait until a calmer moment.

Encourage your child to talk about his anger—afterward. Repressing an intense emotion like anger is not healthy; the anger will go underground only to surface at some other time. While many individuals are not comfortable talking about intense feelings, parents can encourage their children to do so. Marguerite Kelly, author of the syndicated "Family Almanac" column and several parenting books, suggests introducing discussions about anger in situations that feel safe to your child. Try talking with your child on the phone at night, at bedtime, when you're working side-by-side in the kitchen, or in the car—a particularly effective site for privacy.

Don't discount your child's emotions. Kelly observes that children have to be able to express their opinions openly without having a parent discount or dismiss their anger. A parent whose sole reaction is, "Of course your teacher likes you," is, in effect, saying, "You don't know what you're talking about."

Identify the reason for the anger. None of a child's behaviors are without a reason, and Kelly advises parents to get to the bottom of the anger and frustration. Be an active listener; listen beyond the child's words to the true meaning of what he's saying. Check out what you think you hear. "I sense that you're angry because I said you had to come home early. Is that correct?" "I wonder if..."

Beware of reacting to anger. Shouting matches aren't good for anybody, but parents are human and may find themselves reacting to their child's anger. "If you can catch yourself in time," Drobis suggests, "take a deep breath, find a sense of humor, and say, 'Let's erase the beginning of this scene and start over again.'" Other times, you may need to give yourselves time to regroup. Kelly advises we should recognize when it's a good time to withdraw. For example, the parent might say to the child, "We're both saying things we're going to be sorry about later. Let's pull ourselves together and meet back here in fifteen minutes to talk some more." Setting a time is important—it makes it easier for both parties to avoid coming back to such strong emotions at the same time it acknowledges the importance of the issue.

Teach kids to reassess an anger-causing situation. "Our emotions are based on our thoughts," Rathbone points out. "How we assess a situation brings about an emotion." He suggests parents help kids reassess situations that have provoked angry feelings, as in the following:

"You think Alex treats you like a loser. How so?"

"He threw a spitball at me yesterday."

"Has he ever thrown a spitball at anybody else?"

"Well, yeah, he got in trouble for throwing one at Sarah last week."

In this situation, the teen begins to understand that Alex is not singling him out or picking on him alone. Rathbone feels such an approach can help a child achieve some kind of perspective on the incident and determine whether anger is the appropriate reaction.

Help your child problem-solve. After the angry child has calmed down, help him or her find a solution to the problem. Anger is like wax in the ears, Kelly explains, kids can't hear you if they haven't gotten rid of their anger first. When they have, suggests Drobis, parents should be available to help them problem-solve rather than loading them up with advice. Coach them to find their own solutions. Use encouraging statements such as, "I know you'll work this out," or, "You'll make the right choice."

Help your child develop constructive outlets for anger. Show kids how to develop safe ways to express their feelings and understand that the feelings are neither dangerous nor bad. Constructive outlets for anger can include listening to loud music, singing at the top of one's lungs, slamming tennis balls, calling a friend, pummeling a pillow, writing an angry letter (and then throwing it away), or writing in a journal. What's important is that while the angry feelings aren't dangerous or bad, the expression of them needs to be channeled through safe outlets.

Suggest distractions. When adolescents get angry, they may sometimes get stuck on a thought and keep replaying it over and over. Rathbone recommends we suggest they divert themselves by listening to a tape, reading a book, doing homework, or getting together with friends. Chances are they'll come back without that heightened sense of irritation and anger. Returning to the same issue may, however, be a necessary part of the process of working it out. Support whatever process seems to be most productive for your child. If your child is one who needs to stew, coach him or her on how to let go of anger.

Talk about anger. Look for teachable moments, suggests Rathbone. Talk about what you and your teen observe on the street, on television, or in the movies. Get your child thinking about anger with questions like, "What do you think about what he just did? Have you ever done something like that? Is it worth it?" If your child is uncomfortable talking about feelings, draw analogies from something he's interested in. Sports, for example, provide many examples of athletes dealing with anger—help your child identify athletes who handle their anger positively, thinking through their reactions, as well as those whose responses are decidedly inappropriate and discuss how they differ.

Use your own anger as an example. When discussing anger management techniques—those that work and those that don't—use your own experiences as examples. You can tell your child how embarrassed you were when you lost your temper at a motorist who pulled ahead of you and took the parking place you'd been waiting for. Explain how you wished you'd handled the situation differently and ask your child what he would have done in a similar situation.

Help your child maintain balance. Kids who eat the right food and get plenty of rest and exercise are apt to be more emotionally resilient than children who do not. Rathbone observes that when people exercise regularly, they seem to have a higher tolerance for frustration and don't anger as easily. Consider encouraging your teen to learn stress management techniques such as yoga, deep breathing, and meditation.

Don't be afraid of your child's anger. Drobis avers that parents today are afraid of their kids' anger and cave in when the limits they set are challenged. They don't want to face their children's anger or see their kids frustrated. While kids may not be thrilled by limits, parents nonetheless need to set them and be strong enough to tolerate their children's resulting frustration and anger. Giving in when your child is angry shortchanges him of learning the anger management tools he needs.

Keep an anger log. If your child's anger seems out of proportion in both frequency and intensity, it could stem from underlying causes as varied as emotional distress or food allergies. Kelly suggests that recording information about your child's anger for a week or more can provide you both with valuable insights into the causes of that anger. In a journal, record your child's behavior, the apparent trigger, any emotional stress he or she might be experiencing, food eaten, time of the occurrence, and even the weather. Involve your teen in the process if he or she is receptive and interested in learning more about what may be causing the anger. If your child's anger persists in frequency or intensity, seek professional help.

Watch for warning signs. Drobis cautions that anger and irritability in a child can be signs of depression and that parents should look for other signs, such as sudden changes in behavior or in academic patterns, friendships, or activities. Scheininger adds that an increase in addictive behavior—alcohol consumption, overeating, or smoking—may be masking anger or depression. "Any expressions of a child's wishing he were dead need to be taken seriously," Drobis says and continues to caution that if behavior is persistently and consistently destructive and violent, there's something very powerful going on in that child, and the child and the parent may need more help than the parent can provide.

Parents' anger

Manage your own anger. Most of us were not taught to deal with feelings, Drobis points out, but parents can't really help a child learn to deal with anger if they have problems with it themselves. If you find yourself exploding frequently, work at identifying what's triggering your anger. Adolescents' attempts to separate from parents, differentiate themselves, and demand changes in the family can be particularly troublesome for some parents. Getting support from friends and partners can help parents survive a difficult time and manage their anger more effectively.

Get to the source of the anger. Anger can be coming from many sources, Scheininger notes. When parents lose their tempers and yell at a child, for example, their anger may stem from stress on the job or displaced anger at a spouse. It's imperative that parents check in with themselves and ascertain whether they're venting unwarranted anger onto their children in order to prevent the unfair fallout. Kay Abrams, Ph.D., parenting consultant and Maryland psychologist, reminds us that angry reactions to a child's distress can be about our own stress, fatigue, impatience, or disappointed expectations.

Take care of yourself. It's also important for parents to be self-nurturing and to take time for themselves, Scheininger explains, pointing out that doing things that are good for oneself helps manage anger. Parents can use adequate rest, proper nutrition, daily exercise, and stress management techniques such as yoga, meditation, aerobic dance, or tai chi to improve their ability to control their emotions. In addition, she advises that talking with friends, sharing emotional ups and downs, voicing concerns, and getting advice can enable us to restore and bolster our ability to manage difficult situations with our children. These activities also serve to model effective anger management techniques for your teen.

Know when you need help. While parental anger in many situations is natural, understandable, and appropriate, parents should seek professional help if their anger is uncontrollable, or if they find themselves feeling destructive, verbally or physically abusive, or violent. If you're concerned about a spouse's anger management issues, you can encourage him or her to seek professional help. Scheininger warns that sometimes the very people who need help the most don't get it because they don't recognize how abusive they are and people are reluctant to confront their anger. A situation such as this may require another family member to initiate family therapy, ostensibly for themselves. Remember, if one family member is experiencing emotional difficulty, the entire family is affected and all would benefit from counseling.

Learn more about anger yourself. Individual and family therapy, parenting, and anger management classes, and books such as those listed in the resource section at the back of the book can assist you in helping yourself and your child manage anger more effectively.

Final thoughts

We all get angry at times, but how we express our anger and how we respond to it, determine whether it is destructive or creative. Parents can make sure that they and their children have opportunities to express anger and to develop skills to manage this potentially destructive emotion. It you or your teen are chronically angry it is essential that you get assistance to help manage the anger more effectively.

26

Grieving: Death, Disability, Divorce, and Disappointment

A teen asks: A friend of mine just died in a car accident. I still can't believe it really happened. I've never lost anyone before. I feel like everyone expects things to go back to normal, but I can't stop thinking about her and being depressed. How do I deal with this without going crazy?

Q & A, "Dealing with Death," *In the Mix,* Public Broadcasting System website

It is impossible to shield our children from grief experiences no matter how much we parents yearn to do that. Family members die. Teachers and staff die. Sometimes, tragically, our children's peers die. Terrorists strike. Parents divorce. Dreadful injuries result in disability. Even the death of a beloved pet can be devastating.

Young people experience crushing disappointments by failing to make sports teams, win school elections, or be cast in school theatrical productions. Important early romantic relationships end abruptly and painfully. The number one college choice sends a rejection letter. Even progressing from middle school to high school represents an enormous loss of security and familiarity.

Area psychotherapist Ginger Sullivan, M.A., puts it thus, "Life brings change, change brings loss, loss brings pain and grief, and pain and grief give us the opportunity for growth." Given the many opportunities for middle and high schoolers to experience loss, the best thing parents and schools can do is give young people the support, tools, and space to mourn these losses in a healthy way and thus enable them to grow from the experience.

How younger adolescents grieve

Middle- and high-schoolers grieve differently from both younger children and adults. They also grieve differently from each other. Middle-schoolers, aged eleven to thirteen, are at a developmental stage where they are beginning to make commitments to concepts greater than themselves. This is the traditional age for major religious rituals in which children publicly profess their beliefs, such as the Christian confirmation, the Jewish bar/bat mitzvah, and inclusion in the adult Muslim ritual of daily prayer and Ramadan fasting. A major loss at this age is particularly difficult to understand. A child wonders, "If God is good, why did Grandma get cancer?"

"Younger middle school students still think they are the center of the universe," points out Duane Bowers, M.A., grief counselor and trainer in private practice who was formerly with the Wendt Center for Loss and Healing in Washington, D.C. "The first response of an eleven-year-old whose mother has died might be, 'Who is going to cook for me?' Developmentally, this is a normal response, even if it might seem insensitive to the grief-stricken adults in the child's life."

It is also developmentally normal for middle-schoolers to focus on the physical aspects of death, which can be disconcerting for adults. Bowers says that in the aftermath of the September 11, 2001, terrorist attacks, the primary initial focus of many middle school discussions was, "What did the bodies of the people who jumped from the World Trade Center look like when they hit the pavement?" This age group is fascinated by autopsy, for example, and Bowers explains, "They have to start with what happened to that body—but really, they're wondering, 'What if that happened to me?' Once they get through the guts and the gore, then they can get to the emotion."

Middle school children tend to act out their grief in external ways. They can be belligerent and nasty. They may destroy physical objects or even hurt themselves, either wittingly or unwittingly. Sometimes they regress to an earlier age, an age that felt safe, and so may revert to bed-wetting or thumbsucking.

How older adolescents grieve

Bowers notes that older adolescents internalize more and are more subtle in their reactions to loss. Bob Condit, M.Ed., independent consultant and former counselor at the Landon School in Bethesda, Maryland, agrees and says, "Teenagers who are grieving are frightened, but unwilling to show fear. They try to look 'fine' but may long to retreat to safer times. They may act out sexually or by using alcohol or other drugs. They may engage in risk-taking behaviors that can even be life threatening. They may withdraw from friends and experience depression-like symptoms."

Marguerite Kelly, author of the syndicated "Family Almanac" column and several parenting books, writes, "Conformity is critically important to the young, and the death of a parent may be a major embarrassment." Teenagers are deeply invested in their peer group, in wanting to be accepted by the group, as well as in appearing to be just like everyone else in the group. Having a parent or sibling die, or having parents divorce, can be devastating at this age because it renders him different, in his eyes, and in those of his peers.

If a parent's death is due to some stigmatized cause like suicide, HIV/AIDS, or drunk driving (if the parent was the drunk driver), the embarrassment can be even more acute. However, Linda Goldman, Ph.D., area grief and loss counselor and author of *Breaking the Silence: A Guide to Help Children with Complicated Grief—Suicide, Homicide, AIDS, Violence and Abuse*, states that despite the complicated circumstances of suicide, homicide, AIDS, violence, and abuse, the underlying process of grief is universal and timeless.

It is important, reminds Condit, to allow your children to see you grieve. Parents sometimes try to grieve in solitude, imaging that this will be less upsetting to their children. On the contrary, it can be extremely confusing to adolescents who feel devastated by the loss of a parent to assume the surviving parent is handling the situation well because there is little or no evidence of that parent's grief. Visibly grieving, as well as talking about the loss together, validates your child's sense of the magnitude of the loss and allows him to see that his feelings are normal.

Impact of unresolved grief

What happens if we don't allow children to grieve? Experts agree there is a laundry list of possible long-term consequences of unresolved grief, including emotional detachment, fear of intimacy, anxiety and panic, rebelliousness, depression or mania, helplessness, poor concentration, and abuse to self or others. Sullivan notes, "Too often we fail to connect such symptoms with their true source, an unresolved loss."

Dottie Ward-Wimmer, L.P.C., children's grief counselor and play therapist at the Wendt Center for Loss and Healing in Washington, D.C., says simply, "If you don't grieve, it waits. It sits and waits. It is never too late to grieve a loss." She adds, "It is a fact, if you look at histories of people who abuse drugs, there are a large number of them—more than fifty percent—who have had early losses. This is an interesting association, although not necessarily a causal link."

What can parents do? Perhaps the most important thing parents can do when their child is grieving is to listen and talk. Researchers at Memorial Sloan-Kettering Cancer Center in New York City, observing 157 children aged thirteen through seventeen throughout the terminal illness of one of their parents and for fourteen months following the parent's death, found that in every age group, the children and teens who adjusted most successfully had parents who were communicative and shared information about what was going on.

Listening without judging is essential. Adolescents feel losses very intensely and sometimes those losses can mystify adults. How can someone be that upset for that long about breaking up with a boyfriend or girlfriend of just two months? How can being cut from the basketball team be so devastating? Why is a child seemingly more upset about the death of the family dog than about the death of her grandfather?

Ward-Wimmer states emphatically, "It is not up to us to judge how intense the loss is. It is very important that we are aware that loss wears many, many faces and our job as parents and caregivers is to listen to the child tell us how important that loss is. Then we honor it and support her through it. We do not try to talk her out of it or in any way minimize it."

"People have prejudgments about how children and teens grieve," observes Goldman. "They play. They weave loss into their lives. Grief work is as unique as each child. You just cannot judge. It's important to let the child be the expert and let you know where they are in their grief process." By letting go of expectations about "proper" grieving and "appropriate" timetables, parents can be truly present for their children, allowing them the space and time to incorporate this loss into their lives. Bowers advises parents to find out what is developmentally appropriate for their child before responding; don't expect a fifteen-year-old to react like a thirty-year-old.

It is crucial to remember that adolescents, particularly those of high school age, are at a complicated stage of their lives. They are growing up, making important decisions, and are immersed in their social lives. As Ward-Wimmer explains, "At the same time they are grieving they need to maintain growth. It is not unusual to see a profoundly grieving teen going to a dance a week after her mom's death. This does not mean she is not grieving." Parents need to help their grieving child stabilize the one foot walking in the real world while comforting and supporting the other foot walking through the grief field.

Divorce as loss

In the case of divorce, parents have a vital responsibility to minimize the conflict and help the children deal with their loss.

Washington, D. C., clinical psychologist Patricia Dalton, Ph.D., notes that when custody or other issues are in dispute, parents need to stop looking at their grievances against their former spouse and instead ask, "What am I doing to make this situation more difficult?" She suggests seeking feedback from close friends and family members, as it is difficult to view our own behavior objectively. Dalton also stresses, "If at all possible, settle the custody situation between yourselves out of court. The process of going through a drawn-out custody battle is very disturbing to both parents and children."

Death of a pet

The death of a family pet, particularly one that has been with the family since a child was tiny, can be very upsetting for middle- and high-schoolers. While every family member might mourn the death, the loss has particular resonance for adolescents. Often, the pet, particularly a dog or cat, is the first being on which a child practices the giving and receiving of unconditional love. Teens talk to their pets, telling them secrets. Both dogs and cats enjoy and need physical attention and, at a time when teens are shying away from hugging their parents, they still can hug and pet their furry friends. Picture the high school boy who drops to his knees each afternoon to greet enthusiastically the family Labrador or the middle school girl doing her homework with her cat purring on her lap. The loss of a pet, whether suddenly or due to old age, can hit adolescents very hard.

Goldman says, "Pets are near and dear to children's hearts. The death of a pet is the perfect time for children to create a ceremony. Pets teach children how to love and can also teach them how to grieve. Children will be a lot more prepared for grieving other losses if they are allowed to openly grieve and mourn their pets." Parents can help their children—from preschool through college age—mourn the loss of these cherished animals by helping them create a ritual, by honoring their pain rather than diminishing it, and by understanding the developmental reasons the sorrow is so intense.

Loss related to serious injury and disability

Sometimes adolescents experience the far-reaching consequences of unexpected disability due to physical trauma, such as car accidents, diving accidents, or surgical complications. Jeffrey, son of CNN anchor and senior correspondent Judy Woodruff, was born with mild spina bifida, but he could not only walk, he could ski, bike, and swim. He was enrolled in the Edmund Burke School in Washington, D.C., and managed very well. When he was sixteen, Jeffrey went into the hospital for a surgical procedure to correct a small problem. Tragically, he emerged with a brain injury. The injury was global, affecting his speech, vision, mobility, and short-term memory. Jeffrey is permanently in a wheelchair and requires almost constant care, but he returned to Burke after a year of rehabilitation and special schooling and graduated in 2001.

Woodruff says, "What Jeffrey needed most was acceptance from his peers." Many of them were supportive, calling and visiting whenever they could, but given the extent of Jeffrey's injury and the impact it had on his speech, she found some friends stayed away because they didn't know what to say or do. She states, "When someone has a disability, they need friends, need people to engage with them, to stay in touch, to e-mail, to write, to call. Life is all about keeping the lines of communication open."

Woodruff's advice to adolescents who have friends who become disabled is to just be there. "Visit for fifteen minutes, even if you have to keep the conversation going the whole time. Talk, joke, make light, lift their spirits. Deal openly with the loss and how you are feeling. As uncomfortable as you may feel, try hard to accept the person for who he or she is, even though he may look and sound different from before. Don't ever underestimate the impact you can have."

The loss represented by such an injury has a profound impact on the entire family, of course. Woodruff advises other parents facing similar situations to reach out to family and friends and not be afraid to ask for help, for something as small as running an errand, and certainly when you feel you are falling apart. Find other families who have been through a similar experience and talk to them. She says, "Ultimately, an event like this is life changing. Don't expect life to go back to what it was before. What you are striving for is to find a new normal. Brace yourself for the long haul and don't be too hard on yourself. Seek nurturing from faith and friends. Many of your questions are unanswerable, among them, how does God let something like this happen? Whatever you do, don't despair. Your child needs you; your whole family needs you. And a sense of humor is essential; laughter is definitely the best medicine of all."

Daniel Salcedo's thirteen-year-old son Alex sustained a devastating brain injury in August 1999 when he was hit by a car while skateboarding. Throughout the long months in the intensive care unit at the Children's National Medical Center, through rehab and then coming home, and even after his death five months later, information technology had an amazing impact on Alex's family and friends. Salcedo realized early on that it was too painful for him to keep recounting the facts, and yet he knew that a large community of family and friends was eager for information. Using technology familiar to him as the founder and C.E.O. of PEOPLink.org, he put up a website—soon known to all as the Alex Website.

Through this website, the family could post daily, sometimes hourly, updates of Alex's condition and receive messages of sympathy and hope from around the world. The online guestbook quickly became almost a diary for Alex's friends, particularly his female buddies, who regularly wrote messages to be read aloud to him. As Salcedo notes, "The Alex Website was public but anonymous at the same time. Lots of people, adults included, expressed sentiments they wouldn't have otherwise." For everyone touched by Alex's accident, checking the Alex Website became an indispensable and comforting daily ritual.

The importance of ritual

Funeral customs the world over attest to the deep human need to memorialize the death of a family or community member. Goldman explains, "There is a difference between grief and mourning. Grief is how you feel about the loss of a person, thing, or even an idea. Mourning is taking the grief and putting it outside yourself. Rituals help people mourn." Sullivan adds that mourning is grief made public. "For grief to be worked through, it must be done in the presence of at least one other person. There is something about human contact that validates and grounds the healing process."

In the case of death, parents should support their children's desire to attend the funeral or memorial service. This can be an important event for teens, who may rely more on their peers than their parents to deal with a loss. Often boys, as well as girls, weep openly and lean on each other at such services, giving and receiving some comfort.

Ward-Wimmer notes, "It is important to help young people make their own rituals. They might not want to go to the funeral—and that's okay—but then ask, 'What are we going to do to remember your friend?' It might be something as simple as going to McDonald's because that was his favorite restaurant and then talking about him and remembering him. Find out what's meaningful for them. It might not be somber; it might be having a party."

Loss in the school community

Crisis counseling is vital when death touches a school because everyone needs to have an opportunity to express grief. Several organizations in the greater Washington area have trained counselors available to come to a school immediately following a crisis to help the student body and staff through the initial aftermath. Experts agree that all schools should have a plan in place for dealing with a tragedy in the school community.

Within an hour of learning of the suicide of a popular junior at a local school, more than a dozen crisis counselors arrived ready to go to work helping the students deal with the loss. The school's guidance counselor was trained in crisis intervention and had worked at another school where an accident had taken the lives of a teacher and student. Students were counseled as a group and individually, and parents were notified of the death by letter. Counseling sessions were held for the faculty and other adults in the community, and an evening meeting was held for parents of students to share their concerns.

Bowers was pleased when he received a call from a private school in Virginia asking for the Wendt Center for Loss and Healing's help in planning for handling the imminent death from cancer of the former head of the school. "This kind of planning is phenomenal," he says, "Schools are thinking differently about loss and preparing when they can."

Schools have many opportunities to provide platforms for ritual behavior in the event of a death that touches the school community. One school, losing a well-loved teacher to cancer, created an opportunity for children, parents, and staff to purchase recommended books to expand the school library. The books either reflected the teacher's interests or were resource books about death and dying. Another school marked the death of a valued staff member by creating a scholarship fund in her name. At a memorial service held on a cloudy day, the girlfriends of a deceased student wrote messages on balloons, which they then released into the suddenly clearing skies. When a rainbow appeared, the girls felt their departed friend's spirit. Other schools have planted trees or special gardens in remembrance of students or teachers who died, and many parents participated in these projects.

Grieving takes time

Continued recognition of loss and grief is an important consideration for school communities and for parents. Grief lingers. It is imperative that adolescents not feel pushed to "get over it." Condit has counseled parents and teachers over the years with this rule of thumb: Think about the longest amount of time you might imagine it would take someone to no longer feel troubled by a loss. Then triple that estimate and maybe you have come close.

As an example of the long-term effects of a loss, it is instructive to note that several years ago, a local independent school's college guidance counselors reported that the most common college application essay topic of the senior class was the death of a classmate, even though the death may have occurred as many as three years previously. This is not completely surprising, Condit observes. "The loss of a peer is extremely serious for adolescents. When a peer dies, it throws them for a total loop because it points out their own mortality. The death of a classmate can be more difficult to bear than the death of a much older relative."

Parents and school staff must remember that the bereavement process may take weeks, months, and maybe even years. The loss is often felt more intensely at times such as birthdays or holidays, and survivors may go through periods when they are furious at the person who died and, at the same time, feel guilty that they are still living.

Don't shy away from those who have suffered a loss. Take the lead and create the opportunity for them to talk. Those who are grieving need a chance to tell their story over and over until they can integrate it and grow through it. Above all, never minimize the hurt.

What is especially difficult to understand is that the most intense feelings of grief and emptiness often occur three to nine months after the loss—at a time when friends expect the grieving person to be doing better.

Final thoughts

Kelly identifies losses such as death as "the earthquakes of the soul—they shake the structure of your life and they never leave you quite as trusting as you were before." She assures parents that we can support our children by reminding them that "they can get through... with reasonable grace, not because other people have done it, but because, in a sense, you have been preparing for these upheavals all your life. Every time you handled a challenge well, you were teaching yourself to cope with these crises. You will survive, because you always have." We overcome our losses because there are people around us who care.

Parents should take care of themselves and not hide in their children's grief when faced with a seemingly unbearable loss. Bowers reminds parents to take care of their own grief because their behavior is the example for their children. If grieving parents don't help themselves, they inadvertently, through example, instruct their children to focus on others' grief and not work through their own.

| 27 |

Suicide

A sophomore boy, struggling with upheaval in his family, began giving away his prized Latin medals and "It's Academic" trophies to friends—a classic sign of suicidal thinking. Friends also heard him say that he wouldn't be around much longer. Alarmed, his best friend's family called the boy's mother, who was overwhelmed at home in the aftermath of divorce and unaware of her son's behavior at school. Psychotherapy alone was unsuccessful, medication helped, but a residential facility proved to be the turning point. He is now thriving academically and socially in college.

i wake up every morning and wonder why im so sad. its always ur such a pretty girl why dont you smile once in awhile and all I can answer is whats there to smile about? all i thought about was dying and who would care. i didnt think anyone would miss me.

RACHEL, Thirteen-year-old survivor of a suicide attempt

Most teens who attempt suicide don't really want to die. They are hurting deeply and are at a loss for any other way out of their pain. David Jobes, Ph.D., scientist-practitioner and professor of psychology at the Catholic University of America, has observed that there are many reasons for suicidal behavior among young people other than a wish for death, including a desire for attention, a need to change a seemingly intractable situation, or revenge. He says that eighty percent of kids who take their lives told others of their intentions beforehand and weren't taken seriously. Ninety percent of teen suicides have social, psychological, or family problems which could have been resolved or eased with appropriate identification, referral, or treatment.

Friends are essential

Friends are often the first to recognize that a teen may be contemplating suicide. Suicidal teens are far more likely to speak with another teen about feelings of deep unhappiness or suicidal thoughts than with an adult. Peers are often the best, and sometimes the only, early warning system for teens at risk of hurting themselves.

Despite teens' reluctance to broach the topics of depression and suicide at home, parents can take the initiative and work to empower their children to seek help—for themselves, as well as for others—by being alert to signs and symptoms rather than dismissing them as adolescent mood swings. Some adults mistakenly believe that if parents talk of suicide with their children, they will somehow infect them with suicidal thoughts. On the contrary, asserts David Bergman, Ph.D., director of the Yellow Ribbon Suicide Treatment Center in Colorado. He maintains it has long been accepted among professionals that broaching the subject is the first step in prevention, because speaking of suicide pierces the terrible, paralyzing isolation of the person considering it.

Many mental health professionals also emphasize that depression should be the focus of these discussions, as recognition and treatment of depression is the most effective strategy for countering suicidal thoughts and attempts

An increasing number of schools include information about depression and suicide in health curricula, senior seminars, and school-wide wellness programs. Information about depression, suicide, and loss is prominent in peer counseling courses and similar training programs designed to teach teens methods for recognizing troubled peers, techniques for listening as they speak of the cause and extent of their problems, and ways to assist them in making good decisions and finding appropriate help.

Why they do it

Suicidal individuals are consumed with hopelessness and helplessness, and they are filled with the devastating belief that they are utterly unlovable and unworthy of love. This bitter stew of negative feelings results in scalding internal pain and suicide appears the only release. The majority of suicide attempts are expressions of extreme distress from which the victim is trying to extricate himself.

There are two potent feelings in teens, not generally shared by adults, that can tip the balance toward suicide. The first is the belief that they are a disappointment to those they love—usually their parents. The second is the sense that there is something about them or their lives that just doesn't make sense. An example of this feeling of illogical disconnect is teens who feel romantic attractions toward members of their own sex. These young people are especially vulnerable to depression and suicide, and statistics show them to be at greater risk of suicide than their heterosexual peers. Teens who feel they are either homosexual or transgendered quite often fear that, were their true natures exposed, not only would they suffer merciless harassment at school and in their communities, they would also risk parental revulsion and banishment. It is not surprising that an estimated forty percent of all teen suicides are the result of distress about issues of sexual orientation.

Gender and race

Historically, girls have attempted suicide more frequently than have boys, although boys have been more successful at suicide than girls. Boys tend to utilize more lethally fast and effective methods—shooting and hanging. Girls are more likely to overdose on pills or cut their wrists. The latter don't result in instantaneous death and often allow teens to reverse their decision to die and call for help. However, in a recent alarming trend, girls appear to be becoming more efficient at killing themselves as well, making use of guns or jumping from high places.

Many males who attempt suicide are not only depressed, but are also aggressive, quick-tempered, and impulsive, according to a number of area psychologists. Some of these boys tend to drink heavily, use drugs, and have difficulty with interpersonal relations. For many, alcohol—though pharmacologically a depressant—helps erase the suicidal moment, giving depression the slip, and induces a welcome senselessness. One young man who drank heavily before each of several suicide attempts told his doctor, "It's not myself, but my *thinking* that I'm trying to kill."

The per capita suicide rate among some minority groups, until the 1980s, was lower than that of the white population. Among white children between the ages of ten and fourteen, suicides have increased one hundred and twenty percent. African-American suicides in the same age group, however, have increased two hundred and thirty-three percent.

Other risk factors

Suicidal behavior is complex, and the risk factors for suicide frequently occur in conjunction with at least one other condition. More than ninety percent of all teen suicides suffered from depression or some other mental illness or substance abuse at the time of their deaths. Mental health researchers have noted that depression was underdiagnosed and antidepressants underprescribed among teen suicides. Teens abusing alcohol or drugs for more than a year were more likely to have suicidal ideation or to attempt suicide than those who were not drinking or doing drugs.

The more areas of a teen's life that crash simultaneously, the greater the stress, and the more hopeless the situation appears. Family adversity, serious quarrels with parents, break-ups with boyfriends or girlfriends, and difficulties at school all cause the kinds of emotional stress that contribute to suicide. Exposure to the suicidal behavior of others, including family members, peers, and even teen idols like Kurt Cobain, can be a significant risk factor.

Suicide is a permanent, irreversible solution to a temporary problem, and teens need to be made to understand that there is never a time when suicide is an appropriate solution. Suicide is rife with ambivalence, reports Kay Redfield Jamison, M.D., professor of psychiatry at the Johns Hopkins Medical School and author of the acclaimed book, *Night Falls Fast: Understanding Suicide*. Often people want to both live and die simultaneously. Many people attempt suicide fully expecting to be discovered in time to be rescued and survive. It is difficult for adolescents to fully comprehend the permanence of suicide. Their sense of the moment is much more compelling than their sense of the future.

Suicidal thoughts

Robert Roth, M.F.C.C., coordinator of adolescent services at Montgomery General Hospital in Olney, Maryland, says that teens with suicidal thoughts may reveal them indirectly. He identifies clues to their state of mind as including expressions of hopelessness, helplessness, agitation, and apathy, along with mood swings, chronic tardiness, dramatic declines in academic performance, and anhedonia, the inability to experience any pleasure at all.

When teens exhibit multiple suicidal symptoms, and when these symptoms are several days in duration, the teens need concerted intervention and professional help. The Julie Gordon-Sullivan Foundation "Parenting Teens" website recommends parents be observant and note if their teens exhibit the following signs of suicidal thinking.

Divesting themselves of meaningful possessions: The giving away of prized possessions to friends or siblings with the explanation that the teen "isn't going to need them any more."

Change in sleep patterns: Significant changes in teens' normal sleeping patterns, either sleeping all the time or very little, or confessing they're tired in the morning because they were up all night "thinking."

Changes in friends or activities: Formerly busy, outgoing teens closet themselves alone in their bedrooms. Longtime friends no longer calling or stopping by the house could indicate that teens have turned down too many invitations to join friends for them to bother anymore.

Groundless anger or fear: Even-tempered and level-headed teens blowing up at the slightest, or no, discernable provocation, or being frightened of situations not fraught with reasonable threat or danger.

Changes in appetite: Teens known for hearty appetites suddenly stop eating, or those with bird-sized appetites suddenly devour everything in sight.

Physical complaints or chronic fatigue: Frequent, nonspecific physical ailments, such as headaches or stomachaches, or a curtailment of activities due to apparently unwarranted exhaustion.

Self-abusive behavior: The deliberate hurting of one's self by cutting, burning, or mutilating.

Preoccupation with death: Making statements like, "I wish I were dead," or, "You'll be sorry when I'm not around anymore."

Overwhelming sense of guilt or shame: Appearing to carry the weight of the world on their shoulders, or harboring some dark secret.

Despair: Repeated comments such as, "I'd be better off dead," or, "Things will never get any better."

Previous suicide attempts: Teens attempting suicide in the past are at greater risk than others of attempting it again.

Teens responding to a suicidal peer

Taking into consideration that a teen's peers are often the first to be aware of suicidal behavior, and that practically no suicidal teens really want to die, friends are in a unique position to intervene. Most teens, however, don't know the appropriate response to a friend who speaks of suicide. They wonder if they should ignore the threat or assume it's a ploy for attention. Many withdraw from the suicidal teen in shock. Parents can help by teaching their teens the signs that a friend may be headed for trouble and outlining their responsibilities as friends before a serious situation occurs.

Teens should be taught never to ignore a friend's suicidal expressions. While a teen's suicide threat may well be an attempt to get attention, such a drastic ploy is indicative of internal pain or disturbance and should be considered a legitimate cry for help. To ignore a suicide threat, or withdraw from the friend making it, is to further reinforce a troubled teen's feelings of unworthiness by clearly demonstrating that no one cares enough about him to help.

Unfortunately, at the time suicidal teens are most in need of help, they may be treated as pariahs by peers who are unable to cope with their naked pain and don't know what to do. Some parents, in an effort to protect their healthy children, may instruct them to avoid a peer who is depressed or suicidal.

A teen confiding suicidal feelings to a friend often prefaces the confession with a demand for secrecy— "You've got to swear you won't tell anyone." Our teens must be made to understand that such a promise is the one promise that must be broken, no matter what. Teens must tell someone, preferably an adult, but perhaps even another teen whose instincts and resourcefulness they trust, advises Bob Condit, M.Ed, independent consultant and former guidance counselor at the Landon School in Bethesda, Maryland. One cannot sit on this kind of information—the life of a friend may well depend upon sharing it.

Parents

The most powerful warriors in the battle against teen suicide are often, sadly, the ones most unaware of their teens' depression and suicidal thinking—parents. While many parents feel they know their children intimately, the onset of puberty brings about major changes, not the least of which is the hormonal turmoil coincident with a steady increase in the possibility of psychiatric disorders. It is, therefore, not surprising that the suicide rate for this age group takes a significant jump at the beginning of puberty.

Impressionable, vulnerable teens can be influenced by others' suicidal behavior, so parents would do well to take advantage of media reports of suicide to broach the subject with their children, both to sound them out and to teach them what to do should they discover one of their friends is suicidal. Describe depression and its symptoms, pointing out that there are degrees of the illness, and while all need to be treated, depression is not synonymous with suicidal behavior. Ensure that teens understand the importance of their role in recognizing and taking seriously their friends' feeling of hopelessness. Teens are the early warning system that can save lives.

Acknowledge the difficulty of ratting out a friend after being sworn to secrecy, and walk your teens through the ethical process of weighing the relative value of keeping a promise and saving a life. When discussing a suicide, express sadness that no one close to the victim tried, or was able, to take the necessary steps to intervene.

Preventing suicide

Jobes, among many other professionals, believes that problem solving, skill building, and coping-oriented psychotherapies are the essential components in decreasing teens' hopelessness and suicidal thinking and behavior. While he feels family therapy is a potentially strong defense against suicidal behavior in young people, he ardently believes the essential and most effective defense for teens at risk is strong clinical relationships with psychotherapists. Unfortunately, many health insurance companies and groups provide insufficient coverage for psychotherapy, hospitalization, or therapeutic residential centers, and too few professionals are receiving clinical training in the assessment and treatment of suicide risk. Parents of suicidal teens, therefore, must commit to doing whatever it takes to find and pay for treatment to save their children.

Obviously, the most effective method of suicide prevention is early identification and treatment. Ann Howard, Ph.D., consulting psychologist at St. Andrew's Episcopal School in Potomac, Maryland, notes, however, that since "only one-third of depressed kids are ever diagnosed or treated, it is tragic, but not surprising, that some go on to commit suicide." Howard believes suicide is the result of a long chain of events that begins with depression or other mental disorders. The difficulty with many school-based information-only prevention programs that focus solely on suicide is that they may actually increase vulnerable young people's distress. She feels that education about depression is more effective in preventing suicide.

Effective educational programs about depression should be aimed at children, their parents, and teachers and should clearly and objectively teach that depression is a treatable illness rather than a failure of will on the part of the sufferer. This would help lessen the stigma surrounding depression and encourage depressed adolescents to seek help. Parents, teachers, and friends also need to know the facts and symptoms so that they will be able to recognize and get help for depressed teens. Without help, adds Howard, the suffering can escalate quickly to unbearable levels, and that's when young people may make the decision to end their lives.

Medication

Because depressive illness is often biochemical in nature, prescriptive medications are frequently recommended, in combination with therapy, by mental health professionals. The purpose of the medications is not to cure the depression, but to elevate the suicidal teen's affect to a level where mental health counseling can be most effective. Jobes notes that although the depression often preceding suicidal talk or behavior is frequently reduced through the use of medication, no one medication or combination of medications alone should be considered effective against suicidal thinking.

Teens, more than any other age group, are extremely reluctant to take antidepressants, despite the painfulness of their symptoms or the advice of parents and therapists. There are several reasons for this attitude. Teens mistakenly believe they have to tough it out and that taking medication indicates weakness on their part. They also fear medication will alter their minds in a negative manner, causing them to cede control over their conscious selves.

Moreover, by the time teens begin medication, their symptoms may be so acute that they feel the need for, and expect, immediate relief. Unfortunately, the current crop of effective antidepressants may require as much as two weeks or longer before significant effects are apparent, and a trial period of as long as six weeks may be necessary before benefits can be accurately assessed. Once an effective drug with minimal side effects has been decided upon, there is often a period of fine-tuning the dosage, a process teens may find exasperating and discouraging.

Survivors

For the families and friends of someone close who has committed or attempted to commit suicide, survival is fraught with confusion, questions, and a particular kind of lingering grief. Consulting "Grieving: Death, Disability, Divorce, and Disappointment," on page 201 or visiting the websites listed under the heading Suicide in the resource section at the back of the book may provide some guidance and comfort.

Final thoughts

Prevention is essential. We must all understand the risk factors of suicide, know what to do, and be prepared to act quickly. Too many teens view suicide as the only solution to their problems. If your teen appears to be one of these, the good news is that, with your suport and with professional assistance, he or she can find healing and achieve a healthier emotional life.

6 troubles

| 28 |

Out-of-Sync Teens

It is easy to be proud of the child who meets our dreams and expectations, who excels academically, is a star athlete, a gifted musician, a budding actor, or a well-loved volunteer. We feel fortunate when our child has well defined interests and is willing to take our guidance, and feel blessed when our teen willingly spends time with us. But what of a child, who, in spite of our love, seems to be heading towards chaos, turbulence, or turmoil?

KAREN GUBERMAN, Washington, D.C. parent of three

Even the ideal child will encounter rough patches growing up. All children have periods when they struggle to define themselves, suffer from periods of self-doubt, and lash out at parental efforts to help. Some children have experienced difficult periods since early childhood and, as they get into their teens, these rough times can be more wrenching and serious because the consequences can be much more damaging. When our children are out of sync, when their behavior becomes extreme, they need our love and acceptance the most. When our child is at his or her most difficult, and we see the potential for danger, we must find help for ourselves, as well as our teen. The moody, anxious, oppositional, secretive, despondent, explosive, or constantly angry child, or the one who seems unable to regulate or take charge of himself, affects every member of the family.

A challenging child

Out-of-sync teens are a challenge to manage. They may be the ones who cannot organize their lives, or are too intense, or too unique.

They may appear to have no friends, no one to hang out with. They may seem vaguely unhappy or are only happy doing very specific things. They may be good kids who can't, or won't, do well in school. Their parents feel as if they are just chronically out of sync or are avoiding being a teenager. Perhaps they have a style altogether different from what their parents understand. They are troubling. They are difficult to understand and their difficulties are hard to explain. They keep parents awake at night.

The challenge of unconditionally accepting a child's differences can begin at birth. A child can be born with a temperament or personality that is either dramatically different from the parent's own or exactly the same. Or the differences may emerge as the child grows up. It may be difficult for an outgoing and gregarious parent to understand an introverted and cautious child. The child who is physically immature or less physically coordinated may be a challenge or a disappointment to the parent who excelled in sports and sees physical prowess as an important personal attribute. Some children have difficulties with new routines, new foods, or new people and situations. This may be alarming to parents who easily accept and anticipate novel experiences.

Differences in temperament are not the only possible factors to consider when trying to understand and respond to a child who seems out of sync with the world, or at least his family. Sometimes a child is attention-deficit hyperactive disordered (ADHD), exhibits neurological or emotional symptoms, or evidences some other kind of problem.

Many education and health professionals, as well as some parents, are finding that a condition called sensory integration dysfunction (SID) helps to explain at least some children's difficulties. If a child's response to visual or auditory stimulus and physically painful situations is either overly sensitive or underresponsive, or if he feels pain when others would be only vaguely annoyed, is irritable in close quarters and moves away from groups of people, is unusually irritable with clothing seams and tags, is a very picky eater, is overtly distressed by certain smells, or is excessively reactive to transitions, that child may be suffering from SID. This condition can lead to social and behavior problems, according to Lynn Balzer-Martin, Ph.D., pediatric occupational therapist in Chevy Chase, Maryland. She reports that children with SID don't ever know what it's like to feel completely okay; they always feel at the mercy of sensations.

Normal versus crisis

It is not always easy to determine if a teen's behavior and attitude are within normal limits or if there is reason to be alarmed. Parents are forced to reexamine their priorities when their teen starts making choices that push the limits of parental tolerance and understanding. Parents may be tolerant of their teens' body piercings, tattoos, and outré hair color or cut. However, for some teens, those same cosmetic choices may well be evidence of an inner turmoil that should be taken seriously. The teens who begin to fail at school, cut themselves, vomit after meals, disappear overnight, or refuse to talk with family members should always be viewed as in crisis. No single particular parental response is necessarily the right, or best, one. The "rightness" of a parental response may depend upon the parents themselves, what they and their child are willing or able to accept, the nature of their relationship, a good bit of luck, and the luxury of time.

Distinguishing normal teenage behavior—with its usual complement of some defiance, some isolation, some lack of communication, and some argument—from that of a teen in turmoil is not an exact science. "Often parents, as well as professionals, confuse one or more symptoms for the problem," says Carol Maxym, Ph.D., psychologist, educational consultant to the PBS website "Inside the Teenage Brain," and co-author of *Teens in Turmoil: A Path to Change for Parents, Adolescents, and their Families*. She further explains, "For example, parents can blame drugs for their teen's problems without recognizing that drugs are a symptom of an underlying problem. Similarly, parents will blame a new set of friends for leading their teen into bad directions rather than recognizing that their own child is choosing those friends because they are doing and saying what appeals to the teen."

Maxym believes the best way for parents to determine if a teen may be heading toward chaos, turbulence, or turmoil is to follow their gut feelings. She provides the following checklist for parents to assess their feelings about their teen's behavior, saying your teen might be heading for greater problems if:

- you have a feeling you no longer know who your teen is,
- you find fault with your teen's friends, but you excuse your teen,
- you've begun to accept language, standards, attitudes, and behaviors you don't like just because it's too difficult to try to maintain what you believe,
- most times, you decide it's just easier to do the chore yourself than to ask, remind, or nag your teen,
- sometimes you feel as though you have become the resident drill sergeant or nag,
- you often have a sort of scared, angry, or just stressed or depressed feeling when you ask your teen what ought to be a simple question,

- you're always second-guessing and questioning yourself—other parents don't seem to have the same problems as you do,
- you feel angry, hurt, embarrassed, hopeless, and sometimes even helpless in relation to your teen,
- you're worried that your teen may use drugs or alcohol,
- you don't trust your teen, or
- you don't trust him or her to keep him/herself safe.

Your responses to these questions will suggest whether professional help may be in order.

Help for your teen

Most parents faced with such a challenge need help—for their child, their family, and for themselves. Teens may respond to talk therapy or drug therapy, or may require an alternative environment. The best results almost always include all the adults in the child's life, if available, taking a central role in the process.

A few years ago, the U.S. Surgeon General estimated that one in ten American children and adolescents is in need of some kind of treatment for mental, emotional, or behavioral problems. In the Washington, D.C., area, we are fortunate to have many resources to help teens and their families, including therapists specializing in individual and group therapy, as well as those who focus on families. However, the availability of resources and the willingness of teens to utilize them are two different things. Teens are notoriously difficult to treat and often prefer the support of friends to professional counsel. Frequently, they would rather self-medicate than depend on legitimate, and legal, medications. Teens may participate in therapy initially only at the insistence of parents, rather than because they perceive any real need for help.

Finding a therapist with whom your teenager clicks emotionally is essential, and your persistence will be well worth the time and effort invested. Family therapy, individual therapy, group therapy, and parent counseling are all approaches to consider when treating adolescent issues and problems, says Washington, D.C., clinical psychologist Patricia Dalton, Ph.D. It is important initially that the problem is assessed thoroughly, and this may include a complete physical exam, psychological and educational evaluation, individual interviews with the teenager, family evaluation, and a school conference.

The press occasionally reports a dramatic increase in the use of psychotropic medications (prescription drugs that cause changes in behavior or functioning of the mind) for kids, creating provocative headlines and sound bites. Dalton fears that worried parents will refuse or resist the use of medications that could help their children live more normal lives. "My experience, and that of many other therapists, has been that psychotropic medications can be safe to prescribe and very effective in treating some problems in children and adolescents. This is especially true when there is a family history of mood or attentional problems." Most mental health experts agree with Dalton when she points out that untreated mental health and mood disorders in children have developmental ramifications that can last the rest of their lives. Early treatment is usually the most effective treatment. Many problems seen in adults are the result of developmental derailment during childhood.

Parents' perseverance in finding the services that best fit the needs of their families will pay off in the end. If traditional therapies fail, parents may benefit from working with an education consultant who specializes in finding alternatives for struggling teens. Sometimes a more dramatic change in environment may be called for, and educational consultants can be helpful in matching a teenager's individual needs with a particular program outside the home. This might include therapeutic wilderness programs, emotional growth schools, therapeutic boarding schools, as well as local day schools that may be more appropriate for your child. The Independent Educational Consultants Association (IECA) in Fairfax, Virginia, maintains a list of local members who work with families seeking such help for their teens.

Help for parents

Determining whether a child is in trouble and then finding appropriate help for him can be an arduous and draining experience for a parent. A parent may have completed many checklists about difficult child and adolescent behavior and, while their kid may have some of the characteristics of a troubled child, the tools fail to clarify the severity of the problem or whether professional help is indicated. Sometimes a child displays none of the characteristics of a troubled youth, but the parent continues to be concerned despite an inability to even describe the concern. Guberman warns that when a family seeks professional help and is given a diagnosis and recommendations, parents may nonetheless be overwhelmed by the many therapeutic choices and the uncertainty of outcomes. This may be the time for parents to seek individual help and support for themselves. An out-of-sync child can so deplete parents' emotional reserves that they overlook their own need for nurturing.

"A temperamentally difficult child may challenge parents to the point of exhaustion and diminish their confidence," observes Maryland psychologist and parenting consultant Kay Abrams, Ph.D. "Trust and respect may be further undermined as parents react to misbehavior with harsh threats or bribes as their primary means of control." Exhausted, angry parents often resort to reactive, punitive responses that exacerbate a negative, destructive cycle. Parents need to seek support, resources, and guidance for themselves in dealing with their out-of-sync child.

"A good way to help your adolescent through troubled times is to focus on yourself," echoes advice provided by the National Clearinghouse on Families and Youth website, which goes on to say, "By improving your ability to cope with your adolescent's changing behavior, you make it more likely that you will be able to help your child. Seeking help for yourself also shifts the focus away from your teen, who may feel exposed and vulnerable under the scrutiny of a range of outsiders. By getting help for yourself, you are modeling good coping skills and learning new tools for dealing with stress. Perhaps most importantly, you are reassuring your adolescent that the family works through its difficult times without blaming any one family member."

Final thoughts

"No parent would choose a contentious and troubled path for their child," says Susan Reimer, *Baltimore Sun* columnist and parent of two teens, "but that doesn't mean it can always be avoided. We can't trust child-rearing to fate, but we often suffer its vicissitudes."

Our children need our acceptance and love to become fully functioning adults. They need that connection even more when they are feeling or acting chaotic. Being there for them is an essential part of our parental involvement. If you feel you are retreating, giving up, if you feel humiliated, it is really, really time to get help.

Even if out-of-sync children have reached their tenth, or even fifteenth birthday, it's not too late for changes. Parents should never give up on their children—remain involved. Spend time with them; listen to them if they will talk. If not, just be there.

Tell your children you love them and tell them how they are special to you. Tell them you want them to be happy and to find their own way in the world. Tell them you need help to understand them and to be the best parent they can have. Find the professional help that your family needs. Remember, it takes courage to ask for help as well as wisdom to recognize the need for it.

29

Shoplifting and Stealing

Shoplifting is risky business! What happens when a juvenile is caught shoplifting? How does shoplifting affect the family and friends of the shoplifter? Does the school get involved? Can shoplifting lead to more serious crimes?

Shoplifting is not only the act of leaving a store with something you didn't pay for. Shoplifting also includes obtaining goods by charging them to a fictitious person, exchanging cheaper items for expensive ones and paying less, putting an item in a different package, or hiding the item from view in a variety of ways. Theft occurs in schools every day. Teenagers own and carry around so many items of value—calculators, watches, laptops, CD players, expensive clothes, and cash—that temptation abounds. Stealing is often done by teens from affluent families, and rarely is shoplifting or theft the result of real financial need.

Parental reaction

Theft by one's children can embarrass, frighten, or anger parents; some may feel guilty themselves. If the police are involved in the incident, parents can also feel humiliated. They are shocked that a child brought up in their household with their values would even think to steal.

It is very important that parents not respond by shouting at, accusing, or physically punishing a child when he or she is caught stealing. Doing so accomplishes nothing, while at the same time reducing the possibility of parents being able to transform the incident into a lasting learning experience. By the same token, a teen caught stealing must assume responsibility for his or her actions. Parents should make it clear they do not condone the behavior and will be watching the teen closely henceforth. Horror and embarrassment about the incident should never lead parents to coverup the affair. Parents can set new behavior guidelines and make it clear to the child that it will take his consistant adherence to the guidelines, as well as some time, before they can trust him to shop by himself again.

It's a crime

Shoplifting is a crime in all area jurisdictions and, like all crime in our communities, has ramifications well beyond the act of theft itself. Shoplifting affects the prices we all pay for merchandise because merchants recoup their losses and the expense of prosecution by factoring them into the overall cost of goods and services.

Local police say that individual merchants handle shoplifting cases as they see fit, and most merchants at the area's shopping malls report that they prosecute in virtually every case. Some stores have a zero-tolerance theft policy and prosecute even if payment is offered. Detection devices are numerous and sophisticated, and plainclothes security is plentiful. Small, family-owned stores in the area have given way to large chain stores with the money, time, and staff to pursue prosecutions. If the thief is a minor, the parents or legal guardian can be held responsible for any damages incurred. The total value of the stolen items determines whether the thief is charged with a misdemeanor or a felony.

It is usually store or mall security guards rather than the police who apprehend shoplifters. These guards are not always interested in the legal rights of the thief. Reports from around the country indicate that security guards do not always feel obligated to follow proper procedures when apprehending suspected shoplifters. Once turned over to the police, shoplifters are tried in juvenile court, and convictions carry sentences that include probation, community service, juvenile detention, or a combination of the three.

Shoplifting is an issue that calls for parental forethought, guidelines, and rules before it becomes a problem. Let your children know your feelings about stealing and other dishonest and unethical behavior. Talk to them about the consequences and ramifications of shoplifting. Make sure your children understand that a person in the company of a shoplifter may suffer the same penalties as the shoplifter. Psychologists recommend that if parents discover their child has stolen items, the teen should always make restitution, as well as receive an additional penalty such as losing a valued privilege.

Why do children steal?

Children steal for a host of reasons. The very young take things that excite interest. Older children may steal if they feel a sibling is favored by parents over themselves or to gain attention from, or express anger toward or get even with, their parents. Some kids steal to prove themselves to friends, while others do it in order to give their friends presents in a bid for popularity. There are a few kids who steal because they believe it's the only way they will ever obtain coveted items, while others are exhilarated by the rush of getting away with something forbidden.

Parents of shoplifters may feel afraid, outraged, disappointed, or embarrassed. They certainly feel their children have violated their trust. However, as difficult as it may be, parents cannot overlook even an isolated incident of shoplifting because stealing can be addictive. Each time a teenager gets away with it, he is more likely to do it again, warns Neil Bernstein, Ph.D., Washington, D.C., clinical psychologist and author of *How to Keep Your Teenager Out of Trouble and What to Do if You Can't*. If a teen's peers are involved, they may encourage him to take increasing risks.

Indications of stealing

If you suspect your teenager of stealing, area police suggest you watch carefully for the signs below.

- Store tags or package wrappings hidden in the trash.
- Possession of new clothing, jewelry, or other items that you didn't purchase, and your child couldn't afford.
- People reporting items missing from their homes when your child has been present.
- Donning uncharacteristically baggy clothing or an out-of-season jacket when setting out for the mall.
- Carrying an oversize, seemingly empty, purse or backpack when going shopping.
- Speaking admiringly of friends who "get away with stuff."
- Behaving in an uncharacteristically sneaky and secretive manner.
- Going on the offensive and accusing you, the parent, of blaming him or her for everything when confronted with your suspicions.

The more frequently you observe these signs and behaviors, the greater the likelihood your child is stealing, says Bernstein. If the evidence is strong, you must call the child on it.

Preventing and handling theft

Children who steal from their parents, whether it be money, clothing, or other items of value, are likely to steal from others or from a store. Theft within the family needs to be taken seriously. If a child steals repeatedly, professional treatment may be necessary. Sociologists report that children who have engaged in minor delinquencies as adolescents are at a much greater risk of committing serious crimes later in life than children who have not.

To prevent children from shoplifting or from progressing to more serious crimes, parents must give their children clear guidelines for what is unacceptable behavior. Stealing, even of small or inexpensive items, will not be tolerated. Make sure they understand the legal and social ramifications of shoplifting. Explain that a "special discounted price" from a friend working in a store is stealing unless the manager or owner sanctions the discount.

Parents should review with their kids their expectations for behavior while shopping or hanging out at the mall. Parents can review their kids' purchase receipts in the context of budgeting and practical shopping skills. They can teach their children how to save for desired purchases and help them learn to delay gratification.

Kids of all ages need to understand the concept of guilt by association, and that they may be blamed if someone with them or with their group misbehaves. Parents should brainstorm with their children about how to get help if a problem arises or if they inadvertently break merchandise. Don't forget working out what to do if a friend shoplifts and appropriate behavior if your teen is approached by a security guard for any reason.

Final thoughts

When a child gets into trouble, Bernstein says that parents should express their concern for the child, rather than their anger or criticism. This tack prevents the teen from immediately becoming defensive and blocking any opportunity for discussion. If the child repeats the offense, Bernstein recommends that parents "by all means express your frustration and disappointment." Parents can prepare for talking with their teen by reviewing the reasons outlined in this chapter on why children steal. During the exchange, parents can stress to their teen that they don't wish to take action without first obtaining his or her input. If your teen has stolen more than once, it may be advisable to seek professional advice.

| 30 |

Vandalism

A car moved slowly down the street. The mailboxes were planted close to the road, the houses set back on ample lawns. The teen behind the wheel slowed as the car approached a mailbox, and his passenger stretched out from the window and swung the baseball bat. Some mailboxes were impervious to attack, others sagged, or tumbled from their perches. Unbeknownst to the vandals, a ten-year-old boy on a bicycle was following at a safe distance. He dialed 911 on his cell phone and detailed events as they occurred. A patrol car met up with the vandals a few blocks farther on.

It's a popular conception that vandalism is just mischief and doesn't really harm anyone. This notion completely overlooks the anger, fear, frustration, and outrage of the people whose property is destroyed, nor does it take into account the cost of repair, cleanup, and replacement of vandalized property. A rival school's colors or name spray painted before or after a big game not only costs time and labor to cover up, but may also incite retaliation that can result in further property destruction and even physical injuries.

Another common misconception is that teens who destroy property are usually from broken or deprived homes. The reality is that many vandals are from affluent, even socially prominent, families.

Vandalism is an act committed by any person who willfully and maliciously destroys, injures, disfigures, or defaces any public or private, real or personal property of another. Common vandalism includes the destruction of public property in parks, playgrounds, schools, and cemeteries or personal property like mailboxes, flowerbeds, lawn ornaments, and vehicles.

Why they do it

Fitting in and being accepted by one's peer group is of overriding importance to middle and high school students and they may often engage in risky behavior to gain acceptance. Vandalism generally isn't a solo act, it seems to require an audience of fellow vandals.

Neil Bernstein, Ph.D., Washington, D.C., clinical psychologist and author of *How to Keep Your Teenager Out of Trouble*, says some teens may participate in an act of vandalism once, never intending any real harm, feel awful when things get out of hand, and never do it again. They learn an important lesson from their lack of judgment.

Most vandals, however, are young people, work in groups, and damage property out of boredom, anger, revenge, or general defiance of authority. Some may wish to draw attention to a cause, their school, or a particular group. "Some kids trash houses just for the fun of it, because they're angry and want to destroy something," says Rosalind Wiseman, author of *Queen Bees & Wannabees:Helping Your Daughter Survive Cliques, Gossip, Boyfriends & Other Realities of Adolescence* and consultant to area public and private schools. Homes around the Beltway are regularly trashed by teens at unsupervised parties, sometimes under the influence of alcohol, but often just for the thrill of destruction.

Some teens consider vandalism a form of self-expression. A few justify it as a better way to vent anger than harming another person, while still others are malicious and vindictive, their actions premeditated acts of revenge. The most worrisome vandals are those who believe it's exciting to flirt with danger, and Bernstein says these teens are often very troubled and need professional help.

Real damage

Vandalism can have severe consequences. Raw egg on aluminum siding or cars can permanently damage the siding and ruin the paint. A cherry bomb placed in a mailbox as a prank can seriously injure or even kill an unsuspecting passerby. Shattered windshields are expensive and time-consuming to replace. Schools pay out millions of dollars each year to paint over graffiti, repair buildings, and replace vandalized equipment. The cost of vandalism often translates into less money for new books, computers, athletic equipment, and student activities and can be a factor in independent school tuition increases.

Vandalism is a crime!

The penalties for a vandalism conviction are significant. In Virginia, a juvenile convicted of vandalism is required to make at least partial restitution or reparation for property damage, loss caused by the offense, or medical expenses incurred by the victim. Maryland law states that if a juvenile is found guilty of damaging another person or their property, the juvenile court may order the child, or his or her parents, to pay the injured party a prescribed amount as repayment. If convicted, a juvenile's parents can be held responsible, along with their child, for restitution of damages up to $10,000. A young vandal from either Maryland or Virginia may also be required to participate in a court-ordered community service project.

A subset of vandalism is hate crime, which is defined as a criminal act directed against persons because of their race, color, national origin, ethnic background, religion, gender, age, marital status, socioeconomic status, sexual orientation, physical characteristics, or disability. Vandalism to a house of worship, assault on an individual, or the bombing of a building may each be considered a hate crime.

If your child vandalizes

If your child is involved with an incident of vandalism, Bernstein recommends that parents' first step is to determine if alcohol or drugs were involved. Many acts of vandalism are committed while under the influence, predisposing a young person to impaired judgment and reckless behavior. If this is the case, parents must be prepared to deal with a drinking or drug problem.

The next step is to determine if the teen is easily influenced or manipulated by his peers or is unable to refuse them. Parents can help a teen learn to remove himself gracefully from potentially compromising situations with friends as an alternative to banning contact with those same friends.

Finally, Bernstein recommends that parents determine if their teenager has an ax to grind. Does the child feel his actions are justified? Does he feel wronged? Is he inflexible in his view of the event? "If a teen's vandalism is specifically directed, you must make him deal directly with the injured party and understand there are better ways to express his anger."

A teenager who commits destructive acts must experience constructive consequences. If a child's destruction is not reported to the police, perhaps because the target was his parent's property, parents must devise a consequence that will serve as a significant learning experience. If he has been suspended from school, his time at home should be constructive and productive—studying, cleaning, raking, making repairs—rather than a form of holiday. Parents should try to help the teen empathize with the victim and try to view the vandalism from the victim's perspective, asking questions like, "How would you feel if someone spray painted your bike, or threw a rock at our car?"

A teen involved in multiple destructive acts can't be trusted to use good judgment or impulse control, and parents may need to address negative peer pressure. This is also the time to seek counseling for the teen and the family.

Preventing vandalism

In addition to teaching a child vandalism is wrong, it is also important for parents to teach him a respect for property in general, both his and that of others. Baltimore City Police suggest these ideas for parents:

- teach children refusal skills, as an adolescent's ability to say no is the simplest way to prevent his involvement in vandalism,
- never give the impression you condone any form of vandalism,
- know where, and with whom, your children are and what they're doing,
- help your children understand their anger and appropriate expressions of it,
- use media reports of vandalism as the impetus for discussions of the reasons for and consequences of such acts,
- educate your children about the costs and penalties of vandalism,
- keep a watch out for evidence of vandalism—spray paint, large quantities of eggs or toilet paper, paint stained clothing or hands,
- protect your house or apartment with good lighting and locks on gates and garages, and
- do not leave your teenagers home alone overnight—especially on a weekend.

Final thoughts

One of the goals of parenting is to raise confident, self-sufficient people who make good decisions. We, as parents, teach our kids to make those good decisions by communicating with them, establishing rules and consequences, teaching them refusal skills, and modeling responsible behavior. Don't forget that the primary reason teens give for not participating in unlawful acts is not wanting to disappoint their parents. We are the most powerful and persuasive forces in our adolescents' lives. Part of our job is to know our children and to take appropriate action before there is trouble. We have more at risk from vandalism than mere property.

| 31 |

Harassment and Bullying

Picked on, teased, and threatened so much in the ninth grade that she filed a harassment suit and transfered high schools, Erika Harold, Miss America 2003, is now an advocate for youth violence prevention. "I want people to know that if Miss America can be bullied, then it can happen to anyone."

The results of the first national study exploring the phenomenon of bullying suggests that thirty percent of the nearly 16,000 students in grades six through ten interviewed admitted to either bullying others, being the target of bullies, or both. More than eighty percent of kids polled in a recent study sponsored by Centers for Disease Control and Prevention report they have bullied classmates in one way or another. The National Education Association estimates that 160,000 children miss school every day due to fear of attack or intimidation by other students.

Inaction and neglect

A National Mental Health Association study reports that more than three-quarters of teenagers witness the teasing or bullying of class-mates who are gay or thought to be gay. Nearly seventy-eight percent of these teens expressed disapproval of the maltreatment, but only five percent said they try to defend peers who are targets. Most teens fail to intervene, or do so only to prevent bodily harm. Dorothy Espelage, M.A., professor of educational psychology at the University of Illinois, has conducted studies which indicate that bullying, at least in middle school, may be a group activity in which the role of bystanders is to reinforce the bully's actions by declining to intervene. Doing nothing implies approval.

It is sometimes difficult to believe our own communities and schools can be hotbeds of bullying, but the impetus is there in all groups, regardless of socioeconomic level, notes Rosalind Wiseman, author of *Queen Bees & Wannabees: Helping Your Daughter Survive Cliques, Gossip, Boyfriends & Other Realities of Adolescence*, consultant to local public and private schools, and founder and president of the Empower Program, a Washington, D.C.-based, nationally recognized project created to empower youth to end the culture of violence. Our children's safety at school is not determined by the school's neighborhood, tuition, or backgrounds of the student body, but by the ability of the adults—teachers, administrators, and parents—to work together to teach students accountability for unethical behavior in a compassionate but thought-provoking and firm manner.

As parents, we cannot simply automatically deny that our own children may be bullies. Wiseman counsels, "Your child will do things you aren't proud of. It's not a reflection of bad parenting if your child is mean, unless you fail to do something about it." Should you find yourself saying, "I know my kid and he would never do anything like that," stop and seriously listen to what a reporting teacher or other parent is saying.

Popularity

Harassment and bullying are an integral part of the evolving social lives of pre-adolescents and adolescents who are learning to find their place in society, trying to be popular, and seeking acceptance by the in-crowd. Wiseman observes that the rigid structure of the adolescent social hierarchy, coupled with a young person's almost relentless need to find a niche for himself in the greater world beyond his family, can result in meanness, violence, and victimization. Teasing and bullying create a culture of "hurtfulness and hostility, one in which it is more important to fit in than to care or understand," warns William Pollack, Ph.D., clinical professor of psychology at Harvard Medical School and author of many books, including *Real Boys: Rescuing Our Sons from the Myths of Boyhood* and *Real Boys' Voices*.

Popularity, especially in middle school, is about how many people like you or fear you. Boys attain high social status based on evidence of their masculinity. Girls' popularity is tied to their feminine qualities, including appearance and style. In order to fit in, teens abide by a caste system that ranks boys and girls according to individual differences, and adolescent standards can be very harsh. The teen considered too plain, quiet, nonathletic—too anything—might fail to meet the current group standards and be targeted for harassment or bullying. Many teens sacrifice their personal authenticity and values in their efforts to move closer to their group's center of power.

Cliques and bullies have always existed, making life miserable for children who are different, less outgoing, or socially insecure, especially during middle school. Being excluded, teased, threatened, or called names—especially in front of others—erodes any child's self-confidence and can be especially damaging if the child is sensitive or insecure. Social rejection can seriously interfere with a child's education because he focuses on his fears rather than his studies.

The cost of harassment

Harassment at school and in related social situations can cause serious harm to targeted students. Students report that they sometimes stay home from school or don't want to participate as much in class after experiencing harassment, and their grades may take a nosedive.

Harassment can also lead to psychological injury not unlike that suffered by victims of sexual assault. One targeted local boy described days when he would eat his lunch in a bathroom stall to avoid harassment from his male peers. Harassment victims feel afraid, have lowered self-esteem, experience more stress, have a higher rate of eating disorders, and are at heightened risk of depression and suicide. Sexually harassing behaviors hurt a student's ability to benefit fully from educational opportunities, to experience a comfortable social life, and to enjoy a healthy school environment.

Deborah Roffman, M.S., nationally recognized human sexuality educator and author of *Sex & Sensibility: The Thinking Parent's Guide to Talking Sense About Sex*, recently surveyed hundreds of her students in Washington, D.C., and Baltimore, Maryland, and found that nearly every one of the girls aged thirteen to seventeen, and some of the boys in the same age bracket, had been the subject of some form of sexual harassment. In *Sex & Sensibility* she writes, "It was clear that for young girls growing into womanhood in our culture, being the target of sexual harassment is every bit as much a rite of passage as getting their first periods or buying their first brassieres."

Bullying

Sexual harassment is only one type of bullying, which can be defined as one person using his or her power and privilege over another. Bullying ranges from simple name-calling to threats of, or actual, physical harm. Bullying can involve a slur against another's race, ethnicity, sexual orientation, religion, economic class, or physical appearance. The subject of bullying has received much attention recently following a number of highly publicized incidents of student revenge shootings. Some of the perpetrators were described as boys who lashed out after having been regularly taunted, snubbed, or harassed by classmates. Bullied children can suffer lasting scars, and there are even some who are drawn to suicide as a way to end their misery.

Wiseman observes, "In my work with schools, the majority of conflicts that result in kids leaving schools and parents feeling marginalized involve bullying." Bullying is not new, of course, and we all have experienced or witnessed it. We know that contemporary middle and high school teens, both boys and girls, can wield enormous power over their peers. What is new, however, is the attention focused on girls bullying girls and how that interferes with the targeted girls' academic achievement, as well as how the experience can haunt its victims for the rest of their lives.

When school is a nightmare

Young people frequently encounter harassing conduct at school, although many would not label it as such and are seemingly unaware that suffering its effects is both unnecessary and self-defeating. Bullying or harassment can take only a few seconds and much of it is verbal. Clever harassers and bullies act surreptitiously, and most of the time adults aren't aware the harassment is taking place. Sadly, some teens report that the verbal and physical attacks of their peers hurt them less than their teachers' refusal to intervene. One persistently harassed teen is reported to have said, "If high school is a nightmare, your life pretty much is, too."

School is one place where our kids should feel safe. Some teachers—and parents—are unable or unwilling to intervene in a harassment situation. Wiseman suggests this could be the result of an individual teacher's own experiences as an adolescent. An adult who was bullied as a teen may still feel intimated by the young bullies in his or her classroom. Likewise, a teacher who was a bully as a child may fail to appreciate the potential danger and damage bullying poses to his students. Other teachers may have a good sense of what is going on but have no idea how to respond. David Shapiro, M.A., head of the Edmund Burke School in Washington, D.C., says the most important thing is for schools to "make clear, both in writing and in all the kinds of day-to-day practices that really count, that this is a safe, accepting, and inclusive environment."

Programs have been initiated across the country to change school cultures so that students and teachers no longer accept bullying. Information collected for an *Education Week* report shows that thirty-three states now either require or recommend that school districts implement antibullying programs. Some districts may only hang posters displaying the message that bullying is unacceptable, while others design and implement extensive training programs for students and staff. Schools addressing the bullying issue on a case-by-case basis have adopted an ineffective strategy, because it is the school's culture and its rules of social interaction that must be transformed, reports James Garbarino, Ph.D., co-author of *And Words Can Hurt Forever: How to Protect Adolescents from Bullying, Harassment, and Emotional Violence.* Garbarino notes that schools most effective in curtailing bullying have clearly written policies or guidelines that are understood by the entire community and are consistently followed. It is in these schools that most kids will feel protected by adults.

Power and control

Sexual harassment is most accurately defined as unwanted and repeated assertions of power by one individual, or group of individuals, over another. Experts concur that sexual harassment, like rape and childhood abuse, is not primarily motivated by sexual feelings; rather it is an exercise of power and control—an attempt to make the recipient feel uncomfortable and inferior. Too often, however, it's dismissed as harmless flirting.

Young people need to learn how to tell the difference between harassment and flirting. One key is whether the behavior is wanted or unwanted. The recipient of flirting usually feels good about the encounter, finds it flattering, and feels a positive sense of self-esteem. Harassment, on the other hand, feels demeaning and one-sided and can impart feelings of low self-esteem. A person on the receiving end of flirting feels in control; a sexually harassed person does not.

Signs of being bullied

To stop bullying and harassment, we must be able to recognize it. To avoid feelings of shame and embarrassment, a child may actively try to hide the mistreatment. Pollack says bullied teenagers may:

- stop talking about school, a particular class, or school activity,
- try to go to school late each day, by alternate route or transportation, or miss school entirely,
- make radical changes in friends,
- begin to act like bullies themselves, often by teasing or physically taunting younger siblings or children, and
- may appear irritable, socially isolated, sullen, moody, aggravated, and depressed.

Boys and girls as bullies

The weapons wielded by bullying girls—exclusion, gossip, name-calling, rumor mongering—do not result in bloody lips or black eyes. Rachel Simmons, author of *Odd Girl Out: The Hidden Culture of Aggression in Girls*, describes girls' aggression as frequently being covert, consisting of the silent treatment, glaring, rigid fashion guidelines, death stares, note-passing, and being nice to a peer in private and humiliating her in public. Simmons, who grew up in the Maryland suburbs, blames this type of bullying on the cultural restraints imposed on girls, which prevent them from healthy venting of feelings of competition, jealousy, and anger.

Recently, the subtler bullying by "mean" girls has received a lot of press. As parents, we want our daughters to be assertive, and even adaptive or aggressive when necessary; however, the last thing we want is for them to be mean or bullying. Kay Abrams, Ph.D., parenting consultant and Maryland psychologist, warns us not to think in dichotomous terms, pitting "good" girls or boys against "bad" girls or boys, when speaking of nice versus mean behavior. The key, she says, is not to shame girls for being aggressive or controlling, but to channel their energy into socially appropriate avenues.

Boys' bullying, on the other hand, frequently appears to be motivated by homophobia, the fear that some straight people have that others might think they are gay. Boys exert power and control over other boys by policing each other constantly with slurs like, "That's so gay," or, "Sissy," observes Michael Kimmel, Ph.D., professor of sociology at SUNY, Stony Brook and author of *Manhood in America: A Cultural History* and other books on men and masculinity. Roffman says that boys target other boys in supposedly friendly horseplay or as part of institutionalized hazing rituals that can become vicious and even violent. The school lives of boys who seem effeminate or weak, or are even considered gay, can be miserable; as one teen attending a suburban boys' school says, "I would fear for the safety of anyone who was openly gay here."

Pollack warns parents that the "painful set of relentless practices sanctioned by the boy culture, and laughed off by many well-meaning parents and teachers, is not a minor predicament worrying a small subset of boys, but is a constant and widespread problem that is insidiously eating away at the quality of life of so many of America's boys." He describes male bullies as being more than aggressive, suggesting they are most often depressed and are more likely to be sad and lonely rather than bad kids.

Pollock believes the "boy code" perpetuates a terrible injustice. Afraid of appearing less than fully masculine, he says boys often defend themselves by taunting others with hurtful terms. "Many of them don't have an adult to connect to, or the adult in their lives has a skewed view. Like most aggressive boys, bullies are probably fighting their own feelings of sadness, inferiority, or inadequacy." While this must be stopped and the boys made to understand that their behavior is unacceptable, parents and other adults who interact with them need to recognize the pain behind bullies' actions.

Wiseman believes boys who are silent witnesses to the harassment of another are not condoning the behavior so much as they don't know what to say or do. Many fear their own masculinity will be called into question should they intervene. Elinor Scully, M.Ed., upper school associate director at St. Stephen's and St. Agnes School in Alexandria, Virginia, says other boys participate in order to affirm "their heterosexual masculine identity." Their audience is their male peer group. She describes much of the meanness as pack behavior and emphasizes that most of the teens participating are not individually mean kids.

Some bullies target boys and girls from minority groups or other socioeconomic classes. While most area independent schools report they don't believe there is a racial problem at their school, the use of racially and ethnically charged epithets and language does occasionally become part of joking or casual conversation. Even more insidious is the nontargeted use of such language, whether in private or in front of others, to demean or to embarrass. A senior attending the Washington International School reports that he has overheard racist comments about Arab teammates when his team played other independent schools. He cautions school principals to be more aware. Coaches should be more aware, as well.

Intimidation and physical violence are on the extreme edge of the bullying continuum. Hazing activities for clubs and athletic teams often fall into this category. Because victims typically are shamed into silence, the bullies often go unpunished. It is critical that schools and parents take bullying seriously and create a climate in which it simply is not tolerated, in which victims can report it and be confident it will be stopped.

Bullied becomes bully

Surprisingly, sometimes a person can be both bully and victim. Espelage's research, reported in *Education Week*, defines bully-victims as those who are less skilled and more depressed and anxious than the hard-core bullies who often are the more popular and athletic teens.

Many bullies were emotionally or physically abused at home or pushed around or humiliated by stronger kids or adults as they were growing up. In one case, an adolescent bully described to Bob Condit,

M.Ed., independent consultant and former counselor at the Landon School in Bethesda, Maryland, how he had been taunted for being dumb throughout lower school. "Kids laughed when I answered questions wrong in class and made fun of me when I got the lowest grade on a test," he tearfully explained. "So, when I got to eighth grade and had grown to be one of the biggest guys in class, I realized I didn't have to take it anymore and decided to get even." The boy described how good it felt to be finally able to retaliate against the boys who were the source of his feelings of humiliation. "It made me feel so good that I started to push around other kids who had nothing to do with making me feel bad as a kid."

Pollack observes that bullies are often depressed—sometimes, they are the most depressed boys in school. While they shouldn't be forgiven for their actions, we need to realize that they are in a lot of pain and that making others feel bad has become their way of feeling better.

Your child, the bully

Parents of bullies, or of children who are members of exclusionary cliques, often don't realize there is a problem since their children don't demonstrate bullying behavior in their presence. Parents need to question whether attitudes and behaviors that praise children for being tough or insist that they be superior to, or stronger or smarter than peers, might, in fact, encourage inappropriate aggression in their children. If your child persistently bullies or excludes others, it is indicative of a serious social interaction deficiency and an inability to think through behavior options. Without intervention and guidance, bullies may have long-term difficulties succeeding socially.

Although it is often difficult to empathize with a bully, Pollack counsels parents to try to understand the emotional root of the behavior rather than approaching it punitively. He cautions that castigation on the part of a bully's parents results in his feeling even more despondent and isolated, pushing him toward further rebellion. Parents must communicate zero tolerance for violence simultaneously with love and caring for their child in order to help him find better coping strategies for angst and disappointment.

If you realize your teen is, or is perceived to be, a bully, the website *BullyBeware.com* recommends that you listen to your child's rationale for the bullying behavior and try to understand his or her reasoning. This is the opportune time to provide alternative solutions. It is essential that parents make their disapproval of their children's bullying clear—they must never condone abusive behavior or dismiss it as normal. If appropriate, parents may communicate their willingness to be part of a solution to the school or to the family of the bullied child.

If your child is accused of harassment, it is important to help him empathize and identify with the victim, understand the impact of his actions, admit his inappropriate behavior, and agree to change. Should the problem persist, professional help should be sought to help you and your child understand his angry, cruel behavior before it leads to more destructive actions.

Your child, the victim

Parents frequently do not realize their children are being bullied and, when they do become aware, often find that preteens and teens don't want them to take action for fear of either retaliation or escalation of the harassment. Pollack advises parents to be sensitive to the shame that teased or bullied teens may feel. He says not to become hysterical or retaliatory in your response, just firmly and calmly show your resolve to help find a solution. Pollack recommends parents discuss ways of resolving the situation with their children, confirm that bullying is a widespread problem, and reassure them they are no longer alone with the problem.

When your child finally tells you he is being bullied, Wiseman recommends you don't say, "They're just jealous," or, "They'll move on to someone else." The first thing a parent should do is to express sympathy for their child's plight and say something to the effect of, "I'm so sorry this is happening to you. I'll be with you all the way." Whether the harassment warrants a confrontation with the bully or is persistent or outrageous enough to warrant the attention of school staff, help your child strategize. Teach him the skills necessary to stand up for himself. Wiseman confirms that many bullying types avoid bothering people who have stood up to them—they only feel powerful if they're harassing someone they perceive as weaker than themselves. Other experts recommend such nonviolent self-defense strategies as looking the bully directly in the eyes and saying, "If you do not stop, I will tell the teacher," and then walking away.

If your child wants to confront the bully, strategize about the best, and safest, location for such a confrontation to occur. Wiseman recommends a neutral territory where your teen can avoid creating a drama. This is especially important when the action is between girls who may have been friends. Parents can role-play with their daughter to help her effectively state her complaints and request what she wants. She may choose either to salvage and maintain the friendship, or to make it clear she rejects it.

Teach your child that responding in kind makes the problem worse. Talk with him about the power of ignoring negative behavior when he is targeted and the situation is not dangerous. Make sure your child has opportunities for expressing anger. Offer him the opportunity to enroll in a self-defense class. Sometimes feeling more in control, evidencing a more confident walk and posture, and developing better eye contact, help bolster a teen's sense of self.

Recognizing, avoiding, and confronting bullies

The first step parents can take to minimize their children's exposure to harassment is to make sure their kids understand what harassment and bullying are. Linda Goldman, Ph.D., area grief and loss counselor and author of *Breaking the Silence: A Guide to Help Children with Complicated Grief—Suicide, Homicide, AIDS, Violence and Abuse*, offers parents the following definitions to use in speaking with their children.

- A bully is intentionally cruel to others much of the time.
- Bullies come in all sizes, from all socioeconomic groups and ethnicities, and in both genders.
- Bullies are lacking in confidence, picking on people they perceive as weaker than they in order to make themselves feel stronger.
- Bullies often are aggressive as a result of having been victimized by another person, such as a sibling, a parent, or classmate.
- Bullies may not even know why they are cruel; they just do what has been done to them.

Parents can help their children recognize bullying behavior in others and in themselves. Again, Goldman provides a list of common actions associated with bullies:

- picking on smaller, weaker kids,
- teasing or humiliating others,
- deliberately destroying another's belongings,
- cultivating an intimidating look and manner,
- being angry a lot,
- taking revenge if someone hurts them, even if it was unintentional,
- blaming other people when something goes wrong for them,
- needing to win at a game or sport, and
- trying to spoil another's pleasure out of envy for their good fortune.

Children should be cautioned against telling off-color stories in mixed company and warned not to comment on the sexual endowments, physical appearance, or perceived sexual preferences of their peers. Explain how avoiding hurting others emotionally and physically is simply one more aspect of treating others with respect. Discuss with them appropriate responses when their attraction to another isn't reciprocated. Caution your children not to respond to an embarrassing situation by retaliating or by taking out their pain or anger on an innocent, weaker person. Boys who are taunted as gay, for example, sometimes heap this same abuse on another in an attempt to prove their own masculinity.

Always remember that our children model their behavior on what they see at home. In this area, as in many others, parents can lead by setting a good example. What parents say and do, and how they live, provides their children the most lasting impressions. Laughing at a joke or a movie depicting a stereotypical bimbo or an abusive macho figure or commenting derogatorily on the appearance or sexual orientation of others sends the wrong message. Wiseman recommends that parents should "walk the walk" and not gossip about other children; they should apologize when they have hurt someone; and they should reach out to other parents who are wrestling with similar problems.

When kids witness bullying

Parents and educators must display zero tolerance for gay-bashing, racist comments, and sexually demeaning remarks among teens. They must encourage and celebrate sensitive actions, independent behavior, and especially the ability to take a stand against cruel or humiliating behavior toward others. Parents can remind their teens that sometimes it's the action of just one person that breaks a cycle.

Encourage your child not only to report bullying, but to stand up, rather than stand by or ignore it, when a classmate or peer is being mistreated. Avoid a conspiracy of silence about bullying, as it compounds the fear and humiliation. Before taking any action in a case of bullying, help your teen chronicle the abuse so that she can clearly describe the pattern of behavior. This anecdotal report will be essential if you and your teen meet with school personnel or if you write a note to the appropriate school staff member describing the incident.

Parents can urge their children to object strongly to harassment and support them when they do. It's common knowledge that trying to ignore, or go along with, harassment almost guarantees that it will continue—even the Talmud admonishes, "Silence is approval." An assertive response is almost always more effective; one voice can make a difference. A child with a solid sense of self-worth is best able to deal with demeaning comments and actions and to take appropriate action. Such a child is also able to say no persuasively or take no for an answer when dealing with members of the opposite sex.

What schools can do

Parents can check that the school has in place an explicit, well-disseminated policy outlawing harassing behavior together with clear procedures for receiving and processing student complaints, rigorous investigation, and dealing with violators. If your school does not host consciousness-raising programs for students and staff on harassment, suggest to the administration that it do so. Some schools, in an effort to prevent bullying, have established mediation programs. While peer mediation can be appropriate in resolving conflicts between students holding equal power, Susan Limber, Ph.D., developmental psychologist and researcher at Clemson University, notes that "bullying is a form of victimization. It's no more a conflict than child abuse or domestic violence." Bullying is not about a difference of opinions but about power and therefore cannot be viewed or treated as a conflict.

While Limber's point is well taken, Condit notes that school bullies often react more positively to peer influence than to that of adults. Effective peer mediators can bring pressure to bear on bullies, causing them to rethink, and even change, their behavior without the disciplinary intervention of the school administration.

Final thoughts

Roffman advises that the pervasiveness of harassment and bullying should make it clear that this is not a problem for our children to solve by themselves. She recommends that we rear them with respectful and egalitarian attitudes toward sexual orientation, gender, and race in order to minimize the chance that they will ever become perpetrators, and that we require them to own up to their misbehavior if and when it occurs. Because harassment is so big, so pervasive, and so powerful, adults must make sure their school's policies and practices are clear and firm and that proper supports and limits are in place. To overcome bullying, Pollack says we must address not only the perpetrators and victims, but also the whole culture that still allows, and sometimes encourages, the behavior.

| 32 |

Assault and Rape

Last weekend my friend Kate and I went to a party with some upper-classmen. Everybody was drinking and Kate hooked up with one of the varsity lacrosse players. He took her upstairs to make out, but she said that he forced her to have sex, even though she said no. Kate is upset but hasn't told her parents because she's afraid they'll be mad. I want to help her, what can I do?

"FRANCHESCA", seventeen-year-old senior

The first time a woman is hit, she is a victim and the second time, she is a volunteer. Staying must be seen as a choice for only then can leaving be viewed as an option.

GAVIN de BECKER, Consultant on violence and author

Teens all too frequently find themselves in uncomfortable situations, and sometimes those situations escalate into acts of physical violence. Franchesca's friend in the above example was the victim of date rape, a forcible sexual assault at the hands of a social acquaintance, and an all too common event among teens and young adults. Parents need to understand how prevalent assault and rape have become, and that the issue is as relevant to parents of boys as it is to those with daughters.

Recent scandals involving members of the clergy, as well as the many press reports of child abuse, remind us that our children, boys as well as girls, can be vulnerable at the hands of trusted adults and family members. Some teens find themselves in physically abusive dating relationships, in which they become, in effect, battered spouses. Our job as parents is to understand the dynamics of these events, sensitize our children to the issues, equip them with techniques for minimizing their risk, and learn to recognize the signs our teens may be victims and require prompt intervention.

Most of the following discussion concerns sexual assault in the dating context as such acts have become a focus of concern for the parents of middle school, high school, and college students. Victims of other types of assaults, however, exhibit similar warning signs, and many of the suggested steps for preventing sexual assault apply to other forms of assault as well.

Sexual violence

Rape is sexual contact that is forced or coerced, verbally or physically, and includes oral, anal, and vaginal penetration without consent occurring between two or more people, regardless of gender, sexual orientation, or nature of relationship. A sexual assailant can be a friend, acquaintance, date, employer, relative, boyfriend, girlfriend, spouse, or stranger.

Most young victims are raped by someone they know. In one study, ninety-two percent of adolescent rape victims knew their attackers. The frequency of rape in the context of teen dating or partying, often fueled by alcohol and occasionally by date rape drugs, is the primary reason teen rape statistics are so high. Our daughters need to know how to minimize their risk, and our sons need to know that we will not tolerate such behavior.

Rape is a crime in all jurisdictions. According to government statistics compiled by the Wisconsin Coalition Against Sexual Assault, approximately 1.8 million adolescents in the United States have been the victims of sexual assault, and thirty-three percent of all sexual assaults occur when the victim is between the ages of twelve and seventeen. Teens between the ages of sixteen and nineteen are three times more likely to be victims of rape, attempted rape, or other sexual assault, and females comprise eighty-two percent of all juvenile victims. Adolescents are also often the perpetrators. In 2002, twenty-three percent of all sexual offenders were under the age of eighteen, according to the U.S. Department of Justice.

Undoubtedly, these figures dramatically understate the scope of the problem, as it is believed that only a very small percent of victims of sexual assault report an incident to police, and those who have been raped by someone they know or date are extremely reluctant to report the event. Underreporting is especially prevalent in the case of young victims. They, like Franchesca's friend, may be especially hesitant to confide in their parents.

It's about boys and girls

Experts agree that, strictly speaking, rape is not an act of passion. Rather, it is an act of domination and control. In the dating context, however, rape is frequently the result of a common, but dangerous, miscommunication between the sexes about the highly charged issue of sex. Traditionally, boys have been encouraged to be aggressive and actively go for whatever it is they want, in sports and otherwise. Society's traditional concept of masculinity encourages boys to be proud of strong sexual urges, compete with peers in making conquests, and appear in charge at all times.

The media also conspires to teach our sons and daughters that early initiation of sexual behavior is cool. Lisa Gray, M.Ed., director of counseling at the Madeira School in McLean, Virginia, explains that programs and movies that "depict sexual conquest, and even rape, as the measure of manliness, or seduction as a means of manipulation, may lead young viewers to see sex as a route to power rather than as an expression of love. Portrayals in which love and intimacy are absent, and especially where women are shown as the victims of sexual violence or disdain, can influence young viewers' images of their own sexuality and that of the opposite sex in negative ways."

Girls, on the other hand, are often encouraged to be more passive, to please, to be peacemakers, and above all else to avoid making a scene. Often girls are schooled not to appear eager for sexual activity in order to avoid being labeled loose. On the other hand, being popular, which often means winning and keeping a boyfriend, is highly prized among girls. They often feel pressured for sexual favors by boys. When they relent under such pressure, they feel violated but don't recognize the violation as rape. In recent times, some girls, rebelling against the stereotypical role, have opted to become sexual aggressors.

In a climate where young people are bombarded with glamorized depictions of human sexuality in music, videos, and movies—a sexuality which is often portrayed in tandem with violence—it is hardly surprising that some young men would interpret a young woman's tentative or timid no as a coy yes and feel justified in taking charge. Indeed, the Wisconsin Coalition Against Sexual Assault's survey of young men whose actions have met the legal definition of rape found that an overwhelming number of them did not believe they'd committed rape at all. Many of those surveyed expressed the opinion that women enjoy physical roughness, as well as forced sex. On the other hand, the Coalition reported that rape victims frequently blame themselves entirely for the attack.

It's fueled by myths

Surveys of teens revealed that the subject of rape is shrouded by myth and misinformation. Parents must make sure their teens clearly understand the following facts about rape.

- Girls who wear provocative clothing or who drink alcohol are not asking to be raped.
- Taking a girl out to dinner, or even dating her for six months, does not give a boy the right to sex with her.
- A sexual assault has occurred if a girl at first consents to sex and then changes her mind, making that change of heart clear to her partner, who continues anyway.
- A sexual assault has occurred if a boy persists when a girl says no after foreplay. Likewise, sexual assault has occurred if a guy forces sex on a girl who is unwilling, despite having had sex with him in the past.
- Guys do not need to have sex; they have control over their sexual urges.

It's fueled by intoxicants

One out of six college women is the victim, or intended victim, of rape each year, and freshman are the most vulnerable during their first months of school. It is clear that date rape is tied to a college social scene awash in alcohol and drugs. Deborah Roffman, M.S., nationally recognized human sexuality educator and author of *Sex & Sensibility: The Thinking Parent's Guide to Talking Sense About Sex*, tells of one study which found that seventy-five percent of male college students and fifty-five percent of female students involved in reported incidents of date rape had been drinking or using drugs at the time. This is not surprising as alcohol and recreational drugs can lower inhibition, increase aggression, and diminish a victim's awareness of warning signs. To the extent that alcohol and recreational drugs have found their way into the high school social scene, it is safe to say that the risk of date rape has risen in that group as well.

Rape facilitated by drugs such as GHB (gamma hydroxybutyrate), Special K (ketamine) and Roofies (rohypnol) has increased, especially on college campuses. These drugs are colorless, odorless, tasteless, and are easily slipped into unattended drinks. Such drugs lower inhibitions and render the victim semiconscious and helpless, as well as robbing her of most, if not all, memory of the assault. These drugs are increasingly available and may be purchased on the Internet.

It does serious damage

Rape victims must be checked for pregnancy, sexually transmitted diseases (STDs), and HIV. Additionally, most victims of assault and rape suffer severe emotional consequences, including a crippling condition called post-traumatic stress disorder (PTSD), the same affliction suffered by many who return from war or survive life-threatening events.

Other common reactions to rape and assault include sleep disturbances, eating pattern disturbances, phobias, flashbacks, guilt, anger, substance abuse, and suicidal thoughts or attempts. One study has shown that almost twenty-seven percent of women suffering from eating disorders were raped at some point in their lives, as opposed to only about thirteen percent of women without eating disorders. A few rape victims resort to promiscuity or even prostitution as the result of severely injured self-esteem. At the very best, date rape victims report a decline in their ability to trust others and to enjoy normal social and dating experiences.

Parents noticing any of these signs should not hesitate to gently question their teens, and if assault has occurred, promptly seek professional help.

Incest and abuse in the family

Incest is sexual contact between a child and any family or household member, including parents, grandparents, siblings, cousins, aunts, uncles, stepparents, and cohabiting partners of any of these. Incest is the most common form of sexual assault, and the most damaging to its victims. Girls who are abused by family members are vulnerable to being victimized in other relationships as they grow into adulthood, while boys may become aggressive, especially toward women, observes Bob Condit, M.Ed., independent consultant and former counselor at the Landon School in Bethesda, Maryland. Parents are wise to keep a close eye on all domestic relationships and watch for signs of trauma such as those listed above. It is extremely important to believe a child reporting any such activity and provide prompt intervention and counseling.

Other assaults

A teen's relationship with a boyfriend or girlfriend may be accompanied by nonsexual battering. The many excellent websites addressing the bases of domestic violence listed in the resource section of this book provide insight into the root causes of abusive behavior. Be suspicious and intervene, especially if any signs of physical injury are apparent.

Ritual, satanic, and sadistic abuse occurs, often in the context of an ideology or belief structure. Secrecy is paramount to these practices, and severe trauma to the victims, and even torture, is possible. Several web sites providing resources and support to victims of these abuses are also available in the resource section.

Finally, members of certain racial or ethnic groups, or those displaying certain sexual orientations, may become victims of assaults that are, in reality, hate crimes. Such events result in trauma similar to sexual assault and require parental intervention and counseling.

Preparing our children

Prevention of rape and assault should begin long before children are old enough to date. Experts agree that the best protection is a well-developed sense of self-esteem, which is less likely to countenance unhealthy relationships in adolescence. Self-esteem accrues over time through an accumulation of successes.

The girl or young woman who is secure in herself and her own worth doesn't broadcast messages of vulnerability or ambivalence. She knows her wishes and is as assertive as she needs to be in order to communicate them. She doesn't depend upon her date's approval in order to feel good about herself. She is better able to stand up to a relative or authority figure who seeks to take advantage of her.

A young man who believes in his own value isn't pressured to control another or to add a trophy to his collection of sexual experiences. He doesn't need to score and is only interested in a genuinely willing partner. We parents should support, by word and deed, our children's independence and self-love.

It is important we teach our children from an early age appropriate methods for handling frustration and disappointment and to effectively communicate their feelings and needs. We can help children learn the need to communicate their sexual desires and intentions clearly and without ambiguity, as well as to hear and discern another's feelings on the subject. Parents might also want to discuss or role play with both daughters and sons various strategies for exiting situations in which they feel unwanted sexual pressure. Many parents suggest their sons literally ask permission of a girl before each act of sexual contact, as in, "I would really like to touch you there. Is that okay?" and to refrain if his partner says no or is unsure.

We can help our children be secure in their values and decisions about sexual behavior, as well as foster in them an equal respect for others, including others of both genders.

We can urge our children to become knowledgeable about, or even join, organizations striving to end sexual violence. Many independent schools hold assemblies on the subject or support student clubs devoted to it. Students can volunteer at the D.C. Rape Crisis Center or with similar organizations in Maryland or Virginia. Bring Back the Night and Project Safe programs abound on local college campuses, and there are indications these movements have grown in credibility and support among male students. The report of an attempted gang rape at one college fraternity house prompted another house to host a Rape Free Zone party at which revelers were asked to pledge never to commit or condone sexual or domestic violence.

Strategies and observations for avoiding date rape

Parents must ensure their sons understand they can be prosecuted for date rape and that they do not believe a woman should ever have to tolerate unwanted sexual behavior from anyone—including their sons.

By providing an atmosphere that promotes healthy group activities for friends of both sexes, parents give their teens, especially their daughters, opportunities to become better acquainted with dates at home with the family, in group situations, or in public places before the couple spends time alone together in an isolated or secluded environment. Whenever possible, parents should encourage group social activities that include people of all ages.

Parents should counsel children about the impact and illegality of alcohol and other drugs which are often significant factors in date rape, as well as strongly caution daughters not to drink from open containers supplied by their dates or others.

Teens must be taught the dangers of sending mixed signals. Girls should consider whether their mode of dress or manner of presentation broadcasts a sexual attitude that is not, in fact, what they actually feel and that might lead to dangerous misinterpretation. While excessive flirting, off-color joking, or provocative dress never justify date rape, they are things over which a girl has control and can avoid.

Parents can help young people of both sexes define the dating relationships they're seeking. Misunderstandings occur when one party or the other sends a date ambiguous or conflicting signals. Once teens identify their own desires and expectations, they can practice stating those intentions clearly, taking care to determine the expectations of others before engaging in any sexual activity.

Young women should know they are well within their rights to be firm, unpleasant, or even make a scene, if necessary, to avoid what they instinctively feel is trouble. Parents should coordinate with their daughters to develop exit strategies for situations that feel uncomfortable or potentially dangerous. A girl who feels suddenly and inexplicably dizzy and ill at a party should be able to call her parents or 911, rather than accept her date's assistance.

Girls like Franchesca's friend often hesitate to tell their parents they've been victimized in some way. One local teen told a friend that she couldn't tell her mother she'd been raped because she'd never again be allowed to attend a coed party. It is vital that our children understand from an early age that we are always there for them, we won't judge them, and that our aim is simply to protect them rather than to punish them or prevent them from exploring the world.

Get help immediately

Our children, boys and girls who are victims, must be taught that they should seek personal support, as well as counseling and medical help, as soon as possible following rape or attempted rape. Parents need to explain the crucial need for the timely collection of medical evidence validating the assault, as well as testing for STDs. Too often, rape goes unreported and victims are left without critical support when they are most vulnerable. Counseling is usually necessary in order to avoid serious psychological and self-esteem damage. An assault victim and his or her parents should carefully explore and weigh the options of pressing charges. While charging someone from one's school, social circle, or family is extremely difficult and awkward, rape is a criminal act, and offenders must be held legally accountable.

Final thoughts

Most communities have rape or crisis hotlines, which refer victims to trained counselors. The D.C. Rape Crisis Center offers free individual and group counseling to survivors of rape and childhood sexual abuse in the greater metropolitan area.

It is vital for parents to offer their children unconditional love, comfort, and support in the case of assault or rape, and for them to remember that the notion that the victim must have done something to provoke assault is patently untrue. To express such a view is to exponentially increase a victim's trauma. Make sure your child believes that you neither blame her, nor feel she is at fault. Love and support, along with counseling, will help a teen find her way back to physical and emotional health following assault or rape.

7 managing responsibilies

| 33 |

Home Alone

The impact of the "latchkey" experience on kids of all ages depends, to a large degree, on the strength of the parent-child relationship and how deeply the kids feel their parents' presence and concern when the adults are absent. While the number of people working at home is increasing, this does not guarantee that more of us will be home connecting with our children.

In the metropolitan Washington area, as many as three-quarters of households with school-age children are composed of either a working single parent or both parents working outside the home. This is true of both publicly and privately educated children. Many children take care of themselves before or after school, in the evenings, during weekends, or during vacations. When parents say, "We both need to work," the children may believe that staying home alone is their way of contributing to the family's bottom line. Robin Goldstein, Ph.D., Maryland therapist and author of *The Parenting Bible: The Answers to Parents' Most Common Questions*, writes, "Parents either convince themselves that their child will be alright, or they go off to work each day feeling guilty and worried."

"Ten- and eleven-year-olds are too young to be left by themselves regularly or for long periods," admonishes Goldstein. The same can be observed when parents contemplate leaving their teens at home overnight. While older teens may handle after-school and evening hours without parents, they should not be left alone overnight—ever. Some parents become less worried when their children get to be twelve or thirteen years old, assuming that their children have what it takes to be alone. Other parents, perceiving the age group as being at risk of different dangers than those of earlier childhood and believing the value of staying home is imperative, quit their jobs or arrange for part-time employment so they can be home with their adolescents, even though the teens may protest that the parent's presence is more interference than assistance.

Being there

Leah Latimer, author of *Higher Ground: Preparing African-American Children for College,* and the mother of two boys, ten and fifteen, elected to work part-time from a home office in order to maintain the parent-child bond, be on site daily as the dominant role model, and to make sure she followed through on the lessons many parents intend to teach their children but fail to due to the volume of demands on their time. She admits that she is trying to spend more time with kids who are starting to break away, and that she is required to be a yo-yo, to let them push her away only to draw her near again. "I've learned to play the game, but many parents misread the cues. Because they naturally need to be more independent, teens can easily fool us into thinking that they don't need us around as much. The show of apathy about family life and the disdain they seem bound to display toward us fuels this."

When Latimer chose to take "adolescent leave," she had a list of lessons she wanted to teach her sons including, among others, proper manners, how to plan and prepare an entire meal, and the music and literature of the Harlem Renaissance. The goal was to "counter popular culture, mold their character, and give them the moral values and standards they'll need to get through the teenage years." What she has gained in return includes the realization that "my children need me around more than they need me to make more money. The financial sacrifices my husband and I have made will have a big payoff."

Connectedness

Feeling connected to their parents—feeling loved, understood, and trusted—is the most important inoculation teens can have against drug and alcohol abuse, suicide, violence, or early sexual activity. Even if we work outside the home, our children need to have a parent who keeps in touch with them, in addition to their knowing that they are able to reach us quickly in an emergency or just to deal with momentary loneliness. Additionally, children need parents who come home and show genuine interest in their day—sometimes a tall order if our own days are long and stressful.

Research has documented that the psychological connection—family closeness—is more important than the physical one. The impact of the "latchkey" experience on kids of all ages depends, to a large degree, on the strength of the parent-child relationship and how deeply the kids feel their parents' presence and concern when the adults are absent. While the number of people working at home is increasing, this does not guarantee that more of us will be home connecting with our children.

As a result of twenty-five years researching self-care kids aged five to sixteen, Thomas Long, Ph.D., longtime researcher of latchkey kids and professor of psychology at the Catholic University of America, suggests we need a change of attitude to accompany the trend of working from home. Being at home should mean interacting with the kids, actually being there for them. Those of us who are able to work at home must build in time to talk with, listen to, and be involved with our children. Otherwise, to some degree, they will still be in self-care!

Handling time alone

After-school programs. Most independent schools and many recreation centers and sports organizations provide extracurricular activities for young adolescents that can extend the length of time kids are in what their parents may consider care. Most schools have after-school sports practice and programs that can supervise our children for an extra hour or two a day; however, the staff of these programs do not consider themselves to be sitters. They seldom report a child's absence, and they do not wait to ensure that each child is picked up at the end of the activity.

Structuring time. Children who are home alone often have difficulty structuring their time. As a result, they may watch too much television, overeat, spend too much time on the computer, fight with siblings, and experience fear, boredom, or loneliness. Kids also do lots of things they would not be allowed to do if a parent were around. This is especially true when children are alone for long periods of time. Whether seven or seventeen, they are curious, frequently bored,and very inventive with ways to amuse themselves.

Parents may be tempted to keep their self-care child busy with chores, but Goldstein reminds us that "after a day of classwork, he may resent this. He needs a chance to relax and pursue his interests." Older teens can be guided to establish a routine for the hours. They can walk the dog two miles to the 7-Eleven, get a coffee or soda, walk back, check in with friends online for no more than twenty minutes via Instant Messaging, do homework, set the table, etc. Routines are comforting as they set up a framework that is predictable. This framework, suggests Liz Hayes, a Virginia parent with children at National Cathedral, Langley, and Maret Schools, can be posted on a bulletin board where notes, time-filling suggestions, and essential phone numbers provide a reminder system.

Gender differences. "There are definite gender differences when it comes to self-care," reports Long. Two-thirds of girls in self-care report that they stay home and do things around the house. Boys almost universally report that they go out from time to time. Both boys and girls are known to forget to lock the door when they leave the house.

Having a friend of the same sex over may help parents and kids feel safer and more secure. Girls are more likely to stay home and study, talk, cook, paint their nails, listen to music, talk on the phone, or go online. Long warns that when a boy has a same-sex friend drop in to study, however, one thing can lead to another and mischief can occur. Boys are more likely to offer another boy access to the household liquor; the visiting boy may feel there is less danger because it's not his home. In addition, boys often go out—especially if the friend has a car. For teens, time alone without adult supervision is an opportunity for sexual experimentation including intercouse.

Rules. Kids know the rules; they just ignore them, asserts Long. Telling teens "Don't do it!" is just not enough. We say, "Stay in the house," "Don't watch TV for hours," and "Don't answer the phone." They say, "Yeah, yeah, yeah." When parents or other caring adults are not around, children do not necessarily do as they have been instructed. In their burgeoning quest for independence, adolescents are especially likely to ignore or modify their parents' rules.

Necessary nurturing. The pace of our world is fast and stressing. A seldom-addressed reality is that, in some families, no one is getting the necessary nurturing. Many parents work long hours with an average commute of thirty to thirty-five minutes each way, returning home tired, cranky, hungry, and in need of nurturing themselves. This conflicts with their children's need for nurturing and attention. Some parents may feel their children's requests for attention are just too demanding. Parents can build in some rejuvenating relaxation during the daily trip home, such as listening to their choice of music, having a snack, completing some personal calls, or doing some stretching exercises when possible.

Overnight alone

It is never a good idea to leave a preteen or teen at home alone overnight. If we cannot arrange care for our children, we should either not go, or we should take them with us, advises Long. Kids need to have adult supervision. The big danger is not that our child will invite five people to party, but that word will get around that "Jeremy's parents are out of town" and fifty kids show up with a keg. Parents in the metropolitan area should be well versed in their state's or county's statutes concerning underage parties and drinking and the legal ramifications for parents.

Do not make the mistake of believing your teen, and your home, will be just fine if a few "buds" come over, or that your teen will be able to turn away kids should they knock on the door. Teenagers are not able to control what their friends, and particularly a group of other teens, do. They get embarrassed about having to restrain them or are unable to effectively stop fighting, noise, or kids pairing off into bedrooms. We need to help them learn how to avoid problems by communicating strict guidelines for calling a responsible adult to help at the first sign of a party invasion. Their primary protection is an adult consistently on site.

No matter how well we prepare them, children alone face the unknown—alone. We must go over "adult stuff" multiple times to ensure that our teens will integrate rules and precautions. Long reminds us that taking care of oneself is an adult task; it takes years of practice to become good at it. The bottom line is that a minor should never be left alone overnight.

Problems and solutions

Self-care. While most kids of ten years or so say they want to be home alone, few children—even teenagers—would choose to stay alone regularly. They would rather have the comfort of an adult nearby. Many younger children and some older teens left on their own can become bored, lonely, or scared and must contend with household mishaps. They may hear strange noises or worry about frightening events they have seen on the news. Even a parent's warnings can be alarming. "Don't go outside," "Don't answer the door," "Never tell a caller your parents aren't home."

Kids in self-care need to be instructed on how to handle such emergencies as an alarm going off: Is it the smoke detector? Home security alarm? The car in the garage? In case of a power outage, they need to know where flashlights (and candles, for an older teen) are, and what to do if there is a fire in the house. If there are guns in the house, they must be securely locked away.

Children home alone may get harassing phone calls, often from their own schoolmates. Families may find that having the Caller ID option as part of their phone service is a helpful way for their children to monitor unwanted calls and avoid answering the phone if they don't recognize the caller's number.

Children are frequently newshounds and hear vivid accounts of children being stalked—and worse. Girls are especially vulnerable to the fear of being stalked or abducted. "As our daughters mature and blossom sexually, people observe them," cautions Long. Some parents find that a home security system makes them and their children feel safer.

Fear and loneliness can be the most distressing problems for many preteens and teens. While most eight-year-olds will frankly say of being alone, "It's scary," older kids won't tell us they are afraid. Instead, they describe being along as "boring." We need to reassure our children that it's alright to admit they're afraid to be alone too long, or after dark, or when it storms. We then must do everything in our power to be there before it's dark, stormy. or "too long." If circumstances don't allow us to do so, we must have backup in the form of a neighborhood adult or older teen who will come over to be with our child or who will warmly invite our child to come to them.

Sibling-care. Often we view our older children as substitute child-care; however, when we regularly expect our children to care for themselves, as well as for younger siblings, they may feel we are avoiding our adult responsibilities and become resentful. Additionally, children caring for siblings need to be even older and more mature than self-care children without that responsibility. Younger siblings need to be comfortable about staying home with their older brother or sister. Self-care and sibling-care need to be carefully considered if one child has special needs, or if the children are adjusting to new family circumstances such as separation or divorce.

Girls are more often given the responsibility of caring for their younger siblings. When boys are charged with caregiving, they are still more likely to be out and about, leaving younger sibs at home. Adolescent boys may be seen as threatening figures by their sibs, warns Long, as an older brother may sometimes experiment with being rough and even sexual with them.

Siblings at home without adults should each be given instructions so everyone knows what is expected of them. Then, if conflicts arise, the children can collectively call mom or dad to resolve the conflict together. This is important because when an older sibling of either gender is in charge, and trouble with the younger kids ensues, the teen may do what he has seen adults do—threaten, yell, or smack.

Communication

Being in touch with our children is essential to their comfort, confidence, safety, and ability to keep out of trouble. We can call our children frequently from work and as soon as we expect them home.

Some families have a rule that the kids call one of their parents as soon as they arrive home. Long recommends that the very best way to know where our children are and what they're up to is to call them first—not to wait for the kids to call us. Parents should call and say, "I'm thinking of you." "How was your day?" "What did you find for a snack?" "What homework do you have?"

Parents can schedule a specific time each day to call home to speak to their children—a regularly scheduled, uninterrupted "sacred" time to which parents and children can look forward before parents come home in the evening. Periodic calls in the afternoon help ensure that children are home and on task. Children should also know that if they have an important issue they want to discuss with their parents while they are at work, they have priority and it's okay to call their parents. This knowledge goes a long way toward making a child feel more secure and important.

We can be more accessible to our children with the use of pagers, cellular phones, and e-mail. If they know we can always be reached, some of the stress of being alone will be alleviated. Not every parent's job is conducive to periodic or regularly scheduled phone calls with their children, so families should work out a schedule together as a partnership in communication. It is important to remember, however, that teleparenting is but one avenue of parental monitoring; it can never supplant face-to-face contact and conversation.

We should identify a person, preferably in the neighborhood, for children to call if a problem or emergency arises. Prominently post by the home phones your work phone number, as well as emergency fire and police numbers and those of extended family, neighbors, and friends. Some parents also post the home address, believing that, in an emergency, a child could become too emotional to remember this essential piece of information. Our neighbors should know how to reach us at work and by cell phone or pager.

It is wise for children to keep the fact that there is no adult at home from callers. We might consider the content of our phone answering message—instead of a message saying, "We are not home right now," say, "We can't get to the phone," or, "We're on another line." Few children lie well,especially if a caller is persistent in requesting their parents come to the phone. Even teenagers stumble all over themselves when explaining why their parent cannot take the call without revealing the adult's absence.

Prepare for the unexpected. Parents should offer "what if" scenarios to prepare young adolescents for unusual circumstances. Planning should include what to do when feeling bored or lonely; what homework and house responsibilities need to be seen to; how to handle peers or others who show up unexpectedly; how to interact with friends; how to answer the phone. Even teens may have difficulty dealing with the unexpected. Role-play for such occurrences as strangers knocking at the door or the electricity going out. We assume that telling our kids the rules and showing them how to do things once or twice will suffice, but even teenagers don't always internalize our instructions.

Clear instructions should also be provided to a child who is permitted to go outside or leave home. Establish some ground rules regarding where he can or cannot go; the permissible length of time he can be out; how to secure the house before leaving (locking doors, activating the home security system); his mode of transportation; and specific information about with whom he'll be spending time. Work out with him how to keep informed about his whereabouts. This is especially true when a teen has a car—or a friend with a car. We need not accept, "I was just over at Jamie's." Asking questions shows our children that we care and are concerned despite our absence.

A commonplace occurrence that transcends ages and causes kids in self-care distress is the loss of essential items such as keys, coats, and books. A contingency plan for lost keys—a secret hiding place for spares, or keys entrusted with neighbors who are usually available—can remove one cause of stress.

Final thoughts

Being home alone is a real, as opposed to a manufactured, opportunity for our children to learn to take on responsibility, which is a skill developed over time, as opposed to a trait with which they are born. Some children take to responsibility with ease, while others need more help from parents in terms of planning and follow-through. Each success in this area contributes to a child's sense of his own growing competency. Even unsuccessful experiences are helpful if parents use them to help their children learn to review and assess a failure for alternative courses of action which might have been taken for a better outcome, changes that can be made in their future behavior or parental expectations.

Children's successful learning to be home alone is best done in incremental steps in a concerted plan with adult supervision. It involves family discussion of the task, clear understanding of both the parents' and the child's expectations, acceptance of the task and the guidelines by the child, as well as parental coaching, reminders, moral support, and frequent review of the length of time involved and the comfort level of all parties. Perhaps most importantly, parents must be sure their children are not just *old* enough, but also *mature* enough to comfortably and successfully handle the responsibility of being home alone.

| 34 |

Money

Clearly, we are a consumer-driven society in which most of our children want more and more things. On average, teens go to the mall fifty-four times a year—adults thirty-nine times.

LISA GRAY, M.Ed., Director of counseling, Madeira School, McLean, Virginia

Children's spending has roughly doubled every ten years for the past three decades, tripling in the 1990s, with kids' spending exceeding $40 billion in 2002 and expected to exceed $51.8 billion by 2006.

CENTER FOR A NEW AMERICAN DREAM

How do we teach our children, who may carry wallets stuffed with credit cards and cash or who have friends who do, about the value of money when they are accustomed to affluence? How do we instruct our beloved and fortunate kids, to whom we give so much, so often, and so readily, how to live within a budget or develop empathy for others in the community who routinely must make do with less?

One way is by introducing our children to money at an early age, answering questions as they arise rather than postponing discussion until the kids are older. If we help our children learn both values and the value of money gradually and consistently, they will internalize those values and take them on in much the same way they take on language.

Without going into detail about your income and assets, you can be open with your kids about the family budget and how you make budget decisions. Help them learn the vocabulary of finance—invoices, savings, discretionary funds, debits, and credits. Allow them to sit in as you discuss some aspect of the family finances so that they may come to view money in a context of limits, choices, and priorities. Over the course of time, witnessing such discussions will clearly illustrate your values by revealing the process by which you determine how to spend money, particularly your disposable income.

Our children, especially our nine- to fourteen-year-olds, are intensely targeted by advertisers and marketing groups. Many of our "tweens" feel the commercial pressure to buy things that will help them fit in, and they recognize the trouble this causes between their parents and themselves, according to Betsy Taylor, M.P.A., author of *What Kids Really Want that Money Can't Buy* and founder and executive director of the Center for a New American Dream in Takoma Park, Maryland. Teenage girls are prime targets in movies, television shows, and some two hundred magazines for girls—each vying for the buying power that our daughters possess.

Allowances

Many parents are reluctant to give their children allowances, believing they can better control the kids' spending by limiting their access to funds. Janet Bodnar, senior editor at *Kiplinger's Personal Finance* magazine and author of *Kiplinger's Dollars & Sense For Kids*, feels this isn't necessarily a sound practice, as studies indicate that children who don't have allowances still have access to about the same amount of money as those who do. "It's better to have them learn to manage money themselves than nickel and dime you to death," she says. "It is a values issue. You don't want kids to covet money or hoard it, but to see it as a useful tool. Allowances help kids develop a healthy attitude toward money and their ability to manage it."

Delaying gratification and learning to evaluate whether a purchase is really worth the expense are just two of the lessons learned when kids are allowed to manage their own money. Bodnar explains, "By the time kids are eighteen and away at college, they may be managing a semester's, or full year's, worth of funds, sometimes on their own, so learning money management skills must begin early."

The Parent Encouragement Program (PEP) in Kensington, Maryland, advises parents to base allowance amounts on a child's age, interests, needs and wants, family resources, and parents' values. The amount of the allowance and what it covers should increase as the child gets older, along with the responsibility for budgeting it, with parents and children in clear agreement on the expenditures for which it is earmarked, be they clothing, transportation, school lunches, recreation, or other needs. Parents and children should decide how often the allowance is to be granted, whether weekly, monthly, or even twice a year, and the children should be allowed to manage it independently and to learn from their mistakes. For younger children, a more frequent allowance schedule is probably best, while older teens, particularly those away at school or college, are better able to handle a semiannual schedule.

"'Oops' is part of the plan," assures Kathy Griffin, parenting workshop instructor who teaches Methods for Rearing Unspoiled Children in an Affluent Environment for PEP. "The biggest mistake parents make with allowances is giving too little and then turning into the ATM machine to cover their kids' shortfalls. Parents should avoid that so kids can learn from their own mistakes."

Allowances require discipline of parents, as well. Allowances should always be paid in full on the agreed upon day with no exceptions, say the experts. Parents should keep allowance systems simple and easy to administer and may even consider using an online debit card system that automatically deposits the allowance on a regular schedule (see credit card discussion below).

Chores

Should children be required to do chores in exchange for allowances? Again, that is a decision parents make based on their finances and personal values. Some experts believe paying children for chores done well and on time helps them understand what will be expected of them later on in the working world. Others cite surveys indicating some kids count on their parents losing track of whether chores have been performed and paying out the allowance anyway. Another group of experts maintains that children paid for doing chores stop doing those jobs once they can earn better wages outside the home. More important, they believe paying kids for doing chores precludes a golden opportunity to instill in them the responsibility family members accept as a part of living together and caring about each other.

Many parenting experts view an allowance as their child's share of the family resources and not something to be withheld if chores are left undone. However, the consequence of chores left undone could be the denial or revocation of a privilege. Chores can be considered the child's portion of the overall family responsibility, activities they perform as a contribution to living in the family.

Most financial educators agree that children should have opportunities to earn extra cash beyond their allowances by doing extra jobs around the house, yard, and neighborhood. Not only does this help teach delayed gratification, an essential element in money management, by providing savings opportunities, but it also reinforces a child's understanding of the actual cost of popular brands and labels and whether they are worth the money. "I tell my daughter my job is to buy her jeans, but if she wants the designer label, the extra cost has to come out of her budget, not mine," says a Potomac lawyer and mother of a fourteen-year-old.

Jobs: when they are good...

A recent U.S. Department of Labor study indicates a record percentage of teenagers in Washington, D.C., and across the country are forsaking the learning experiences of year-round and summer employment to work on academic or athletic skills, travel, or simply work on a tan. "We have a spoiled labor force," Stephen S. Fuller, Ph.D., professor of public policy at George Mason University in Northern Virginia, and observer of the Washington area economy, told the *Washington Post*. "There is a wealth effect which has taken the kids out of the labor market. Today's middle-class kids have two working parents, and they get a pretty good allowance. They don't even have to cut lawns anymore, because Daddy hires a lawn service."

Should adolescents be expected to work, even if the family is affluent? A growing consensus of research has found that a modest amount of paid work—ten to twelve hours a week on weekends or after school during the school year—has a positive impact on young people. Adolescents who work these kinds of hours actually have higher grades than those who don't work. They learn to organize their time more efficiently and develop responsibility, resourcefulness, empathy, diligence, and the ability to work with others.

Jobs: when they are bad...

There is also, however, ample evidence that students pay a price when they work more than fifteen hours a week during the school year. Studies by the National Research Council and by professors at Stanford University, Temple University, and the University of Minnesota found that when teens work long hours, they often do not have enough time or energy for homework or family life. They miss out on the important social and intellectual development of participating in drama, music, athletics, and personal interests.

According to a study by the Centers for Disease Control and Prevention, there is a distinct correlation between teens working more than eleven hours a week and smoking and drinking. The same correlation occurs between teens working more than twenty-six hours a week and marijuana or cocaine use. An earlier CDC study found that students who worked more than eleven hours a week had significantly higher rates of sexually transmitted diseases and unwanted pregnancies.

With these statistics in mind, parents need to understand the value of work as both a learning experience and supplemental income for their teens at the same time they recognize the difficulties and conflicts a job can pose. Parents can help their teens achieve a healthy balance by limiting the number of hours worked so that the job is a positive arena in which young people can grow rather than become demoralized or get into trouble.

Parents can also require that students spend their wages responsibly. Plans for money earned at a summer job should be discussed and agreed upon with teens before the first day of work. Some families earmark summer job wages as bankable discretionary college expenses funds. Others feel the additional stress of an after-school job frequently outweighs either the learning experience or the money and believe the best approach is to reassure their teens that, "Your job right now is school." Children whose parents instilled in them the habit of regularly allotting a percentage of their allowances and cash gifts to savings, charity, and the like, will be more apt to do so with their wages when they begin working.

Matching funds

Many parents don't want their children to go without the material things they might have gone without during their childhoods, and they misguidedly shower their children with all that they missed. The experts agree this is a grave error, often resulting in ungrateful kids with an overdeveloped sense of entitlement and an underdeveloped sense of responsibility. An equally serious error is for parents to do the opposite and, in attempting to foster a sense of realistic fiscal sense in their teens, require children to work for every dollar, resulting in children developing a poverty mentality. The poverty mentality is a negative mindset, central to which is the feeling that there is not enough money and there will never be enough money to meet one's needs. This mindset can result in one hanging onto money too tightly out of fear, rather than learning to view money as a tool, as something to use both to meet needs and to purchase enjoyment.

To avoid either outcome, some experts suggest parents contribute toward their kids' purchases of coveted items by matching their teen's earnings and/or savings. If, for example, a child achieves the goal of working and saving toward a new tennis racket, the parent will provide matching funds for lessons or new shoes. Parents can provide matching funds to a child who has saved for an expensive trip or camp with friends. Working toward a specific goal and the pride of achievement are strong motivations for banking hefty gifts of cash from birthdays, graduation, or summer paychecks, with parental matching funds providing an extra incentive to stay on track and save.

Another way in which parents can help with matching funds is to create an individual retirement account (IRA) for their child and deposit an amount matching their teen's earnings up to the allowable IRA ceiling. Annual holiday gifts to the IRA provide additional work incentives, as well as valuable lessons about saving and investing, compound interest, and tax-free money growth.

Credit cards

When thinking about teens and credit cards, there are two important facts to take into consideration. The first is the finding by the Jump$tart Coalition for Personal Financial Literacy that financial literacy about credit card use, taxes, or saving toward retirement has declined among twelfth graders from 57.3% to 51.9% in the past three years. The second is, as author and correspondent Tracy Rozhon reported in the *New York Times*, that in 1995, there were only 4,000 stores in the country that exclusively targeted teens. At present, there are almost 10,000. Understanding that children must be taught money management, particularly in an environment where they are targeted consumers, is extremely important in parents' determination of if, and how, they will give their children credit cards.

In two-income areas like metropolitan Washington, D.C., family time is limited and incomes tend to be higher. It is not at all uncommon for parents to allow their children to use their credit cards to buy clothing and other necessities without adult supervision. Parents do this as a sign of trust and because they can monitor the expenses on their monthly statement.

Some financial experts suggest that while limited, controlled use of parents' credit cards by teens can be a positive learning experience, unlimited use, or cards of their own, should be avoided. Uncontrolled teen use of credit cards can contribute to the unrealistic belief that they have unlimited financial resources. To avoid this mistaken impression, experts advise parents to consider giving their teens credit cards for specific purchases and set the highest price they are willing to pay. "Teens know how to use a credit card to buy things, but they're not always clear about how the bill gets paid," Bodnar says. "They think plastic is just another form of currency and don't understand that using a card is like taking out a loan." Financial experts also say parents can help their children make the clear and unassailable connection between credit card purchases and the inevitable payment by having their teens join them in going over monthly credit card bills and writing the payment checks.

Often, parents don't allow their children the use of their credit cards until they are college students, where the cards are designated in advance for emergency or travel use only. Other parents believe a credit card is a must for their teens. They want to allow their teens the experience of managing a credit card; they trust their kids' ability to handle one; or they fear their kids will apply for their own cards as soon they are legally able without researching the best terms. In response to this trend, some credit card companies and organizations enable parents to acquire a credit card on behalf of a student. Parents set the credit limit, and use the Internet or a toll-free phone number to monitor how the card is being used. The cards are initially sent to the parents, providing them the opportunity to discuss the terms and responsibilities with their teens before turning the cards over to them.

Parents can either allow their teen to put the card in his own name, or they can co-sign for the card, which, if the teen runs into credit trouble, impacts on the parents' credit rating. Other major credit card companies offer cards designed expressly for teens that carry no annual fees and have a $1,000 credit ceiling to limit potential losses.

Some financial advisors recommend debit cards over credit cards for teens because they decrease the risk of overspending while being safe, convenient, and easy for parents to monitor. Many colleges and universities offer such debit cards to their students. Some prepaid debit card programs have been created especially for teens with monetary limits set by the parents. When a teen makes a purchase the cost is deducted from the card balance. When the card balance gets low, parents deposit, or "reload" the card, from their credit cards, check cards, or checking accounts (transferring money using a checking account can take five to seven days). Parents can even schedule automatic deposits weekly, biweekly, or monthly, for example, to cover an allowance or for college. Parents can then review a teen's account to ascertain spending patterns and amounts. A growing number of banks also provide these cards with varying fees and charges.

While many parents choose not to give their kids credit cards, they can nonetheless help them learn to budget with bank books/statements, personal finance notebooks, money management software, and money-review sessions.

Philanthropy

Parents do a fairly good job of teaching earning, spending, and saving, but often neglect the areas of investment and philanthropy, observes Griffin. To counter that situation in her own family, she and her husband established a donor-advised fund when they sold their successful computer consulting business. The fund evolved from a tax strategy into a family foundation, offering their two teenagers an opportunity to help conduct research and decide which environmental and social causes to fund.

Most donor-advised family foundations can be established with a required minimum of $10,000 seed money. Parents interested in learning more about creating and maintaining family foundations can check out one of the many websites on the subject, including two Washington, D.C., area sites: the Council on Foundations and the National Center for Family Philanthropy.

Families with less to donate can participate in altruism through what Susan Price, Washington, D.C., area author of the Council on Foundations publication *The Giving Family: Raising Our Children to Help Others*, calls a "dinner table foundation." She suggests parents hold a family meeting, with members bringing to the table an easel, markers, memo pads, pencils, mailings requesting donations, and their ideas about what charities or causes they would like to fund. The family determines how much they can realistically afford to donate to worthy causes for the year, be it $50 or $500, agrees upon how selections will be made, lists preferences, votes on which organizations to fund and in what amount, and participates in writing the checks.

"Most of our kids growing up in this area are learning about volunteering their time for community service, but we need to be deliberate about teaching kids to be generous with their money too," says Price, whose book offers numerous examples for ways in which children and their families can work together on philanthropic endeavors.

Creating a family culture of altruism by expecting your children to serve and give; letting your children decide what projects to support with their money and time; teaching them to manage money; and praising them for their philanthropic actions early on will establish a habit of giving that will serve them for a lifetime.

"A lot of people don't talk about their own philanthropy, but it is important for parents to both show their kids what and how they give and to talk to them about it as well, even if in the end the kids choose other causes," Price says. "What is important is that the kids make their own decisions about where to give their charitable money."

When children are determining which charitable endeavors they wish to fund, parents can take part in teaching strategic philanthropic planning by helping the kids research where and how a given charity spends its money, the number of people benefiting, and the overall wisdom of the organization's policies.

Investment

There is no better gift a parent can give than the life skill of financial management, financial experts agree. Many vehicles exist to help parents teach their children about the fundamentals of investment, but Bodnar advises that buying your children shares in the stock market, beginning with owning stock in companies in which they have interest, teaches a priceless lesson. Parents and kids can discuss prospective investment opportunities, purchase products from those companies, and follow trends to see which stocks may be worth buying.

Developing fiscal responsibility

Teenage Research Unlimited has identified the eighteen- to twenty-five-year-old age group as comprising the fastest growing segment of bankruptcy filings in the country. The danger of fiscal irresponsibility among the young is very real, but early training by parents can help them develop good sense about money and avoid serious trouble when out on their own.

Parents can learn effective tips and strategies for helping their children develop sound fiscal responsibility by reviewing Bodnar's *Kiplinger's Dollars & Sense for Kids*, in which she outlines methods of fostering healthy financial attitudes and management skills for parents of pre-school through college-age children.

Money managers and parenting specialists suggest a number of tips and strategies for teaching children fiscal responsibility.

Allowance. Prior to giving your child an allowance, have him keep track of his spending for a few weeks. The amount of his allowance can then be based on his actual needs. Review allowance amounts at least annually, perhaps at the beginning of each school year.

Loans. Consider carefully before lending children money for impulse purchases. Some experts say such lending can result in the birth of a credit-spending habit. Instead, delay the purchase until the next time you're together at that particular store. This allows children time to review and perhaps rethink the impulse to buy and determine if they can afford the purchase on their budgets.

Choices. Teach your children that they can't have everything. Even affluent adults generally can't have everything they desire, expensive cars, exotic vacations, memberships in prestigious country clubs, exclusive schools. They prioritize their desires and choose which are most important to them and then accept responsibility for their choices. Parents can walk their children through their own prioritization and selection processes and thus show their kids how adults arrive at spending decisions.

Quality versus quantity. Consider cutting back on the quantity of things you give your children and instead make sure the items you do give them are imbued with broader value and meaning. Create memories and experiences by giving less stuff, but doing more together.

Savings. Deposit savings at regular intervals into bank accounts in your children's names so they can observe the transactions and watch balances grow.

Investments. If you don't regularly study the stock market, learn how to do so and allow your children to be part of that learning process. If you are adept at investment research, introduce your kids to the market and help them understand how you analyze market information and determine your investment strategies.

Work for hire. Use the family bulletin board, refrigerator door, or other prominent spot to post a list of household jobs available for your children and the fee you're willing to pay, along with the date or time of day by which the work must be completed. Your children may then contract with you to do a particular job for the stated price, understanding that you will pay only for a job well done and on time, and not for sloppy or late work.

Model the desired behavior. Remember that parents provide children an indelible template for money management and fiscal responsibility. Parents' attitudes about money, and their ability to manage it skillfully for both fun and profit, are invaluable tools to pass on to children. Many family financial advisors report that the best thing parents can do is to set limits on their children's access to money, thus encouraging kids to be decision-makers, and learn from their mistakes, so they won't evolve into passive spenders by default, which often happens when kids' access to money is unlimited.

Final thought

Children who are gradually given more responsibility and funds will develop a healthy attitude toward money and the ability to manage it. Talk to your children about how you and others use money. Especially in the environment where teens are targeted consumers by advertisers, they must learn to make choices, set priorities, and understand the need for limits.

| 35 |

Computers

I don't know what I'd do without the Internet or a computer. It just makes all my schoolwork easier. Actually, it makes my life easier.
SEVENTH-GRADER, Northern Virginia

The newest street corners, arcades, and malls that serve as teen hangouts can be found right within the walls of the homestead. They are electronic mock-ups of the real thing—accessed easily by the family's computer. For many adolescents, these cyberspace hangouts are no less treasured or real than the "real" thing.
JOHN SULER, Ph.D., Professor of psychology, Rider University

The evolution of the Internet and the wealth of information available to anyone who can go online have changed both the way many educators teach and the way students learn. At home, parents have to deal with the new challenges technology continues to present, including squabbles with their children over computer use, Internet access, and acceptable work and study habits. Parents are inclined to use the Internet as a source of information or news, while their teens are more inclined to see it as a place to meet friends, relax, and have fun, observes John Suler, Ph.D., professor of psychology at Rider University and author of the online book *Psychology of Cyberspace*. It isn't surprising that the Internet has so much appeal for teenagers—they are the first generation to have grown up with computers.

Suler feels that the fact that cyberspace is so attractive to teens can be a blessing in disguise. He says that typical adolescents don't want to simply chat—they want to write scripts that automate their online activities, create their own web pages, scan pictures and e-mail them to their friends. They love the sense of accomplishment and mastery, and when they are able to teach other kids these skills, it reinforces their own knowledge and builds their self-esteem. Suler admits cyberspace is great, and seductive, but parents need to help their teenagers remain involved in real world activities as well.

It is common knowledge that a highly-motivated middle or high school student can find out about almost anything on the Web, a situation that worries many parents. Rita Schonberg, Ph.D., a Maryland psychologist specializing in adolescents, identifies the major concerns parents should have about their children's access to the Internet as:

- the ease with which a child can access the outside, adult world from the comfort of the family room,
- the accessibility of information about hate groups, bomb making, pro-anorexia groups, and similar material that is unsuitable for children,
- the ease with which a child can be offered unsolicited information that is titillating, disturbing, or too mature for them to handle, and
- the prevalence of sexual, financial, and identity predators exploiting children and young teens.

Impact of technology

The age-old question of how much is too much, the concern of many parents about the amount of time their children spent watching TV during the 1970s, has now expanded to include concern about the amount of time spent at the computer. The frequent TV news stories of Internet predators and the growing numbers of pornography and hate sites prompt many parents to consider purchasing stronger filtering systems or banning their children's Internet use entirely.

And what of the children themselves—how have computers and the technological revolution changed them? As one seventh-grader so clearly stated, computer technology has changed the way she learns, gathers information, and generates her schoolwork. The fact that kids today use computers in ways that neither their parents nor their teachers ever imagined doesn't mean that doing so is wrong.

Some thoughtful adults worry that technology threatens a child's development of such qualities as self-discipline, sustained concentration, critical thinking, thoughtful writing, reasoned discourse, and in-depth deliberation. When our children are learning so much about the world via the exciting global technology, the slow pace of real life can seem boring to some of them. Almost a decade ago, Sherry Turkle, Ph.D., professor of sociology and founder and director of the M.I.T. Initiative on Technology and Self, wrote in her book *Life on the Screen: Identity in the Age of the Internet*, "The technology changes us as people, changes our relationships and sense of ourselves." Turkle's research examines how computers have, and will, change the way children and adults interact with the world and how they view themselves.

Other voices questioning the impact of technology include Richard Restak, M.D., Washington, D.C., neuropsychiatrist, therapist, and author of *The New Brain: How the Modern Age is Rewiring Your Mind.* He believes the sensory overload resulting from the new technology may be permanently altering our brain development. Likewise, Michael Gurian, Ph.D., psychologist, social philosopher, and author of *The Soul of the Child: Nurturing the Divine Identity of Our Children*, counsels parents that computer use, especially before the age of fourteen, negatively affects the brain development of our children.

Jane Healy, Ph.D., author of *Failure to Connect: How Computers Affect Our Children's Minds—And What We Can Do About It*, is curious as to "how computer use will change the developing brain, and how we can maximize its positive effects without neglecting aptitudes we value, such as reading, reflection, original thoughts, or internally driven motivation and sustained analysis."

Enhanced learning

While the impact of this technology is being debated, the computer has established a firm presence in our lives. As a new tool it provides new avenues to time-honored learning skills.

Research skills. The Internet is a "vast library covering any topic imaginable," notes Suler, and he suggests that it is a positive dilemma for teenagers to decide for themselves what is good information and what isn't. They have to "learn how to search for the information they want, to use a web search engine, to learn about Boolean logic and the nuances of how to phrase a keyword. It makes them think about their topic before they even find the information."

Marcy Cathey, M.S., mother of two tech-savvy daughters and director of technology at the Madeira School in McLean, Virginia, advises that whatever search engines students use, it is important they understand search logic and employ some basic search strategies to the task. The best way for a parent to help is to sit with the child during a search session and provide suggestions for a more efficient search, recommends Cathey, although in some families the teenagers have skills far superior to those of their parents.

Organizational skills. While the notions of file management and maintenance don't sound very exciting, being able to find one's work when needed, track changes and versions of work accurately, and ensure nothing important, be it a term paper or a personal best version of a challenging game, is lost or erased is an important skill for students. Organizational skills cannot be taught too early, and it's never too late for older students or adults to learn. For most people, avoiding the heartache and panic of lost data is a strong motivation for adopting sound file management and maintenance practices.

Parents can encourage children to develop their own file management system by identifying the kinds of work they will be doing on the computer—daily homework, term papers, tests, and reports—and creating separate folders for each within a general subject folder. Make sure kids are aware of where a given file actually goes when saving information.

Computer proficency

Cathey has this advice for successful computer use by all students.

Learn to type well. It is surprising how many people use hunt and peck typing, especially high school students. Typing is a skill that can be learned as early as first or second grade, and it is in children's best interest to insure they do so. Thirty typed words per minute exceed one's speed writing longhand, and is an adequate minimum typing speed.

Know your productivity software well. Typical students' school reports now include tables, graphics, and diagrams. Many students are required to give oral presentations accompanied by computer-generated multimedia displays. While learning to use Word, Excel, and PowerPoint may not be glamorous, the efficient and effective use of these programs will benefit students throughout middle and high school, as well as in college. Attractive, neat work always earns higher grades.

There are dozens of how-to books published annually to guide students and parents as they work to learn specific application skills as well as Internet research skills. Check your local or online booksellers for the best guides, being sure to read the customer reviews, and select the book most appropriate to the skill level of the student or parent.

Computers and information literacy

Healy warns that the Web is increasingly dominated by organizations guiding consumers toward their products or ideas. She encourages parents to work on "information literacy" with their children, helping kids learn to question material seen on the Web in order to "distinguish information from opinion or propaganda." When children are researching something via the Web, she suggests parents coach kids to ask the source of information and the motivation for posting it by posing questions like those that follow:

- Is someone trying to sell a product or a point of view?
- What possible biases may be detected?
- Does this information represent theory or fact?
- Why might some sources be more accurate than others?
- How do the visuals influence the way the information is received?
- Is the information designed to appeal to the emotions?
- Are sound effects intended to influence one's thinking?
- Do the visuals and text convey the same message?

Games kids play

Parents need to be vigilant in monitoring the quality and quantity of their children's video games. Elementary school children should not spend hours playing mindless games, rather they should be encouraged to play a variety of fun but educational games. For older kids, the need for monitoring is pronounced. Many preteens and teens, especially boys, spend countless hours playing violent computer games. While many nonviolent children and teens play these games, there is evidence that doing so results in desensitization and undermines the ability of children to empathize with victims of violence. "But all my friends play it," is not a reason for allowing children to own or play unsuitable video games. A simple kitchen timer can help parents enforce time limits on computer use.

Parents can minimize problems associated with the playing of violent video games by setting limits on games rated mature by the Entertainment Software Rating Board. These ratings are analogous to, but slightly different from, the Classification and Rating Administration ratings for movies, and it is worthwhile for parents to familiarize themselves with the rating system. However, "the ratings on many games can be misleading," says Daphne White, founder and executive director of the Lion & Lamb Project, a national parents' organization dedicated to halting the marketing of violence to children. White reports that obscene levels of violence are being marketed directly to children and teens, "mostly bypassing the parents." She suggests that labels could include such information as, "This game includes decapitation, evisceration, shooting, bombing and other illegal acts."

Games can be addictive, and gender may influence what kids find addictive. Girls are much more interested in relationships than boys, so it is not surprising they find The Sims family of simulation software fascinating. For the same reason, girls participate as much as, or more so than, boys in Instant Messaging (IM) and chat rooms. By contrast, "While boys are also heavy users of e-mail, chat rooms, and IM, their messages tend to be shorter, and they are less likely to be interested in using them to build lasting relationships," observes Jeffrey Hart, Ph.D., chair of the political science department at Indiana University, father of a teenage boy, and student of technology. Hart notes boys tend to get addicted to combat simulations and shooting games. They are particularly attracted to playing the networked versions of these games.

Instant Messaging and e-mail

Our kids seem to be using the phone lines less and less and using Instant Messaging more and more. Deborah Tannen, Ph.D., professor of linguistics at Georgetown University and author of many books on communication, says that speed is only one reason teenagers prefer IM shorthand to lengthy, articulate messages. She observes that a kid using IM-speak correctly shows that she knows the lingo, belongs to the group.

While many adults are concerned about children's use of IM, others note the ease of communication. A teacher, for example, spoke recently of how much she enjoyed IM for answering homework questions or queries from students the night before an exam.

Instant Messaging and chat room conversations are as much a part of many students' evening routines as brushing their teeth or taking showers. A number of students admit to watching TV, IMing, and keeping up with conversation in a chat room while doing homework. Many parents are convinced that this practice decreases comprehension and efficiency and should feel comfortable requiring their children hold off on Instant Messaging and joining a chat room discussion until their homework is finished or they have free time.

Cathey observes that a ratio of three-fourths homework to one-fourth IM or chat seems to work for many families. Children who spend more than half of their free time Instant Messaging or chatting may be using the computer as an escape, an aid to procrastination, or to avoid responsibilities. Some teens, particularly those who are socially awkward, are more comfortable relating to others via the computer rather than interacting face to face in social situations, thus depriving themselves of opportunities to develop the social skills live encounters provide. When a teen would rather spend time online than with family and friends, things may not be alright in the real world. The teen and his or her parents may need professional help to kick the habit and enhance the appeal of live interaction.

Parents should monitor their children's use patterns and talk with them if they observe dramatic behavior changes. It is also important children understand that e-mail is never entirely private, nor is it completely erased when deleted, so they should be extremely careful about what they write online. It's not a bad idea for adults and children to remember not to write anything online that they couldn't bear to have made public.

Unfortunately, says Suler, many kids approach chat rooms as if they are computer games, behaving as if other people are robots. Some may also use inappropriate sexual remarks, profanity, and abusive language. Online anonymity provides a safe, easy method to satisfy the desire to inflict abuse, vent frustrations, or express prejudice. Suler suggests that the more intensely teens act out, the more likely they are having problems in their real lives and are using the Internet to ventilate and escape from those real life tensions.

Keeping safe online

Adolescents need, and even want, rules. In the same way that parents don't let their teens stay out all night or drive everywhere they want, there have to be guidelines and consequences for computer use and abuse. Among your family rules should be clear restrictions on harassing others online or attempting to hack online systems. Suler counsels that it's not a good idea to let adolescents treat other people online as if they are not real people.

Being aware of children's behavior while using the computer is important to insuring their safety. While both parents and children are aware of Internet predators, peer harassment and aggression are a much more common source of discomfort. Children have the right, and the technology, to block IMs from someone who is harassing them. Parents should encourage children to talk about their online communications and reinforce basic safety rules, such as not chatting or Instant Messaging with someone they don't personally know and not giving out personal information.

Some online service providers provide parental controls that allow parents to set limits on their children's online use and behavior. Knowing what can and cannot be limited is essential for the cyber-savvy parent. All software controls, however, have loopholes that a technically sophisticated teen can exploit. Suler notes that the last thing parents want is an ongoing technical battle of wits with their children.

As observation, awareness, and a good working relationship with their children are parents' best tools for ensuring their kids' sound and safe use of the computer and the Internet, many technology specialists and adolescent experts suggest that both the television and computer be located in a community area of the home, such as the family room, rather than in children's bedrooms. Children are less likely to get involved in negative activities online while surrounded by other family members. Having the computer and television in a common area also provides for teaching the benefits of sharing and negotiating for their use. Most of all, the location of the computer has much to do with the degree to which parents can observe and be aware of their children's computer use. In multi-computer households, it is a useful practice to network the computers together, thus mirroring computer systems in the real world and accustoming children to system oversight.

Caught in the Net

Many teens will always be just casual computer users, some may go through phases of consuming Internet use, and a few will become addicted to it. In her book, *Caught in the Net: How to Recognize the Signs of Internet Addiction—and a Winning Strategy for Recovery*, University of Pittsburgh assistant professor and expert on Internet addiction Kimberly Young, Ph.D., describes some of the warning signals of excessive computer use among teens:

- lying or denial about the amount of time spent on the computer or the type of activity engaged in,
- withdrawal from friends and declining interest in hobbies as online activities and online friends take the place of the real world,
- extreme irritability when cut off from computer use, and
- chronic fatigue, or changes in sleeping habits, as a teen stays up later and later, or gets up early in order to spend more time online.

Final thoughts

The personal computer has already fundamentally altered the pace at which our children learn about their world, as well as the amount of information to which they are exposed. Because the Internet can be a place to escape, act out, or vent, as well as to find information, it can satisfy needs of many adolescents and be very seductive and even addictive.

What parents really need to be thinking about, cautions Healy, is how to prepare their children for life in an information-loaded, but depersonalized, world landscape. Instead of asking what our children will learn with computers, she posits we may also need to ask what they will become, and suggests that the best preparation may be simply to help them become as human as possible. She reminds us of Thoreau's warning that, if we are not careful, we could all become "tools of our tools."

| 36 |

Sports: What's the Goal?

In Washington...affluence means that many parents don't think twice about dropping hundreds of dollars on a coach or a clinic. An obsession with politics makes us fixated on winning and losing, some say. We're a population of strivers, and our workaholic habits spill into sports, leading to five-day-a-week practices and year-round training.

DREW LINDSAY, Parent and *Washingtonian* magazine features editor

A group of parents taking part in an informal survey was asked, "What goal do you have for your child's participation in sports?" The answers varied—some parents said their goal was for their children to have fun, others replied, "To learn discipline," and still others explained they wanted to increase their children's chances of acceptance at good colleges, maybe even to be awarded athletic scholarships. Many others looked to sports participation to help their children burn off energy, develop better focusing skills, learn about teamwork and good sportsmanship, make friends, and come to understand that winning isn't everything or even the only thing—and neither is losing.

Not surprisingly, the children of these parents used many of these same words when asked about their goals for sports participation. Several teens agreed that it's a lot more fun to win than to lose, and it's not fun to be on a sports team that doesn't compete to win, especially at the high school level. One teen answered that sports provide opportunities to learn about adults as well as peers, and he cited some examples, one of which was of a talented teammate whose parents' enthusiasm for his play, to the exclusion of that of his teammates, had embarrassed him. Another was of a coach who, during an early season game, ordered a player to feign an injury so that he could substitute a more talented player. These replies and others—"keeping fit," "trying something different," "gaining self-esteem"—illustrate that in sports, parents and children share many of the same goals.

That said, understand that children modify and change their sports objectives over time, and parents need to be sure they are cognizant of their children's current feelings about participation. Given these many, and sometimes conflicting, goals and mindful of the prominence sports play in adolescent lives and society at large, how should a parent guide a child in this area? Should parents place their children in sports at an early age? What about parents holding back an academically qualified middle-schooler, as one local independent school has recommended, so that the child will be more physically developed and thus more equipped to compete in high school athletics? Is it wise for a parent to encourage a focus on sports, or a single sport, to the exclusion of academics, drama, art, music, or other sports?

The American Academy of Pediatrics notes there is no evidence to support the notion that starting children in athletic activities at two or three years of age results in better athletes than if they begin at later ages. The Academy also discourages having children specialize in a single sport before adolescence: kids who play multiple sports appear to suffer fewer injuries and perform better overall than those who specialize early. Another advantage of fostering children's interest in a variety of athletic endeavors before adolescence is that doing so will provide them with options should they later not make the team in their favorite sport, or if they should suffer an injury which prohibits their continued participation in their primary sport.

Other experts warn that holding back an academically qualified child to enhance his or her athletic opportunities later may send the signal that only sports count. Consider the plight of a gifted middle school athlete who suffered a freak injury. Despite several surgeries and countless hours of physical therapy, he was never able to participate in sports during high school. His parents now wish they had encouraged their son to develop other interests.

Not all children are meant to be athletes, reminds Karen Epstein, physical education department chair and coach at Georgetown Day School in Washington, D.C. Forcing them into competitive sports may lead to early negative experiences that discourage them from pursuing a lifetime of healthy activity. Parents can suggest and encourage other avenues of physical exercise and exploration through activities focusing on fun, play for play's sake, and skill improvement. Biking, rock climbing, skateboarding, martial arts, and rollerblading are, to many children, preferable to organized team sports.

Parents of athletes

Parents should be alert for certain kinds of competition that may impact negatively on the family. The Williams sisters of tennis, Venus and Serena, appear to be exceptions to the general wisdom that it is best to encourage siblings to play different sports or, at least, play in different leagues if they play competitively.

For many people, sports bring the competitive juices to a boil, often along with an attendant loss of emotional control. It's easy to say that the behavior of adults should be exemplary no matter the situation, but Washington, D.C., area writer Herbert Rosen says that "some parents—otherwise somewhat rational people—act as if they have no brains when it comes to the overheated atmosphere of sports."

If paying attention to your child is the most important thing, running a close second is paying attention to your own goals, motives, and behavior in relation to sports. Experts encourage parents to consider their own motives in urging a child to participate in athletics to the exclusion of other activities. Are they seeking to bask vicariously in the glory of the child's success? What of the motives of high school coaches who penalize players for being involved with other sports?

It is useful to remember that we parents serve as role models for our children in the context of sports, as well as in other areas of life. Who has not seen or heard about parents who scream at players, shout meaningless instructions to a pitcher, or, worse still, abuse referees, coaches, or the parents of other players?

Like it or not, intensely competitive sports play a profound role in society, observes Rosen. "Sadly," he says, "it's how too many kids define themselves. Sadly, too, many parents' sense of self-worth comes from how well their kids play." This is even more the case with parents of children seriously involved in the more solo competitions like gymnastics or skating. In these sports, a child essentially competes against everybody in his area for a slot on a temporary, ranked "team" attending a particular competition. Lacking the input and feedback from regular teammates, a child and his participating parent then function as a very small, intense team with the parent much more intimately involved in transportation, interacting with coaches, and the child's performance. At the same time, they are far more isolated and alone than parents and children participating in more traditional team sports.

It is virtually impossible to resist the pull of our culture's obsession with sport and sports figures—the impact of all the slickly evocative athletic shoe and clothing commercials, the array of televised games, the endless programs of pre- and postgame commentary on television, as well as the elevation to cultural icons of both deserving and less than deserving athletes.

Unless asked, parents should resist offering advice to their children about skills or strategy before a game. If asked, advising your child in that situation often serves to indicate you don't trust your child to do what he or she needs to do. It is better to back away, demonstrating your faith in your child's judgment. As difficult as it may be, leave the coaching to the coach.

Levels of participation

There are many levels of participation in children's sports. The degree of athletic prowess differs at each level, as do the expectations and relationships between coaches and players, players and parents, and parents and coaches. That is as it should be, notes Rosen, for what is appropriate for a child taking part in a rec league program designed to provide exercise and socialization may not be so for a highly skilled young person who plays in a select league or on a varsity team. Likewise, conversations about play, technique, strategy, and skills between a teen and a knowledgeable and caring parent will be quite different from conversations with a younger child who's just having a good time playing a couple of seasons of rec league ball.

Even recognizing differences in ability and aspirations, there is still no foolproof formula for finding the ideal balance between a child's ability and desire, and the appropriate level and venue of competition. What works for one child fails utterly with another. Attorney and National Presbyterian School parent Liz Nadeau observes that for some children, being the star on a mediocre team or league may be more satisfying than sitting on the bench of a more skilled team. It is incumbent upon parents to know their children and be realistic about them, not only in terms of their ability but also in terms of their emotional makeup, goals, and desire. Rockville parent Marc Bastow points out that just as there are kids who excel academically, the same is true of athletically gifted children. They need to be challenged and provided opportunities to grow and hone their skills. Meeting the challenge requires commitment from both child and parents, with the latter prepared to provide support and devote evenings and weekends to practice and competition around the region.

Learning in a team environment

Coping with expectations. Adolescents generally haven't much of an arsenal of coping skills they can use to deal with, and learn from, their performance errors in the athletic arena. Epstein notes that research suggests boys more often react to stressful sports situations with avoidance strategies, while girls tend to seek social support. She recommends that both parents and coaches avoid being judgmental about mistakes and be corrective instead. Abilities are not fixed—we can, and do, learn from our mistakes. Children also need to know that their parents believe in them and love them regardless of how they do on the playing field.

Probably the most important thing parents can do is to pay close attention to their children's sports involvement. Are they growing from the experience? Are they attaining the objectives they have set for themselves? Although there is no absolute guide for ascertaining the answers, most experts agree that it is a subject worth exploring with your children, and suggest checking in on the subject with them periodically. Rather than a frontal assault such as, "Are you having fun playing on the team, this year?" a better approach is an open-ended statement like, "Tell me what it's like playing for Coach Smith." Often a parent can tell from even a nonresponsive answer how their child feels about playing for Coach Smith.

What are parents to do if their child is not achieving his or her objectives? In the most extreme case, where participation is physically or emotionally abusive or destructive, there is but one solution—participation must end. Find another team to join. The critical challenge is how to determine when, or whether, that extreme has been reached. Parents have several ways to tackle the problem. One is to seek information on your own, without first consulting your child. Another is to advise your child about what you plan to do and why and then listen to your child's reaction. Yet another course of action is to encourage your child to bring the matter up with the persons involved.

If, for example, your child is not having fun or is not developing his or her skills because of limited playing time, the coach needs to be consulted in order to determine what your child can do to effect a positive change. Confronting the problem is usually far better than sidestepping it and letting your child's feelings fester. Perhaps some guidance through role playing or scripting will help to calm the adolescent's fear of addressing the matter with the coach. Such sessions can also help the child refine the questions to be asked, and be aware of, and govern, tone of voice. Should your child be dissatisfied with the resulting conversation with the coach, then it is appropriate to schedule a meeting of you and your child with the coach. In certain cases, a conversation with the school's athletic director should be considered, as well.

Coping with a team. A frequently identified objective for sports involvement is that kids learn the value of playing by the rules. If you observe that all the players on a team are disciplined for poor sportsmanship but the coach routinely makes exceptions for the star player, then the team is clearly operating under a double standard. Perhaps the best course is to discuss the inconsistent treatment with your child and solicit his reaction. Often you will find that your child is also aware of the double standard and may be confused or conflicted about it. Discussing the various options for dealing with the situation will be beneficial in both the immediate and long term as it will help your child learn how to deal with the complexities, and sometimes downright unfairness, of the human experience.

While the result of such discussion may not bring you satisfaction for the outrage you feel, it may allow your child to better understand your values, at the same time encouraging him to sort out for himself how to respond. Sports participation can be the venue in which your teenager learns about dealing with difficult people, both adults and peers, as well as about blunt criticism and rejection. Some teens may learn early that they don't have to automatically accept or agree with feedback about their performance and thus learn not to take criticism personally.

Some behavior among teammates can lead to problems. Hazing is one such case, meriting a conversation with the coach and perhaps the athletic director, advises Elizabeth Hall, physical education and athletic department chair at the Maret School in Washington, D.C. Although many players think of hazing as a team ritual, such behavior is patently unacceptable. Parents should discuss hazing with their child, making it clear that such conduct should not be tolerated, let alone encouraged, and should the hazing recur, they should not hesitate to bring the matter to the attention of the coach or athletic director. Hall states unequivocally that children should be able to enjoy their athletic experience without being humiliated by the coach or peers.

Epstein acknowledges that there are still lingering connotations of masculinity attached to sports and athletic endeavor in general. It is important our sons grow to understand that their masculinity is not dependent upon being an athlete and our daughters grow to accept that "real women" are, and should be, as strong, fast, powerful, cooperative, and achievement-oriented as they wish to be. Epstein suggests we ensure our children observe a variety of male and female role models—including ourselves—engaged in a broad range of activities. "Above all," she says, "talk to your teens when they suggest that some activities are less appropriate for one gender than the other. Sports will not 'make' girls gay, nor will they 'make' boys straight." As long as we allow children to harbor these misconceptions, many girls will continue to reject sports, and many boys and girls who do not conform to sex-role stereotypes will experience negative social consequences.

Winning—handling the glory

Americans love winners—indeed, we glorify them and frequently choose to overlook their contemptible behavior. This is particularly true of our forgiving attitude toward professional athletes, both on and off the field. Unfortunately, this unquestioning glorification of winning athletes has found acceptance in the world of pre-adolescent sports.

Because athletic achievement is highly valued and visible, sports success can determine social status on our campuses. A seldom addressed issue is the manner in which athletes treat other, nonathletic students. Does athletic status in school translate into socially acceptable or unacceptable behavior? Do athletes function as a jock clique? Are athletes treated preferentially by adults? Does this status encourage bullying—or pressuring for sex? Parents of these successful kids should remind their children that their talents are more in the nature of a gift. We and our children must be alert for signs of "jock entitlement" within the school culture.

Athletic success can lead to monetary rewards such as scholarships to independent secondary schools and colleges. Such rewards are available to only a limited few and the competition for them is fierce. Moreover, the result of such competition can be dictated by pure chance. If your child has a bad game on the day the scouts are watching, chances are a coveted scholarship will not be offered. It is important to realize that, according to statistics collected by the Positive Coaching Alliance, only one-tenth of one percent of high school athletes will attend college on an athletic scholarship.

On the other hand, teens who are not "high skill" athletes are not enticed to participate in sports solely by the prospect of winning, says Epstein. She observes that these children are motivated by task orientation: How much have I improved? Is it fun? I am good at this! Are my friends playing? In addition, she points out, "Children ages ten to eighteen years are more likely to stay involved in a sport when the coaching style is democratic in nature. They need to feel a degree of autonomy, social connectedness, and self-control. They tend to want coaches who will provide an environment that fosters these things."

Losing—learning from defeat

"It doesn't matter who won or lost; it's how you played the game that counts," is unlikely to comfort a child who has just experienced a defeat, no matter how deeply you hold that conviction or believe that often more can be learned from failure than success.

There are, however, ways parents can help children deal with defeat. Most important is to recognize that if a parent is angry or upset about a game's outcome, then, no matter how hard he or she tries to disguise it, the child will pick up on it. In that situation, it is wise to avoid attempting to ease a child's pain until one's own emotions are less vivid. Similarly, experts say parents should not try to talk their children out of the feelings of anger, disappointment, and frustration that are often by-products of losing. Instead, parents should acknowledge and accept those feelings—it's okay to be upset after a loss. The important thing is for the child to learn to cope with disappointment.

This does not mean that a parent cannot have an active role. A parent can help a child find time and appropriate outlets for venting anger. A parent should not, however, tolerate a child's threats, or those of her teammates or classmates, to "get even" with, or punish, the opposing school, team, or a team member who screwed up. If your child seems unable to let go of her anger over several hours or days, you must carefully appraise the level of hostility and prevent any antisocial behavior.

While such vigilance is warranted, immediate action is generally not required. Indeed, in dealing with defeat, it is sometimes better to let the moment pass and not to comment immediately on either your feelings or those of your child. Both of you can, with a little time and space, process the event better and put a greater emphasis on the things your child did well, both mentally and physically. Although it is often easy to illustrate these things by contrasting your child's actions with those of her teammates or opponents, experts warn against using this approach as such comparisons send the wrong message, emphasizing competition rather than your child's conduct and feelings. Denigrating others to lift one's own esteem should always be avoided.

When you do find the right time to talk, it's better to begin by asking open-ended questions such as, "What do you think you did well in that game?" or, "What do you think you can do to make things better?" These questions, even if posed after the heat of the moment has cooled, may be answered with, "Nothing—I just suck," a response that can rapidly degenerate into a lightning round of "No, you don't," "Yes, I do," ending in both parent and child feeling even more frustrated. Instead, experts advise us to listen rather than comment. "Be a witness, not a judge" is how one puts it. Not only is your child unlikely to accept your opinion of his play, it is much more important that he explore his feelings and make his own assessment of his performance. Following up with questions like "What makes you think that?" can be more constructive and beneficial in the long run than any immediate attempt to ease a child's pain.

School spirit versus animosity

Competition between schools, whether centered on academic, athletic, or artistic endeavors, is normal and healthy. However, athletic competitions appear to be the primary impetus for almost all incidents of school rivalry that get out of hand. Results of academic and artistic competitions don't generate the same emotional intensity.

Intense athletic rivalries of decades, even generations, in length, fierce competition on the playing field, and strong school spirit can all be positive and healthy. Good athletes play by the rules and play to win in order to achieve honor for their school, for their teammates, and for themselves. For the majority of athletes and spectators, being proud of one's school and playing one's heart out on the field or cheering loudly for friends and school alike from the stands are important elements of character development, team building, and school spirit. Yet, parents need to be able to differentiate between school spirit and traditional athletic rivalries on the one hand, and animosity and the potential for violence on the other—and we need to make sure that our children know the difference as well.

Mature and rational athletes and fans leave the struggle on the playing field after the final whistle has blown. A very small number of students may harbor irrational, deep-seated animosity toward other schools, and by extension, toward students of those schools. Ironically, these children are rarely athletes themselves but are more often described as hangers-on, wannabes, and attention-seekers. They are the most vocal and most apt to cause trouble with students from another school, invariably after school hours and outside of school-sanctioned events. Students who compete fiercely on the playing field are playing a game—students who engage in violence off the playing field are breaking the law.

Party crashing, brawling, and the destruction of personal property are decidedly unhealthy and unlawful. Be clear that no incidence of vandalism or reprisal by your child will be tolerated. Tell your child never to assume that if unlawful acts occur, a grown-up with connections can "fix" things. This is usually untrue and is always unwise.

Final thought

The late tennis champion Arthur Ashe wrote in his book *Days of Grace*, "Sports are wonderful; they can bring you comfort and pleasure for the rest of your life. Sports can teach you so much about yourself, your emotions and character, how to be resolute in moments of crisis and how to fight back from the brink of defeat." By emphasizing these aspects of sports, parents can help their children achieve the ultimate goal of a happier and healthier life.

8 school

| 37 |

Cheating

What is important is getting ahead...cheating is a shortcut and it is a pretty efficient one in a lot of cases.

ALICE NEWHALL, Northern Virginia high school student

...Integrity may earn [teens] a pat on the back, but honors and diplomas are strictly reserved for academic achievement. So kids are quick to recognize that cheating offers an easy way to win the prize, with a minimal chance of getting caught.

JOSEPH GAULD, Founder, Hyde Schools, Bath, Maine

Back when we parents were growing up, cheating was rather simple—kids would write formulas or vocabulary words on the insides of their hands or on smuggled crib sheets. Occasionally, someone would be caught looking at another student's test to copy answers. Today, cheating is a lot more sophisticated. Students log onto websites offering fully-researched term papers. Tech-savvy students hack into school records to modify grades electronically. Other kids log into chat rooms to get answers to math problems or exchange science lab data. Using e-mail, pagers, and the text messaging function on their cell phones, students transmit test answers to others, while still others complete foreign language assignments by using Internet translator services.

The media is full of stories about new instances and types of cheating. At the University of Virginia, a physics professor, suspicious of remarkably similar test responses from a number of students, designed software to detect cheating. He identified 154 students in his class who had cheated—and this at a school with an historic and highly touted honor code. In the Washington area, ten students at a well-respected, private boys' school were recently found to have cheated on an SAT test. The motivation for several of the students was baffling as they had already been accepted to colleges.

A Duke University study of high school students found that ninety-seven percent admitted to cheating or plagiarizing at least once. In 2001, the Center for Academic Integrity at Rutgers University conducted a study of 4,500 high school students that revealed seventy-four percent had cheated at least once on an important test, seventy-two percent cheated on written work, and ninety-seven percent admitted to having committed at least one questionable activity, such as copying someone's homework. One-third of those surveyed acknowledged engaging in frequent cheating.

Are students cheating more, or is there just a lot more publicity about cheating? Has there been some fundamental change in our morals that excuses cheating or finds it more tolerable? Are the honor codes at our schools a deterrent to cheating, or are they merely an empty standard?

Michael Daigneault, Esq., adjunct professor of business ethics at Georgetown University's McDonough School of Business, says that while he doesn't know if cheating happens more often these days, he can posit a psychological reason for it. "Young people see no harm in cheating," he says. "It is a victimless crime in their perception. They see their peers doing it, and they are subject to peer and parent pressure to do well. Both good and poor high school students are cheating because they know that if they don't do well on a test or a course, it will have an impact on getting into college." Daigneault says kids rationalize cheating by saying to themselves, "Why not do it, when the stakes are high and the odds of getting caught are low?" Some students feel they have no choice but to cheat—"I'll be at a disadvantage if I'm the only one not doing it. I'd love to stop if you can get everyone else to stop."

Parents as models

Kids who cheat and get away with it at school are more likely to carry this behavior over into their professional and personal lives when adults. A *U.S. News & World Report* poll revealed that one in four adults feel they must cheat and lie to succeed, and this mentality is all too frequently communicated to our children. So what should we do to instill a sense of honor and integrity in our students? The following are some strategies to consider.

Demonstrate your belief in the core value of honesty in their daily lives. We must model personal integrity to our children so they understand that this value is at work even when no one is watching.

Find teachable moments to reinforce your beliefs. Comment approvingly on a TV show, movie, or book with a positive message about honesty. Show your kids real life examples of heroes who try to do the right thing.

Restrain yourself when it comes to helping your kids, especially younger ones, with homework. While parental involvement in children's education is a goal to be encouraged, your writing papers and solving problems does not ultimately help the student learn.

Lighten the pressure on your child to get good grades at any cost. Encourage your children to do their best and don't subject them to unnecessary competitive pressure to get into the best high schools and colleges. Try to maintain a healthy perspective about homework, exams, and school admission.

Congratulate your children when they try hard, but fail or fall short of their goals. An honest C grade representing hard work and a good faith effort may be disappointing, but it is a better reflection of a student's effort and/or capability than a dishonest A. Encourage your kids to use good judgment in resisting the temptation to cheat, to report cheating by others, and to rebuff a request to cheat.

Resist the temptation to fly immediately to your child's defense if he should be accused of cheating, or if the school concludes that he has cheated. Too often, parents try to excuse their child's cheating by protesting that everyone does it, with the addition of, "So why are you singling out my child?" They may also attempt to deflect blame away from the child, as in, "The test was poorly proctored," or, "The teacher is overreacting."

Honor codes

Teachers and schools need to have clear rules about cheating and honesty for students of all ages. An honor code means that the school trusts students to behave honorably, and if they violate that trust, the consequences are clear. Some schools have adopted a "one chance to confess" standard to make their honor code more realistic and effective. When a student is suspected of cheating, he is given the opportunity to admit the transgression and accept a punishment that is less severe than expulsion. This policy teaches that cheating is wrong, that one can be caught and punished, and that one will have an opportunity to rehabilitate one's self.

Some schools provide clear definitions of various types of academic fraud and an outline of the protocol to be followed when a student is accused. Punishments range from corrective action, such as redoing the work, to expulsion, with repeat offenders treated more severely than first-timers. In the "Edmund Burke School Family Handbook," it is made very clear that it is a violation to copy homework from others, to provide homework to be copied by others, or to receive excess assistance. The handbook further states that plagiarism occurs when a writer takes the words or ideas of another and passes them off as his own. Should there be any question about the definition of cheating on tests and quizzes, both unpremeditated and premeditated cheating are clearly described for students.

In addition to defining various forms of cheating, David Shapiro, M.A., head of the Edmund Burke School in Washington, D.C., strongly advises teachers to take the time to make sure their students fully understand the various forms of unacceptable academic behavior. It is important that parents review such information with their children as well, so that students are clear about what is honorable and honest performance.

Joseph Gauld, founder of the Hyde Schools in Bath, Maine, takes an opposite view of school honor codes believing they do not teach integrity, but are designed to protect the integrity of the school. He feels honor codes overlook kids' innate sense of honor and fairness, and the fact that, at their best, kids are committed to each other's welfare. Gauld says, "Honor codes force kids to choose between protecting the school, by ratting on their peers, and protecting their classmates," and his four schools have no such codes. Citing Theodore Roosevelt's dictum, "To educate a person in mind and not in morals is to educate a menace to society," Gauld explains that the Hyde Schools promote character development—courage, integrity, concern, curiosity, and leadership—and establish a learning environment based on trust in which the schools truly value and honor character more than academic achievement.

Fighting back

Schools are fighting back against rampant cheating. New websites are being developed to help teachers combat Internet plagiarism, one of which, Turnitin.com, allows faculty to submit students' papers for assessment of their originality. Within forty-eight hours, the site responds and indicates whether any Internet documents or resources have been copied in the students' work.

A more Draconian approach is being tried out by the educational testing service center of a local university. Digital and video cameras are located in the testing room to record every student's moves during an exam. Fifteen computers create customized exams with the test questions arranged in a different order on each in order to prevent cheating among the examinees. In the works for the future are biometric scans of thumbprints to prevent a student taking an exam for another. The downside of these approaches to cheating is that they bypass moral education in favor of efficient enforcement.

The best approach is for parents and schools to talk about honesty and integrity with young people so that it becomes a part of their individual and school character. Character education programs and strict academic integrity policies should be encouraged at our schools. Teachers should discuss academic integrity in their classrooms, clearly delineating the rules, unacceptable behaviors, and their consequences. The reinforcement of these standards may help undermine the typical motivations for cheating, such as feeling the work to be too much of a hassle, lack of study time, desire for better grades, or not caring.

Final thoughts

The bottom line is involvement and modeling behavior by parents, adults, teachers, and students themselves. We need to instill integrity in children during their school years in order to enhance the chances of their becoming good citizens in the future.

| 38 |

Changing Schools

You may have been considered a really talented guitarist at your old school, but let the students at your new school determine for themselves how good they think you are. If your new peers decide that you aren't quite as good as you bragged, you might be kept as an outsider.

BOB CONDIT, M.Ed., Independent consultant and former counselor, Landon School, Bethesda, Maryland

Changing schools is scary and stressful for most kids. Moving up to high school is a major life event, as is changing schools mid-year for any reason. Attending a new school because your family has recently moved to a new area can be especially challenging. Leaving behind old friends and needing to make new ones; assimilating a different culture, rules, and procedures; finding comfortable places to hang out; and getting accustomed to new teachers and their expectations all contribute to the worry and stress of adjusting to a new school environment.

How schools help

Children attending schools that end at eighth grade have the comfort of an entire class of peers wrestling, usually silently, with similar worries and emotions. Most schools provide programs designed to help eighth-graders and their parents deal with the transition to high school.

It is common for high schools to provide programs during the spring of senior year to help seniors and their parents recognize and talk about the range of emotions associated with graduating and moving away from home to live on college campuses. These programs usually provide information to reassure graduates and their parents that they will be able to make a smooth and successful transition to college. Often, schools sponsoring such programs will ask recent graduates to provide their insights and experiences, and these speakers are often remembered as the most important part of the programs. If your school does sponsor a transition program, don't pass it up. Even if you learn only a few new things, it can be worth the evening, and the shared experience of attending with your child can form the basis for hours of subsequent helpful discussion.

How parents can help

Parents need to be sensitive to the fact that changing schools is stressful for children and, despite a show of bravado, or an assurance from your child that this will be "no sweat," the kid may actually be anticipating the change to be extremely difficult. Mark Stein, Ph.D., former program director of the Children's National Medical Center Hyperactivity, Attention, and Learning Problems Clinic in Fairfax, Virginia, advises that parents help their child "understand that not all stress is bad and, in fact, some stress can prepare him to face unfamiliar situations in the future." For some children it may be necessary for parents to monitor their teen's stress levels as much as possible, especially during transition periods. Stein suggests that one way to alleviate some of your child's worry is to take care of details like completing school forms and purchasing required school supplies well in advance. Waiting until the last minute can add significantly to a child's stress.

Discuss changing schools with your adolescent at times when he or she is away from brothers and sisters and when you both are relatively relaxed. This might occur around the dinner table, riding in a car, or late at night before going to bed—three particularly good scenarios for meaningful conversation with an adolescent. If your son or daughter has changed schools, or even summer camps, before or has a friend who has done so, ask how it went. Try to help your child talk about what seemed to go well and what could have been done differently to make for an easier transition. Encourage your child to build on past experiences.

Support your children's efforts to make friends, as they may be much more concerned initially about fitting in socially at the new school than they are about academic success. Rita Schonberg, Ph.D., a Maryland psychologist specializing in adolescents, reminds us that friendships are essential during early adolescence. Young teens have an "urgent need for friends who define the child's self-worth. This is not a good time to have to tolerate loneliness." While this may require a certain increase in parents chauffeuring their children to the homes of new friends scattered around the Beltway, it will contribute to a smoother social transition.

If the new school has preseason sports practice in August for a sport your child will be playing in the fall, encourage him or her to take part and adjust your vacation schedule so that your child can participate. Then, by the first day of class, your child will have a head start both on making friends and on making a place for himself, and the actual beginning of school won't feel quite so daunting.

Make every effort to attend the orientation session for parents of new students even if all you do is listen. You can learn a lot about the culture of the new school from such a meeting, and you will meet adults from the school, as well as parents of other new students who could be important resources in the future.

Don't begin the new school year by setting a performance standard for your child, as in an arbitrary level of grades or achievement you expect of him. Also, bite your tongue if you have to, but don't remind your child of how much the family is sacrificing financially to send him to this new school.

Expect to see your child work hard and praise him for the effort put into academic studies. For the first months in a new school, your child's grades may dip a bit. Empathize with your child and discuss the need to understand what each teacher expects from homework and on tests. Encourage him to seek out teachers for extra help or to talk about course material and test design, perhaps even role-play or script appropriate ways to begin a dialogue with a particular teacher. In addition, encourage your child to talk with an advisor, dean, or counselor if he seems discouraged by the new workload or a lower than normal performance level. Most importantly, praise your child's effort! If the effort and the desire to learn are there, higher grades will eventually follow.

Advice for teens

Condit offers teens these suggestions for making a more comfortable transition when changing schools or moving up to high school.

When it comes time to plan an academic schedule, don't fill your day with the toughest courses offered. Leave breaks in the day if the school and the schedule allows and know that taking at least one easy, or easier, course is okay. The physical and emotional stress experienced by many students during the first four to six months at a new school is roughly the equivalent to carrying at least one additional academic course, so be careful not to overextend yourself.

If your school has an orientation session for new students before classes begin, be sure to sign up and attend. Often, as part of the orientation process, new students are paired up with a classmate buddy who serves as a guide for the first few days of the term. Use this buddy as a resource for information and the inside scoop on classes, teachers, and school issues.

When starting at a new school, make a real effort to be yourself. You are probably a great kid with a fine personality, a pretty good sense of humor, and generally fun to be around. You don't need to pass yourself off as someone you're not. If you do try to be someone different, it's almost certain your new classmates will eventually see through the act and label you a phony. Watching and listening in the beginning will help you learn the lay of the land and see how you can fit in just as you are.

Try to look as though you are happy to be at your new school. Showing by your attitude, expression, and body language that you enjoy your new surroundings will invite new friendships and encourage others to include you in their groups. Even if you're feeling miserable during the first few weeks of school, putting on a happy face will bring out the friendliness in other students and may help you feel better and more confident about being in a new situation. Looking unhappy or ill-tempered will only serve to drive your classmates away from you.

This said, however, it's extremely important to let an adult at school, or better yet, several of them, know if you are, indeed, unhappy. None will be able to help you or work to turn your unhappiness around if they don't know how you really feel. Tell them early on and allow them the opportunity to help well before your unhappiness becomes so bad you want to leave school. If you have an assigned buddy from the school's orientation program or have made friends with a peer counselor or advisor, talk with them, too, and be honest about your feelings.

Begin your new school year trying to make same-sex friends first, rather than charging after peers of the opposite sex. If you're a girl, don't play up to the boys or make an effort to find a boyfriend immediately. If you're a boy, don't begin by going after the girls. This will very probably alienate peers of your own sex and can make developing same-sex friendships much more difficult. Getting a boyfriend or girlfriend can happen later, after you've established yourself in your new school.

If your new school has peer counselors (or peer helpers or advisors), use them. Seek out one or more of these older students and get to know them. Develop a friendship and ask for help or advice if you feel you need it. Learn where the counselor's office is located and get to know your counselor. If you're assigned a faculty advisor, a homeroom teacher, or a class dean, get to know that person as well.

Allow each of these people to get to know you, too. Tell them how you feel about coming to this school and talk about your interests. Let them know about your strengths and weaknesses, your likes and dislikes. The better they get to know you, the more able they will be to help you to fit in, make friends, become involved in school activities, and learn the ropes.

One of the toughest things about making friends at a new school is knowing what to say to people and how to act. Avoid telling other students how good you are at something. This may be the most important piece of advice of all, advises Condit. Let them find out for themselves. In other words, don't brag. It's normal to want to tell potential new friends what you're good at—"Baseball is my best sport, and I'm a really good pitcher." You may have been considered a really good pitcher at your old school or on a community team, but let your new classmates determine for themselves how good they think you are. Classmates resent it when they feel you don't live up to your self-proclaimed reputation and may ostracize you. Boys seem to fall into this trap more often than girls and should remember that their new classmates are going to measure them by their standards, not those of your old school friends.

To rework the baseball statement cited above, you might try this:

New friend: "What do you play?"

You: "I really like baseball."

New friend: "Are you good? What position do you play?"

You: "I've pitched in the past. I'm okay, I guess." (Or "I'm not too bad.") "I'm just hoping to make the team."

Shaping responses about any of your interests in this way keeps you from establishing a standard or level of proficiency to which you might not measure up. If they later tell you, "Hey, you really are good!" respond graciously with, "Well, I really love baseball and try to play it a lot." If it turns out your new teammates are better than you are, you won't look ridiculous, and they'll be more willing to help you improve.

Final thoughts

Although the process of changing schools may seem confusing and anxiety-provoking, the transition will be greatly eased by parental support and patience. The experience will help you grow as a family and be an important start to the next stage of your lives together.

39

Choosing College

All this emphasis on advanced placement classes, grades, and tests has brought anxiety to high school students all over America and for no good reason. There are more than enough slots to go around—and in good colleges, too.

MARGUERITE KELLY, Author and syndicated columnist

Selecting and attending a college, or choosing not to go to college can feel like the most significant decision in a young person's life, observes Sylvia Stultz, Ph.D., a Washington, D.C., psychologist specializing in friendships and social relationships. It is best accomplished when the process is enjoyable and accompanied by a caring supportive cast that includes parents.

For both parents and students, the college search is a time of excitement and trepidation as they plan for the future. It is important, however, not to allow the college search to become the consuming focus of the teen years. The goal of high school is not simply to get into college, anymore than the goal of college is to be admitted to graduate school. The teen years are a time of self-discovery, identifying goals and strengths, and honing decision-making skills. Parents must accept that their child's entire adult future does not rest solely on his choice of colleges; rather that college, now or later, is simply another step in life's journey.

The college selection and application process is most successful when it is a partnership among students, parents, high schools, and colleges, advises Leonard King, M.A., director of the college counseling department at the Maret School in Washington, D.C., and Nina Marks, assistant head and director of college guidance at the National Cathedral School in Washington, D.C. Each participant plays an important role in identifying the best match. Students create an academic, testing, and extracurricular record in high school and fill out the application forms to reflect the interests and values that shaped that record. Parents determine their parameters, including financial, regional, ethnic, and religious considerations, and discuss them candidly with their teens and the college counselors. It is helpful for parents to accompany their teens to visit prospective colleges, comparing their knowledge of their children with their impressions of each school to minimize the possibility of a poor choice. College counselors listen carefully to both teens and their parents and offer advice and support, maintaining a dialogue with the students, parents, and, to some degree, with the colleges. Colleges assess the application material and accept, wait list, or deny students admission based on the school's needs and expectations. If the process is well done, students, parents, the high school community, and the colleges achieve a win/win conclusion.

Early in the process, it is important for parents to make their college preferences clear to their teens. It is extremely frustrating when an adolescent realizes his parents have a hidden agenda. Bob Condit, M.Ed., independent consultant and former counselor at the Landon School in Bethesda, Maryland, recalls a very frustrated senior who spent an agonizing six months trying to figure out where his parents wanted him to go to college. "Each time I make a decision, they find something wrong with the school and tell me I shouldn't be thinking of going there. But when I ask them where they think I should go, they just say it's my decision. I feel like I'm in the middle of some game I can't win." Parents can give guidance, but the senior must make the final decision, reminds Nancy Rosenberg, M.Ed., an independent college counselor who specializes in advising students with learning differences and attention deficits.

Advice for teens: selecting colleges

As you conduct your research, not only will you learn about colleges, you will also learn quite a bit about yourself. And, as you will quickly realize, the more astute you are about yourself, the better you will be at identifying colleges that match your needs. If you are not a student of a foreign language, determine which colleges do not have a language requirement for graduation. If you will benefit from an environment that assists students with learning disabilities by allowing extended-time tests and providing note takers, ask the college's learning support center to provide you with names of current learning disabled students who would be willing to speak with you about their experiences at the school. Consult with a college counselor who specializes in helping students with special needs. If learning support services are your most important consideration, begin your college search with an up-to-date list of colleges providing comprehensive support services.

If you have an anticipated major, reviewing the *U.S. News and World Report* annual college rankings will provide current information on the top colleges in each field. You may be surprised to learn that not all fields of study are dominated by Ivy League schools. Some relatively small or lesser-known schools, as well as some large state universities, have earned top marks in specific fields.

There are many excellent print resources for information about colleges; however, one of the best and most easily accessible resources is the Internet. A college website is an extremely useful source of information. You can take a virtual tour of the campus, email questions to the admissions office or a specific department, view the entire course catalog, and download application and financial aid forms. You and your parents can learn online of informative seminars arranged by colleges across the country and held at Washington area hotels or independent schools that you might wish to attend.

Advice for teens: taking the tours

Once you have formulated an initial list of colleges to consider, arrange, if possible, to visit some or all of the campuses. If you can travel, by all means do, but if you cannot, a trip to several local colleges and universities will give you an excellent sense of the options and opportunities you will find in other colleges around the country. Even if you are certain you will be leaving the area for college, one educator recommends that all area high school students tour both a large state school and a small private school here in the Washington area. Touring the University of Maryland will give you a taste of a large state university and a feel for the dormitories, the advantages of a big school, and a sense of the challenge of maneuvering between buildings during the course of a day. Virginia Vogel, Ed.S., independent college counselor and former college counselor at Georgetown Visitation School in Washington, D.C., also suggests that when touring, you should "practice listening to what is being emphasized by the student leading the tour, the kinds of questions others are asking, and sensing what you like or dislike about the college."

Whenever and wherever you visit, ask questions and observe carefully. Are students actively engaged in class? Is this an environment where you will be intellectually challenged? Are faculty members accessible outside of class? Is there a core curriculum, and if so, does it appeal to you? How much do students study? Does the social life revolve around fraternities and sororities? Is the food good? Do people study in their rooms or the library? How easy is it to get into the classes you want at registration? Is the campus well maintained? Are the dormitories pleasant? Is the neighborhood safe and welcoming? What support services are available? What is special about this school?

Vogel recommends students be brutally honest with themselves when visiting colleges. Look at a school not through the lens of who you would like to be, but rather who you are. Can you deal with this academic/social/geographic environment? Ask if the school provides a learning environment in which you feel you can succeed. Try to ascertain the comfort of fit between yourself and a school before examining a school's program in your anticipated major, as the latter frequently changes over the course of a college career.

If you are touring two or more schools in one day, or five or six in a couple of days, you should make detailed notes during or after each visit in order to avoid attributing information to the wrong school later. Rosenberg provides students with a checklist or chart with which to rate each school, and you can create your own customized chart with spreadsheet software. Don't eliminate a college simply because your campus tour guide isn't impressive or informative, or whose answers to your questions are vague or superficial. Rosenberg advises you talk with other students and probe further to get the information you need.

Hang out at several locations where students congregate on each campus; listen to conversations and imagine yourself fitting in. Are these people with whom you could be friends? Check kiosks and bulletin boards for posters and announcements of upcoming events and activities. Read the campus newspaper. Together, the official tour, your notes and photos, conversations with students, and your observations should provide an idea of the social and intellectual life on campus.

Advice for parents: selecting colleges

As colleges are eliminated from consideration for one reason or another, parents may need to remind themselves to be both flexible and patient. Vogel consoles, "It is not lost time to visit campuses you find you don't like—as long as your teen can identify what she did not like about them." Eliminating a college from consideration only serves to narrow down the parameters of the subsequent search.

Making a list. As families research, tour, and consult, a final college list will evolve. Marks recommends that a sound college list consists of some long shots, some likely bets, and some schools that are sure to accept your child. Other college counselors note that while the final list of colleges might contain a few long shots, the majority of schools should be ones at which your teen has at least a fifty percent chance of being accepted. King suggests that students be sure they really like all the schools on their list and would be happy to attend any of them. He further advises seniors to think not only about where they would like to go to college, but also where they are likely to be accepted.

Applying to colleges. The college selection and admission process is a rite of passage in which our teens' sense of self-worth is tested as probably never before in their short lives. We do our children a terrible disservice to publicly identify their first choice school, or speak in terms of schools that are sure bets or easy to get into, contends the author of a recent *Independent School* magazine article. To do so, the writer warns, sets in motion the psychological forces for failure. The author, both a parent and independent school assistant headmaster, suggests parents encourage their children to answer the question by identifing the group of colleges in which they are interested.

Getting help. Whether members of your teen's school faculty or independent consultants, college counselors play significant, yet limited, roles in the college selection process. It is important for parents and teens to understand that college counselors do not get kids admitted to colleges. Students do it themselves. Counselors work behind the scenes. They are not matchmakers who, for a fee, can guarantee college acceptances. Counselors help identify the selectivity of colleges and the factors that best predict a good fit. Vogel emphasizes that while a counselor can guide the process, the student will feel most competent and in control if he or she takes the lead.

The Test

The Scholastic Aptitude Test (SAT) is a three-hour exam designed to measure two sets of skills--verbal reasoning and mathematical problem solving. Most colleges require students to submit either SAT or ACT (formerly the American College Test) scores as part of a student's application package. A perfect combined score is 1600, or a possible score of 800 on each of the two sections. According to the test designers, the scores are used for college admission purposes "because the test predicts readiness for college work."

Test scores can change how teens feel about their friends and themselves. One student lamented, "The SATs made me see myself differently...stupid as compared to my friends. It's a huge threat to kids to see others naturally get 1600, and others struggle to get 1000. Schools should do something to stop kids from comparing scores." Another student proclaimed, "The SAT is a big, fat joke that shows nothing... I would get rid of them." When students addressed the issue of SAT prep classes, some expressed outrage at the pressure and the amount of money spent by some parents. Summing up, a student declared, "These tests just measure how much money people have." Generally, the students agreed that "there's too much pressure in general about college and scores. You get paranoid about others finding out scores. It's the parents of friends asking what schools are you applying to, which adds to the pressure."

Advice for teens: applications and essays

To be considered for acceptance by a college, you have to apply. Several hundred colleges and universities accept the common college application form available online at *www.commonapp.org*, while many others require you to complete a customized form you can download from their website. The purpose of the application is to convince the school that you are someone the college would be pleased to include in its community, who would be successful academically, and who would make a positive contribution to the institution.

Admissions officers read hundreds of applications and are highly sensitive to messy penmanship and spelling and grammar errors. They are suspicious of grandiosity and fantastic resumes of extracurricular activities. Their most important advice to students is to carefully follow the directions in completing the application. Jay Matthews, a Washington, D.C., education writer, provides some observations and suggestions gleaned from his daughter's recent college application process. He says to report your most outstanding extracurricular activities, summarizing your greatest strengths, in the spaces provided on the form. Include a resume outlining additional activities. Avoid decorative type fonts and eye-catching typography. Tell the truth and do not exaggerate—not even a little white lie. It is quite likely a college admissions officer will contact your school counselor to confirm the details of your application.

The application process may be less stressful if you keep a chart for each college to which you're applying that lists the required components of the application, including the application form, transcript, teacher recommendations, essay, test scores, and any other required information. You can then check off each item as it is sent out. It's also a good idea to keep photocopies of everything, just in case something goes astray in the mail or the admissions office. Make sure your transcript is accurate by requesting an unofficial copy and checking the accuracy of courses, internships, and grades before including it in an application package.

Many selective colleges fill substantial portions of each freshman class with early applicants. November 1 is the deadline for early-decision (ED) applications, which provide seniors guaranteed admission in return for a firm commitment to attend. November 1 is also the deadline for early-action (EA) admission, which provides nonbinding acceptance of seniors. Some colleges are reconsidering their ED and EA policies. Supporters of ED and EA argue that seniors who know in December where they'll be going in the fall avoid prolonged acceptance anxiety and thus have a far more enjoyable final year of high school.

Detractors point out that the ED policy forces teens to make binding college choices six months earlier than the traditional May 1 deadline and that it works to the disadvantage of minority and low-income students. Colleges are the primary beneficiaries of the policy. By committing attractive applicants early on, schools raise their acceptance rates and thus their rankings in the college surveys. Schools are judged, in part, by how many students they turn down.

Now we come to that "most unnerving of all special projects, the essays on college applications," as Matthews terms them. He passes on the best advice he has been given and the best he has given out—parents can help as long as they never touch pen to paper. A good college essay is not boring and vividly portrays the applicant. Never write anything that might be interpreted as boastful. In fact, the occasional confession of weakness or error, may be apealing, Matthews assures students. Keep the sentences short and use active verbs. Get feedback from others, however, the essay has to be your own work.

College criteria for selecting students

Colleges consider many factors in selecting each freshman class. Most importantly, they want to be certain that each candidate has demonstrated the ability to be academically successful at their institution. They are also looking for people who will contribute to their communities and campus activities. Most colleges seek a homogenous balance of ethnic, regional, and socioeconomic diversity, legacies, athletes, special academic and artistic talents, and students who may contribute financially to the school in the future.

While each college determines the weight attached to particular factors, all colleges begin by looking for academic achievement. Rosenberg notes that some colleges give more weight to considerations such as test records, recommendations, essays, extracurricular activities, personal interviews, and special status (minorities, first-generation college students), based on the school's particular admission priorities.

Each year the college acceptance process changes. The College Board recently approved major changes in the SAT I, effective as of 2005. Some colleges are reviewing the wisdom of their ED and EA policies to determine if amendment is called for. More colleges are offering courses online. Nevertheless, one thing remains constant—colleges accept students who demonstrate an active interest in learning and in their communities.

Acceptances, rejections, and decisions

Some rejection is inevitable in the college application process. The disappointment of not being accepted by one's first choice college, or even many of them, is an example of what Judith Viorst, Washington, D.C., author of fiction and nonfiction books reflecting both child and adult development, terms an "everyday loss." King counsels, "Do not evaluate your own worth or let your senior evaluate his or hers by which school he or she will be attending."

Parents' and teens' most important decision in the entire process is deciding which of the schools accepting a student is the one the student will attend. "Just because you got accepted, doesn't mean it's the right choice for you—academically or socially," counsels Rosenberg. "Look into your heart and choose a college where you will be successful." Many graduates will have to face, and accept, that they were not chosen by their top choice colleges. It is sad to see a teenager unhappy with the acceptances he received. It is much worse to see parents who shamefacedly mumble the name of the college their child will be attending. Inevitably, Rosenberg counsels, although it sounds trite, most students thrive at and love their college.

How parents can help

Parents are critical to the college selection, application, and acceptance process. They can either help the process go more smoothly and comfortably, or they can make a complex and complicated endeavor much more difficult, depending upon the manner in which they handle it. It can be difficult for parents to determine the most appropriate role to assume in order to best help their teens. Teenagers can become annoyed if parents are too involved or not involved enough, frequently accusing parents of being both on the same day, often in the same conversation! The following are some suggestions to help parents better support their teens through the process.

Keep the process child-centered. Look at your child's needs, strengths, and interests rather than at your own priorities. Remember that the college search, application, and admission process may be an emotional one for you, as well as for your child. You may experience surprising feelings: anxiety, fear, anger, and even jealousy, if your child is being offered opportunities that weren't available to you.

Don't serve college with every meal. If the subject of college seems to dominate every conversation you have with your teen, call a moratorium on it and instead, schedule a specific time of the week to discuss developments on the college front and confine your involvement to that allotted time. You may also find the discussion is most fruitful when done with the help of a counselor.

Be realistic and flexible. Taking your child to tour only colleges at which his or her chances of acceptance are long shots sends the message that you expect him or her to get into one of those colleges. Instead, visit a wide range of schools. Similarly, be enthusiastic about the offers of admission your child receives. Don't make your child feel like a failure if he or she wasn't accepted by the schools you desired. It's an excellent idea to celebrate the first letter of acceptance, even if it the school sending it was not at the top of your teen's list.

Do not use your influence to obtain an acceptance. There are many powerful people in the Washington, D.C., area, and many of them are parents. Before bringing professional power to bear to engineer your child's acceptance by the college of your choice, Rosenberg advises parents to consider the impact such an admittance could have on teens' self-worth. They may find it difficult to ever believe a school found them worthy of acceptance in their own right. Our college-bound teens need to feel that they were accepted on their own merit, are perceived to be assets by the colleges of their choice, and deserve to be there.

Do not brag about all the colleges that accepted your senior or lament those that didn't. Joe Queenan, in a *New York Times* article on what he describes as the "neurotic gabbiness that afflicts parents of the college-bound," observes that he finds "almost all conversations about the college selection process to be banal, self-aggrandizing, self-flagellatory, or punitive."

Not college bound?

Sometimes, a student may decide he's not really ready to go to college immediately following high school. Kaye Cook, M.P.A., a Bethesda, Maryland career counselor who works with adolescents and adults, believes parents should give credence to such feelings on the part of their teens. "The truth is that some kids are just not ready for college at seventeen or eighteen, and need more time to think through what they really want, and maybe should not go to college at all." Some parents fear that if their teens take time off after high school, they may never attend college and complete a degree. "I cannot relax and feel that my job is done until my child has a least a baseline college education," one area mother says.

There are a few young people, however, who come to see the value of college only after knocking about in the adult world until they find a specific area of career interest that requires a degree, and then they put themselves through school, with or without the support of their parents. Others profit from taking some well-planned time off before beginning a college program. Taking off, "not in a hedonistic sense, but in the realistic sense that their work lives will be long and stretched out," explains Cook. She points out that "life expectations will reach eighty to ninety years of age for the next generation, so there is time to take a break, as long as they do this with a plan."

Some graduating seniors consider such alternatives to college as the Peace Corps, AmeriCorps, or perhaps corporate or community service internship programs. They might pursue an opportunity to hone specific skills or work independently. Any of these pursuits serve to provide teens with new skills and windows onto career fields under consideration, as well as foster confidence, maturity, and insight. Other students seek out such opportunities after a year or two of college. Most colleges support students taking some time off after high school or at some point during an undergraduate career, because students generally return from such breaks with new focus and energy to complete their education.

Even if your child is considering not attending college immediately following graduation, Condit recommends that your family continue the college search while at the same time you investigate alternative programs. "If the draw of an alternative program looks less exciting in April when friends are deciding which school to attend in September, students need to be prepared with a college acceptance," he advises. It should be remembered that researching colleges and working with a college counselor are much more easily done while a student is still in high school than it is after graduation. Once accepted to a college, a teen can then advise that college of alternative plans. It is quite common for colleges and universities to allow a student to defer matriculation for either a semester or a year.

Final thoughts

Although the college search and acceptance process may seem long, confusing, and anxiety-ridden, or the choice not to go to college difficult to accept, parents and students can not only survive, but thrive during this time. The experience will help you grow as a family and is an important beginning to the next stage of your lives together.

40

Senior Year: Pulling Away, Letting Go

The irony is that this year of separation is also a year in which parents are very involved in their child's life—driving to colleges, helping with applications, making sure they have the domestic experience necessary for dorm living (changing sheets, doing laundry, etc.). In fact, it is hard to be involved without being overinvolved.

RITA SCHONBERG, Ph.D., Maryland psychologist specializing in adolescents

Preparing a child to leave home following graduation from high school is a family process affecting not only the teenager, but parents, too—it's interactive. Michael Brody, M.D., psychiatrist, parenting consultant, and former Maret School parent, reminds us, "All stages of development require parental guidance and nurturance. The transition from home is a 'really big deal' and parents are necessary participants. Letting go is something parents and their child must do together. If the adults express doubt and trepidation about the future, the teen's anxiety will increase too."

"Many families face profound changes as a child leaves home," observes Leonard King, M.A., director of the college counseling department at the Maret School in Washington, D.C. "Working through that process, not surprisingly, often complicates family dynamics, highlighting conflicts and concerns, as well as the struggle for independence that a family may have been working through since a child was born."

Senior slump

The final year of high school is famous for the "Senior Slump," that tricky period when a senior's mind is more focused on the future than on the classroom in the here and now. Many school counselors consider the slump to be a part of an overall separation anxiety, but Rita Schonberg, Ph.D., a Maryland psychologist specializing in adolescents, suggests that teachers and parents overestimate, and teens underestimate, the impact and length of "senioritis," or the interruption of the ability to do hard work. Some seniors actually work harder during the last year of high school, while others learn better when they feel the pressure is off. "The final semester is no time to slack off," advises local parent Leah Latimer in her thoughtful book *Higher Ground: Preparing African-American Children for College*. "For one thing, it can bring down class rank and overall grade point average. As seniors get their acceptances and decide which opportunity they will follow, a certain let-up is almost inevitable." Colleges, however, expect seniors to maintain the level of achievement that earned them their acceptance. An area senior whose grades deteriorated dramatically during second semester of senior year managed to keep his place at Carnegie-Mellon, but found he was denied access to the honors program.

Schonberg observes that many high school seniors expect school to be easier in their final year. They realize there will be some crunch periods, but they generally expect the year to go well. Even some kids who have performed poorly in school expect to miraculously shape up in their senior year and to find studying less arduous. She says, "Many expect the school to 'cut them a break.' Everyone knows that they are the seniors and that they have been at this school forever and it is their turn to cut corners, miss classes, and decide for themselves what is reasonable and what is not."

When senioritis, boredom, or indifference sets in during the final school year, seniors might be enthusiastic about attempting an entirely new venture—volunteering at a fire station or hospital, taking up tennis, arranging for an internship, or planning an ideal family vacation to pass time while waiting to graduate. Subsequently, some teens are embarrassed to find they finished school with poor grades at the very time they were trying to convince themselves, their teachers, and parents that they were mature and responsible.

Seniors may suddenly ask themselves: Am I good enough? Will I know how to present myself properly? How will I know which choice is the best one? Unconscious concern about their competence and ability to function away from their families can affect seniors' relationships, as well as their ability to be reasonable and productive. Many seniors believe they are the only ones who are unsure and confused. Parents can diffuse some of their children's fears by letting them know that feeling inadequate or depressed at times is normal. Reassure teens by pointing out their many past successes and express confidence in their abilities to cope and succeed.

Separating

A child begins the natural and necessary process of separating from parents during the very first years of life. "Separation is part of the process of living and takes place throughout the human life cycle," advises Brody who, along with his wife, Shelly Brody, M.A., a college counselor and humanities teacher at the Maret School in Washington, D.C., and Leonard King, M.A., the director of the college counseling department at Maret, have created an annual presentation for seniors and their parents called "Transition from High School to College."

The anticipated separation at the end of high school is increasingly complicated in this time of blended families and single parent households. Single parents may have difficulty with the anticipated departure of a child into the world, and the child, in turn, may worry about leaving the parent alone. For teens of divorced parents, the normal separation issues of senior year may resonate with echoes of the separation and loss that surrounded their parents' divorces.

For some families, the process of separating will be more complicated and difficult. Families who have recently suffered the death of a member or undergone a divorce, as well as teens who have been adopted, undergone a premature boarding school experience, or have an emotional or physical disability are more likely to find separation daunting.

Seniors pulling away

Adults often fail to realize that for many seniors, the anticipated separations at the end of senior year feel almost global in scope. Teens will be separating from parents, siblings, pets, and home, of course, but also from schools they may have attended for as many as fourteen years, teachers who have nurtured them, and friends who have been mainstays since many were literally toddlers.

Some teens, anticipating the looming changes, may cut class or fail to turn in assignments in an unconscious attempt either to break ties with high school or to signify that it is not longer relevant. Friends are often the people from whom teens have the most difficulty separating, and some seniors, overwhelmed by the impending separation, break off relationships, depriving themselves of invaluable peer support.

Parents can point out to their teens that although their friends may scatter across the country following graduation, e-mail and Instant Messaging allow them to stay in touch almost effortlessly. Once college begins, old friends will be home for the holidays and breaks, often bringing with them new college friends who may settle in the area after graduation.

Nancy Faust Sizer, M.A., author and lecturer at the Harvard Graduate School of Education, observes that our teens' teachers, responsible in part for helping seniors prepare for the upcoming changes, may also have difficulty letting go of their students. She writes, "They [teachers and students] are trying not to need each other, but they have seen each other daily." She admits she has a "familiar springtime dream in which I am on a riverbank helplessly watching as my students float downstream toward the sea." Many parents have similar dreams.

Seniors often behave like Dr. Doolittle's Pushmi-Pullyu, of two minds and with two heads pointing in opposite directions. One parent describes the behavior as being akin to having her son hold tightly to her shoulders while pressing his foot into her belly and pushing off. Senior year is poignant and bittersweet, and all seniors will be sad from time to time and some may struggle with depression.

Parents letting go

Karen Coburn, M.A., and Madge Treeger, M.A., authors of *Letting Go: A Parent's Guide to Understanding the College Years*, write, "Parental ambivalence about sending a child off to college, particularly a first-born, is common. The sense that family life will never be the same again, a sense of loss, even jealousy—all are likely to be mixed with the anticipated satisfaction of launching one's offspring." Parents send their "children off with a mixture of anticipation and anxiety, a sense of loneliness and freedom, fantasy and reality."

Parents shouldn't be surprised if their teens procrastinate about corresponding with colleges, requesting final transcripts, ordering graduation invitations or similar senior obligations; these symbolize the inevitability of their uncertain futures. Brody observes, "We try so hard to regulate our children's anxieties that they may have a limited capacity to do this themselves once away from home." Difficult though it may be, we should not be afraid to allow our teens to make final decisions and trust that they will turn to us for help when their plans don't work out.

It is important that parents don't overreact or take their teens' moods and behavior personally. Remember that parental love includes letting go so that your children can achieve independence and freedom. Foster an attitude of optimism and anticipation of positive and exciting change for your teens and yourselves.

The pattern of family life does change once teens are out on their own. Whether parents have one less child at home or none at all, they will now be able to plan their time and commitments differently. Marital relationships come under renewed focus and may even go through a period of readjustment, while single parents may feel freer to expand their social lives or commit more time to a steady companion.

We should make a point of reassuring our teens that when we tell them, "I'm really going to miss you," we're not laying a guilt trip on them or think they are not ready for the next big step in their lives. We can point out that just as they will miss family, friends, and pets, we're allowed to miss them, too. Likewise, we can let our teens know that we understand that they're excited to get out and get on their own, and that we are looking forward to doing some personal exploration as well. By doing so, we can help them validate the bittersweet flavor of their own feelings.

Parents who feel they are losing too much, too soon as senior year rolls by may need to examine their feelings closely. Those whose sense of self has been defined by parenthood may have lost sight of themselves as individuals. Senior year may be a marvelous opportunity to rediscover one's self, identify interests, set goals, and invest energy in one's own development

Information cramming

Susan Reimer, *Baltimore Sun* columnist and parent of two teenagers, writes of senior year, "I am engaging in what I call 'speed parenting,' my attempt to tie up eighteen years of instructional loose ends in a little more than a few weeks. I feel like the teacher who suddenly realizes that finals are just days away, and two weeks' worth of lesson plans are untaught. Where did the time go?"

During the course of senior year, parents are sure to remember essential survival skills they feel they may have failed to teach their eighteen-year-olds. Reviewing, or cramming, all those practical, essential lessons can be a major effort. Much of the information is rudimentary in terms of the grand scheme of things—how much detergent to use in the washer, how to determine if refrigerated or frozen food has gone bad, how to change sheets, arrange for dry cleaning, schedule appointments. Imparting these helpful hints can help parents weather the separation process better by knowing they have enhanced their teens' competence to handle everyday demands and stresses. Godfrey

Taylor, a student at William and Mary, advises parents, "Just don't overwhelm your senior with every life lesson you've picked up over the years. Give them that knowledge you think crucial, but let them learn some things from experience."

This said, there is no guarantee that seniors will enthusiastically embrace the "Adult Life 101" lessons. Reimer says that our children are trying to "drain the last drops of adolescent fun from their lives while we are still trying to get their attention for a review of parenthood's major talking points."

Final thoughts: planning ahead

Mary Pipher, Ph.D., author of *Reviving Ophelia: Saving the Selves of Adolescent Girls* and *The Shelter of Each Other: Rebuilding Our Families*, observes that our culture could use a new model of family life beyond the high school years. We place such value on autonomy that both parents and teens get the message that once one reaches a certain chronological age and is healthy, then one breaks with the family and doesn't see them or need them all that much. This is patently untrue. Parents who are emotionally close to their children when they are young can continue to enjoy regular contact after the children are young adults living on their own by talking often, getting together for dinners out, attending events of mutual interest, and perhaps traveling together.

For parents of teens going off to college, reassure the young people of regular e-mail and telephone correspondence and make sure to follow through. Make plans to attend Parents' Weekend, making reservations early to ensure your attendance. Let teens know you are looking forward to their coming home during the school year and that a friend from school is welcome, too. What to many parents may loom as an achingly empty and lonely time just after teens go off to college will seem, between Parents' Weekend, Fall Break, and Thanksgiving, to almost fly past.

Finally, college breaks and holiday schedules, as well as summer job opportunities, may interfere with your family celebrating and vacationing together with the same ease as when your teens were still in high school. Condit advises parents to plan a special family trip for the summer immediately following high school graduation, It may be the last time the family can easily get together.

RESOURCES

Every attempt has been made to provide accurate resources. We apologize for any incomplete or inaccurate entries.

1 | MOVING TOWARD ADULTHOOD

Chapter 1. The Adolescent Brain: Not Yet Adult

PUBLICATIONS: BOOKS

JoAnn Deak, Ph.D. and Teresa Barker, *Girls Will Be Girls: Raising Confident and Courageous Daughters*. Hyperion, 2002.

Marian Diamond, Ph.D. and Janet Hopson, *Magic Trees of the Mind: How to Nurture Your Child's Intelligence, Creativity, and Healthy Emotions from Birth through Adolescence*. Penguin USA, 1999.

Howard Gardner, Ph.D., *Intelligence Reframed: Multiple Intelligence for the 21st Century*. Basic Books, 2000.

Daniel Goleman, Ph.D., *Emotional Intelligence*. Bantam, 1997.

Jane Healy, Ph.D., *Failure to Connect: How Computers Affect Our Children's Minds--and What We Can Do About It*. Touchstone, 1999.

Dharma Khalso, M.D. and Cameron Stauth, *Brain Longevity: The Breakthrough Medical Program that Improves Your Mind and Memory*. Warner Books, 1999.

Richard Restak, M.D., *The New Brain: How the Modern Age is Rewiring Your Mind*. Rodale, 2003.

Barbara Strauch, *The Primal Teen: What the New Discoveries about the Teenage Brain Tell Us about Our Kids*. Doubleday, 2003.

ARTICLE

Karen Young Kreeger, M.S.,"Deciphering How the Sexes Think." *The Scientist*, Jan. 21, 2002.

WEBSITE

www.luinst.org/brainexplorer
The Lundbeck Institute's online interactive atlas of the human brain.

Chapter 2. Adolescent Identity: Who Am I?

PUBLICATIONS: BOOKS

Mary Collins, *The Essential Daughter: Changing Expectations for Girls at Home, 1797 to the Present*. Praeger Publishers, 2002.

David Elkind, Ph.D., *Ties that Stress: The New Family Imbalance*. Harvard University Press, 1994.

Erik Erikson, *Childhood and Society*. W. W. Norton, 1993.

H. Paul Gabriel, M.D. and Robert Wool, M.D., *Anticipating Adolescence: How to Cope with Your Child's Emotional Upheaval and Forge a New Relationship Together*. *iUniverse.com*, 2001.

June Tangney, Ph.D., Editor, *Handbook of Self and Identity*. Guilford Press, 2002.

Beverly Tatum, *Why Are All the Black Kids Sitting Together in the Cafeteria? And Other Conversations about Race: A Psychologist Explains the Devvelopment of Racial Identity*. Basic Books, 2003.

Sherry Turkle, Ph.D., *Life on the Screen: Identity in the Age of the Internet*. Touchstone Books, 1997.

PUBLICATIONS: INTERNET

www.rider.edu/~suler/psycyber/adoles.html
"Adolescents in Cyberspace: The Good, the Bad, and the Ugly," article by John Suler, Ph.D., Rider University. Explores the psychological dimensions of environments created by computers and online networks.

Chapter 3. Body Image

PUBLICATIONS: BOOKS

Joan Jacobs Brumberg, Ph.D., T*he Body Project: An Intimate History of American Girls*. Vintage Books, 1998.

Ophira Edut and Rebecca Walker, *Adios, Barbie: Young Women Write About Body Image and Identity*. Seal Press Feminist Publications, 1998.

Rita Freedman, Ph.D., *Bodylove: Learning To Like Our Looks and Ourselves: A Practical Guide for Women*. Gurze Design and Books, 2002

Jean Kilbourne, Ed.D., *Deadly Persuasion: Why Women and Girls Must Fight the Addictive Power of Advertising*. Free Press, 1999.

Jean Kilbourne, Ed.D. and Mary Pipher, Ph.D., *Can't Buy My Love: How Advertising Changes the Way We Think and Feel*. Touchstone Books. 2000.

Abigail Natenshon, M.A., L.C.S.W., *When Your Child has an Eating Disorder: A Step-by-Step Workbook for Parents and Other Caregivers*. Jossey-Bass, 1999.

Virginia Beane Rutter, M.S., *Embracing Persephone: How to be the Mother You Want for the Daughter You Cherish*. Conari Press, 2001.

WEBSITE

www.edreferral.com/body_image.htm
The Eating Disorder Referral and Information Center
Information for eating disorder prevention and treatment. International references and articles on body image relating to eating disorders.

Chapter 4. Communication Between Parents and Teens

PUBLICATIONS: BOOKS

Eileen Bernstein, M.Ed, LCPC, *Middle School and the Age of Adjustment: A Guide for Parents*. Bergin & Garvey, 2002.

Adele Faber, and Elaine Mazlish. *How To Talk So Kids Will Listen & Listen So Kids Will Talk*. Avon Books, 1999.

Robin Goldstein, Ph.D., with Janet Gallant. *The Parenting Bible: The Answers to Parents' Most Common Questions*. Sourcebooks, Inc., 2002.

Edward Hallowell, M.D., *The Childhood Roots of Adult Happiness*. Ballantine Books, 2002.

Edward Hallowell, M.D., *When You Worry About the Child You Love*. Simon and Schuster, 1996.

Rod Wallace Kennedy, Ph.D., *The Encouraging Parent: How to Stop Yelling at Your Kids and Start Teaching Them Confidence, Self-Discipline, and Joy*. Three Rivers Press, 2001.

Dan Kindlon, Ph.D. and Michael Thompson, M.D., *Raising Cain: Protecting the Emotional Life of Boys*. Ballantine Books, 2000.

Kenneth Rubin, Ph.D., with Andrea Thompson. *The Friendship Factor*. Viking Press, 2002.

Martin E. P. Seligman, Ph.D., *The Optimistic Child: A Proven Program to Safeguard Children Against Depression and Build Lifelong Resilience*. Houghton Mifflin Company, 1995.

Susan Morris Shaffer and Linda Perlman Gordon, *Why Boys Don't Talk and Why We Care: A Mother's Guide to Connection*. Mid-Atlantic Equity Consortium, Inc., 2000.

Douglas Stone, Bruce Patton, and Sheila Heen, *Difficult Conversations: How to Discuss What Matters Most*. Penguin Books, 2000.

Ron Taffel, Ph.D., with Melinda Blau, *The Second Family: How Adolescent Power Is Challenging the American Family*. St. Martin's Press, 2001.

Deborah Tannen, Ph.D., *I Only Say This Because I Love You*. Random House, 2001.

Anthony E. Wolf, Ph.D., *Get Out of My Life, But First Could You Drive Me & Cheryl to the Mall: A Parent's Guide to the New Teenager*, Revised and Updated. Farrar, Straus, and Giroux, 2002.

WEBSITE

groups.yahoo.com
Under subheadings "Family & Home" and "Parenting," Yahoo! Groups provides thousands of message boards and clubs for a multitude of parent and family issues.

2 | TEENS ON THE MOVE

Chapter 5. Friendships

PUBLICATIONS: BOOKS

Fred Frankel, Ph.D., *Good Friends Are Hard to Find*. Perspective Publishing, 1996.

Kenneth H. Rubin, Ph.D., with Andrea Thompson, *The Friendship Factor*. Viking Penguin, 2002.

Michael Thompson, Ph.D., Catherine O'Neill Grace, and Lawrence and J. Cohen, Ph.D., *Best Friends, Worst Enemies: Understanding the Social Lives of Children*. Ballantine Books, 2002.

Chapter 6. Hanging Out

See chapters: 5. Friendships, 8. Dating

Chapter 7. Driving

PUBLICATIONS: BOOKS

Phil Berardelli, *Safe Young Drivers: A Guide for Parents and Teens.* Nautilus Communications, Inc., 2002. *www.safeyoungdrivers.com*

Spiral-bound book designed to be read by parents and teens: preparing for the driver's test, quick reference to be kept in the car afterwards.

J. Marlene Snyder. Ph.D., *AD/HD & Driving: A Guide for Parents of Teens with AD/HD.* Whitefish Consultants, 2001. Available through Children and Adults with Attention-Deficit/Hyperactivity Disorder (CHADD), 800/233-4050, *www.chadd.org.*

ORGANIZATIONS

Automotive Association of America, 800/327-3444

Call for AAA's "Teaching Your Teen to Drive: A Partnership for Survival."

AAA Mid-Atlantic, 703/222-4104

Publications include "Alcohol," "One Drink Can Be Too Many," and "Choosing a Driving School," includes a handbook and the choice of a video or CD-Rom.

WEBSITES

www.highwaysafety.org, www.iihs.org

Insurance Institute for Highway Safety, Highway Loss Data Institute Data on car crashes, licensing legislation, vehicle research tools.

www.nhtsa.gov, National Highway Traffic Safety Administration

Auto and traffic safety and vehicle and equipment safety studies, regulations, and crash test results.

www.saddonline.com, National Office: 877/SADD-INC

Students against Destructive Decisions/Students against Driving Drunk (SADD) Organization information, legislation, calendar of events, organizing.

www.truckline.com/safetynet/howtodrive/blindspot_tips.html

American Trucking Association, "Staying Out of the 'No-Zone': Tips for Eliminating Blind Spot Accidents," a tip sheet for sharing the road with trucks.

Chapter 8 Dating

PUBLICATIONS: BOOKS

William Pollack, Ph.D., with Todd Shuster, *Real Boys Voices.* Random House, 2000.

Deborah Roffman, M.S., *Sex & Sensibility: The Thinking Parent's Guide to Talking Sense About Sex.* Perseus Publishing, 2001.

Chapter 9. S-e-x

PUBLICATIONS: BOOKS

Jane Annunziata, Ph.D. and Marc Nemiroff, Ph.D., *Sex and Babies: First Facts.* Magination, 2002.

Deborah Roffman, M.S., *Sex & Sensibility: The Thinking Parent's Guide to Talking Sense About Sex.* Perseus Publishing 2001.

ORGANIZATIONS

National Campaign to Prevent Teen Pregnancy, Washington, D.C.
202/478-8500, *www.teenpregnancy.org*
Collaborates with media leaders about preventing teen pregnancy.

Parents, Families, and Friends of Lesbians and Gays (PFLAG)
Washington D.C., 202/467-8180, *www.pflag.org*
Health and interests of gay, lesbian, transgendered persons and their families.

Chapter 10. Home Parties and School Dances

See chapters : 8. Dating, 9. Sex, 16. Alcohol

Chapter 11. Clubs, Concerts, and Music *See chapters: 5. Friendship, 16. Alcohol*

Chapter 12. Beach Week

TELEPHONE CONTACTS

Ocean City Police Department, 410/723-6600
Ask for: Community Relations Coordinator

Ocean City Parent Network, 410/723-3700
24/7 hotline from mid-May through June.

Ocean City Visitors Center, 800-OCOCEAN (800/626-2326)

Rehoboth Beach Police Department, 302/227-2577

WEBSITES

www.bethanybeachde.com, Bethany Beach, Delaware
"At The Beach," events, rentals, and maps for Bethany and Fenwick Beaches.

www.ococean.com, Ocean City, Maryland, Calendar of events, places to stay. Click on "Senior Week Housing" for approved lodging for teens.

www.cityofrehoboth.com, City of Rehoboth Beach, Delaware
Maps, rules, links to cultural, educational, and recreational activities.

www.beach-fun.com, Rehoboth Beach and Dewey Beach, Delaware
Listing of events, accommodations.

3 | UNDER THE INFLUENCE

Chapter 13. Media

PUBLICATIONS: BOOKS

Jean Kilbourne, Ed.D., *Can't Buy My Love: How Advertising Changes the Way We Think and Feel*. Touchstone Books, 2000.

Jean Kilbourne, Ed.D., *Deadly Persuasion: Why Women and Girls Must Fight the Addictive Power of Advertising*. Free Press, 1999.

ORGANIZATIONS

Institute for Mental Health Initiatives, Washington, D.C.
202/467-2285, *www.imhi.org*
Brings mental health issues to the media through the newsletter, "Dialogue"; Research-based examples and suggestions for applying current knowledge about mental health to media story lines, character development, and scripts.

Media Education Foundation, 800/897-0089, *www.mediaed.org*
Education videos on media, culture, race, and sexuality.

WEBSITES

www.dadsanddaughters.org. Dads and Daughters, 888/ 824-DADS
Advocacy organization for strengthening father-daughter relationships and transforming the media's impact on their daughters.

www.frameworksinstitute.org
The Frameworks Institute. Reports concerning adolescents and the media.

Chapter 14. Eating: An Issue of Control

PUBLICATIONS: BOOKS

Joan Jacobs Brumberg, Ph.D., *Fasting Girls: The History of Anorexia Nervosa.* Vintage Books, 2000.

Ann Litt, M.S., R.D., L.D., *The College Student's Guide to Eating Well on Campus.* Tulip Hill Press, 2000.

Abigail Natenshon, M.A., *When Your Child Has an Eating Disorder.* Jossey-Bass, 1999.

WEBSITES

www.edreferral.com/body_image.htm
Eating Disorder Referral and Information Center
Information for eating disorder prevention and treatment, international referrals and articles on body image as it relates to eating disorders.

www.nationaleatingdisorders.org
National Eating Disorders Association (NEDA), 800-931-2237
Dedicated to eliminating eating disorders and body dissatisfaction. Information and referral services for parents, professionals, girls and women, boys and men, and athletes and coaches. "Go Girls" and "Media Watchdog Programs."

www.somethingfishy.com
Site has an extensive list of web links describing eating disorder treatment options, as well as numerous web links for many health issues about which parents of adolescents may seek information.

www.eatright.org American Dietetic Association, 202-775-8277
Offers information to promote optimal nutrition and health with ample content focused on adolescents.

www.cnmc.org
Children's National Medical Center Eating Disorders Clinic, 202-884-2164
Search, Eating Disorders: information for parents, adolescents, and professionals; description of outpatient and inpatient treatment programs and group therapy programs.

www.renfrew.org Renfrew Center, 800-RENFREW
Education, prevention, research, and treatment of Eating Disorders. Printable educational materials and a comprehensive listing of recommended books, magazines, and videos.

Chapter 15. Smoking

PUBLICATIONS: INTERNET

www.cdc.gov/tobacco/educational_materials/parenting/gotaminbrochure.htm
Centers for Disease Control and Prevention's online brochure for parents; information on helping kids quit smoking; 30-minute video about how to keep children free of tobacco, alcohol and drugs. Order: *www.cdc.gov/tobacco/educational_materials/mykids.htm* or by mail from CDC's Office on Smoking and Health Publications, Mail Stop K-50, 4770 Buford Highway, NE, Atlanta, GA 30341-3717.

WEBSITES

www.artfultruth.fiu.edu Healthy Propaganda Arts Project
Reducing tobacco use among young people through art education.

www.ash.org, www.no-smoking.org Action on Smoking and Health
Information on antismoking activism, smoking risks, and quitting smoking.

www.cdc.gov/tobacco Centers for Disease Control and Prevention (CDC)
CDC's Tobacco Information and Prevention Source (TIPS). Resources for parents, educators, and youth on tobacco facts and reports from the Surgeon General. Under "TIPS for Youth," see SLAM, a 15-minute video for young people to make them more aware of cigarette advertising and ways to resist influences of tobacco industry.

www.communitiesofconcern.org Communities of Concern
Partnership of parents, students, and schools. Encourages the prevention of substance abuse with its publication "A Parent's Guide for the Prevention of Alcohol, Tobacco and Other Drug Use," customizable web document.

www.kickbuttsday.org Kick Butts Day sponsored by the Campaign for Tobacco-Free Kids, an annual initiative encouraging activism and leadership among students in elementary, middle, and high school.

www.quitnet.com QuitNet
In association with Boston University's School of Public Health, personalized support, advice, chat rooms, and products devoted to quitting smoking.

www.notobacco.org Foundation for a Smokefree America
Resources, information, and anti-smoking "adbuster" posters. Video, "The Truth about Tobacco" to aid young people to remain tobacco-free and empower smokers to quit successfully. Special pages for middle and high school students.

www.thetruth.com
Information about the tobacco industry, including names, incomes, and research compiled, organized, and published online after the tobacco industry was required to release internal information and research on the health risks and addictiveness of cigarettes.

www.tobaccofreekids.org Campaign for Tobacco-Free Kids
Information, resources, and support for the anti-smoking movement.

Chapter 16. Alcohol and Other Drugs

PUBLICATIONS: BOOKS

Richard Bonnie and Mary Ellen O'Connell, *Reducing Underage Drinking: A Collective Responsibility*. National Academies Press, 2003. *www.nap.edu*.

ORGANIZATIONS

Al-Anon and Alateen, *www.al-anon.alateen.org*
Washington, D.C. and Maryland, 202/882-1334
Virginia, 703/764-0476
Anonymous resources and support groups, as well as a twelve-step program of personal recovery for friends and family of alcoholics.

Alcoholics Anonymous, *www.alcoholics-anonymous.org*
Washington, D.C. and Maryland, 202/966-9115
Northern Virginia, 703/876-6166
Men and women dedicated to helping one another quit drinking.

American Council for Drug Education and Children of Alcoholics Foundation, New York, New York, 800/488-3784
www.acde.org; www.drughelp.org
Drug education, prevention tips, treatment options, a referral and drug information database; advice about how to prevent use of drugs in homes.

Campaign for Tobacco-Free Kids, Washington, D.C.
202/296-5469, *www.tobaccofreekids.org*
The Campaign for Tobacco-Free Kids provides information, resources, and avenues of support for the anti-smoking movement.

Communities of Concern, Bethesda, Maryland
301/656-2481, *www.communitiesofconcern.org*
Partnership of parents, students, and schools encouraging the prevention of substance abuse by distribution of the booklet, "A Parent's Guide for the Prevention of Alcohol, Tobacco and Other Drug Use."

Family Support Center, Bethesda, Maryland
301/718-2467, *www.fscone.org*
Nonprofit organization helping independent and public school staff and families prevent, recognize, and overcome mental health and behavior problems in children and adolescents.

Mothers Against Drunk Driving (MADD), *www.madd.org*
Montgomery County Chapter, Rockville, Maryland, 301/949-1222
Northern Virginia Chapter, Fairfax, Virginia, 703/352-3944
Supports grassroots activism for prevention of underage drinking and drunk driving; support services for victims of violent crime.

U.S. Department of Health and Human Services (HHS)
Substance Abuse and Mental Health Services Administration

National Clearinghouse for Alcohol and Drug Information (NCADI)
800/662-HELP, *www.health.org*
Access to research and databases from HHS on drug and alcohol use and addiction and preventative measures. Also maintains a NCADI Update listserve.

Partnership for a Drug-Free America
New York, New York, 212/922-1560, *www.drugfreeamerica.org*
Nonprofit coalition of communications industry professionals dedicated to advertising the realities of drug and alcohol use to kids and teens.

Addiction treatment centers. Please check hospitals in your area for addiction treatment programs for adolecents.

4 | FOCUS ON PARENTS

Chapter 17. Saying No, and Meaning It

PUBLICATIONS: BOOKS

Neil Bernstein, Ph.D., *How to Keep Your Teenager Out of Trouble and What to Do if You Can't*. Workman Publishing, 2001.

Chapter 18. Push for Success

BPUBLICATIONS: BOOKS

Wendy Mogel, Ph.D., *The Blessing of a Skinned Knee: Using Jewish Teachings to Raise Self-Reliant Children*. Penguin USA, 2001.

Barbara Schneider, Ph.D. and David Stevenson, Ph.D., *The Ambitious Generation: America's Teenagers, Motivated but Directionless*. Yale University Press, 2000.

Martin E. Seligman, Ph.D., *The Optimistic Child: Proven Program to Safeguard Children from Depression and Build Lifelong Resistance*. Perennial, 1996.

Chapter 19. Gender: Rearing Boys and Girls

PUBLICATIONS: BOOKS

Evelyn Bassoff, Ph.D., *Between Mothers and Sons: The Making of Vital and Loving Men*. Plume, 1995.

Joan Jacobs Brumberg, Ph.D., T*he Body Project: An Intimate History of American Girls*. Vintage Books, 1998.

Mary Collins, *The Essential Daughter: Changing Expectations for Girls at Home, 1797 to the Present*. Praeger, 2002.

JoAnn Deak, Ph.D., and Teresa Barker, *Girls Will Be Girls: Raising Confident and Courageous Daughters*. Hyperion Books, 2002.

Elizabeth Debold, Marie Wilson, and Idelisse Malave, *Mother Daughter Revolution: From Betrayal to Power.* Addison-Wesley Publishing Co, 1994.

Carol Gilligan, Ph.D., *In a Different Voice: Psychological Theory on Women's Development.* Harvard University Press, 1993.

Michael Gurian, Ph.D., *A Fine Young Man: What Parents, Mentors, and Educators Can Do to Shape Adolescent Boys into Exceptional Men.* J.P. Tarcher/Putnam, 1998.

Michael Gurian, Ph.D., *The Good Son: Shaping the Moral Development of Our Boys and Young Men--A Complete Parenting Plan*. J.P. Tarcher/Putnam, 1999.

Michael Gurian, Ph.D., *The Wonder of Boys: What Parents, Mentors, And Educators Can Do To Shape Boys Into Exceptional Men*. J.P. Tarcher, 1997.

Michael Gurian, Ph.D., *The Wonder of Girls: Understanding the Hidden Nature of Our Daughters*. Fireside, 2003.

Harris Interactive, *Hostile Hallways: Bullying, Teasing, and Sexual Harassment in Schools*. American Association of University Women Educational Foundation, 2001.

Mavis Jukes, B.A., J.D., *The Guy Book: An Owner's Manual*. Crown Publishing, 2002.

Michael Kimmel, Ph.D., *The Gendered Society*, Oxford University Press. 2001.

Michael Kimmel, Ph.D., *Manhood in America*. Free Press, 1995.

Daniel J. Kindlon, Ph.D., and Michael Thompson, Ph.D., *Raising Cain: Protecting the Emotional Life of Boys*. Ballantine Books, 1999.

Eleanor Maccoby, Ph.D., *The Two Sexes: Growing Up Apart, Coming Together*. Belknap Press, 1999.

Peggy Orenstein, *School Girls: Young Women, Self Esteem, and the Confidence Gap*. American Association of University Women, Doubleday, 1995.

Mary Pipher, Ph.D., *Reviving Ophelia: Saving the Selves of Adolescent Girls*. Ballantine Books. 1994.

William Pollack, Ph.D., *Real Boys: Rescuing Our Sons From the Myths of Boyhood*. Henry Holt, 1999.

Deborah Roffman, M.S., *Sex & Sensibility: The Thinking Parent's Guide to Talking Sense about Sex*. Perseus Books, 2000.

Myra Sadker, Ph.D., and David Sadker, Ph.D., *Failing at Fairness: How America's Schools Cheat Girls*. Touchstone Books, 1995.

Olga Silverstein and Beth Rashbaum, *The Courage to Raise Good Men*. Penguin Books, 1995.

Susan Morris Shaffer and Linda Perlman Gordon, *Why Boys Don't Talk and Why We Care: A Mother's Guide to Connection*. Mid-Atlantic Equity Consortium, 2000.

Rachel Simmons, *Odd Girl Out: The Hidden Culture of Aggression in Girls*. Harcourt Inc., 2002.

Michael Thompson, Ph.D. and Catherine O'Neill Grace, with Lawrence J. Cohen, Ph.D., *Best Friends, Worst Enemies: Understanding the Social Lives of Children*. Ballantine Books, 2002.

Rosalind Wiseman, *Queen Bees and Wannabes: Helping Your Daughter Survive Cliques, Gossip, Boyfriends & Other Realities of Adolescence*. Crown Publishers, 2002.

WEBSITES

www.Ritualwell.org, 215/576-0800

Creates and implements innovative programs, including "Rosh Hodesh: It's A Girl Thing!" for the strengthening of self-esteem and Jewish identity in adolescent girls.

www.aauw.org, American Association of University Women, 800/326-AAUW
Advocates and lobbies for education and equity for girls and women, and provides financial and legal aid for women in higher education.

www.dadsanddaughters.org, 888/ 824-DADS
Advocacy organization aimed at strengthening father-daughter relationships and transforming the cultural message that values daughters more for how they look than for who they are.

www.girlsinc.org, 800/374-4475, Girls, Incorporated
Eeducational programs and opportunities for girls in high-risk areas.

www.ms.foundation.org, 800/676-7780, Ms. Foundation for Women
Promotes girls' and womens' right to govern their lives and influence the world around them through effecting change in public consciousness, law, philanthropy, and social policy.

www.wcwonline.org, 781/283-2500, The Wellesley Centers for Women
Research alliance of the Stone Center and Center for Women, nation's largest women's research organization. Promotes positive change for women and girls; publications including *How Schools Can Stop Shortchanging Girls (and Boys): Gender Equity Strategies*.

Chapter 20. Communication: Parent to Parent

PUBLICATIONS: BOOKS

Brad Sachs, Ph.D., *The Good Enough Child: How to Have an Imperfect Family and Be Perfectly Satisfied*. Quill, 2001.

Chapter 21. Learning from Diversity

PUBLICATIONS: BOOKS

Sharon Bush, *Loving Across the Color Line: A White Adoptive Mother Learns About Race*. Rowman & Littlefield, 2000.

Lisa Delpit, *Other People's Children: Cultural Conflict in the Classroom*. New Press, 1996.

Lynn Duvall, *Respecting Our Differences: A Guide to Getting Along in a Changing World*. Free Spirit Press, 1994.

Jeffrey Garadere, Ph.D., *Smart Parenting for African Americans: Help Your Kids Thrive in a Difficult World*. Citadel Press, 1999.

Darlene Powell Hopson, Ph.D. and Derek S. Hopson, Ph.D., *Different and Wonderful:Raising Black Children in a Race Conscious Society*. Prentice Hall, 1990.

Darlene Powell Hopson, Ph.D. and Derek S. Hopson, Ph.D., *Raising the Rainbow Generation:Teaching Your Children to be Successful in a Multicultural Society*. Fireside, 1993.

Leah Latimer, *Higher Ground: Preparing African-American Children for College*. Avon Books, 1999.

Sara Lawrence-Lightfoot, *Respect: An Exploration*. Perseus Publishing, 2000.

Stuart Matlins and Arthur Magida, editors, *How to be a Perfect Stranger: The Essential Religious Etiquette Handbook*. Skylight Paths, 2002.

Barbara Mathias and Mary Ann French, *40 Ways to Raise a Nonracist Child*. Harper Collins, 1997.

Beverly Tatum, *Assimilation Blues: Black Families in a White Community*. Basic Books, 2000.

Beverly Tatum, Ph.D., *Why are All the Black Kids Sitting Together in the Cafeteria? And Other Conversations about Race: A Psychologist Explains the Development of Racial Identity*. Basic Books, 2003.

Gayle Colquitt White, *Believer and Beliefs: A Practical Religious Etiquette for Business and Social Occasions*. Berkeley Publishing Group, 1997.

ORGANIZATIONS

Black Student Fund, Washington, D.C., 202/387-1414, *www.blackstudentfund.org* Financial assistance and support services to DC area African-American students and families.

Eastern Educational Resource Collaborative (East Ed), Washington, D.C. 202/ 464-1996, *www.easted.org*

Offers services on diversity to schools, including consulting to administrators, teachers, and boards; Multicultural Seminar series, institutes, and conferences; and online services and newsletter on Equity and Justice.

Latino Student Fund, Washington, D.C., 202/ 244-3438
www.latinostudentfund.org

Provides scholarships and resources to help Hispanic children in the Washington area reach their highest potential through education.

Gay, Lesbian and Straight Education Network (GLSEN), National Capitol Area, 202/ 253-2441, *www.glsennca.org*

Straight and sexual minority teens and adults, educators and others concerned about sexual orientation issues in our public and private schools.

Parents and Friends of Lesbians and Gays (PFLAG), DC chapter
202/ 467-8180, *www.pflag.org*

National organization promoting the well-being of sexual minority teens and adults through education, resources, and advocacy.

Sexual Minority Youth Assistance League (SMYAL), Washington, D.C. 202/ 546-5940, *www.smyal.org*

Supports and enhances self-esteem of sexual minority youth, thirteen to twenty-one years of age; works to increase awareness and understanding of their issues.

Teaching for Change, Washington, D.C., 800/763-9131
www.teachingforchange.org

Resources for teachers and families to promote social and economic justice.

Tolerance.org, Montgomery, Alabama, 334/956-8200
www.teachingtolerance.org

Southern Poverty Law Center, supports K-12 educators to promote respect for difference and appreciation of diversity.

5 | EMOTIONS

Chapter 22. Stress: Living with the Inevitable

PUBLICATIONS: BOOKS

Elisabeth Guthrie, M.D. and Kathy Matthews, *The Trouble with Perfect: How Parents Can Avoid the Overachievement Trap and Still Raise Successful Children*. Broadway Books, 2003.

Brad Sachs, Ph.D., *The Good Enough Child: How to Have and Imperfect Family and Be Perfectly Satisfied*. Quill, 2001.

Chapter 23. Afraid, Anxious, and Just Worried

PUBLICATIONS: BOOKS

Gavin de Becker, *The Gift of Fear: Survival Signals that Protect Us from Violence*. Dell Publishing Company, 1998.

Linda Goldman, Ph.D., *Breaking the Silence: A Guide to Help Children with Complicated Grief, Suicide, Homicide, AIDS, Violence and Abuse*. Brunner-Routledge, 2001. *www.childrensgrief.net*

Stanley I. Greenspan, M.D., *The Secure Child: Helping Children Feel Safe and Confident in a Changing World*. Perseus Publishing, 2002.

Edward M. Hallowell, M.D., *Worry: Hope and Help for a Common Condition*. Ballantine Books, 1998.

INTERNET PUBLICATIONS

www.nasponline.org
National Association of School Psychologists site: information for parents and educators, including "Helping Children Cope in Unsettling Times."

www.redcross.org/services/disaster/keepsafe/unexpected.html
"Terrorism—Preparing for the Unexpected." Sensible and inclusive suggestions on natural disasters; "man-made" events addressed.

ORGANIZATIONS

American Academy of Pediatrics, Washington, D.C., 202/347-8600
www.aap.org/terrorism
Through their national Task Force on Terrorism, provides information and resources on biological and chemical agents and their affect on children.

American Psychological Association, Washington, D.C., 800/964-2000
www.helping.apa.org/daily/traumaticstress.html
Suggestions for handling anxiety and stress after a traumatic event.

Freedom from Fear, Staten Island, New York, 718/351-1717
www.freedomfromfear.org
Provides information and resources on anxiety and depression, as well as a national referral network of clinical psychologists.

Institute of Mental Health Initiatives (IMHI), Washington, D.C. 202/467-2285 *www.imhi.org*

Transforms mental health research into useful information and resources for the everyday American.

Moving Past Trauma, 800/455-8300, *www.ywca.org/html/ptsd.asp*

Post Traumatic Stress Disorder Community Outreach Program, sponsored by YMCA and Pfizer; information, resources about PTSD and types of trauma.

National Center for Children Exposed to Violence, Yale University Child Study Center, New Haven, Connecticut, 877/496-2238, *www.nccev.org*

Information for the treatment of children who have experienced or witnessed violent trauma. Methods for educating children about war and terrorism.

National Institute of Mental Health, Bethesda, Maryland, 888/ANXIETY *www.nimh.nih.gov*

Brochures and pamphlets on phobias, post traumatic stress disorder, obsessive compulsive disorder, panic disorder, depression, and anxiety disorders.

Chapter 24. Depression: When Is It Over the Edge?

PUBLICATIONS: BOOKS

Bev Cobain, R.N.C. and Elizabeth Verdick, editor, *When Nothing Matters Anymore: A Survival Guide for Depressed Teens*. Free Spirit Publishing, 1998.

Maureen Empfield, M.D. and Nicholas Bakalar, *Understanding Teenage Depression: A Guide to Diagnosis, Treatment, and Management*. Owl Books, 2001.

Barbara Ingersoll, Ph.D. and Sam Goldstein, Ph.D., *Lonely, Sad and Angry*. Specialty Press, 2001.

Harold Koplewicz, M.D., *More Than Moody: Recognizing and Treating Adolescent Depression*. Putman Publishing Group, 2002.

Marilyn Martin, M.D., *Saving Our Last Nerve: The African American Woman's Path to Mental Health*. Hilton Publishing, 2002.

INTERNET PUBLICATIONS

menanddepression.nimh.nih.gov, 866/227-6464

"Real Men, Real Depression," a National Institute of Mental Health (NIMH) initiative; information on male depression, personal stories, and treatment.

www.groups4kids.com, 202/686-4084

The Washington Metropolitan Area Guide to Therapy Groups for Children, Adolescents, and Parents; cooperative listing on Web and brochure.

ORGANIZATIONS

The Adolescent Depression Awareness Program, 410/955-0518

Johns Hopkins Department of Psychiatry and Behavioral Sciences Baltimore, Maryland, Affective Disorders Consultation Clinic

Professional community outreach in high schools to inform teens of depression symptoms and treatment in preparation for national school curriculum.

WEBSITE

www.nimh.nih.gov, National Institute of Mental Health

Information on all divisions and projects of NIMH for public, researchers, and medical practitioners.

Chapter 25. Anger

PUBLICATIONS: BOOKS

Adele Faber and Elaine Mazlish, *How to Talk So Kids Will Listen & Listen So Kids Will Talk*. Avon Books, 1999.

Bernard Golden, Ph.D., *Healthy Anger: How to Help Children and Teens Manage Their Anger*. Oxford University Press, 2002.

Harriet Lerner, Ph.D., *The Dance of Anger: A Woman's Guide to Changing the Patterns of Intimate Relationships*. HarperCollins, 1997.

Brian Luke Seaward, Ph.D., *Hot Stones & Funny Bones: Teens Helping Teens Cope With Stress & Anger*. Health Communications, 2002.

Carl Semmelroth, Ph.D., with Donald E. P. Smith, Ph.D., *The Anger Habit: Proven Principles to Calm the Stormy Mind*. Universe Writer's Showcase Press. 2000.

Carl Semmelroth, Ph.D., *The Anger Habit Workbook: Proven Principles to Calm the Stormy Mind.* Writers Club Press, 2002.

Elaine Whitehouse and Warwick Pudney, *There's a Volcano in My Tummy: Helping Children to Handle Anger: A Resource Book for Parents, Caregivers and Teachers*. New Society Publishers, 1996.

VIDEOS

"Anger Management for Parents: The RETHINK Method".
Research Press, Champaign, Illinois. 800/519-2707, *www.researchpress.com*

"Learning to Manage Anger: The RETHINK Workout for Teens".
Research Press, Champaign, Illinois. 800/519-2707, *www.researchpress.com*

Chapter 26. Grieving: Death, Disability, Divorce, and Disappointment

PUBLICATIONS: BOOKS

Helen Fitzgerald, C.D.E., *The Grieving Teen: A Guide for Teenagers and Their Friends*. Fireside, 2000.

John C. Friel, Ph.D. and Linda D. Friel, M.A., *The 7 Best Things (Smart) Kids Do*. Health Communications,2000.

Linda Goldman, Ph.D., *Breaking the Silence: A Guide to Helping Children with Complicated Grief*. Taylor & Francis, 2001.

Linda Goldman, Ph.D., *Life and Loss: A Guide to Help Grieving Children*. Taylor & Francis, 2000.

Earl A. Grollman, *Bereaved Children and Teens: A Support Guide for Parents and Professionals*. Beacon Press, 1996.

Warren Hanson, *The Next Place*. Waldman House Press, 1997.

William C. Kroen, Ph.D., L.M.H.C., *Helping Children Cope with the Loss of a Loved One: A Guide for Grownups*. Free Spirit Publishing, 1996.

Pat Schwiebert, R.N. and Chuck DeKlyen, *Tear Soup. Grief Watch, 2001.*

Enid Samuel Traisman, M.S.W., *Fire in My Heart, Ice in My Veins: A Journal for Teenagers Experiencing Loss*. The Centering Corporation, 1992.

J. William Worden, Ph.D., *Children and Grief: When a Parent Dies*. Guilford Press, 2001.

ORGANIZATIONS

Hospice of Northern Virginia, Fairfax, Virginia, 703/538-2044
www.hospicepg.org/home.asp
Point of Hope Family day and weekend, spring and summer camps, counseling services, and groups for children, teens, and adults dealing with grief.

Jewish Social Service Agency, Rockville, Maryland, 301/881-3700
www.jssa.org
Individual and group therapy and peer support groups for bereaved parents, spouses, and children.

Montgomery Hospice Society, Inc., Rockville, Maryland, 301/279-2566
www.montgomeryhospice.org/index.php
Group sessions and individual bereavement counseling for children and adolescents, with concurrent groups for parents, parental loss for adults.

National Family Resiliency Center, Inc. (NFRC), Columbia, Maryland
410/740-9553, *www.divorceabc.com*
Rockville, Maryland, 301/384-0079
Individual, family, and group therapy for understanding and acceptance of separation and divorce; parenting seminars dealing with separation and divorce, and activities around other parenting issues.

Wendt Center for Loss and Healing, Washington, D.C., 202/624-0010
www.lossandhealing.org
Child and adolescent programs dealing loss, including: death, trauma, divorce, chronic and life threatening illnesses; individual, group and family counseling, and play therapy; education, support, and community outreach to Washington area schools. Sponsors Camp Forget-Me-Not, a weekend-long grief camp for children ages six through sixteen years of age.

WEBSITES

www.childrensgrief.net
Helping children deal with grief, useful information and resources.

www.griefwatch.com
Ministry of Metanoia Peace Community of the United Methodist Church in Portland, Oregon; resources for bereaved families and professional caregivers.

www.medicalstatus.com
Free service for people with friends or family in the hospital. An easy-to-update web page where news of the loved one's condition can be posted, enabling friends and family to keep apprised of the patient's status.

Chapter 27. Suicide

PUBLICATIONS: BOOKS

Bev Cobain, R.N.C. and Elizabeth Verdick, editor, *When Nothing Matters Anymore: A Survival Guide for Depressed Teens*. Free Spirit Publishing, 1998.

Barbara Ingersoll, Ph.D. and Sam Goldstein, Ph.D., *Lonely, Sad and Angry*. Specialty Press, 2001.

Paul D. Meier, M.D. and Jan Meier, *Happiness is a Choice for Teens*. Thomas Nelson, 1996.

Gerald Oster, Ph.D., and Sarah Montgomery, M.S.W., *Helping Your Depressed Teenager: A Guide for Parents and Caregivers*. John Wiley and Sons, 1994.

Kay Redfield Jamison, Ph.D., *Night Falls Fast: Understanding Suicide*. Vintage, 2000.

Gary Remafedi, editor, *Death by Denial: Studies of Suicide in Gay and Lesbian Teenagers*. Alyson Publishers, 1994.

Tonia Shamoo, Ph.D. and Philip Patros, Ph.D., *Helping Your Child Cope with Depression and Suicidal Thoughts*. Jossey-Bass, 1997.

Andrew Slaby, M.D. and Lili Frank Garfinkel, *No One Saw My Pain: Why Teens Kill Themselves*. W.W. Norton, 1996.

Kate Williams, A *Parent's Guide for Suicidal and Depressed Teens: Help for Recognizing If a Child is in Crisis and What to Do about It*. Hazeldon Information Education, 1995.

ORGANIZATIONS

American Association of Suicidology (AAS), Washington, D.C.
202/237-2280, *www.suicidology.org*
Strives to prevent suicide by promoting research, education, and training for the public, professionals, and volunteers. Trains crisis workers, publishes information on suicide, and offers support services to survivors of suicide.

American Foundation for Suicide Prevention, New York, New York
888/333-AFSP, *www.afsp.org*
Supports research and education about suicide prevention and survivor treatment, and provides and publicizes information on depression and suicide.

Maryland Youth Crisis Hotline, Community Crisis Services, Inc.
800/422-0009 (Maryland only), *www.communitycrisis.org*
24-hour crisis counseling hotline, support groups, community outreach programs, referrals, and resources for people considering suicide or facing a personal crisis.

National Hopeline Network, 800/SUICIDE
Connects callers with the closest suicide crisis center and trained counselors.

National Organization for People of Color Against Suicide (NOPCAS)
Washington, D.C., 202/549-6039 or 866/899-5317, *www.nopcas.com*
Scholarship and research on suicide prevention and survivor treatment among the traditionally ignored minority communities.

Suicide Prevention Advocacy Network (SPAN USA), 770/998-8819 or 888/649-1366, *www.spanusa.org*
Promotes community organization and action to bring suicide prevention to national awareness.

The Trevor Project, 866/4-U-TREVOR, *www.TheTrevorProject.org*
Support for gay, lesbian, bisexual, transgendered, and "questioning" youth to aid in suicide prevention. Free 24-hour Trevor Helpline dedicated to counseling gay and questioning youth. Oscar-winning short special program, "Trevor", a funny, touching look at one 13-year-old's coming to terms with his sexuality.

Yellow Ribbon Suicide Prevention Program, 303/429-3530, *www.yellowribbon.org*
Teaches teens and adults necessary tools to prevent suicide and save lives.

WEBSITES

www.nimh.nih.gov, National Institute of Mental Health (NIMH)
Information on projects of the NIMH for the public, researchers, and medical practitioners.

www.parentingteens.org, The Julie Gordon-Sullivan Foundation
Cape Porpoise, Maine, 207/967-0001
Fosters understanding and mutual respect in adult-adolescent relationships, by providing information and resources to parents and teens, including PERC, Parent Effectiveness in Resolving Conflicts with Your Teen.

6 | TROUBLES

Chapter 28. Out-of-Sync Teens

PUBLICATIONS: BOOKS

Neil Bernstein, Ph.D., *How to Keep Your Teenager Out of Trouble and What to Do if You Can't*. Workman Publishing, 2001.

Jane Bluestein, Ph.D., *Parents, Teens and Boundaries: How to Draw the Line*. Health Communications, 1993.

Marshall P. Duke, Ph.D., Elisabeth A. Martin, M.Ed., and Stephen Nowicki, Jr., Ph.D., *Teaching Your Child the Language of Social Success*. Peachtree Publication, 1996.

David Elkind, Ph.D., *Ties That Stress*. Belknap Press, 1994.

Jan Goldberg and Miriam Adderholdt-Elliot, Ph.D., *Perfectionism: What's Bad about Being Too Good*. Free Spirit Publishing, 1999.

Robin Goldstein, Ph.D., *The Parenting Bible*. Sourcebooks, 2002.

Daniel Goleman, Ph.D., *Emotional Intelligence, Educational Implication*. Basic Books, 1997.

Ross W. Green, Ph.D., *The Explosive Child*. HarperCollins, 2001.

Carol Stock Kranowitz, M.A., *The Out-of-Sync Child: Recognizing and Coping with Sensory Integration Dysfunction*. Perigee, 1998.

Anthony E. Wolf, Ph.D., *Get Out of My Life, but First Could You Drive Me & Cheryl to the Mall: A Parent's Guide to the New Teenager*. Farrar, Straus, and Giroux, 2002.

ORGANIZATIONS

Independent Education Consultants Association (ICEA)
Fairfax, Virginia, 703/591-4850, *www.educationalconsulting.org*
Training and workshops, aiding consultants and families in education choices.

Parent Encouragement Program (PEP), Kensington, Maryland
301/929-8824, *www.parentencouragement.org*
Classes and workshops for parents geared to child's developmental stages.

WEBSITES

www.groups4kids.com, 202/686-4084
The Washington Metropolitan Area Guide to Therapy Groups for Children, Adolescents, and Parents. A cooperative listing on the Web and in print.

www.ncfy.com, 301/608-8098
Information and resources on issues for young people, parents, communities.

Chapter 29. Shoplifting and Stealing *See chapts: 5.Friends, 34.Money, 37.Cheating*

Chapter 30. Vandalism *See chapters: 5.Friends, 25.Anger, 31.Harassment*

Chapter 31. Harassment and Bullying

PUBLICATIONS: BOOKS

James Garbarino, Ph.D. and Ellen DeLara, Ph.D., *And Words Can Hurt Forever: How to Protect Adolescents from Bullying, Harassment, and Emotional Violence*. The Free Press, 2002.

Harris Interactive, *Hostile Hallways: Bullying, Teasing, and Sexual Harassment in Schools*. American Association of University Women Educational Foundation, 2001.

William Pollack, Ph.D., with Todd Shuster, *Real Boys Voices*. Random House, 2000.

Rachel Simmons, *Odd Girl Out: The Hidden Culture of Aggression in Girls*. Harcourt, 2002.

Rosalind Wiseman, *Queen Bees & Wannabes: Helping Your Daughter Survive Cliques, Gossip, Boyfriends & Other Realities of Adolescence*. Crown Publishers, 2002.

WEBSITES

www.aauw.org/ef/harass/index.cfm
American Association of University Women
"Harassment-Free Hallways: How to Stop Sexual Harassment in Schools," Interactive guide by the American Association of University Women for students, parents, and administrators; survey and online resources on sexual harassment and bullying in schools.

www.bullybeware.com, Bully B'Ware
Hosted by teachers and administrators, information and materials on bullying.

www.bullying.org
With a slogan of "Where You are Not Alone," bullying.org provides resources, information, and support groups aimed at raising awareness of the problems of bullying and to find nonviolent solutions to conflicts associated with bullying.

Chapter 32. Assault And Rape

PUBLICATIONS: BOOKS

Lori Robinson, *I Will Survive: The African-American Guide to Healing from Sexual Assault and Abuse*. Seal Press Feminist Publications, 2003.

ORGANIZATION

D.C. Rape Crisis Center, Washington, D.C., 202/333-RAPE
www.dcrcc.org

Information on what to do if raped, rape myths, long-term effects of abuse, date rape drugs, self defense techniques, what men can do to stop rape.

WEBSITES

www.childhelpusa.org, Childhelp USA, 800/422–4453/ 4-A-CHILD
Cconfidential, 24/7 National Child Abuse Hotline for children who have been abused and the people who want to help them.

www.fvpf.org, The Family Violence Prevention Fund, 800/656-HOPE
Education, media advocacy, preventative support, and public policy; seeks to end domestic violence and help victims.

www.ncadv.org, National Coalition against Domestic Violence
Legislative support of battered women and children.

www.ndvh.org, National Domestic Violence Hotline, 800/799-SAFE
Support services and information on domestic violence and victims' rights for kids, teens, and adults

www.ra-info.org, Ritual Abuse, Ritual Crime and Healing
Information on ritualistic abuse for survivors and professional counselors.

www.rainn.org, Rape, Abuse and Incest National Network (RAINN)
National Sexual Assault Hotline; programs to prevent sexual assault, support victims, and prosecute sexual assaulters.

www.survivorship.org, Survivorship
Helping survivors of ritualized abuse, mind control, and torture.

www.vday.org, V-day
Distributes funds to grassroots, national, and international organizations and programs in the prevention of violence against women and girls.

www.wcasa.org, Wisconsin Coalition Against Sexual Assault
Public awareness and policy development, training support counselors, and information though its quarterly journal.

HOTLINES

National Sexual Assault Hotline, 1/800/656-HOPE

D.C. Rape Crisis Center, 202/333-RAPE

Montgomery County Victim Assistance and Sexual Assault Program 240/777-4247

Prince George's County Sexual Assault Center, 301/618-3154

Alexandria Sexual Assault Response and Awareness Program (SARA) 703/683-7273

Fairfax County Victim Assistance Network Hotline, 703/360-7273

7 | MANAGING RESPONSIBILITY

Chapter 33. Home Alone *See chapters: 4. Communication: Teen/Parent, 5. Friendships*

Capter 34. Money

PUBLICATIONS: BOOKS

Janet Bodnar, *Dollars & Sense for Kids*. Kiplinger Books, 1999.

Susan Price, *The Giving Family: Raising Our Children to Help Others*. Council on Foundations, 2001.

Marie Sherlock, *Living Simply with Children: A Voluntary Simplicity Guide*. Three Rivers Press, 2003.

Betsy Taylor, M.P.A., *What Kids Really Want That Money Can't Buy*. Warner Books, 2003.

ORGANIZATIONS

Jump$tart Coalition For Personal Financial Literacy, Washington, D.C. 888/45-EDUCATE, *www.jumpstartcoalition.org*
Promotes financial literacy in young adults and the teaching of personal finance in schools: free educational materials for students, parents, and teachers.

The National Association of Investors Corporation (NAIC), Royal Oak, Michigan, 248/583-6242, *www.better-investing.org*,
Information and resources to aid people in becoming smarter investors

College Parents of America (CPA), Vienna, Virginia, 703/761-6702 *www.collegeparents.org*
Guidance and resources for families preparing and putting a child through college. Financial advice, services, and resources in partnership with financial institutions and colleges.

WEBSITES

www.capitalistchicks.com
Financial information and a discussion room for girls who are prospective entrepreneurs. Edgy, hip information encouraging young women.

www.kiplinger.com
Keyword "Janet Bodnar" to reach Kiplinger's Personal Finance's column on child finance, access past articles for a fee.

www.ncee.net, National Council on Economic Education (NCEE) 800/338-1192
Sponsors the It All Adds Up website for high school age students; online games and simulations to help teens learn about credit management, car buying, paying for college, budgeting, saving, and investing.

www.practicalmoneyskills.com
Provided by Visa, Practical Money Skills for Life addresses budgeting, saving, and investing for young adults. Includes banking information for teachers and parents, available in Spanish.

www.visabuxx.com, Visa Buxx, 866/354-9302
A prepaid money card alternative to cash and traditional credit cards for teens. Visa Buxx allows kids and parents plan and track budgets more effectively and foster financial responsibility.

www.yacenter.org, Young Americans Center for Financial Education
Online banking services for young people aged twelve to eighteen; includes online banking for checking, savings, and borrowing.

www.youngbiz.com, Young Biz, 888/543-7929
A partner of the National Association of Investors Corporation (NAIC); online resources including internships, summer camps and workshops to educate youth on entrepreneurship and investing.

www.younginvestor.com, Liberty Funds
Interactive guide to allowances and investing aimed at children; student and parent questions to investment experts; entertainment and games for children.

Chapter 35. Computers

PUBLICATIONS: BOOKS

Jane Healy, Ph.D., *Endangered Minds: Why Children Don't Think—and What We Can Do About It*. Touchstone, 1999.

Jane Healy, Ph.D., *Failure to Connect: How Computers Affect Our Children's Minds—and What We Can Do About It. Touchstone*, 1999.

Sherry Turkle, Ph.D., *Life on the Screen: Identity in the Age of the Internet.* Touchstone, 1997.

Kimberly S. Young, Ph.D., *Caught in the Net: How to Recognize the Signs of Internet Addiction—and a Winning Strategy for Recovery.* John Wiley & Sons, 1998.

PUBLICATIONS: INTERNET

www.kff.org
Key Facts: Teens Online, study by Henry J. Kaiser Family Foundation: fact sheets by gender, age, and ethnicity, time spent online, and favorite activities.

www.ouc.bc.ca/libr/connect96/search.htm
"Sink or Swim: Internet Search Tools & Techniques," by Ross Tyner of Okanagan University College: online workshop on search engines and search techniques.

www.rider.edu/~suler/psycyber/adoles.html
"Adolescents in Cyberspace: The Good, the Bad, and the Ugly," from *The Psychology of Cyberspace*, hypertext book by John Suler, Ph.D. of Rider University; psychological dimensions of environments created by computers.

WEBSITES

www.esrb.org, Entertainment Software Rating Board
Helps parents choose video and computer games by appropriate age group rating; rating symbol and content descriptors on the packaging.

www.grrl.com
Savvy girl-friendly advice, news, and entertainment, helps modern teenage girls to educate themselves about feminist issues.

www.learnthenet.com
An online Internet help desk.

Chapter 36. Sports: What's The Goal?

PUBLICATIONS: BOOKS

Bob Bigelow, Tom Moroney, and Linda Hall, *Just Let the Kids Play: How to Stop Other Adults from Ruining Your Child's Fun and Success in Youth Sports*. Health Communications, 2001.

Jordan Metzl, M.D. and Carol Shookhoff, Ph.D., *The Young Athlete: A Sports Doctor's Complete Guide for Parents*. Little Brown and Company, 2002.

WEBSITES

www.nays.org, The National Alliance for Youth Sports (NAYS), 800/729-2057
Encourages good sportsmanship among parents; advocates for safe sports and suggests questions to ask coaches.

www.positivecoach.org, Positive Coaching Alliance (PCA), Washington D.C. 202/338-4843
Information for coaches and parents about rewarding effort and learning, as well as winning.

8 | SCHOOL

Chapter 37. Cheating *See chapters: 17. Saying No, 18. Push for Success*

Chapter 38. Changing Schools *See chapters: 5. Friendship, 23. Afraid,*

Chapter 39. Choosing College

PUBLICATIONS: BOOKS

Josaih Bunting III, *All Loves Excelling*. Berkeley Publishing Group, 2002.

Karen Levin Coburn, M.A. and Madge Lawrence Treeger, M.A., *Letting Go: A Parents' Guide to Understanding the College Years*. HarperPerennial, 1997.

Howard Greene, M.A., M.Ed. and Matthew W. Greene, Ph.D., *Greenes' Guides to Educational Planning: The Hidden Ivies: Thirty Colleges of Excellence*. Cliff Street Books, 2000.

Leah Y. Latimer, *Higher Ground: Preparing African-American Children for College*. Avon Books, 1999

Colin Hall and Ron Lieber, *Taking Time Off: Inspiring Stories of Students Who Enjoyed Successful Breaks from College and How You Can Plan Your Own*. Princeton Review, 2003.

Jay Mathews, *Harvard Schmarvard: Getting Beyond the Ivy League to the College that is Best for You*. Prima Lifestyles, 2003.

Marjorie Nieuwenhuis, *Kaplan Parent's Guide to College Admissions*. Kaplan, 2000.

Loren Pope, Ph.D., *Colleges That Change Lives: 40 Schools You Should Know About Even If You're Not a Straight A Student*. Penguin USA, 2000.

Bonnie Rubin, *Time Out: How to Take a Year (Or More or Less Off Without Jeopardizing Your Job, Your Family, or Your Bank Account)*. W.W. Norton, 1987.

Jacques Steinberg, *The Gatekeepers: Inside the Admissions Process of a Premier College*. Penquin USA, 2003.

PUBLICATIONS: INTERNET

www.ed.gov/pubs/Prepare
Preparing Your Child for College: Resource Book for Parents.

WEBSITES

www.gapyear.com, Gapyear Company
Resources for taking time out for travel between schools and careers.

www.nacac.org, National Association for College Admission Counseling
Resources for school counselors, college admission, and financial aid administrators. National College Fair dates, and information for parents, students, and college exhibitors.

www.takingtimeoff.com
Links to travel resources, study abroad programs, jobs and career advice, volunteer work, and tips for settling back into school.

Chapter 40. Senior Year: Pulling Away, Letting Go *See chapter: 39. College*